ZIMBABWE INDEPENDENCE MOVEMENTS

Select Documents

ZIMBABWE INDEPENDENCE MOVEMENTS

Select Documents

Edited and selected by
CHRISTOPHER NYANGONI & GIDEON NYANDORO

BARNES & NOBLE
BOOKS
10 East 53d St., New York 10022
(a division of Harper & Row Publishers, Inc.)

Published in the USA by
Harper & Row Publishers Inc.
Barnes & Noble Import Division

ISBN   0 06 495222 3

Library of Congress Number
LC   79-51834

Typesetting by Malvern Typesetting Services
Printed in Great Britain by
The Pitman Press, Bath

CONTENTS

CHRONOLOGY—KEY DATES

1890	Royal Charter granted to Rhodes's British South Africa Company.
1890 12 September	Occupation Day. British flag raised at Fort Salisbury by Pioneer Column.
1893	Occupation of Matabeleland. Matabele rising.
1894	First Matebeleland Order-in-Council.
1896	Mashona 'rebellion'.
1898	Second Order-in-Council.
	Introduction of the franchise system.
1914	BSA Co Charter renewed for ten years.
1920	Rhodesia Bantu Voters Association (RBVA) founded.
1923 23 September	End of Company rule. Southern Rhodesia became a self-governing British colony after a referendum. Vote: 8,774 for and 5,089 against.
1927	The Rhodesian Industrial and Commercial Workers' Union formed.
1930	Land Apportionment Act—the Magna Carta of white economic control in Rhodesia. 48% land allocated to Africans; 52% to Europeans.
1934	The African National Congress founded.
1947	The British African Voice Association (BAVA) founded.
1951	Land Husbandry Act, dispossessing a great number of Africans of their land, passed.
1953	Federation of the Rhodesias and Nyasaland established.
1955 13 May	The City Youth League formed.
1957 12 September	The Southern Rhodesia African National Congress (SRANC) launched.
1959	Unlawful Organizations Act.
29 February	SRANC banned.
1960 1 January	National Democratic Party (NDP) formed.
1961	London Constitutional Conference. Proposals rejected by NDP.
9 December	NDP banned.
17 December	Zimbabwe African Peoples' Union (ZAPU) formed.
1962 20 September	ZAPU banned.
1963 July	Split in African nationalist movement. Peoples' Caretaker Council (PCC) and Zimbabwe African National Union (ZANU) formed.
10 August*	
8 August*	
31 December	Federation dissolved.
1964 13 April	Ian Smith became prime minister.
	ZANU and PCC banned.

*ZANU formed on 8.8.63
PCC formed on 10.8.63

	20-26 October	Domboshava 'Indaba'. Chiefs and headmen supported Smith in calling for independence under the 1961 Constitution.
1965	25-29 October	Harold Wilson in Rhodesia.
	5 November	State of emergency declared.
	11 November	Unilateral declaration of independence (UDI). Imposition of economic sanctions against Rhodesia.
	12 November	ZANU announced the formation of a people's government inside Zimbabwe. Headquarters at Sikombela where its leaders were detained.
	19 November	UN economic sanctions imposed.
	15 December	Ghana broke off diplomatic relations with Britain over Rhodesia.
1966	January	Lagos Commonwealth Conference—the first to be held outside London—called specifically to discuss measures to bring down the illegal regime. British Premier declared that sanctions would bring down the rebellion in 'weeks rather than months'.
	28 April	ZANU launched the battle of Sinoia which marked the beginning of armed struggle.
	December	Abortive HMS *Tiger* constitutional talks between the British and Rhodesian governments.
1967		South African troops in the Zambezi valley.
1968		ZAPU-ANC of South Africa military alliance.
	October	Abortive HMS *Fearless* constitutional talks.
1969	21 February	Rhodesian government proclamation forcibly moved the Tangwena people from their land—the Gaeresi Ranch. The Land Tenure Act passed.
	September	The Lusaka Manifesto urged talks rather than armed struggle in southern Africa.
1970	2 March	Rhodesia became a republic under the 1969 Constitution.
1971	1 October	Front for the Liberation of Zimbabwe (FROLIZI) formed.
	24 November	Anglo-Rhodesian Settlement Proposals signed in Salisbury.
	16 December	African National Council (ANC) formed to oppose the proposals.
1972	11 January	Arrival of the Pearce Commission in Rhodesia to test the acceptability of the proposals.
	10 March	The Commission left Rhodesia. The ANC became a political party.
	3 May	The Commission reported overwhelming rejection of the proposed settlement.

1973	9 January	Rhodesia-Zambia border closed.
1974	7 December	The Lusaka Declaration of Unity signed, bringing ANC, FROLIZI, ZANU and ZAPU under a new organization—the enlarged ANC.
1975	20-23 August	Kaunda-Vorster meeting and the abortive Victoria Falls bridge constitutional talks between the Rhodesian regime and African nationalists.
1976	3 March	Rhodesia-Mozambique border closed.
	19 March	Breakdown of Smith-Nkomo talks which had been going on since the end of October 1975.
	22 March	New British settlement terms put forward by Foreign Secretary James Callaghan: majority rule within two years.
	27 April	Kissinger's 10-point 'message of commitment and co-operation' delivered in Lusaka setting out US policy towards southern African minority regimes.
	23-24 June	Kissinger-Vorster meeting in Bavaria, West Germany.
	4-6 September	Second Kissinger-Vorster meeting in Zurich, Switzerland.
	19 September	Kissinger-Vorster-Smith meeting in Pretoria.
	24 September	Smith accepts majority rule principle.
	28 October	The Geneva Constitutional Conference opens.

LIST OF ABBREVIATIONS

AFP	p. 170 Agence France Press
ANC	African National Council/African National Congress
ANC-Z	African National Council-Zimbabwe
BAVA	British African Voice Association
BSAP	British South Africa Police
CDC	Colonial Development Corporation
CP	Centre Party
FAO	Food and Agriculture Organization
FRELIMO	Front for the Liberation of Mozambique
FROLIZI	Front for the Liberation of Zimbabwe
ICU	Industrial and Commercial Workers' Union
JMC	Joint Military Council
KANU	Kenya African National Union
MIU	Mounted Infantry Units
NDP	National Democratic Party
NPU	National Peoples' Union
OAU	Organization for African Unity
PAIGC	African Party for the Independence of Guinea-Bissau and Cape Verde
PCC	Peoples' Caretaker Council
RBC	Rhodesia Broadcasting Corporation
RBVA	Rhodesian Bantu Voters' Association
RCC	Revolutionary Command Council
RF	Rhodesian Front
RICU	Reformed Industrial and Commercial Workers' Union
RISCO	Rhodesia Iron and Steel Company
RP	Rhodesia Party
SWAPO	South West Africa Peoples' Organization
TANU	Tanganyika African National Union
UNIP	United National Independence Party
UFP	United Federal Party
UNO	United Nations Organization
ZANLA	Zimbabwe African National Liberation Army
ZANU	Zimbabwe African National Union
ZAPRA	Zimbabwe African Peoples' Revolutionary Army
ZAPU	Zimbabwe African Peoples' Union
ZIPA	Zimbabwe Peoples' Army
ZLA	Zimbabwe Liberation Army
ZLC	Zimbabwe Liberation Council
ZRP	Zimbabwe Republic Police

INTRODUCTION

The struggle for freedom in Zimbabwe is as old as colonialism itself. But one of the first notable political movements was the Rhodesian Bantu Voters' Association (RBVA) launched in 1920, which drew influence from South African Africans. At that time, European registered voters were 19,000 out of a total population of 35,000 while Africans numbered 30 out of a population of 1 million. RBVA was formed to campaign for voting rights for the emerging African élite. It was not much concerned with the participation of the masses in the political process.

However, the formation in 1927 of the Rhodesian Industrial and Commercial Workers Union (ICU), marked the beginning of mass political campaigning by African urban workers. ICU was run on an extra-tribal basis and was a forerunner of the later mass nationalist movements. In 1944 ICU was transformed into RICU: the Reformed Industrial and Commercial Workers' Union. Some of the leaders of RICU (Charles Mzingeli, S. Masoja Ndhlovu and Job Dumbutshena) continued to take an active part in politics.

1934 saw the launching of the first African National Congress (ANC) in Southern Rhodesia. This was led by Aaron Jacha. It was essentially an elitist organization, like RBVA. The Congress campaigned for equal rights with Europeans, such as exemption from the pass and liquor laws, and permission to join white clubs.

The post-war period witnessed a rapid growth in African politics in Zimbabwe as elsewhere in Africa. The continued decline in African work-force gave impetus to African politics. In 1945 the Rev Samkange revived the ANC and in 1947 the British African Voice Association (BAVA) was founded by Benjamin B. Burombo. These movements concentrated their efforts in urban areas. In 1948 a country-wide strike broke out which almost paralysed the Rhodesian economy. Congress and BAVA leaders acted as spokesmen for the strikers. In 1952 BAVA was banned by the Southern Rhodesian government.

Late in 1951 the British Government convened a conference in London to discuss federation. The Southern Rhodesian delegation included two Africans, Joshua Nkomo and Jasper Savanhu. All other Africans boycotted the conference because of opposition to the federal scheme.

Nkomo denounced the federal scheme when he returned home, but later sought election to the first federal parliament; he failed.

In 1953 Federation was imposed. The Federal Constitution left political power with the white settler minority. The first Prime Minister was Godfrey Huggins (Lord Malvern), the architect of Rhodesia's *apartheid* system. As Prime Minister of Southern Rhodesia he advanced his theory of the 'two pyramid policy' of separate development on racial lines.

To the African elitist of Southern Rhodesia, Federation with its declared policy of 'partnership' was an opportunity for political advancement and the ending of racial discrimination. In Southern Rhodesia Mike Hove and Jasper Savanhu became the first African Federal members of Parliament.

However, the formation in 1955 of the City Youth League in Salisbury by George Nyandoro, Edson Sithole, Paul Mushonga, James Chikerema, and Dunduza Chisiza who was from Nyasaland, produced a strong challenge to élitist politics—the politics of participation in European dominated structure. In 1956 the League successfully organized a bus boycott against increased fares. The boycott became a strike after Garfield Todd, the so-called liberal, had applied ruthless measures to suppress it.

The need for a nation-wide mass organization was strongly felt in both Salisbury and Bulawayo, where the old ANC was still in existence. Amongst its leaders were Joseph Msika, Jason Moyo, Francis Nehwati and Knight Maripe. On 12 September 1967 the two organizations united in Salisbury to form the new Southern Rhodesia African National Congress (SRANC). Joshua Nkomo, then a member of the United Federal Party, was chosen as a neutral member to chair the meeting but he emerged as leader of the new organization. Chikerema was elected deputy-president, Nyandoro secretary-general and Mushonga treasurer-general. Capitalizing on the unpopular land legislations, the SRANC grew rapidly, its influence and acceptance penetrating all corners of Zimbabwe.

Later African political parties—the National Democratic Party (NDP), the Zimbabwe African Peoples' Union (ZAPU), the Zimbabwe African National Union (ZANU), the Front for the Liberation of Zimbabwe (FROLIZI) and the African National Council (ANC)—were all to take their roots from the SRANC of 1957, the year when mass African politics began in Zimbabwe. Most of the present political leadership is connected with that movement.

Against this brief historical background can be understood the development of African politics in Zimbabwe. That is the central theme of this book. It is an attempt to present the African viewpoint and attitude towards the Rhodesian constitutional problem—how African requests of 'please rule us well' have evolved into the demands 'leave us to rule ourselves or face the consequences'. Many books have been written about African politics and political development in Zimbabwe which cover the same period. But this book attempts to let the leaders and the leading participants speak for themselves. The record reflects their own thinking and approach. Through their own words they expose their own consistencies or inconsistencies. Furthermore, the record attempts to present the achievements, failures, problems, intrigues and crises that various Zimbabwean nationalist movements have experienced since 1957. The failure of British policies towards Rhodesia is also dealt with.

The Western mass media have not helped much in clarifying the complex nature of the Zimbabwe problem, its international implications, the political objectives of the African majority, and the reaction of the 'settler' minority to the true aspirations of the Africans. It is hoped that this book will help to reveal the complex nature of the situation and particularly the African point of view.

Most of these documents were traced in libraries, especially in London. Individuals also helped in locating some of them.

The book consists of about seventy-five documents, selected from the speeches, memoranda, resolutions, press releases, writings (including letters), party constitutions, policies and programmes, proposals and submissions, made by various African nationalist leaders, political parties, international organizations, and by some leaders of independent African countries who are deeply involved in the Rhodesian question. The documents range from the formation of the SRANC in 1957 up to the Geneva conference, 1976. The selection was influenced by the book's central theme. Hence each leading participant has a fair share of representation, so that the book contains various shades of opinion. It is hoped that the book completely represents the African viewpoint.

The book is divided into four main sections:
1 The period of protest, 1957-64.
2 The period of direct confrontation, 1964-71.
3 The period of armed struggle, 1971-4.
4 The period of armed struggle and detente, 1974-6.
Each section is introduced separately, and is divided into chapters.

The documents are arranged chronologically where possible, although this sequence is violated in one or two cases where necessary. Where the documents overlapped or were out of context it was necessary to omit some sections.

This collection of documents becomes available to the academic community and to the general public at a time when international attention is focussed on the situation in Rhodesia and southern Africa. No doubt some of this material has appeared elsewhere: in some obscure journals, fugitive leaflets and pamphlets. But put together it is hoped that this collection will be valuable as a source of information and as a reference book on the subject.

CHRISTOPHER K. NYANGONI

SECTION I

THE PERIOD OF PROTEST
1957–64

The period of 1957–64 was characterized by the emergence of the Southern Rhodesia African National Congress (SRANC), the National Democratic Party (NDP), the Zimbabwe African People's Union (ZAPU) and the Zimbabwe African National Union (ZANU). These movements indicate the development of political consciousness that was gradually taking shape among Zimbabweans.

The SRANC was a reformist movement, through which Africans were to plead with the settler minority for a just society. The belief that African advancement in all spheres would come about by securing the vote gradually gained ground.

However, African politics suffered a big setback when a split occurred in the nationalist ranks.

CHAPTER ONE

THE POLITICS OF REFORMISM

1 Southern Rhodesia African National Congress: statement of principles, policy and programme. Salisbury, 1957

PRINCIPLES AND POLICY

The African National Congress of Southern Rhodesia is a people's movement, dedicated to a political programme, economic and educational advancement, social service and personal standards.

Its aim is the NATIONAL UNITY of all inhabitants of the country in true partnership regardless of race, colour and creed. It stands for a completely integrated society, equality of opportunity in every sphere and the social, economic and political advancement of all. It regards these objectives as the essential foundation of that partnership between people of all races without which there can be no peaceful progress in this country.

Congress affirms complete loyalty to the Crown as the symbol of national unity.

It is not a racial movement. It is equally opposed to tribalism and racialism.

It welcomes as members all of any race who are in sympathy with its aims and are prepared to fulfil the conditions of membership.

It recognizes the rights of all who are citizens of the country, whether African, European, Coloured or Asian, to retain permanently the fullest citizenship.

It believes that this country can only advance through non-racial thinking and acting, and that an integrated society provides the only alternative to tribalism and racialism.

Congress believes that individual initiative and free enterprise are necessary to the life of a young country and must be fully encouraged, but that a considerable measure of Government control is necessary in a modern state.

The immediate economic concern of Congress is to raise the standard of living of the underprivileged. The peaceful development of the country demands above all things that the gap between the lowest and highest in the social and economic order should be greatly reduced.

Congress believes that in the whole of Southern and Eastern Africa there are three outstanding needs which it is supremely important to meet:

(a) the standard of living of millions of people must be raised in a short space of time through their rapid social, economic and political advancement;

(b) this is only possible with the aid of skills, techniques and capital from overseas. These must be attracted to this country not only by the offer of material advantages but also by appeal to the altruism and sense of service prevalent in the world. This is a challenge to the more advanced and privileged people in the world whose help is required in the interests of world peace and the total development of mankind.

(c) in view of the inevitable uprising of national feeling among the peoples of Africa and the need to enlist the full co-operation of the mass of the people in this great enterprise, full participation of African people must be provided for in Government and the legitimate political aspirations of the people be thus fulfilled.

Congress realizes that to meet these three needs is a task of gigantic proportions, but believes that nothing short of this can ensure the people development of this country for the benefit of all the inhabitants. Congress is therefore dedicated to the fulfilment of these needs and regards it as a matter of the most urgent necessity.

POLITICAL PROGRAMME

1. Land
Congress believes that the land belongs to the people. Thus the use of land must be controlled and administered by Government. Government must ensure that the use of land is not limited by undue speculation in land values. Government must promote the fullest freedom for the economic use of land by competent people regardless of race, and must provide for this now largely through the system of freehold land tenure. It is, however, both uneconomic and also socially undesirable that land should be apportioned racially. Congress therefore believes that the Land Apportionment Act must be repealed and the land of this country freed from racial restrictions for economic development in both rural and urban areas. Unjust distribution of land is one of the fundamental causes of social discontent, and Congress regards measures of land reform as of the utmost importance.

2. Agriculture
Congress believes that this country must become self-supporting in all

agricultural produce and may well become an exporting country. It recognizes the need for large scale agriculture, but does not believe that this should be confined by law to a particular racial group. A rural economy for the country must be founded primarily on the small farmer. Government must therefore support the peasant farmer strongly with land settlement schemes, research, and the provision of capital so that his farming may develop along modern lines. Agriculture will benefit greatly if racial restrictions are removed and the large and small farmer are permitted to farm side by side to their mutual advantage. Agriculture must become increasingly intensive and undeveloped land in any areas must be freed for economic use. Farming must become as attractive an occupation as industry and a proper balance must be maintained between rural and urban development. Government efforts to open up overseas markets, arrange for orderly marketing schemes and regulate and maintain price levels and a price structure in the interests of both the producer and the consumer must be motivated by economic considerations alone. The change over to modern intensive farming methods requires the utmost encouragement from Government for the benefit of both producer and consumer regardless of race.

3. Urban areas
Congress believes that urban areas must be freed from racial restrictions and that industry and housing must be planned according to the best modern considerations in the interests of the community as a whole. Every effort must be made to promote the development of industry, but also to decentralize it, and to avoid large agglomerations of population. Government must promote the development of housing estates on an economic, not a racial basis and, whether through ownership or tenancy, security of occupation must be provided for people of all races who elect to live and find employment in urban areas.

4. Local government
Congress believes that the same pattern of local government must prevail in all areas and for all races, and that separate communal administration must cease. The Ministry of Native Affairs must be abolished and government by 'Native Commissioner' and the 'Native Affairs Department' must give way in all areas to a system of local government authorities elected on a democratic franchise. Local government services must develop and the fullest opportunity must be open to all people according to ability and regardless of race in the local government service.

5. Social services

Congress aims at the rapid development of modern social services, including social insurance, and their application to all people regardless of race. It regards community development and adult education services as of great importance in the task of enabling the adult population to develop rapidly in both urban and rural areas. It believes not only in government initiative in the provision of social services but also in voluntary effort. Voluntary associations must be encouraged and given the fullest freedom in the religious, cultural and social spheres. The initiation and extension of social services is most necessary for those in the lower income groups, who are predominantly African, and Congress is primarily concerned to promote them there. The cheap labour of the African and non-European is the major source of the wealth of the country, and it is from that accumulated wealth that provision must be made for full social security for all workers, for unemployment pay, for sickness allowances and for adequate pensions. Until such facilities are available, it is a dangerous step for any African to leave the Reserve and opt to become an urban worker, for he has thereby forfeited his right to return to and live in the Reserve, and in unemployment, sickness or old age no provision is made for him in the town.

Full social security must be the terms upon which the African workers contribute to the development of the country.

6. Education

Congress wholly supports the principle of free compulsory universal primary education on a non-racial basis. No child must be deprived of educational opportunity from which he or she will benefit. Secondary education must be greatly expanded with no lowering of standards. New secondary schools must be established on a non-racial basis and must accept pupils on grounds of academic ability alone. In this way the younger generation will be educated for an integrated society. Technical colleges must be started on the same non-racial basis, offering equal opportunity to all in the ability to make use of it. Education at the university level must be unrestrictedly available to all who attain the required standards and if this involves a quicker growth of the University College than is at present planned, this growth must be facilitated. Opportunities for further education, study and training overseas must be opened up by the generous establishment of State bursaries and scholarships awarded to qualified ability without distinction of race. Government must provide equality of opportunity in education regardless of race and colour and a single educational system taking no account of race must be the objective.

Government should at the same time give the greatest encouragement to private schools maintained by voluntary bodies so that they may make their contribution to education in co-operation with the state.

Congress realizes that education is expensive and must be paid for. No state can make light of the difficulty of doing so. But it is the most important single need confronting the country and must have top priority in its claim on revenue and resources. This is not a poor country; it is prospering greatly, and the redistribution of resources required to finance the educational programme will prove the best possible investment for the prosperity of citizens of all races.

7. Health

Congress believes that in order to provide adequate health services throughout the country for the whole population, provision must be made for greatly increased medical staff, for training doctors, nurses and medical orderlies. The selection, training and service conditions of these must be without discrimination as to race, if enough competent candidates are to be received into the medical services.

The difficulties of financing increased health services are not to be underestimated, but the increase in production to which this would lead would rapidly offset the cost. Congress believes that a further way to meet this cost is by making all hospitals multi-racial, and the savings effected by ceasing to maintain separate institutions can be used in the provision of the additional services required.

8. Industry and trades unions

Congress believes in the necessity of the rapid development of industry, yet under such conditions that rural economy and social life will not be destroyed but improved. In particular, secondary industries must be based on the products of the primary industries of the country. Conditions must be promoted under which the establishment of industry will be encouraged: these conditions include appropriate financial arrangements, provision of efficient transportation, of cheap power, of adequate housing for employees and of an efficient labour force. Capital skills and techniques must be attracted from overseas, yet it is necessary to make the fullest use of the capital resources and potential of the population of the country. Education and training in crafts and trades must therefore be strenuously promoted by Government through training schemes and through the encouragement of apprenticeship. Opportunities to acquire skills must be open to all people equally regardless of race and according to ability. Trade Unions must be encouraged to participate in these schemes so that they may fulfil the role of maintaining and increasing the efficiency of industry as well as that of improving the working conditions of their members. Congress believes in collective bargaining and in the Trade Unions and Employers' Organizations which make this possible; these must be organized on an industrial and not a racial basis, and must not exist to maintain an artificially high standard of living for one class of persons at the expense of another.

9. Cost of living

Congress believes that the basic costs of living should be controlled and kept low. A reasonable basic standard of living must be assured for all people, and to this end capital must be applied to the increase of productive effort within the country and not to the import of luxuries from overseas. There must therefore, be in the present stage of development of the country a strict control of imports. Congress believes in the full development of natural resources, both human and material, within the country so that the basic costs of living may be reduced for all people.

10. Taxation

Congress realizes that more widespread social services mean a higher rate of taxation but regards such services as a necessary insurance for the future. It believes in indirect taxation falling most heavily upon luxuries, in the present situation of the country where necessities have yet to be spread widely throughout the population. It is against Poll Tax and Hut Tax and favours direct taxation according to means through income tax, which must begin at a low income level in order to raise income from the majority of citizens of all races.

Taxation must not be levied nor its proceeds spent on a racial basis; both collection and spending of revenue must be administered to meet the needs of the people of the country as a whole.

11. Foreign investment

This country greatly needs capital investment from overseas. Congress recognizes that to obtain this security must be provided for both public and private investment. Government must therefore establish conditions under which capital may be invested and industry established with sufficient security to encourage investors. Congress believes that solving the racial problem by developing a fully integrated society on non-racial lines will give the greatest encouragement to investment from overseas.

12. *Immigration*

Congress believes that any policy of immigration aimed at increasing the non-indigenous population of the country for political reasons or from relieving other parts of the world of their surplus population is economically, politically and socially unsound and dangerous to peaceful development. Yet Congress recognizes that people with capital, ability and techniques which are not available in this country in sufficient quantity are needed from overseas. Those who have such assets must be encouraged to bring them into this country as and when they are needed provided that these immigrants are people of good character, prepared to enter fully into the life of this country on a basis of equality with the existing population, and to become integrated into a society in which there will be no discrimination as to race or colour. Immigration must therefore be strictly regulated and immigrants be very carefully selected both for their character and their abilities. In this way the country will become populated as fast as it can be developed and the immigrant population will become absorbed gradually and integrated in a stable social order.

13. *Freedom of movement*

Congress believes that, while a system of registration of all citizens of all races is necessary, there must be freedom of movement for all people on their lawful business throughout the country, without regard to race and without special passes. To make this possible, the Pass Laws must be repealed and ordinary administrative measures used for controlling the population.

Visitors to this country from overseas and from other African territories must be encouraged, and inhabitants from this country must only be refused permission to travel out of it or their movements otherwise controlled on grounds which can be challenged by appeal to the highest judicial authority.

14. *Police*

Congress believes in the necessity of a police force but considers that the growth of the modern state and the political conditions of the mid-twentieth century have given the police and security services an influence which too easily becomes a threat to individual freedom. No modern country is free from this danger. Congress therefore believes that an emerging modern democratic government must take the most careful precautions to control the activities of the police and security services and to make them subject in all things to the prompt scrutiny of an independent judiciary.

15. *Political representation*

Congress can see no justification for continuing any limitation of the franchise on grounds either of income, educational standard or race. The only form of government now acceptable to the vast majority of people in the British Commonwealth is parliamentary democracy based on universal adult suffrage, since this alone can produce a government responsible to all inhabitants of the country and aware of the needs of all. Further, only by this system can the enthusiasm of the whole people for government enterprise and national development be evoked and only by this system can we arrive at that fully representative government which, in the eyes of the United Kingdom and the world, is the condition of complete national independence. The real danger to future stability lies in keeping the majority of the people voteless, not in extending the franchise.

Congress believes that the present electoral arrangements are designed to keep political power in the hands of one small racial section of the population, and that the continuation of a racial alignment of political forces will be disastrous. The vote must be cast for the good of the whole country, not to promote the sectional interests of any one race. Racial politics will be disastrous for all. They can be avoided by universal suffrage NOW.

16. *Citizenship*

Congress believes that full citizenship must be extended to all those of any race or colour who are lawful and permanent inhabitants of the country, and have demonstrated this through their satisfactory residence and integration in the life of the community over the course of five years residence in the country.

17. *Racial discrimination*

Congress totally rejects the whole idea and practice of discrimination or segregation according to race or colour. It believes that this country can only develop peacefully as a society in which the different races become increasingly integrated in social, cultural, economic and political life, and in which there is no discrimination according to race, colour, creed or political opinion. Congress believes that such integration is both practicable and urgently necessary. It is in fact not an idealistic dream but the only practical way through existing racial problems. Present discriminations which exist, and which are a grave menace to society, must be strongly discouraged by government and government publicity services, and must be eliminated from all public institutions. All clauses in legislation which are directly discriminatory or are discriminatory in effect, must be repealed, and racial discrimination must be abolished entirely throughout the field of public administration. It must be made illegal by statute for racial discrimination to be practised in any institution holding a public licence. If such measures are taken, backed by a widespread government propaganda campaign, such racial discrimination as is of significance can be eliminated from society within a short space of time.

18. *Federation*
Congress believes that the Federation of Central African territories against the will of the vast majority of the inhabitants was both a moral and political error. It recognizes the need for consultation and closer association between neighbouring territories, but believes that a federation can only endure in so far as it is acceptable to the majority of the population and is voluntarily entered into by governments representative of the people of the territories. Such governments can only be elected on a wide franchise through which the will of the people can be expressed. Congress is primarily concerned to promote the establishment of popular representative government in Southern Rhodesia. When this is achieved questions involving Federation can be faced, and will then be found to take on a quite different aspect.

19. *Independence within the Commonwealth*
Congress believes that at present any question of granting greater independence to Southern Rhodesia, either directly or through the Federation, is wholly premature. Until racial problems are completely solved and an integrated society is well advanced, the Government of the United Kingdom must be strongly discouraged from relinquishing any further control over the affairs of this country or any of the territories incorporated in the Federation. It should, in fact, be strongly encouraged to exert its influence to the utmost in favour of the creation of a non-racial integrated society with a government responsible to the people, as the first essential step towards the granting of greater independence.

20. *Defence*
Congress believes that history has shown in modern times that the best form of defence against external aggression is internal strength. The settlement of the racial problem through the provision of equality of opportunity for people of all races in all spheres will produce an integrated society, which is the essential foundation to defence policy. In any form of conscription for necessary National Service for defence, recruitment and conditions of service must be according to ability and

without regard to race or colour.

Defence forces must at no time be used either in this country or beyond it to silence the legitimate aspirations of the uprising peoples of Africa or elsewhere.

21. *Foreign affairs*

Congress believes that this country should remain within the British Commonwealth of Nations playing such part as is appropriate and practicable in the affairs of the Commonwealth and in the relationships of the United Kingdom Government with foreign powers and the United Nations Organization.

Social programme

Congress encourages hard voluntary work for the development of community life. It will attempt to promote the following social organizations and will co-operate in their formation with all other bodies interested and devoted to non-racial principles:

Community associations, neighbourhood centres and settlements, to develop improved facilities for education, recreation, housing, health, and social, moral and intellectual advance in co-operation with local authorities and voluntary organizations,

Adult education facilities including literacy classes, evening classes, courses and discussion groups,

Public libraries and reading rooms to make available good books, periodicals and general information to local communities,

Mens' and womens' clubs for educational, social and recreational purposes,

Youth clubs and youth organizations for the provision of healthy leisure occupation for young people,

Children's nursery schools and play centres to aid parents in the upbringing of their children and to provide facilities for early education and play for children.

Personal programme

Congress encourages all members in their daily lives to offer to all people, regardless of race, colour, creed, class or political affiliation, a good example in habits of:

Friendship, courtesy, good manners and respect, in all dealings with individual people,

Honesty in all dealings with other people and in all money transactions,

Hard work with hand and brain in industry, agriculture and all services of benefit to the community,

Temperance, economy and simplicity in personal living,
Avoidance of violence or provocation to violence in all relations with
other people or organized bodies,
Vigorous effort to promote the social, economic and political welfare of
all men and service to the community as a whole.

CONGRESS WILL TAKE ALL POSSIBLE ACTION IN THE SOCIAL, ECONOMIC AND
POLITICAL SPHERES TO ESTABLISH THESE PRINCIPLES, PURSUE THESE POLICIES AND
CARRY OUT THESE PROGRAMMES.

IT WILL CO-OPERATE WITH ALL OTHER BODIES PURSUING SIMILAR AIMS, IN THE
BELIEF THAT THROUGH CO-OPERATION ADVANCE WILL BE MADE *TOWARDS THAT
SOCIETY IN WHICH PEACE, SECURITY AND PROGRESS WILL BE ASSURED TO THE
WHOLE POPULATION, REGARDLESS OF DIFFERENCES OF RACE, COLOUR AND
TRADITION.*

2 *Southern Rhodesia African National Congress: presidential report on progress and expansion during 1957-58. First Annual Delegates Conference, 12-14 September 1958*

INTRODUCTION

I welcome you all to the first annual conference of the Southern
Rhodesia African National Congress. On this day a year ago delegates
representing the Bulawayo branch of Congress and the Southern
Rhodesia African National Youth League met in Salisbury, at the
Community Centre in Harare, to approve the draft constitution and to
inaugurate the formation of the Southern Rhodesia African National
Congress. On that historic day this people's organization was born.

Your delegates elected a National Executive to govern, and to build
the foundation and structure of the Congress movement throughout
Southern Rhodesia and, through it, to implement vigorously the policy
and aspiration of the Southern Rhodesia African National Congress.
Your delegates honoured me with the privilege of leading your Congress.
Having set ourselves the task of defending the rights and supporting the
aspirations of the under-privileged people of this country, we concerned
ourselves in the first place with the examining of legislation that affects
the social, economic and political progress of these people.

Our examination of this legislation convinced us more than ever that
laws based on racial discrimination and racial differences are the chief
causes of our suffering. All our present misfortunes and the decaying
dignity of our race are directly, or indirectly, produced by such laws

which have subjected the African to the position of a serf, both physically and mentally. The greatest crimes committed by the rulers of this country, through the legislative monopoly and power which they have are the Acts of Parliament and regulations that are of a discriminatory nature.

Beginning with the Franchise laws of this country, it is sad to observe that the settlers have devised elaborate schemes to bar Africans from participating in the Government of the country. A qualitative Franchise such as the one enforced in this country has only one result—the complete deprivation of the African people from the exercise of their right to vote. Hence, in the Legislative Assembly, the African people are not represented, and all laws made therein threaten the security, progress and peace of the African people as a whole.

The monopoly of the settlers for making laws that govern this country has corrupted the democratic parliamentary institution renowned the world over. And not only has it done that, it has also destroyed the human values of the settlers themselves, in that it has made them believe that they alone as a race are capable of ruling this country. It has made them forget that here in Southern Rhodesia, and in Central Africa as a whole, there are millions of other people who have legitimate claims to participate in the Governments of these territories. But I would be failing in my duty as President-General of Congress were I to omit mentioning to you the devastating effects resulting from the settlers' political and economic domination over the non-Europeans in this country.

In the course of our organizing and expanding of Congress in all parts of this country, we have come across a section of the African community convinced in its theories relating to the problems of African advancement. This section believes, as the settlers do, that African advancement should be a gradual process controlled by Government and other powers that-be. They fear freedom and all the good things freedom may give. They have resigned from any attempts to demand their birthrights and, may I say, they have given up all hope of serving themselves and their people. It is in this section where you will find the so-called African moderates, who have taken it upon themselves to propagate the policies of the European-dominated political parties, knowing full well that there is no salvation for the African people in the present political parties.

The Todd crisis proved more than ever that African advancement is the bone of contention, and a subject loathed by all the European-dominated political parties. It is evident that all these political parties required Africans as members, in order to endorse their anti-African advancement policies and to divide and dilute African nationalism. But let us be clear, after all is said and done, that the African people of Central Africa hold all these African fellow-travellers in the present political parties responsible for whatever small or big misfortunes shall befall or retard African political, social or economic advancement. That is the verdict that awaits all those Africans who are supporting the present undemocratic political parties.

Native Land Husbandry Act

Your National Executive, in compliance with its mandate as the watchdog of the under-privileged people, has laid bare the ruthlessness in the implementation of the Native Land Husbandry Act in the reserves. The information before us has led us to one firm conclusion, that the Land Husbandry Act is a vicious device whose primary aims and objectives are to uproot, impoverish and to disperse the African people. It was meant to hit at the security of the Africans' Land Rights, and to violate their constitutional land security as envisaged in the Reserve Act which constituted the reserves in this colony. I do not intend to go into details as regards our observations and experience of the implementation of the Land Husbandry Act. Suffice it to say that any law, Act or measure whose effects undermine the security of our small land rights, dispossess us of our little wealth in the form of cattle, disperse us from our ancestral homes in the reserves and reduce us to the status of vagabonds and a source of cheap labour for the farmers, miners and industrials—such a law, Act or measure will turn the African people against society to the detriment of the peace and progress of this country.

I say this with all seriousness, because I have observed the effects of the Land Husbandry Act in those reserves where it is being enforced. I venture to call upon the Government of Southern Rhodesia to suspend immediately the implementation of the Native Land Husbandry Act, and to appoint a Commission of Inquiry to report on the effects of the Land Husbandry Act in all reserves where it has been enforced so far. If, after such an inquiry, the Government and the country are satisfied with the results, let the implementation of the Act be continued. I give this challenge to the Government on behalf of Congress.

The Native Affairs Department

In keeping with its old policy of spying on the progress, attitude and general political development of the African people, the Native Affairs Department has since the formation of Congress displayed a very hostile attitude towards us. In the first place, it was the Native Affairs Department that was instrumental in the enactment of the Native Affairs Amendment Bill, a fascist-type measure aimed at the leaders of Congress and their supporters. This Bill was intended as a Magna Carta for the Native Commissioners to enable them to deal with the leaders and members of Congress. But I am pleased to say, in spite of its vicious intentions, your Congress leaders and organizers throughout this colony are all the more determined to organize and spread the activities of Congress. Today we are proud of the many branches of this organization in various parts of Southern Rhodesia; no previous organization in this country has ever achieved so much within the short space of one year.

But I would like to remind the Native Affairs Department that the African National Congress is a political organization with the same status, rights and privileges as any other political party in this country; to interfere with its machinery of organization, its leaders and members, is in essence interfering with the basic principles of party politics. I submit that this is beyond the jurisdiction of the Native Affairs Department. Instead of going into politics, the Native Affairs Department should concern itself with its own affairs. It is no secret that, due to ignorance and not keeping up with the march of time, this Department no longer serves a useful purpose. It has failed to advance Africans into positions of responsibility. There is not a single African Native Commissioner or Assistant Native Commissioner in this country. Why? Instead, we find that this Department has become a convenient hide-out for incapable, inefficient people; rejects of commerce and industries, and other professions. These people earn higher salaries in the Native Affairs Department than they would otherwise be capable of earning. We demand an immediate end to their parasitic existence on the poor African tax-payer in this country. The Native Affairs Department must be abolished.

Chiefs, Headmen and Congress
Our chiefs and headmen have been subjected and intimidated by the Native Affairs Department during the past year. But despite all that, Congress has received invaluable co-operation from the chiefs and headmen in many parts of the country where Congress has established its branches. I am pleased to say that we have been assured by many chiefs that the indoctrination and intimidation that goes on at Seke, and in other reserves, from time to time, directed against the Congress movement in the reserves, will have no influence on them against Congress.

Contact with other organizations
A high level Conference between leaders of the Southern Rhodesia African National Congress, the Northern Rhodesia African National

Congress and the Nyasaland African National Congress was held in Lusaka early this year. This was a very important Conference. Valuable interchange of information concerning the activities of Congress in the three territories took place at this conference. Leaders discussed their political tactics and agreed on the various ways of facing the problems in their territories. The success of this conference marked the beginning of an interchange of information between the three Congresses. It was agreed that similar conferences should be held every year, more so before 1960, in order to coordinate one general policy of the Congress movement to be presented by the three Congresses at the 1960 Conference.

Team work in the National Executive
I am proud of the team you elected me to lead. It is in my opinion one of the best national executives that can be found anywhere in the Congress movement in Central Africa. We face the national problems of this country without fear. Whenever we are confronted with difficulties, we face these difficulties as one man. There is no going back. This is possible because of the vigour and determination that is characteristic of the officers and members of our National Executive.

Attempts to hold a Round-Table Conference with Government
At the beginning of this year, a grave and serious problem of education faced the African children throughout the country. Reports from all over the country poured into the office requesting Congress to take the matter up with the Government. We accordingly drew the attention of the Government to this educational problem and requested an opportunity to present to and discuss with the Government our Educational plan. In reply the Government directed us to submit our plan to the Education Department authorities. This we could not do because our plan not only concerned itself with minor details and problems of education, but viewed the whole African educational problem against the background of Government policy as a whole. Negotiations came to a standstill, for the Ministry of African Education and the Government would not agree to hold a round-table conference with the representatives of Congress on the subject of African education. We intend once more to press the Government to allow us the opportunity to discuss with them our educational plan.

The Great Task Before Us
Racial discrimination practised in this country is a sin against humanity. No self-respecting people can bow down to this iniquitous soul-

destroying practice. We have experienced the fruits of this disease, and we are satisfied that it is our duty as oppressed people to do everything in our power to get rid of the practice of racial discrimination in this country.

It is against the laws of God and the laws of nature to discriminate against a person because of the colour of his or her skin. To fulfil the great principles of God, and the United Nations Charter on Human Rights, the great task before us is to fight the evils of racial discrimination in this country. With that in mind Congress has requested all its branches to submit detailed information with regard to all public places where Africans are discriminated against on grounds of colour. We need this detailed information. It is very important in our campaign.

Identity Cards

It is the policy of Congress to fight all racial discrimination. Therefore we regard the identity card system in Southern Rhodesia as a discriminatory measure against the dignity of the African people. We cannot accept it. Africans are being asked to pay £1 for these discriminatory documents which leave them in exactly the same position as they were before.

Our attitude towards Federation

1. We regard Federation as a failure because racial discrimination still goes on and is now worse than before.
2. Practices in the Federation are contrary to the preamble of the Federal Constitution.
3. Deportation of African leaders by the Southern Rhodesia Government has proved that geographically the three territories and their peoples are not one.
4. Difficulties in obtaining passports by the Africans in the Federation have proved that geographically the three territories and their peoples are not one.
5. Interference by the Federal Government in the internal Constitutional changes in Northern Rhodesia and Nyasaland has shown us that it is the settlers who are intended to control the political destiny of these territories.

The above facts have shown what form the Federation is taking. The attitude of Congress will be discussed by the delegates at this Conference and results will be published.

I have told you during my opening speech some of the things that the delegates will discuss during the sitting of this Conference. They are matters that affect you who are present here, and all the people who claim citizenship of this country. They are matters that need serious consideration by us all. We live in a beautiful country, a country with wonderful prospects, a country with enough resources for all of us if we are prepared to live together as a family, recognizing our similarities rather than our differences. We may be of different colours, different races and different religions, but the most important thing is that we are all human beings with human dignity, the dignity that must be recognized and preserved and respected by all of us. It is on that basis that we can develop this country peacefully and contribute to the welfare of humanity throughout the world.

We are in a country in a continent which is attracting world attention today. We are in a unique position in that we can demonstrate to the world that people of different colours can live together in mutual respect and understanding. That is the task to be undertaken by you and me and every other person in Southern Rhodesia. To be able to do so we have to examine and re-examine ourselves. We must satisfy ourselves that all we do in this country is in accordance with the Universal Declaration of Human Rights. It is not easy to live up to these declarations, but if we are interested in the future of our country and the welfare of our children we must sacrifice all temporary advantages there may be for enjoyment, for the good of the future of our children and our country.

Congress as a national organization stands for that. It recognizes certain forces in our country that may destroy the very foundation of goodwill and mutual understanding in the country. It offers a programme that will destroy such forces.

Racial Discrimination
I would like to re-affirm and emphasize that Congress totally rejects the whole idea and practice of racial discrimination. It believes that the country can only be developed peacefully in a society in which the different races become integrated in social, political, economical and cultural life in which there is no discrimination according to colour, race, creed or political opinion. Congress believes that such integration is both practicable and urgently necessary.

The present discrimination which exists in our country today is a grave menace to our society and is a terrible disease which is eating away the intelligence and energy of our people. It is a disease that has warped the minds of those who practise it and damaged the attitude of those against whom it is practised.

I therefore call upon all the people of goodwill in Southern Rhodesia in the name of humanity and decency, to fight and eradicate this menace without any compromise. I call upon the Christian church, whose principles are diametrically opposed to this shameful and sinful practice, to join hands with us in destroying this monster.

Our attitude towards the church is that we believe in freedom of worship. It is important for a nation to recognize the existence of God or a supernatural being. We have no quarrel with the Christian church, but only with their practices. We have no quarrel with any religious groups or sects.

Self-Rule

There has been a lot of talk about self-rule in this country. Southern Rhodesia is a self-governing colony, but only a few people share in that self-government. What Congress wants is self-government for all the inhabitants.

Ladies and gentlemen, this a brief report of the activities of the Southern Rhodesia African National Congress during the past year.

3 National Democratic Party: statement of appeal by interim President Michael Mawema and Secretary-General Sketchley Samkange. Salisbury, 1960

The National Democratic Party is a political party initiated and led by Africans. It is the only such party existing today in Southern Rhodesia since the banning of the African National Congress in February, 1959.

The party was launched on January 1st, 1960 at Highfields, in Salisbury after six weeks of drafting the aims and objects behind closed doors. It enjoys the support of all the classes of Africans in Southern Rhodesia.

The party aims at:

(i) pursuing the struggle for, and the attainment of freedom for the African people of Southern Rhodesia,

(ii) establishing and granting one man one vote for all the inhabitants of Southern Rhodesia,

(iii) working in conjunction with other freedom organizations in Africa for the establishment and maintenance of full democracy in Africa and the achievement of Pan-Africanism.

Since its inauguration on New Year's day, the Party has opened seven branches, covering the main towns of the country—Salisbury (Highfields, Harare, Mabvuku—African Townships), Bulawayo, Umtali, Gwelo and Marandellas.

The present National Executive is interim, composed mainly of foundation members of the Party. The Party seeks the support of all but by the nature of its task it is bound to make its appeal first to Africans.

By and large the Africans are poor. We cannot count on any large donation of funds to begin our work as European parties usually are able to. The Party has strong support of the Africans and we believe that after overcoming the initial stages the Africans themselves will bear the burden. We must find the initial sum to enable the organization to take root.

As a basic minimum we need:

1. An office in Salisbury at—£5 rent per month.

2. A typewriter—£35.
3. A duplicating machine—£200.
4. A fund to meet the cost of stationery.
5. A fund to pay a full time Secretary—£20 per month.
6. A fund to enable us to hire halls for meetings at about £3 to £5 per meeting, with about £10 deposit for the hall.
7. Transport for organizing from place to place.

We estimate that at least £1,500 would see us through our initial stages. We hope after that the Organization will be able to continue on its own.

We hereby appeal for any help in cash or kind and any such help will greatly be appreciated.

4 *National Democratic Party:* Reserved Powers in the Southern Rhodesia Constitution *(SR Letters Patent, 1923); memorandum submitted to the British Government, 1960*

1. We, the African people of the Colony of Southern Rhodesia, cognizant of our rights as British subjects and deeply conscious of the paramount importance and necessity of the powers reserved to Her Majesty's Government in the United Kingdom in the Southern Rhodesia Constitution Letters Patent, 1923, view with the greatest alarm and perturbation recent moves and demands by the European-controlled Government of Southern Rhodesia to secure the removal of those powers. We hold it to be the sacred duty and moral obligation of Her Majesty's Government to retain intact all the reserved powers as embodied in the aforesaid constitution and listed in Paragraph 2 of this memorandum, as long as the majority of the people of the colony do not have the requisite power to elect and control the government of their country. It is our sincerest and deepest conviction that the removal of these powers without the prior fulfilment of the above condition would not only constitute a breach of faith but would also, and what is more, hand over the lives of the overwhelming majority of the Colony's people to the complete control of an ethnic and reactionary minority whose political philosophy and socio-economic policies are clearly opposed to the democratic system of government based on the political equality of individuals regardless of race, colour or property, and on majority rule. It is our conviction, and developments in other parts of Africa confirm

that conviction in large measure, that any removal of these reserved powers, without parallel political and constitutional changes acceptable to the majority of the country's inhabitants, cannot but be interpreted, and would be so interpreted by the Africans of Southern Rhodesia in particular and the world in general, as an endorsement by the British Government of the racial policies of Southern Rhodesia and of continued European domination. Anxious to avoid racial bitterness and eventual calamity in our country, determined to avoid the emergence of another South Africa, aware that in the recent history of British colonial policy in Africa the British Government has not relinquished control over any territory without the prior consent of the majority of its inhabitants, and desirous of creating in our country a system of government based on majority rule and popular consent, we beg to submit to Her Majesty's Government this memorandum in the humble and confident hope that British justice and fairness will not fail the people of Southern Rhodesia and that no further constitutional changes will be made in the Southern Rhodesia constitution without the effective participation of Africans through their representatives duly returned under a democratic electoral system based on one man one vote. We are aware that Southern Rhodesia is self-governing and has been so since 1923, but we are equally aware of the numerous obstacles that have been placed in the way of the political advancement of the African, particularly through the means of a highly restrictive franchise system which has made democratic rule impossible. As long as government of the many by a monopolistic and ethnic minority obtains, the chances of inter-racial amity must remain bleak and any further devolution of power to the minority must further alienate African loyalties.

THE RESERVED POWERS:

2. Under the provisions of the Southern Rhodesia Constitution Letters Patent, 1923, the British Government, with the full consent of the European community of Southern Rhodesia, reserved to itself the following powers, both for the protection of the interests of the native inhabitants and for purposes of general overall control:

A. *Section* 27, that—

When any Law has been passed by the Legislature it shall be presented for Our assent to the Governor, who shall declare according to his discretion, but subject to this Constitution and any instructions in that behalf given him, under Our Sign manual and Signet or through a Secretary of State, that he assents in Our name, or that he witholds assents, or that he reserves the Law for the signification of Our pleasure.

B. *Section* 28, that—

Unless he shall have previously obtained Our instruction upon such Law through a Secretary of State, or unless such Law shall contain a clause suspending the operation thereof until the signification in the Colony of Our pleasure thereupon, the Governor shall reserve:

(a) any Law, save in respect of the supply of arms, ammunition, or liquor to natives, whereby natives may be subjected or made liable to any conditions, disabilities or restrictions to which persons of European descent are not also subjected or made liable.

(b) any Law which may repeal, alter or amend, or is in any way repugnant to or inconsistent with such provisions of these Our Letters Patent, as may under these Our Letters Patent be repealed or altered by the Legislature.

(c) any Law constituting the Legislative Council passed in pursuance of Section 2 of these Our Letters Patent.

C. *Section* 31, that—

It shall be lawful for Us, Our Heirs and successors, to disallow any Law within one year from the date of the Governor's assent thereto, and such disallowance, on being made known by the Governor by Speech or Message to the Legislative Assembly or by Proclamation in the Gazette, shall annul the Law from the day when the disallowance is so made known.

D. *Section* 32, that—

A proposed Law reserved for Our pleasure shall not have any force unless and until, within one year from the day on which it was presented to the Governor for Our assent, the Governor makes known by Speech or Message to the Legislative Council and the Legislative Assembly, or by Proclamation in the Gazette, that it has received Our assent.

E. *Section* 41, that—

No conditions, disabilities or restrictions which do not equally apply to persons of European descent shall, without the previous consent of the Secretary of State, be imposed upon natives (save in respect of the supply of arms, ammunition and liquor), by any Proclamation, Regulation, or other instrument issued under the provisions of any Law, unless such conditions, disabilities, or restrictions shall have been explicitly prescribed, defined and limited in such Law.

F. *Section* 61, that—

We do hereby reserve to Ourselves, Our heirs and successors, full power and authority from time to time to revoke, alter or amend Sections 26, 28, 39-47, and 55 of these Our Letters Patent as to Us or Them shall seem meet.

3. These powers of reservation, disallowance and overall control, held

by the British Government as listed in Paragraph 2 above, constitute the main powers any alteration or removal of which the majority of the people of Southern Rhodesia must necessarily view with the greatest concern and alarm, unless and until the Government of Southern Rhodesia is elected by the majority of the people of the country.

THE COMMITMENT:

4. In submitting this memorandum we are aware, and fully acknowledge, that the Constitution Letters Patent in question, because made under the Royal Prerogative, can be altered in part or in whole, or completely repealed unilaterally or otherwise, by Her Majesty's Government, and that such action could not be questioned either in English Law or International Law. We fully accept the legitimacy and plenitude of Her Majesty's Government's right and power.

5. We submit, however, that Her Majesty's Government has a paramount moral and political obligation which it seems to us must counterbalance the right and power acknowledged in Paragraph 4 above. The majority of the people of Southern Rhodesia have always looked and still look to Her Majesty's Government for the protection of their interests. Her Majesty's Government deemed fit and freely extended their protection both during the days of the rule of the British South Africa Company and since 1923 when Southern Rhodesia became a self-governing Colony. We further submit that the political hazards of any relinquishment of the reserved powers enumerated in Paragraph 2 above, without a previous or accompanying redistribution of political power enabling the majority of the people in the Colony to elect and control their government, are difficult to overestimate and must undermine the whole basis of African confidence and racial amity in Central Africa and the prospect of peaceful political settlement.

6. It will be recalled—and this is a matter which inspires confidence in us—that Her Majesty's Government will unfailingly uphold their high moral and political obligations to all British Subjects whatever their race or colour—that from the very cradle of the Colony till now the British Government and people have regarded as important and vital the protection of the interests of the native inhabitants of our country. Thus, for example:
(a)   Article 80 of the Southern Rhodesia Order in Council, 1898, contained the provisions for the protection of the natives, and these provisions were retained under Section 28 (a) and Section 41 of the

Southern Rhodesia Constitution Letters Patent, 1923.

(b) In 1921 Lord Buxton's Committee advised that the restrictions of Article 80 of the Order in Council of 1898 should be incorporated in the Constitution of a self-governing Southern Rhodesia. The British Government accepted this advice and incorporated those provisions in the Letters Patent of 1923. Significantly, Sir Charles Coghlan, Southern Rhodesia's first Premier, speaking with the approval of the members of the Legislative Council, stated that the settlers would accept 'all the guarantees which the Imperial Government might choose to lay down' (cf. Cmd. 5218, p.6). The reserved powers were regarded as necessary by the British Government and were accepted by the European leaders. We contend as we shall show hereunder, that the reserved powers still remain necessary and are necessary as long as the natives of the country are under a settler-dominated government.

(c) In 1934/35, in response to proposals made by the Prime Minister of Southern Rhodesia for the removal of the restrictions and reservations in the Constitution, the then Secretary of State for Dominion Affairs replied that:

    (i)   the time had not come for Her Majesty's Government in the United Kingdom to agree to the removal of all the safeguards;

    (ii) any relaxation or removal of those safeguards could not include at present a waiver of Section 28 (a) and Section 41 of the Constitution Letters Patent, since the development of native policy in the Colony might well have repercussions beyond the Colony's borders (cf. Cmd. 5218).

(N.B. We submit that the racial policies of Southern Rhodesia and the complete control in particular of the government by the European minority, render even more necessary that the British Government retain its present powers, unless and until a political system acceptable to the majority of the people of the Colony is effected. We further submit that any waiver of those powers, against the wishes of that majority, is bound to have serious consequences in the whole of Central Africa and a most damaging effect on the future of race relations. We are completely convinced, and there is every evidence to show that, the sole reason for the demand by the ruling European minority, is the complete control of African affairs and the entrenchment of a socio-political system characterized by race discrimination and European control (cf. Paragraphs 11 and 12 below).)

(d) The British Government in agreeing to the Constitution of the Federation of Rhodesia and Nyasaland insisted on the inclusion of safeguards for the Africans (although we fully realize that the safeguards have proved largely ineffectual and we reject the present Federation as an imposition and an instrument of domination by the European minority).

(e) We interpret repeated statements by Her Majesty's Government that no final political and constitutional settlement regarding the present Federation of Rhodesia and Nyasaland will be effected without the wishes of the inhabitants of the territories concerned, as referring not only to the wishes of the inhabitants of Northern Rhodesia and Nyasaland, but also to wishes of the inhabitants of Southern Rhodesia. For although Southern Rhodesia is self-governing, we cannot see in what sense the wishes of the inhabitants of Southern Rhodesia can be said to have been expressed or to be expressed when the Government which acts on their behalf is controlled by less than ten per cent of the total population and is opposed by the remaining majority. Thus, just as the British Government has insisted on the wishes of the inhabitants with regard to the Federal Constitution, we think it must equally insist on the full expression of the wishes of the majority of Southern Rhodesia. There can be no final and peaceful solution without the active support of the majority. Only Government by consent, and consent of the majority under a democratic system, can achieve the desired goal of a racially harmonious society in Central Africa. Any further concession or devolution of power to the European minorities we must regard with every gravity and we cannot fail to warn Her Majesty's Government of the disastrous consequences such a policy would entail.

EUROPEAN DEMANDS — AND THEIR REASONS:
7. The reserved powers in question have been repeatedly attacked and demand made for their removal. Thus, for example:
(a) Both in 1934 and 1935 the Prime Minister of Southern Rhodesia proposed to the Secretary of State that the restrictions and reservations be removed. But, as we have stated above in paragraph 6 (c), it was the view of the Secretary of State that the reservations could not be removed yet.
(b) In 1951, after sustained pressure on the Southern Rhodesia Government by the Opposition, a Select Committee of the Legislative Assembly was appointed and it drew up a report recommending the setting up of a second chamber (Legislative Council or Senate) to take over the reserved powers over native legislation. But as the

issue of federating the two Rhodesias and Nyasaland soon began and eclipsed for the time the Committee's report, the matter was not proceeded with. The control which the European minority would have over the whole Federation and the prospects of the Federation attaining dominion status under European control gave a substantial section of the European community in Southern Rhodesia no cause to press on with their demand for the removal of the reserved powers in question.

(c)   And now again the demand has been renewed. At the end of 1959, while in London, Sir Edgar Whitehead, the Prime Minister of Southern Rhodesia, stated that he would propose to the British Government that the reserved powers be removed. At a Press conference which was held in Southern Rhodesia on 19 January, 1960, Sir Edgar repeated the demand, broadly hinting that a multi-racial second chamber would be substituted for the British Government regarding the reservations in the Colony's Constitution (cf. *Federal Newsletter*, London, 12 February 1960). Subsequently, following the recent visit of the Secretary of State for Commonwealth Relations to Southern Rhodesia, Sir Edgar announced that he would himself be visiting London in April to hold negotiations about the removal of the veto power of the Secretary of State with a view to replacing the latter by a second chamber. (cf. *Federal Newsletter,* London, 11 March 1960). We cannot but be alarmed at such negotiations taking place without the participation of accepted African leaders, nor can we fail to draw attention to detrimental effect on African confidence such a move must inevitably have. The Southern Rhodesia Government is not representative of the majority of the Colony's population and cannot accordingly know and express the wishes of that majority.

8. The reasons which have been given for this demand at various stages may be summarized as follows:

(a)   that Southern Rhodesia has proved herself competent to govern herself and must be accorded an increased international status;

(b)   that the present protection by the British Government was no protection at all, for oftener than not officials in London knew little about the subject of any legislation submitted to them for the signification of Her Majesty's pleasure;

(c)   that the process of consulting between London and Salisbury was time-consuming and wasteful;

(d)   that the powers in question have never been used by the British Government to disallow any legislation and that they are therefore unnecessary.

9. For these reasons and others the European-controlled Government of Southern Rhodesia has sought and seeks the abolition of the powers concerned and the substitution of a second chamber instead.

10. We, on the other hand, beg to submit that no safeguard whatever can be possible for the majority of the Colony's population through any institution which is either directly controlled by the overwhelmingly European electorate or pitted against the European-dominated Legislative Assembly.

OUR SUBMISSION

11. We contest the reasons given in paragraph 8 above, on the following grounds:

(a) Southern Rhodesia may have proved competent to govern within the framework of a system acceptable to the European minority, but it has undoubtedly failed to gain the confidence of the majority of the Africans and has resorted to repressive and restrictive measures to prop the existing oligarchical system of government and to muzzle African political aspirations and their unmistakeable rejection of policies of race discrimination and European domination. We cannot but regard the following laws, for example, as infringements of the Rule of Law and as constituting unquestionable political subjugation and social degradation of the Africans:

(i) The Southern Rhodesia Electoral Act, which sets extremely high education and means qualifications, thus making it impossible for the electorate to be broad and representative of the majority of the people. We need not remind Her Majesty's Government of the details of these qualifications, which are well known to them. But we must question on what grounds the Southern Rhodesia Government, with an entirely white Assembly, an electorate which is composed of more than 65,000 European voters and less than 2,000 African voters, and a racially restrictive civil service—a Government which, in brief, is a settler oligarchy in a country of 2,500,000 Africans and only 200,000 Europeans—can claim to speak on behalf of the people of Southern Rhodesia?

(ii) The Preventive Detention Act, 1959, in terms of which people can be summarily arrested and detained without recourse to the normal courts of law, and under which several African leaders are still detained following the emergency of last year.

(iii) The Unlawful Organizations Act, 1959, under which the

African National Congress and other political organizations are proscribed, and under which any political party which did not accept the government of the day is regarded as subversive, as if to challenge the policies of the governing party is to challenge the State, as if the party in power is the State.

(iv) The Land Apportionment Act, 1930, which effects an inequitable racial distribution of land and which is the basis of a rigid system of geographical segregation of the races.

(v) The Natives Registration Act, 1936, and related Acts which create a 'pass system' affecting most deeply the freedom of movement and labour contract of the Africans, a system hardly distinguishable from the pass system of the Union of South Africa.

(vi) The many other laws, such as the Movement of Persons (Control) Act, the Subversive Activities Act, the Native Affairs Amendment Act, 1959, which makes it an offence for an African to criticize the Government of Southern Rhodesia and the Federation of Rhodesia and Nyasaland and any of their officials and the many practices of social segregation such as the provision of segregated cinemas and restaurants and even ambulances, which are either sanctioned or connived at by the Government. We cannot indeed see in what sense the Southern Rhodesia Government can claim to have proved itself competent to govern, unless government is synonymous with restrictive and repressive measures, and we cannot see in what sense it can claim to be given even more powers to be independent of supervision by Her Majesty's Government, without bringing the majority of the population even more ruthlessly under a sectional system of government.

(b) It may be true that officials in London know little about any legislation which may be submitted to them from Salisbury, but it does not appear that knowledge of the actual conditions by the Europeans in Southern Rhodesia has made them less biased. On the contrary, we contend that the European minority is determined to maintain its dominant position and the various Acts quoted above and other measures amply support our contention. We believe, on the other hand, that British officials from their wide experience are in an eminently better position to act more impartially on any measures which might be submitted for the signification of Her Majesty's pleasure.

(c) The only alternative way to effect an acceptable government is not the substitution of the proposed second chamber for the reservations in the Constitution, but the substitution of majority rule for the said reservations. Nothing less will do.

(d) The fact that these powers of disallowances have never been used does not argue that they are unnecessary, but merely that they have not been used by the British Government, though we submit that the powers should have been invoked and used when such Acts were enacted as the Land Apportionment Act, 1930, the Natives Registration Act, 1936, the Natives Affairs Amendment Act, 1959, the Preventive Detention Act, 1959, and others, and when African representations were made to the British Government to use the reserved powers whenever discriminatory legislation was made in the Colony. Although the British Government has not used its powers, circumstances may yet arise when it may be necessary to use them. The powers have not elapsed either, because they have not been used or because they may be difficult to use. We submit that they are still legally tenable and could be so used; and that they constitute, in addition, a moral restraint, a factor strongly in favour of their retention as long as a sectional minority regime exists in the Colony.

12. We suspect, and submit, that the real motive for the demand by the European-dominated Government of Southern Rhodesia for the removal of these powers is their desire to bring Africans even more effectively and completely under an oligarchical, European-dominated type of Government. For surely, if the desire of the European minority in the Colony is to build a nation in which all people, regardless of their race or colour, who have chosen the country as their home, shall look to Salisbury and not to London for any redress of grievances and for the location of their loyalties, we fail to see why the European community should seek to do so under a political system which is clearly rejected by the majority of the population and which must inevitably destroy the basis of inter-racial amity.

13. The reserved powers in the Constitution Letters Patent constitute, we suggest, the last constitutional and political bargaining power for Her Majesty's Government to influence desirable and overdue changes in Southern Rhodesia. Her Majesty's Government can relinquish those powers any time if they so wish, and we would have no objection whatsoever, *provided* political power in the Colony devolved on a government which is democratically responsive; *provided* this was accompanied by a radical reform of the Colony's electoral laws, basing them on the principle of 'one man, one vote'. Any other position taken by the British Government in the way of a final settlement, which would be a capitulation to the settlers, must be regarded, and we would have no

alternative but to so regard it, as amounting to complicity by Her Majesty's Government in the settler scheme for racial discrimination and settler domination. We would wish not to be driven to this position, particularly as we believe that it is Her Majesty's Government's intention, as evidenced by recent constitutional developments in Kenya and Tanganyika, to steer clear of policies based on race discrimination and minority rule.

BASIS FOR AGREEMENT:

14. The future cannot be made secure by a political system based on a monopoly of power by the European minority or on an electoral system which entrenches European and therefore minority preponderance, and therefore disenfranchisement of the majority of the population. On the contrary, we believe that such a system will never and can never secure for the European any future in Africa. The only just and acceptable democratic basis for agreement is their acceptance of the political equality of individuals regardless of race or colour, and of government by majority rule. 'One man, one vote' can be the only basis for final agreement.

15. The present Government of Southern Rhodesia cannot in justice commit the country to any final settlement, for it is responsible only to less than 70,000 voters out of a total population of nearly 2,700,000. Further, we are not impressed by the argument that because Southern Rhodesia has been self-governing since 1923, the British Government cannot interfere in the Colony's affairs. The argument is irrelevant and overlooks the fact that the future of 2,500,000 people is at stake and would be left at the mercy of an ethnic minority whose desire to entrench its own position might prove most disastrous to Central Africa. Just what the exact constitutional arrangements should be, should be the subject of a constitutional conference representative of the accepted leaders of both the European community and the African community. Delegates to such a conference must command the support of their communities, be elected by them, and not appointed by a Government which is responsible to a small minority of the population, nor should they be elected by the present European-dominated electorate.

16. Under a system of majority rule, we would accept a second chamber to carry out the normal functions of second chambers under the parliamentary system and, provided always that the democratically elected Legislative Assembly remains the repository of sovereign power as the British House of Commons is to the House of Lords.

17. In conclusion, we beg to submit in all humility to Her Majesty's

Government that the hour has long struck for a bold and imaginative British policy and stand to exert influence in Southern Rhodesia. The wind of change which is blowing over Africa cannot miss Southern Rhodesia. Unless the British people and Government wish to see Southern Rhodesia sink into racial chaos, which we believe it is by no means their wish, it is imperative that the whole weight of British justice and fairness be thrown in the cause of democracy and not in support of policies which in one way or another support continued minority rule. The choice in Southern Rhodesia is not between an efficient European-dominated Government on the one hand and an incompetent corrupt African-dominated Government on the other, as Europeans in Southern Rhodesia would make the world believe. No, on the contrary, the choice is not between these alternatives. The choice is between a fearful reactionary European-dominated government relying inevitably more and more on restrictive and repressive measures on the one hand, and a popularly-supported democratic government on the other, whatever its initial shortcomings might be. These are the alternatives and the British Government can immeasurably influence the right choice and the safe course, standing by their historical obligations to the African people of Central Africa until the majority of the people of Southern Rhodesia control the government of their country. If it is probably the easier way for Her Majesty's Government to yield to the demands of the European minority, it is also the easiest way to racial antagonism and catastrophe, to say nothing of the loss of British prestige and influence in the world generally and in Africa in particular—a loss whose consequences it is difficult to underestimate.

18. We submit this memorandum with all confidence in the broader visions for racial harmony and Commonwealth understanding which we know Her Majesty's Government to cherish and to be deeply concerned with, but which must remain or become illusory were race discrimination and European domination of African majorities not abjured.

5 National Democratic Party: proposals for a new and revised constitution for Southern Rhodesia. 1960

PART I

Fundamental Rights

1. The provisions of this part of this constitution shall form the basic law of Southern Rhodesia and supersede the provisions of any law made by the legislature of Southern Rhodesia.

2. All persons born or naturalized in Southern Rhodesia who are subject to its jurisdiction are citizens of Southern Rhodesia.

3. All citizens are equal in their rights and before the law, and no law shall discriminate directly or indirectly between citizens on the grounds of their race, their religious beliefs or affiliations, or their colour.

4. Subject to other provisions of this constitution, all citizens shall have the right to vote for members of the legislature and to be elected to membership of the same.

5. All citizens shall be eligible to take part in the Government of the country and no discrimination shall be made between citizens on the grounds of their race, colour or creed in their eligibility for employment in the public service of Southern Rhodesia.

6. No citizen shall be exiled out of Southern Rhodesia or forbidden to return to Southern Rhodesia.

7. Subject to the provisions of sections 2 and 3 all citizens shall be free to reside anywhere in Southern Rhodesia where citizens may lawfully reside.

8. No person shall be deprived of life, liberty or property without due process of law, nor shall any person be denied the equal protection of the laws.

9. The legislature shall make no laws abridging the right to freedom of speech or of the Press, or the right of the people peaceably to assemble and petition the Government for the redress of grievances.

10. The right of the people to be secure in their persons, houses, papers and effects against unreasonable searches and seizures shall not be violated nor shall warrants for the search of any person or property issue except upon reasonable and probable cause supported by oath or affirmation and particularly describing the place to be searched and the person or thing to be seized.

11. In criminal trials the accused shall be considered innocent until proved guilty and he shall have a right to speedy trial by an impartial jury, judge and assessors or magistrate; to be informed of the nature

of the charge against him; to be confronted with the witness against him; to have compulsive process for obtaining witnesses in his favour and access to legal advice and representation.

12. Excessive bail shall not be required nor shall bail be refused except for good cause shown, nor shall excessive fines be imposed or cruel and inhuman punishment inflicted.

13. The prerogative writ of habeas corpus shall not be suspended or abridged in any way except in times of rebellion or invasion.

14. No person shall be deprived of his property compulsorily except according to law or for just and reasonable compensation.

15. No person shall be denied employment on the grounds of race, colour or religious belief (the legislature shall make laws to give effect to this provision).

16. The right to acquire, lease, occupy or use shall not be restricted on the grounds of race or creed or colour.

17. Every person has the right to form and join trade unions or other associations for the protection of his interests.

18. All people have a right to education. All children without regard to race, colour or religion shall be entitled to such free education as the state provides. The Government of Southern Rhodesia is charged with the fundamental obligation to provide education for all children.

PART II

The Governor

19. The Governor shall be appointed by the Queen on the recommendation of the Cabinet of Southern Rhodesia.

20. He shall serve for a term of five years, which period may only be extended by another period of five years.

21. The Governor shall assent to all bills duly passed by Parliament and presented to him for his signature on behalf of the Queen.

22. The Governor may return to the Legislative Assembly any bills so presented to him and may transmit therewith any amendments which he may recommend, and the Legislative Assembly may deal with such recommendations provided that he shall sign the bill when it is presented to him unaltered a third time or within thirty days, whichever is the shorter period.

PART III

The Legislature

23. There shall be a Legislative Assembly consisting of 60 members who shall be elected by voters in and for the several electoral districts

as hereinafter provided for and for the purpose of constituting the Legislative Assembly, the Governor shall issue writs under the Public Seal of Southern Rhodesia for the general election of members to serve in the Legislative Assembly.

24. All citizens of Southern Rhodesia of the age of twenty-one years and above who are not otherwise disqualified under the terms of this constitution shall be entitled to be voters at any election of members of the Legislative Assembly.

25. The following persons are disqualified from being registered as voters and from voting:

(a)   certified lunatics or idiots or persons undergoing treatment in mental institutions;

(b)   persons convicted of any offence who have not completed their punishment or been pardoned, provided that they were sentenced to imprisonment for more than twelve months;

(c)   persons convicted of corrupt and illegal practices at elections;

(d)   persons who have not been registered as voters 90 days before the date of the election.

26. All citizens who have attained the age of twenty-one years shall be eligible for election as members of the Legislative Assembly, provided they are not illiterate and understand the official language of the country sufficiently to be able to take an active part in the proceedings of the Legislative Assembly; provided, further, that they are not disqualified under one or more of the following classes:

(a)   civil servants;

(b)   insolvent persons;

(c)   persons guilty of corrupt or illegal practices at elections, provided that this disqualification shall be for a period of five years only following the date of conviction;

(d)   persons convicted of any offence who have not completed their term of punishment or been pardoned, provided that they were sentenced to imprisonment for more than twelve months;

(e)   persons holding commissions or undertaking contracts for or on account of the public service;

(f)   persons appointed to statutory bodies responsible for any nationalized industry.

27. Subject to the provisions of Sections 24, 25 and 26, the registration of voters, the preparation of lists of voters, the nomination of candidates, the conduct of elections and the hearing of election petitions shall be carried out in accordance with the existing electoral laws of Southern Rhodesia.

28. The registration of voters shall be continuous and voters' rolls shall be compiled quarterly and annually.

29. As often as may be deemed necessary and always before each general election, the Governor shall appoint a delimitation

commission to divide Southern Rhodesia into 60 electoral districts, each of which shall retain one member of the Legislative Assembly.

30. The commission shall consist of not more than five and not less than three members.

31. The chairman of the commission shall be the Chief Justice of Southern Rhodesia and other members shall be appointed by the Governor upon recommendation of the Chief Justice.

32. In determining the boundaries of each of the constituencies, the Commission shall give due consideration to the following;
(a)   community of interests,
(b)   means of communication,
(c)   physical features,
(d)   approximate equality of all constituencies in number of voters, but shall not consider the racial character of any constituency or part thereof.

33. The Commission appointed under the provisions of this Constitution shall submit to the Governor:
(a)   a list of electoral districts, with the names given to them by the Commission and a description of the boundaries of every such district;
(b)   a map or maps showing the electoral districts into which Southern Rhodesia has been divided;
(c)   such further particulars as they consider necessary.

34. The Governor shall proclaim the names and boundaries of the electoral districts as finally settled and certified by the commission or a majority thereof, and, thereafter, until there shall be a re-division, the electoral districts as named and defined shall be the electoral districts of Southern Rhodesia.

If any discrepancy arises between the description of the electoral districts and the aforesaid map or maps, the description shall prevail.

35. Any re-division of Southern Rhodesia made as aforesaid shall come into operation at the next general election held after the completion of the re-division, and not earlier.

36. The Legislative Assembly shall, on their first meeting, before proceeding to the despatch of any other business, elect one of their members to be Speaker and another to be Deputy Speaker and Chairman of Committees (hereinafter called the Deputy Speaker) of the said Assembly (subject in both cases to confirmation by the Governor) until the dissolution thereof, and in case of vacancy in either office another Speaker or Deputy Speaker, as the case may be, shall be elected in like manner and subject to such confirmation as aforesaid. Notwithstanding the provisions of the preceding sub-section, it shall be lawful for the Legislative Assembly, if they see fit, to elect any suitable person other than one of their Members to be Speaker, and any person so elected shall be entitled to exercise and perform all the

powers and duties by this Constitution, including the power and duty to exercise a casting vote as provided in section 46 thereof, or by any Standing Rules and Orders from time to time in force under the provisions of section 48 thereof, or otherwise howsoever vested in the Speaker of the Legislative Assembly.

37. The Speaker, or, in his absence, the Deputy Speaker, and in the absence of both Speaker and Deputy Speaker, some member elected by the Legislative Assembly, shall preside at the meetings thereof.

38. The Legislative Assembly shall not be disqualified from the transaction of business on account of any vacancies among the members thereof, but the said Assembly shall not be competent to proceed to the despatch of business unless a third of members be present.

39. Any member of the Legislative Assembly may resign his seat therein by writing under his hand addressed to the Speaker and upon the receipt of such resignation by the Speaker the seat of such member shall become vacant:

> provided that no member shall, without the permission of the Legislative Assembly, resign his seat while any proceedings are pending in respect of his election if it is alleged in those proceedings that any corrupt or illegal practices took place at that election, or while any proceedings are contemplated or pending in respect of his conduct in, or as a member of, the Legislative Assembly.

40. Whenever a vacancy occurs in the Legislative Assembly from any cause, other than as the result of an election petition, the Speaker shall, upon a resolution of the said Assembly declaring such vacancy, inform the Governor thereof.

Provided that if such vacancy occurs when the Legislative Assembly is not in session, the Speaker, or, in the case of the death, incapacity or absence from Southern Rhodesia of the Speaker, the Clerk to the Assembly shall, on a certificate under the hands of two members of the Assembly, stating that such vacancy has occurred and the cause thereof, inform the Governor thereof.

The Governor on receiving such information shall, without delay, cause the necessary steps to be taken for filling such vacancy in accordance with the law for the time being in force in Southern Rhodesia.

41. There shall be a session of the legislature once at least in every year, so that a period of twelve months shall not intervene between the last sitting of the legislature in one session and the first sitting thereof in the next session.

The first session shall be held within eight months of the coming into force of this constitution.

42. Every session of the legislature shall be held in Salisbury at such time as may be notified by the Governor by proclamation in the *Gazette*.

43. The Governor may, from time to time, summon, prorogue or dissolve the legislature by proclamation, which shall be published in the *Gazette*.

The Governor shall dissolve the Legislative Assembly at the expiration of five years from the date of the first meeting thereof.

44. The Governor may transmit by message to the Legislative Assembly the draft of any Bill which it may appear to him desirable to introduce, and all such drafts shall be taken into consideration by the Assembly in such convenient manner as shall be provided in that behalf by Rules of Procedure.

45. Every member of the Legislative Assembly shall, before being permitted to sit or vote therein, take and subscribe the following oath before the Speaker or before such person as may be appointed thereto by the Governor should such oath be required to be taken before the appointment or election of a President or Speaker, as the case may be:

'I, A.B., do swear that I will be faithful and bear true allegiance to Her Majesty Queen Elizabeth the Second, her Heirs and Successors, according to Law. So Help me God.'

Provided that any person authorized by law to make a solemn affirmation or declaration instead of taking an oath may make such affirmation or declaration in lieu of such oath.

46. Subject to the provisions contained in this constitution, all questions in the Legislative Assembly shall be determined by a majority of the votes of members present, other than the Speaker or presiding member, who shall, however, have and exercise a casting vote in case of an equality of votes.

47. If any member of the Legislative Assembly—

(1)   shall be absent, except on the ground of illness, from the sittings of the Legislative Assembly for a period of one month during any session without the leave of the Legislative Assembly; or

(2)   shall take any oath or make any declaration or acknowledgement of allegiance, obedience or adherence to any foreign state or power; or

(3)   shall do, concur in or adopt any act whereby he may become the subject or citizen of any such state or power; or

(4)   shall become an insolvent or take advantage of any law for the relief of insolvent debtors; or

(5)   shall be attainted of treason, or be sentenced to imprisonment without the option of a fine for a term of not less than twelve months, or

(6)   shall become of unsound mind; or

(7)   shall accept any office of profit under the Crown other than that of a Minister or that of an officer of the naval, military and air forces of Southern Rhodesia on retired or half-pay, or that of an officer or member of the defence forces of Southern Rhodesia

whose services are not wholly employed by Southern Rhodesia; his seat shall become vacant, and if any person under any of the disqualifications herein mentioned shall, whilst so disqualified, knowingly sit or vote as a member of the said Assembly, such person shall forfeit the sum of twenty-five pounds, to be recovered by the Attorney-General for the benefit of the Treasury by action in the High Court:

provided that a person in receipt of pension from the Government of Southern Rhodesia shall not be deemed to hold an office of profit under the Government of Southern Rhodesia within the meaning of this section.

48. (1) The Legislative Assembly shall adopt and confirm standing rules and orders for the regulation and orderly conduct of the proceedings and the despatch of business.

(2) Provided that the standing rules and orders of the Legislative Assembly as now subsisting shall, until altered, added to or amended, be the standing rules and orders of the Legislative Assembly.

49. The salary of the Speaker of the Legislative Assembly shall be such as may be prescribed by any law of Southern Rhodesia. The Chief Clerk of the Legislative Assembly shall be removable from office only in accordance with a vote of the House.

50. It shall be lawful for the legislature of Southern Rhodesia by law to define the privileges, immunities and powers to be held, enjoyed and exercised by the Legislative Assembly, and by the members thereof:

provided that no such privileges, immunities or powers shall exceed those for the time being held, enjoyed and exercised by the House of Commons of the United Kingdom.

PART IV

Legislation

51. The Legislative Assembly shall have power, subject to the provisions of this constitution, to make laws, to be entitled 'Acts', required for the peace, order and good government of Southern Rhodesia.

52. The Governor shall cause every law to which he shall have assented in the name of the Queen or to which she shall have given her assent to be printed in the *Gazette* for general information.

53. As soon as may be after any law shall have been assented to in the Queen's name by the Governor, the Clerk of the Legislative Assembly shall cause a fair copy of such law signed by the Governor to be enrolled on record in the office of the Registrar of the High Court, and such copy shall be conclusive evidence as to the provisions of

every such Law:

provided, however, that the validity of any such Law shall not
depend upon the enrolment thereof.

PART V

The Executive
54.
(1)   There shall be a Prime Minister of Southern Rhodesia, who shall
be appointed by the Governor.
(2)   Whenever the Governor has occasion to appoint a Prime
Minister he shall appoint a member of the Legislative Assembly
who appears to him likely to command the support of the
majority of the members of the Legislative Assembly.
(3)   There shall be, in addition to the office of Prime Minister, such
other offices of Minister of the Government of Southern
Rhodesia as may be established by Parliament or, subject to the
provisions of any Act of Parliament, by the Governor, acting in
accordance with the advice of the Prime Minister.
(4)   Appointments to the office of Minister of the Government other
than the office of Prime Minister shall be made by the
Governor, acting in accordance with the advice of the Prime
Minister.
(5)   No Minister shall hold office for a longer period than four
months unless he is or becomes a member of the Legislative
Assembly.
(6)   No Minister shall vacate his seat in the Legislative Assembly by
reason of his appointment to or retention of an office in the
Ministry.

PART VI

The Judiciary
55. There shall be a department of the Judiciary.

56. All judicial officers shall be members of the Judiciary, provided
the chiefs shall be *ex officio* members of the Judiciary.

57. A judicial officer is any person who presides over any Court of
Law established by Parliament.

58. The judges of the High Court shall be appointed by the Governor
in Council from a list of advocates of ten years' standing
recommended by the Chief Justice and other judges.

59. The judges of the High Court shall not be removed except by the
Governor in Council on an address from the Legislative Assembly in
the same session praying for such removal on the ground of proved

misbehaviour or incapacity.

60. The judges of the High Court shall receive such remuneration as shall from time to time be prescribed by law, but the remuneration of a judge shall not be diminished during his tenure of office and the remuneration of the present judges shall not be diminished, and their commissions shall continue as heretofore.

61. The power to appoint persons to hold judicial office or act in a judicial capacity, to dismiss or exercise disciplinary control over persons holding judicial office and to promote or transfer them shall vest in the Judicial Service Commission of Southern Rhodesia.

62. There shall be a Judicial Service Commission for Southern Rhodesia whose members shall be:

(a)   The Chief Justice, who shall be the Chairman.
(b)   The Chairman of the Public Service Commission.
(c)   One other member appointed by the Governor in Council and who must be a person who—
       (1) has been or is a judge of a Court with unlimited criminal and civil jurisdiction.
       (2) His term of office shall be for five years.
       (3) He may be removed by the Governor only for failure to perform his duty or for misbehaviour.

63. The High Court shall have exclusive jurisdiction to interpret this constitution, and all courts shall have the power and duty to enforce all the rights secured by this constitution.

PART VII

The Land

64. Notwithstanding anything to the contrary in this constitution, the lands now known as the Native Reserves, together with all unalienated Crown land, shall henceforth be known as the Public Trust Lands and shall vest in the Board of Trustees.

65. The members of the Board of Trustees shall be the Chief Justice and two other members appointed, one by the Governor in Council and the other by the Chief Justice.

66. The present occupiers of the Public Trust Lands shall have a right to continue to occupy and use the same.

67. The Governor shall, after the first general election under this constitution, appoint a Commission to consider and report on Land Settlement in the Public Trust Lands on terms of, and in accordance with, the provisions of Section 29 of this constitution.

68. This Constitution may be amended by a two-thirds' majority of the members of the Legislative Assembly.

Where two-thirds' majority of the Legislative Assembly have passed an amendment to any of the provisions of Part I of this constitution, then the amendment shall not come into operation until a referendum to the voters has been held, and has confirmed the amendment by a simple majority.

69. The rights secured under Part I of this constitution may be suspended during a period of public emergency, but the question whether an emergency does or does not exist shall be capable of determination by the High Court.

6 National Democratic Party: Southern Rhodesia Constitution a Fraud. Statement, London, 9 March 1961.

We make no bones about our part in the Southern Rhodesia constitutional conference. It was, to say the least, bad political performance. Whitehead out-manoeuvred his opponents. As a result the National Democratic Party was twisted like molten iron until the delegation accepted or gave tacit approval to a constitution that leaves Africans worse than they were before the conference.

The people reacted sharply and condemned the tacit approval given to the new constitution by the delegation. What our delegation failed to realize was that the franchise and representation were the two crucial issues before the conference and not the Bill of Rights. They had a Bill of Rights. Sir Edgar Whitehead, Prime Minister of Southern Rhodesia, had no Bill of Rights. The Bill of Rights was discussed first and accepted and was unwritten. There was only the promise that the British and Southern Rhodesia Governments would write one.

By the time the franchise and representation were discussed our delegation had been flattered into believing that they had, by having the Bill of Rights accepted, won a major victory. Then they compromised on the franchise and representation. They did not accept them but they said nothing, thus giving tacit approval to these two iniquitous measures. It was a fraudulent act on the part of those who schemed this clever and diabolical arrangement.

Basic to any democratic constitution is the franchise system and not a Bill of Rights. A Bill of Rights based on an undemocratic constitution is valueless.

It will take Africans in Southern Rhodesia from 15 to 20 years to equal the number of European voters if the B qualifications in the new constitution are put into effect. At present there are 70,000 white electors and a little over 2,500 African voters. With £120 as the least income qualification and two years secondary education as, coupled with the £120, the least educational qualifications, 70,000 can only be reached after 20 years. (There is an educational qualification requiring standard six but to use this one must be 30 years of age which makes it impossible for a child leaving school at the age of 13 or 14 years to take part in elections for 16 years.) In 1960 only 774 Africans passed Form II in Southern Rhodesia and in 1959 there were only 1,163 students enrolled in Form II. In the same year a mere 18 were in Form VI. In the towns of Southern Rhodesia African workers married or single receive £6.50 a month and the average annual wages of African workers is £81. Compare this with the £120 required to qualify on the B Voters Roll. On the A Voters Roll incomes vary from £300 plus matriculation and £720. The average wages of white workers in Southern Rhodesia is £1,134 a year. How will African voters ever overtake European voters? This is the kind of political arrangement Sir Roy Welensky calls non-racial.

While the British Government retained the 'Reserved Powers' in the constitution, Africans had a moral right to petition them to look into the affairs of Southern Rhodesia. It is true they did nothing to stop the settler governments of Southern Rhodesia from following policies that deny Africans fundamental human rights. They did nothing to stop the passing of 63 discriminatory bills. But it was because of these powers that the National Democratic Party successfully appealed to the British Government to hold a constitutional conference. The new constitution removes these reserved powers.

Sir Edgar Whitehead has secured his complete independence with powers to legislate extra-territorially. He has agreed, in place of the British Government, to the appointment of a Constitutional Council with advisory and delaying powers. This body is worse or less effective than the African Affairs Board of the Federal Assembly. It has less powers than those of Councils of State suggested by the Monckton Commission. It can only delay bills which are declared by itself discriminatory. Such bills can be reintroduced in the House immediately the Council declares them discriminatory and be passed by a two-thirds majority or by a simple majority after six months from the time the Council declares such bills. Fifteen Africans in a House of 65 will not affect that two-third majority. And who says these Africans in rigged elections and constituencies will not be supporters of Whitehead? Why then did the NDP allow Whitehead to get his independence?

Having lost our chance to influence an immediate transfer to the people and not to a white ruling clique, what do we do next? The answer is simple: 'Organize and organize and let the voice of the people speak out. Be tough and uncompromising. Be honest and live and grow in the spirit of the party.' No better advice can be given. Mr Joshua Nkomo, the President-General has told the world that NDP did not accept the Southern Rhodesia constitutional agreement. On 19 March their party is holding an emergency conference to consider the agreement. The verdict of the conference is already known: 'Rejection of the agreement.' From that conference Mr Nkomo will get a mandate from his people and it will be clear and simple. 'Get the whole black population behind you and be tough.'

In a country where every able-bodied white man and woman is armed to the teeth. Africans are militarily at a disadvantage. They know that they intend to use their knowledge to the best advantage. With Welensky's white troops showing their menacing fangs in every African township, it is perhaps foolish and penny wise to resort to violence and invite the fangs to be struck in deadly earnest. But the strength of the people is in their numbers and in their moral right to govern that which is theirs. The NDP will march forward to victory in spite of these obstacles and even in spite of Welensky's South African white troops and British trained paratroops. The fire of freedom has never been watered and gunned by submission. People die and are forgotten but the yearning for freedom lives on.

Political butchers hedged with force-maintained privileges jeer at the only democratic franchise: one man, one vote. That is not strange, criminals defend the code by which they live, so do the political criminals. The difference is that the political criminal once caught up with never raises his head again. One man, one vote is now gathering the strength of a religious belief.

7 All African Peoples Conference: resolutions on the Federation, passed by the third conference. Cairo, March 1961

WHEREAS the undemocratic imposition by British imperialist of a Central African Federation on the nine million Africans of Northern Rhodesia, Southern Rhodesia and Nyasaland has resulted in a barbaric savage and outrageous domination of the Africans by colonialists led by Roy Welensky;

WHEREAS it is the inherent right of the Africans of Central Africa to choose their own government and mode of life;

WHEREAS the existence of British rule over Central Africa is nothing but an accident of history;

WHEREAS the recent tendencies in Britain and among the governing Party as regards the Northern Rhodesia Southern Rhodesia and Nyasaland, is contrary to the spirit of the recent expulsion of South Africa from the Commonwealth;

WHEREAS the recent constitutional changes in Northern Rhodesia and Southern Rhodesia fall far short of the aspirations of the people and are a ghostly reflection of barbaric intentions of the British Government over the African people of Central Africa;

WHEREAS the continued detention, imprisonment and detentions of African Nationalists by Colonialists and Imperialists is contrary to Democratic Principles;

It resolved therefore that this conference

(a) condemns the present constitutional changes in Northern Rhodesia and Southern Rhodesia and demands the immediate grant of independence of the two Rhodesias on the principle of One Man One Vote

(b) demands the immediate dissolution of the Central African Federation unconditionally and the consequent independence of the Central African territories of Nyasaland, Northern Rhodesia and Southern Rhodesia; who by their right will decide their political future

(c) calls upon all Commonwealth countries to eject the imposed Central African Federation from the Commonwealth as it is in fact a pocket edition of the *apartheid* policies of the Union of South Africa;

(d) calls upon all African and Commonwealth countries not to fraternize with the imposed Central African Federation through diplomatic exchanges, trade relations, touristical or other socio-cultural exchanges;

(e) demands the immediate release of all political prisoners and detainees in Nyasaland and the two Rhodesias such as George Nyandoro, Chikerema and Masuki Chipembere whose only crime is their dedication to the struggle against imperialism and colonialism;

(f) calls upon the All-African Peoples Conference and the independent African states to redouble their aid and support to the Africans of Central Africa against British imperialism;

(g) calls upon all African independent states to see to it that:

(i) no independent African state should export nor import anything to or from this Federation;

(ii) Federal airlines should not be allowed to use African independent states' territorial air space nor be accorded landing facilities;

(iii) that Afro-Asian states should raise the issue of Central African Federation at the forthcoming United Nations General Assembly;

(h) appeals to the freedom loving countries of the world to condemn British imperialism in Nyasaland and the Rhodesias as vigorously as possible.

8 National Democratic Party: press statement by Moton Malianga, deputy-President. London, 14 June 1961

During the Southern Rhodesian constitutional conference in February, our delegation was promised that the ban on meetings in the native reserves would be looked into to enable us to report to our supporters and the chiefs in the reserves the proceedings of the conference. At this conference, it was also agreed that the land question as a whole and not only the native land or the Land Apportionment Act would be discussed. We took these promises in good faith and hoped that the people responsible for the fulfilment of these obligations would honour them. We were deceived. None of these obligations have been carried out.

We made a special request to the Southern Rhodesia Minister of Native Affairs to permit us to meet the chiefs so that we could discuss with them the report of the conference and our own proposals. This request was refused. In spite of the Southern Rhodesia government refusing us permission to meet our supporters, other delegates to the conference were afforded the opportunity to meet their supporters and report to them the proceedings of the conference and to hear their reactions to them.

We attach great importance to the land question because on it rests the solution to the vote. Immovable property owned by Africans in native reserves, or rented houses occupied by Africans in towns are not recognized as qualification for the vote even if their value was a million pounds. On the other hand ownership of immovable property by Europeans either in the country or in towns is recognized as qualification for the vote. This permanently excludes the African from the vote and therefore from participation in shaping his own destiny.

We have put these arguments to Mr Sandys, Secretary of State for Commonwealth Relations, but he has refused to appreciate them. I have been sent by Mr Joshua Nkomo, our President, and the party which represents the entire African population of three million, and a number of Europeans to ask the Right Honourable Harold Macmillan to intervene in this crisis. The present constitution governing Southern Rhodesia contains powers reserved to the British Government for the protection of the African people against discriminatory laws. Our contention is that the proposed constitution discriminates against the African people and therefore we are asking Mr Macmillan to prevent the implementation of the constitution on the grounds that it discriminates against the African by refusing him the vote even under equal circumstances, as a European.

I have been informed by the Secretary of State for Commonwealth Relations that Mr Macmillan is too busy to see me. Mr Sandys however, says he is prepared to see me but I find no useful purpose in seeing him.

9 Michael Mawema: Why I resigned from the NDP to join the Zimbabwe National Party. Salisbury, September 1961

Dear Freedom Fighters,

Some people are confused about my political activities in this country with the result that some accusations have been circulating about what I did and what I am doing now. I have been accused by the leaders of the NDP for very many things as from February 1961.

I decided to resign from the NDP because of the treachery, dishonesty, inconsistency and betrayal of the mandate and demands of our people at the last constitutional conference. We demanded one man one vote but Nkomo agreed with the UFP and signed for a qualitative franchise of £720; we demanded a majority representation in parliament but Nkomo signed for 15 seats in a house of 65; we demanded our land but Nkomo signed a document which excluded our Zimbabwe. Besides that he chose to tell the country a lie that he had not agreed when in actual fact he had told the country previously that the constitution was 'REVOLUTIONARY AND A STEPPING STONE TOWARDS INDEPENDENCE'. Being a true son of Zimbabwe I made a public condemnation of the Nkomo-Whitehead-Sandys constitution as utterly unacceptable and I was suspended for having rejected that constitution.

At the Bulawayo Congress of the NDP, I explained the evils of the constitution to the delegates as I saw it and the delegates rejected it. The NDP executive had endorsed Nkomo's agreement to the constitution at the council meeting of 12 February 1961, at which I was driven out and later suspended—see their minutes. I would have told the country at that time but as you will all remember I was on bail pending hearing at the High Court and one of the conditions was that I did not address a public meeting, so those who wanted the constitution took advantage of my having been silenced by the UFP Government and continued to sell you by telling you false stories. I was called a Tshombe because I had not accepted the constitution which the great Nkomo had signed for.

You have been told that I was paid by the government quite large sums of money as Tranos Makombe said at Highfields, 'in order to split African unity', and that I am power-hungry etc. This is the truth: I have never, at any time, received money from any quarter for the purpose mentioned nor have I ever received a bribe in order to sell the people. Our God and great-grandfathers will not forgive anyone of us who shall betray this land or fear to suffer for it because of wanting pleasures and money. Those who still believe and continue to support the NDP leadership are committing sins against those who suffered and died for this country because by such actions you are doing them injustice when you compromise with what they did not compromise on. I cannot protect the interests of a few people in the NDP because they have the money. Many of those who speak against me are paid by the NDP from the money paid by the ordinary man who wants this money to be used for restoring Zimbabweland to the African people. How on earth can a true son of Zimbabwe follow men who are dishonest to the African cause? We demanded one man one vote but they signed for a qualitative franchise of £720. Is that one man one vote? Are 15 seats in a house of 65 the majority representation? We wanted our Zimbabweland back to us but they signed a constitution without the land provision and when it was time to discuss about our land they decided to walk out and left the decision to Sir Edgar the imperialist.

What moral right have they in the name of Zimbabwe to continue to sell us for luxury and money which they have already? Of recent times many people are going about without food and jobs after being misled to go on strike; many lay in prisons, some died, but the people who asked them to violate the laws are free, enjoying themselves without worry or giving help to the people who are suffering.

It has been said I was forced to resign from the presidency of the NDP because I had embezzled party funds; that is not true. I challenge anyone to bring me to court to prove such accusations. The fact is that I resigned from the NDP presidency simply because at that time I had fallen ill and since I realized that the party was to be engaged in strenuous constitutional negotiations I decided to hand over to someone who was fit enough to serve the people. My resignation was accepted by the party and I remained a National Councillor up to the time I resigned from the party altogether. Why was the question of having embezzled party funds not raised during that time and only now when I had left the party? This is the dishonesty manifest in the NDP leadership.

I will continue to disagree with anybody who betrays our people and compromise with the UFP Government until Zimbabwe is free. I do not fear prison. You all know that I still have six months imprisonment hanging on my head. Our people are being arrested and imprisoned in their hundreds but the said leaders are putting on more weight which is to be reduced by useless fasting in the name of Zimbabwe whilst in actual fact they are finding means of not being imprisoned. Those who share the loot in the NDP will continue to sell you, but the honest sons and daughters will seek for the truth and join us in the Zimbabwe National Party.

Yours in the struggle,

M. A. MAWEMA
Secretary-General, ZNP

10 All African Peoples Conference: letter to the Rt Hon Harold Macmillan, MP, Prime Minister of the UK, 21 October 1961

Your Excellency,
The All-African Peoples' Conference is greatly concerned about the trend of events in Southern Rhodesia and, for reasons later disclosed herein, appeal to your Government to concede the demands of our people in that territory.

Southern Rhodesia is an African country whose fate is bound with that of the rest of our continent. The population there is 3,000,000 Africans and 280,000 immigrants and other races.

Since 1922, you will remember, this part of our continent has been governed by a responsible government representing the interests of the non-African minorities. This, no doubt, has been 37 years of undemocratic rule without consultation with nor the consent of the governed indigenous people.

We wish to remind you that the African peoples have taken seriously the 'Wind of Change' speech delivered in Cape Town on 3 February, 1960 in which, among other things, you said: 'It has been Britain's aim in the countries for which she has borne responsibility not only to raise the material standards of life but to create a society which respected the rights of the individuals—a society in which men were given the opportunity to grow to their full stature, and that in Britain's view must include the opportunity of an increasing share in political power and responsibility; a society in which individual merit, and individual merit alone, was the criterion of a man's advancement'.

We further wish to observe that the National Democratic Party, an affiliated member of our organization, is the recognized spokesman of our people in Southern Rhodesia and we do not consider their demand for 'one man one vote' as being inconsistent with the sentiments expressed in your speech above-quoted nor is it in conflict with the Declaration of Human Rights to which United Kingdom Government is a signatory.

It is fitting to note that during the constitutional talks held in London and Salisbury the spokesman of the majority, the NDP, rejected in no uncertain terms the proposed constitution. Yet the representative of the white minority, Sir Edgar Whitehead, and the representative of the UK Government, Mr Duncan Sandys, came to an agreement in defiance of and contempt for the majority viewpoint. This blatantly unjust agreement was endorsed on 26 July 1961 by a referendum in which only the settler minority participated. The outcome, even then, was that a substantial number of the settlers came out against the proposed constitution as indicated by the figures: 41,940 Yesses and 21,826 Noes.

You will recall that prior to this exclusive minority referendum the National Democratic Party undertook to and did organize a referendum which further strengthened our objection to the proposed constitution. By an overwhelming majority of 467,189 as against 584 the African people have made their attitude to this proposed constitution unmistakably clear.

All African peoples, therefore, call on your Government to exercise the sacred democratic principles in the light of these figures for we know that the final decision rests with your government. We urge you as the top representative of the UK government to set aside this constitution and negotiate a constitution acceptable to the majority.

Finally, we consider, in our assessment of the African struggle for immediate liberation, that the problems confronting us in Southern Rhodesia can be solved by negotiations.

Hoping, Mr Prime Minister, that you will do all in your power to bring about the negotiations for a constitution acceptable to the people of Southern Rhodesia,

I remain,
Yours faithfully,

Secretary-General,
All African Peoples' Conference

11 Zimbabwe African People's Union: memorandum to United Nations Organization by Joshua Nkomo, President. New York, February 1962

Your Excellencies,

In a series of treaties our hereditary rulers did, under pressure from the British government and the representatives of the British South Africa Company, grant certain mining concessions in the late 1880s to the above company.

The operation of these concessions brought a considerable number of immigrant races (mainly of British stock) to our motherland. The immigrant races quickly organized themselves into powerful economic and political groups; so much so that in 1923, the British government, without consultation or consent of the indigenous people, granted the white minority some form of self-government.

This so-called self-government was granted after a referendum involving 13,000 white settlers had voted . . . while the 2,000,000 indigenous African people and their chiefs took no part whatsoever.

It must be stated here that the 1923 Constitution left the function of foreign affairs, defence, and the power of concluding treaties firmly in the British government's hands. Further, Britain reserved to herself the power to legislate and also to take complete control of the government of the colony at any time if, in her opinion, it was desirous for her to do so. This power carried with it the right for the British government to disallow any law if, in her opinion, that law discriminated against the indigenous people; or was not in the spirit of the constitution. This makes it perfectly clear that Britain still has great responsibilities towards the indigenous people, and, therefore, Southern Rhodesia cannot be said to have reached a full measure of self-government, and this renders Britain responsible for the submission of reports and information to the United Nations Organization.

Since 1923, up to the present day, the successive governments of Southern Rhodesia have been returned by an entirely European electorate, under an Electoral Act which sets extremely high educational and property qualifications, thus making it impossible for the electorate to be broad and representative of the majority of the African people. The present Southern Rhodesia settler Parliament, with an entirely white Assembly of 30, was elected by an electorate composed of 80,000 European voters and less than 2,000 African voters, in a country of 3,000,000 Africans and 240,000 European settlers.

The white settler oligarchy, assisted by a racially restricted civil service, police force and army, and a judiciary which is entirely white, has resorted to repressive and restrictive measures to muzzle and stifle African political and economic aspirations.

We regard the following laws, for example, as infringements of the rule of law and as constituting unquestionable political subjugation and social degradation of the African peoples:

1. The Southern Rhodesia Electoral Law, which has kept power and government in the hands of a white minority; and has denied the indigenous people expression through freely elected Parliaments based on universal franchise.

2. The Preventive Detention Act, 1959, in terms of which people can be summarily arrested and detained without recourse to the courts of law, under which several African leaders were arrested in 1959 and detained, and some of whom are still detained today.

3. The Unlawful Organizations Act, 1959, under which the African National Congress was banned in 1959; and the National Democratic Party in December 1961, for the purpose of eliminating African opposition.

4. The Law and Order Maintenance Act, under which over 10,000 Africans, including 2,000 African women, were arrested during the course of 1961 for opposing a white imposed constitution and sentenced to terms of imprisonment ranging up to 20 years.

5. The Land Apportionment Act, 1930, under which over 53% of the best land has been sold to white people.

6. Native Affairs Act, which created a Native Affairs Department and gives dictatorial powers to ruthless native commissioners (white officers). Under this law, in December 1961, over 5,000 leaders were served with restriction orders, refusing them entry into African areas.

7. Native Education Act, created to give limited education to Africans so as to avoid their 'invading' European spheres of employment.

During the 39 years of this fake self-governing status, the white settler minority government used the above laws to demoralize and degrade the African majority in preparation for a quick and final move into independence and permanent white domination, as exemplified by the 1961 Constitutional Proposals. These sinister proposals, which were concocted by Sir Roy Welensky and the White Settler Government of Sir Edgar Whitehead, but flatly rejected by the 3,000,000 African people, if allowed to pass shall turn Southern Rhodesia into another South Africa within the next year or two. The British Government have, all of a sudden, become aware that this so-called self-governing status which settlers are said to have enjoyed since 1923 is a fake, and is not based on the will of the people. These 1961 Constitutional Proposals, therefore became necessary to complete the political plot to give independence, by the back door, to a white minority and condemns Africans to perpetual political slavery.

They propose a Parliament of 65 members, elected through a dual roll system. That is, there shall be an A Roll and a B Roll, both based on a high qualitative franchise. The A Roll voters shall elect 50 of the 65 members. So far, of the 240,000 European settlers, 80,000 are registered on the A Roll. Of the 3,000,000 Africans, only 1,000 qualify for the A Roll. The disparity is too obvious to demand any explanation. The 15 other members of the 65-member legislature shall be elected by the B Roll voters. May it be stated here that the proposed constitution does not state that the 15 shall be Africans. It merely stipulates that these shall be elected by the B Roll voters.

The settlers maintain that at least 50,000 Africans shall qualify for the B Roll, but our estimates show that hardly 15,000 Africans can qualify for the B Roll. May it also be stated here that from the total of 240,000 white settlers, 80,000 are registered on the A Roll, 160,000 are unregistered, and even if we give an allowance of 60,000 non-qualifying people, we still have 100,000 who may, if they wish, or are told to do so, register on the B Roll and thereby easily outnumber the African voters . . . even if the 50,000 Africans, as estimated by the settler government, did register.

Because of the aforesaid reasons, we, the 3,000,000 African people of Southern Rhodesia, have thus resolved:

(a)   *To reject the present constitution for Southern Rhodesia;*

(b)   *We have organized that no African in our motherland—Southern Rhodesia—should register as a voter on the basis of the present arrangements. Because of this stand and the support given to us by the toiling 3,000,000 African masses, our national movement, the National Democratic Party, was banned on 9 December 1961, and not only was the Party banned, but the national leaders, plus provincial and district as well as branch leaders numbering 5,000 are prohibited to appear in public, or address any public gatherings.*

Apart from all this, the settlers went further, with the paternal sanctions of the British Government, and confiscated our party property valued at approximately £80,000. On 16 December 1961, we created a new party—the ZIMBABWE AFRICAN PEOPLE'S UNION under the banner of genuine democracy—the principle of ONE MAN, ONE VOTE. The ZAPU stand is clear on this particular principle; it includes the boycott of elections, and the refusal to get any African on the fake Voters' Roll; not only do we dispute it as being impolite, but we dispute it fundamentally on the basis that Southern Rhodesia is an African country. As such, we stand for no compromise, but universal franchise.

We have uttered our complaints to the British government, but they have been unattended to and met only by alleging the peculiar circumstances of the country. All hope of a favourable change in the government of our country is thus extinguished in our bosoms, and we are now beginning to look to you for help by:

1. Bringing the matter before the General Assembly;
2. And declaring Southern Rhodesia as a dependent and non-self-governing territory;
3. That the present proposed constitution must not be proceeded with, and that a fresh constitutional conference be convened to draft a constitution transferring power to the majority on the basis of ONE-MAN, ONE-VOTE.

Our demand is simple: A constitution based on the principle of 'One man, One vote'. Therefore, in the name of humanity, in the name of freedom and justice, in the name of peace and security, we appeal to Your Excellencies; and earnestly and respectfully ask that our case be regarded with the urgency and seriousness to which the peculiarities of our struggle entitle us.

In the name of our suffering people and their party, the Zimbabwe African People's Union, we humbly submit this memorandum of ours for your consideration.

12 Joshua Nkomo; press statement, 9 January 1963

I cannot institute any negotiations with Mr Field who as Whitehead's successor has inherited the long-standing dispute over the constitution of Southern Rhodesia. We maintain as strongly as ever, that Southern Rhodesia is a dependent territory of Britain and, as such, Britain has the power, indeed the responsibility, to legislate for the territory without prior consent of the Southern Rhodesia settler government. If Britain can do so in respect of the whole Federation of Rhodesia and Nyasaland, then the oft-repeated convenient argument that Britain has no power to intervene in the constitutional affairs of this country, has further been proved to be not valid.

To avert disaster, now impending over our country, Britain must act immediately by legislating for majority rule.

There has been some speculation as to whether I shall meet Mr Field on the question of lifting the ban on ZAPU. To me, this is not at all an issue on which negotiations of any kind are necessary and I leave it to Winston Field, who has inherited the sins of the Whitehead regime, to take immediate steps in lifting the ban. This is the demand of my 4,000,000 supporters and indeed of the whole world as represented by UNO. To ignore this demand, at this hour, is fatal and disastrous for the future of this country.

Settler minority rule which has now gone uninterrupted for more than 70 years—all the time in flagrant defiance of my people's wishes and in open war against their aspirations—must now be forced to a halt.

The political history of this country, beginning with white settlement, is one long stretch of political swindles. The 1923 Constitution was an imposition; and so was the 1953 Federation and the present Southern Rhodesia constitution. In spite of the vigorous African opposition, the 1961 constitution has now been imposed. In their own referendum of 1961 and at subsequent Congresses of my party, my people demonstrated their unanimous rejection of the Constitution. Again by refusing to register as voters and recently by abstaining from the polls, they have openly indicated they cannot be party to instruments of their own oppression. My people cannot, therefore, be expected to continue respecting institutions created under imposed constitutions.

WE HAVE BEEN PATIENT FOR TOO LONG.

CHAPTER THREE

THE FIRST INTERNAL CRISIS

13 Joshua Nkomo: statement to the National Peoples' Conference. Salisbury, 10 August 1963

ZAPU was banned on 20 September 1962. I was in Lusaka on that day on my way back to Southern Rhodesia from West Africa. Mr Sithole was in Greece where he was attending a conference. Mr Aggripa Mukhahlera was on his way back from Europe and Mr Dan Ncube was in the Copperbelt in Northern Rhodesia. All these men were on party duty. The rest of the Committee was at home.

With the ban of the party a crisis had arisen. As President of the party then, I had to take a quick action in conformity with a decision that was taken before the ban of the party that no new party was to be formed and that the ban of the party had to be resisted. I appointed those of my men who were outside the country to take over control. The Rev Sithole was appointed the leader of the group. I made the announcement on a Saturday and I was to return home on Monday.

When those of my colleagues who had not been rounded up at the time heard I was returning to Southern Rhodesia, they sent Mr Joseph Msika to tell me not to return yet for reasons they knew better than I.

With this delayed return, I decided to get back to Dar-es-Salaam so as to contact the Rev Sithole and others there to work out our plan of action. Mr Msika came with me to Dar-es-Salaam. When we arrived and the Rev Sithole arrived two days later, Mr Mukhahlera had already arrived. After a thorough discussion with the Rev Sithole and the others, it was agreed that the Rev Sithole leads the group outside the country based in Dar-es-Salaam. This group was composed of the Rev Sithole, Messrs Aggripa Mukhahlera and Joseph Msika. I then left Dar-es-Salaam for Nairobi accompanied by the Rev Sithole where I boarded a plane bound for Salisbury. When I arrived in Salisbury, I was collected by the police at the Salisbury Airport and taken to Simukwe Reserve where I remained for three months under restriction.

I left my restriction area on 2 January 1963. Most of my colleagues had been released before that date. Immediately after that date those of us who were at home met to review the situation. We agreed that the decision that was made before the party was banned should be proceeded with. That is to say there was going to be no new party formed. Plans to carry on the struggle were formulated within that policy and each one of us was given duties to perform.

During the month of January, Messrs Robert Chikerema and George Nyandoro joined us after their release from Gokwe. They were put into the picture as to the plans of the group. It was felt that contact should be made with the Rev Sithole and those colleagues who were in Dar-es-Salaam. Accordingly Mr W. Malianga and Mr J. Z. Moyo were sent to Dar-es-Salaam. Arrangements were made by Moyo and Malianga at their request that I and Chikerema meet the Rev Sithole at Tunduma in Southern Tanganyika to discuss certain matters.

At the agreed date, Chikerema and I arrived at Tunduma but the Rev Sithole was not there. We then proceeded to Dar-es-Salaam. In our office in Dar-es-Salaam, we were told that the Rev Sithole had left for Egypt towards the end of January and had not returned. I chose not to report in writing the state in which our affairs were when we arrived in Dar-es-Salaam, but I am prepared to report verbally to the conference.

On our way to Dar-es-Salaam, it was reported on radio that the British government had invited Mr Field to come to London. Mr Chikerema and myself felt that it was important that we get to London before Mr Field gets there in order to put our point of view to Mr Butler. We then sent a cable to our colleagues in Salisbury informing them that under the circumstances we felt it was to the best interest of our country to proceed to London to see Mr Butler before Mr Field does so.

In London, together with our representatives there, Mr Dumbutshena and Mr Chirimbani, we saw Mr Butler. While we were in London, a message came from the Committee of 17 that I should come to the United Nations to give the latest information about Southern Rhodesia, as the Committee was at the time discussing the affairs of the country. At this juncture, we were told by Mr Dumbutshena that the Rev Sithole had been in London for about a week and that he had left for some unknown country in Europe. In London the state of our affairs was chaotic, as Mr Dumbutshena can testify to this conference.

I then left for New York where I remained for three days. During these days, accompanied by Mr Joseph Msika, I addressed the Committee of 24. I also addressed the Afro-Asian group and met the Secretary-General of the United Nations, Mr U Thant. The whole trip was very essential. Miss Jane Ngwenya was at the time on a visit to the United States of America. I took the opportunity of consulting them regarding the action we intended taking due to moves that were being taken by Mr Field. I was satisfied after the discussion that both Miss Ngwenya and Mr Msika agreed with the projected action.

I then returned to London where I met the Rev Sithole who had returned from his trip to Israel. Here I had full discussions with him and he completely agreed with the projected action. I then requested the Rev Sithole to come with me to Dar-es-Salaam in order to complete all our arrangements, and also to get a full report of his activities outside the country as he had not given it to me at that time.

The Rev Sithole said he could not come with me on the same plane as he had a few appointments to attend to in London, but said he would be joining me in Dar-es-Salaam a day later. I remained in Dar-es-Salaam for three days but the Rev Sithole never showed up.

In Dar-es-Salaam I was joined by Mr Chikerema again. Together we saw and discussed with the people there. We were satisfied with all our discussions. We then left for Salisbury. We reported to our colleagues all we had done during the trip. Most of all we presented the plan of action as we had discussed it with others. We had altogether three meetings. I must emphasize here that there was a thorough discussion of the plan. We were all completely agreed. It was agreed that all the members of the ex-national executive leave the country for Tanganyika on a specified day and by various specified routes. Only Mr Chikerema was to remain for a specified period.

In Dar-es-Salaam we were joined by Mr Joseph Msika, Miss Jane Ngwenya who were returning from their American trip. We were also joined by Mr Mukhahlera who was away in Asia.

Mr Sithole's whereabouts were unknown. We were later told he was in the United States. Cables were sent to London and New York asking him to come and join us in Dar-es-Salaam without success. Ten of us who were in Dar-es-Salaam, then discussed. Duties were allocated to each one of us. After full consultations with everyone concerned, we all got down to carrying out our respective tasks. One of the important duties of our plan was that after a certain stage, I and a certain number of my colleagues had to return home. This, it was agreed, would be after the Addis Ababa Conference. Up to this point all efforts to contact the Rev Sithole had failed.

Mr Takawira and I then left to visit certain African countries which were to be visited before the Addis Ababa Conference. The trip was a great success. During these visits we were to have special discussions with Commonwealth countries. This included seeing representatives of countries like Canada, New Zealand and Australia.

After our return from West Africa, we went to the Addis Ababa conference. Six of us attended the conference, Takawira, Sithole, J. Z.

Moyo, W. Malianga, R. Mugabe and I. This was the first time to meet Sithole since parting in London. The conference went off very well. Our case was well received, first by the Foreign Ministers and finally by the Heads of States. To suggest that there was any form of reluctance by any of the independent countries because of one reason or another, is the biggest lie ever told about our political and diplomatic relations with African countries. The resolution passed at this conference was a clear indication of the unqualified support the conference gave to our plan of action. I would like to emphasize here that we had not gone to Addis Ababa to get a plan, but to get support for our plan. No one can design for us what to do in our own country. What we sought for and got was support and not direction.

As I have said above, at Addis Ababa there were six of us. At no time was there a suggestion or any indication that there was dissatisfaction among my colleagues.

After the conference, I sent two of my colleagues to two different countries. The Rev Sithole to the Congo and Mr L. Takawira carried a letter from me to Mr R. A. Butler. Mr Sithole was to return to Dar-es-Salaam within five days and Mr Takawira as soon as was possible. From Addis Ababa, Mr Mugabe, Mr Malianga and I travelled back to Dar-es-Salaam. Mr Moyo was left behind to complete some of our work. I stayed in Dar-es-Salaam for about 14 days waiting for the Rev Sithole and Mr Takawira to return. When they failed to return as expected I requested that cables be sent to them to return. There was no response.

At this stage it was reported that the Federal Conference was to be held at the Victoria Falls, and also that Mr Field was returning to Southern Rhodesia without his independence. I therefore felt it was time for me to get back home. I met members of my group who were in Dar-es-Salaam with me and it was agreed that Mr W. Malianga and I should leave for home. I left by car on a Wednesday and Mr Malianga was to follow by plane on Sunday.

I arrived in Bulawayo on Saturday and found Mr Chikerema there. He proceeded to Salisbury and I followed him a few days later.

When I finally arrived in Salisbury, I found that Mr Malianga had not arrived. No explanation was given for his failure to follow me.

When in Salisbury we discovered that a number of meetings had been held in houses of a number of people who once held prominent positions in the nationalist movement. These meetings were, we were told, held at the instigation of people like Shamuyarira, Hamadziripi, Matute, Chikowore, etc. We were told that messages had been sent to a number of centres, asking people to come into Salisbury to discuss the formation of a new party and change of leadership.

At some stage, we were told, it was decided that recommendations be sent to Dar-es-Salaam for consideration. But these recommendations were never given to us.

Mr Chikerema and myself then left for Northern Rhodesia where we had an appointment with Dr Kaunda. While in Northern Rhodesia we met Mr L. Takawira and Mr J. Z. Moyo. Mr Moyo had come to Northern Rhodesia accompanying Mr Mukhahlera who was returning home due to ill-health. Mr Takawira, we were told, had come by truck to collect students to go to Dar-es-Salaam. We were told by Mr Takawira that he had brought with him Mr Marondera, and that he had sent him to Southern Rhodesia for some students who had not come with others in Lusaka. When we pointed out that we had substitutes for those students, Takawira said we would recall Marondera.

During our three days in Lusaka, we agreed that an executive meeting be held in Northern Rhodesia on 10 July. During all these days with Takawira at no time did he mention that there was any dissatisfaction among the members of the National Executive. Before leaving for Southern Rhodesia we were joined by Zvobgo who said he was on his way to Dar-es-Salaam, then back to New York.

When we arrived back in Salisbury, we were shocked to discover that Marondera had been sent to Salisbury with letters from Takawira and Mugabe to a number of people in all the African townships in Salisbury. These letters grossly abused me and urged the formation of a new political party. We discovered the people who were connected with the holding of meetings in Salisbury were involved in this letter plot and that they held a number of meetings with Marondera during his few days in Salisbury. Mr Chikerema and myself called these men and told them of our discovery. When we failed to get any satisfactory explanation from them we decided to suspend them from political activity.

Having observed the harm that had been caused by Marondera's activities and by letters sent from Dar-es-Salaam by Mugabe and Takawira, we felt we could not go to Northern Rhodesia for the meeting we had arranged for 10 July before crushing the damage caused. Thus we decided to get the meeting postponed. So we sent the following telegram:

'Meeting of 10th postponed until mess created Marondera's activities here and activities of one or two of members in Dar-es-Salaam is cleaned. Signed Nkomo.'

The telegram was sent on 7 July. On Saturday, 6 July we received a telephone message from Mr J. Z. Moyo telling us that Sithole, Takawira, Malianga and Mugabe had decided to do away with me as leader and had installed Mr Sithole in my place and that Mr Takawira had been made deputy. On the same day I addressed a meeting in Harare, and at that meeting I named people who were behind the formation of a new party. But despite the fact that I had been told by the people in Dar-es-Salaam that the four men in Dar-es-Salaam had also taken that move, I only said I understood that they too were involved, but I said, I do not believe it.

On Sunday, 7 July, I received a message from a friend who had just arrived from Dar-es-Salaam informing me that he had travelled from Dar-es-Salaam with Zvobgo and Zvogbo had brought a number of letters for people in Salisbury from Sithole, Takawira, Mugabe and Malianga and that Zvobgo was instructed by the aforesaid not to contact either me or Chikerema.

We immediately set out to find Zvobgo. We finally discovered him on Monday morning, 8 July. After questioning him for some time Zvobgo agreed that he was sent to a number of people in the country to prepare them for the formation of a new party on 10 July. We finally got him to make the following statement, which we read to the press:

> 'In Dar-es-Salaam, Tanganyika, a serious turn of the tide has taken place among the former executive members of the banned ZAPU. Messrs Ndabaningi Sithole, Robert Mugabe, Leopold Takawira and Washington Malianga have now made a decision not to follow or support Mr Nkomo as President of their former nationalist movement. They decided that Mr Nkomo should step down as leader and be replaced by Rev Sithole. Mr Leopold Takawira is said to be their choice for vice-President. Mr Malianga and Mr Robert Mugabe are, according to that decision, supposed to maintain their present posts.
>
> An announcement is expected from Dar-es-Salaam on either Wednesday or Thursday this week.
>
> At the meeting that took the decision in Dar-es-Salaam Mr J. Z. Moyo is reported to have walked out and Mr Msika abstained.
>
> These are the people I saw at Mr Chikowore's house last night: Mr Chikowore, Mr Marere, Mr Pote, Mr Chikowore, Jr, Mr Hamadziripi.
>
> There were many others who I did not recognize were also there.'

After getting first hand information from a man sent by the four men in Dar-es-Salaam I sent them and Dr Nyerere the following telegrams:

> 'To Ndabaningi Sithole,
> Messrs Sithole, Takawira, Malianga and Mugabe, you are hereby suspended until decision of a conference of people's representatives. You will be informed of the date and place of conference.
>
> NKOMO.'

'To Dr Julius Nyerere, Dar-es-Salaam, Tanganyika,
 Serious misunderstandings within our group in Dar, I have
 suspended all activities of Messrs Sithole, Takawira, Malianga and
 Mugabe stop pending decision of people's representatives conference to be held soon here at home.'

After sending the above telegrams, I made the following statement to
the press:

'I am calling on the nation to remain cool and should not be disturbed
by these reports. Within the next few days I will call the people to
make their own decision. An opportunity shall be given to the
gentlemen in Dar-es-Salaam to present their own case. Meanwhile to
prevent them making further disquiet in the minds of the people I
suspend forthwith all their activities until a representative conference
is summoned. This conference will cover the whole country. I want
every opinion to be represented at this conference.'

After deciding to call the national conference on 3 August 1963 (now
10th) I wrote the following letter to Rev Sithole:

'Dear Mr Sithole,
 As I told you by telegram that I will inform you of the conference to
be held here at home to decide on what has happened between us, I
hereby inform and invite you and the other three men, Messrs
Malianga, Mugabe and Takawira, to the conference which is to be
held here in Salisbury on 3 August 1963, at 9 a.m.
 Your presence will be greatly appreciated.
                            Yours sincerely,
                            JOSHUA NKOMO.'

Because of the importance of the matter and for the purpose of affording
Mr Sithole the opportunity of discussion and suggestions I sent the letter
by hand. And the man I sent to Dar-es-Salaam, and I am grateful to him
for his co-operation, is Mr Chinamano. Mr Chinamano is here himself to
give you the story of his mission. The following is the reply to my letter
from the Rev Sithole:

'Dear Mr Nkomo,
                    re: *Suggested Conference*
 I refer to your letter of 16 July 1963, brought by Mr Josiah
Chinamano. Your idea of a conference is wholly unrealistic and
impracticable. To me and my colleagues, a genuine conference must
conform to every one of the following requirements:
 First, it must be summoned, not by you or by me alone, but by the
National Executive in terms of our constitution. Its agenda must
similarly not be the dream of one person but the joint work of the
National Executive.

Secondly, the choice of delegates to such conference must accord to the requirements of the constitution, whereby only properly constituted branches of the party exercise the function of selecting who will represent them, such function being exercised at a members-only-meeting called for the purpose.

Thirdly, such conference can only be held under the auspices of an existing organization and its machinery.

Fourthly, the legal circumstances, unless a defiance of the law is deliberately planned, must be favourable.

With these requirements in mind, it is obvious that the Executive has not been consulted on the issue of a conference. The decision is a unilateral one taken by you in the usual dictatorial manner, and in utter defiance of other people's rights.

Further, we do not see how the majority of the 4,000,000 people, exercising no right of *choosing candidates and giving them a mandate*, can be represented by a thousand individuals, hand-picked by you alone. What we seek is not the opinion of 1,000 but of 4,000,000 people of Zimbabwe. Unless you wish to suggest that you have gone into a secret pact with Mr Winston Field, we fail to see how a conference of a banned organization can be held under the auspices of that organization or indeed of any other. Do we understand you to say the ban on ZAPU has been lifted? If not, please do stop fooling the people at home and abroad.

If the people's opinion is your genuine desire, I challenge you to appear on the same platform with me when I return home and address public meetings in every possible centre of the country, from Chipinga to Plumtree. This is the best way of assessing the feelings of the people on your deposition. A conference of your hand-picked delegates will not solve anything.

Yours faithfully,
NDABANINGI SITHOLE.'

In short ladies and gentlemen, this is the story as I know it.

14 Zimbabwe African National Union: policy statement. Salisbury, 21 August 1963

1. THE ZANU DECLARATION OF POLICY

Zimbabwe is an African country in the context of an African continent in various stages of the relentless process of overthrowing the yoke of colonialism, imperialism and settlerism. As such Zimbabwe must be considered as participating in this tremendous process of inevitable change.

Therefore its institutions—political, social and economic—must reflect the will of the African people who form over 96% of the population while at the same time recognizing and respecting the rights and aspirations of the various minorities within its borders.

The Zimbabwe African National Union is a non-racial Union of all the peoples of Zimbabwe who share a common destiny and a common fate believing in the African character of Zimbabwe and democratic rule by the majority regardless of race, colour, creed or tribe.

ZANU, which in the words of its President—the Rev Ndabaningi Sithole—ushers in 'the new politics of confrontation', seriously intends to confront the voting white minority, the minority-elected government and the British government with a positive programme that can only result in bringing about equal opportunity and full citizenship to every one regardless of the colour of one's skin, race, religion or sex.

2. THE ZANU STATE

(a) ZANU will establish a nationalist, democratic, socialist and Pan-Africanist republic within the fraternity of African States and the British Commonwealth of Nations.

(b) The only form of franchise that the ZANU republic will recognize is one based on 'One man, One vote'.

(c) In the organization of the ZANU state the principles of the rule of law and separation of powers shall be strictly adhered to.

(d) The ZANU republic shall be a unitary and indivisible state.

(e) The ZANU republic shall be based on the principle of non-racialism.

3. ZANU AND CITIZENSHIP

All people born in Zimbabwe or who have been citizens of Zimbabwe shall be citizens of the republic. Foreigners may qualify for citizenship under conditions prescribed in accordance with the Law of the Republic.

4. BILL OF RIGHTS

(a) There shall be entrenched in the Constitution of the Republic a Bill of Rights guaranteeing the rights and freedom of every citizen.

(b) The Bill of Rights shall have retrospective effect from 12 September 1890.

(c) In a ZANU Republic, the judiciary—apart from its normal functions of administering justice, shall test the constitutionality of all legislation.

5. THE ZANU LAND POLICY

(a) All land shall belong to the Zimbabwe nation, and the Government shall merely be the trustee on behalf of the people.

(b) The Land Apportionment Act and its corollary—the Land Husbandry Act—shall be repealed and replaced by a new Land Distribution Law.

(c) A National Land Board shall be created to effect an equitable redistribution of land.

(d) Absentee ownership of land by foreigners shall be forbidden.

(e) Owned but unused land shall be declared communal.

6. ZANU AND AGRICULTURE

(a) A land bank for the purpose of financing agricultural projects shall be established.

(b) For the purpose of improving livestock, and rendering available educational materials to all farmers, a Veterinary Research Agency shall be established.

(c) Destocking shall be abolished.

(d) Incentive to farmers engaged in intensive Agriculture shall be established throughout the country.

(e) In order to increase production, co-operative societies shall be established throughout the country.

(f) Serious effort shall be made by the ZANU government to increase the volume of our exports of tobacco, maize, sugar, citrus fruit and other products.

7. ZANU AND EDUCATION

(a) ZANU believes in complete integration of all educational institutions.

(b) ZANU believes in free and compulsory education for all children up to Form II.

(c) ZANU shall launch an adult and mass education programme to wipe out illiteracy.

(d) A ZANU Government shall encourage and assist higher education. A programme of scholarships and loans shall be instituted.

(e) A Zimbabwe Institute of Technology shall be established.

(f) More Teacher Training Institutions shall be established in order to provide the kindergarten, primary and secondary schools with better qualified teachers.

(g)   The present Unified African Teaching Service shall be abolished and all teachers shall be part of the civil service establishment.

8. ZANU AND LABOUR

(a)   The Industrial Conciliation Act, the Masters and Servants Act and all such industrial and labour laws that discriminate on the basis of colour, shall be repealed.

(b)   A new labour law that will treat all labour matters without racial discrimination shall be enacted.

(c)   ZANU will accord legal recognition to all organized and registered labour unions.

(d)   ZANU Government shall uphold the right of trade Unions to assemble and organize all workers.

(e)   A ZANU Government will establish a high national minimum wage.

9. ZANU AND UNEMPLOYMENNT

(a)   A National Employment Bureau shall be set up for the registration of the unemployed and the implementation of a relief fund for the unemployed.

(b)   Unemployment shall be tackled by the creation of more economic projects which may include: (1) communal farms; (2) opening of postal agencies in rural areas; (3) establishment of communal and co-operative societies; (4) housing schemes in rural and urban areas; (5) irrigation projects; (6) national Army.

10. ZANU AND JUSTICE

(a)   A ZANU Government shall declare unconditional amnesty for all political prisoners at once.

(b)   Every citizen of Zimbabwe shall have the option to be tried by or without jury.

(c)   African courts enforcing African customary law shall be instituted throughout the country.

(d)   The Zimbabwe law courts shall consist of the lower courts, the High Court and the Supreme Court.

(e)   The ZANU republican government shall establish the Zimbabwe Republic Police (ZRP) to replace the BSAP.

(f)   ZANU shall repeal the Unlawful Organizations Act, the Law and Order Maintenance Act, the Preservation of Constitutional

Government Act. Preventive Detention Act, Curatorship Act and all other repressive laws enacted by the white minority Settler-Governments.

11. PAN-AFRICAN AND FOREIGN POLICY

(a)   A ZANU Republic shall adopt Pan-Africanism as the foundation of its foreign policy.

(b)   A ZANU Republic shall seek membership in the Organization of African States and shall participate fully in all Pan-African Conferences.

(c)   The liquidation of colonialism, settlerism, neo-colonialism and Imperialism in Africa shall be the major goal of ZANU's Pan-African policy.

(d)   In foreign affairs, the policy of positive neutrality and non-alignment shall be pursued with vigilance.

(e)   ZANU shall participate fully in mankind's search for a lasting peace through disarmament and freedom from hunger, but it will not seek co-existence between oppressor and oppressed in any country. Co-existence can only be between free people.

12. ZANU AND DEFENCE

(a)   A ZANU republic regime will maintain a strong national Army for defence and liberation of Africa from colonialism, settlerism and imperialism.

(b)   Special inducement will be introduced so as to encourage capable soldiers to pursue military service as a career.

13. ZANU AND WELFARE AND HOUSING

(a)   ZANU shall spearhead social schemes for juvenile delinquents.

(b)   ZANU will introduce a training programme in the arts and skills for all prisoners in order to facilitate their rehabilitation.

(c)   Creches and child welfare centres shall be established in all places.

(d)   A training and re-training programme for the unemployed shall be established in conjunction with the Ministry of Labour.

(e)   A ZANU Government shall establish a Freedom Fighters Council which shall administer special education and life insurance funds for the dependants of those who died, or were partially or wholly incapacitated in the national struggle for liberation.

(f)   A ZANU government will ensure that every person has a suitable house in urban or rural areas.

(g) ZANU shall repeal 'The Native Status Determination Act' and disband the present racial Social Welfare Department.

14. ZANU AND IMMIGRATION

(a) Immigration from overseas shall in principle be prohibited except for technicians and investors.

(b) The ZANU Government shall pursue an open-door policy with regard to immigrants from other parts of Africa except South African and Portuguese whites who shall be prohibited.

15. LOCAL GOVERNMENT

(a) The municipal franchise, under a ZANU Government, shall be based on 'One man, one vote'.

(b) The present Local Government Act shall be repealed, and a new one enacted.

(c) Chieftainship as an Institution shall be protected by the Constitution.

(d) A College for the training of Chiefs and their heirs-apparent shall be established.

16. ECONOMIC PLANNING

(a) Under ZANU government, a Ministry of Economics shall be created and charged with the responsibility of preparing long-range development schemes for every government department, taking into account the economic implications of departmental policies and intended projects.

(b) The Ministry of Economics shall study and propose ways and means of raising capital on home and foreign markets for national and economic developments.

(c) Private enterprise shall be encouraged as an economic mainstay in the private economic sector.

(d) Foreign investment shall be vigorously encouraged.

(e) ALL major industries that form the basis of our main economy shall be nationalized.

17. ZANU AND TRADE AND COMMERCE

(a) A ZANU Government shall create a Board of Trade and Commerce to step up the Republic's trade with the outside world.

(b) A favoured nation policy in respect of tariffs and customs in trade with the African sister-states shall be pursued.

18. POWER AND WATER DEVELOPMENT

(a) A ZANU government shall encourage the use of all available electric power for industry, lighting and cooking in urban and rural areas.

(b) Irrigation schemes along the major river valleys shall be initiated to improve farming.

(c) A ZANU government shall supply water to all villages and communities.

19. TRANSPORT AND COMMUNICATION

(a) All railways and passenger aircraft shall be public property.

(b) Urban passenger-transport shall fall under Government management.

(c) An improved communications system will be maintained.

(d) Radio Zimbabwe shall be the national broadcasting system.

(e) Tourism shall be encouraged.

20. YOUTH AND CULTURE

(a) A ZANU Ministry of Youth, Sports and Culture shall be established.

(b) Public youth centres and recreational facilities shall be established in conjunction with the Department of Social Welfare.

(c) A National Youth Brigade shall be formed to spearhead voluntary work.

21. NATIONAL SHRINES AND MONUMENTS

(a) A ZANU Regime shall ensure that all ruins, caves and other shrines and monuments are honoured and respected.

(b) All statues and other images that symbolize colonialism and settlerism shall be demolished.

22. NATIONAL HOLIDAYS

(a) A ZANU regime shall abolish colonial and imperialist holidays.

(b) A National Day of Heroes shall be named and observed in honour of national martyrs such as Dr Parirenyatwa and others who died for national liberation.

23. ZANU AND NATIONAL HEALTH POLICY

(a) A ZANU government shall attach great importance to the Medical School at the University of Zimbabwe.

(b) An inducement consisting in scholarships and allowances as well as better conditions of service upon the completion of training shall be offered to all doctors.

(c) More training centres for State Registered Nurses will be established throughout the country.

(d) All hospitals, clinics, dispensaries and places of confinement throughout the country shall be open to people of all races.

(e) A ZANU government shall establish a new system of mobile clinics that will bring medical treatment and care to all villages and other remote places every day.

(f) The National Health Service will be free for people of all races.

SECTION II

THE PERIOD OF DIRECT CONFRONTATION 1964–1971

This period can be traced back to the NDP Congress held in October 1961 when, among other things, it was decided to resort to violence in order to get an acceptable constitution. That decision was reinforced by the Reverend Ndabaningi Sithole's 'We are our own liberators' Presidential speech at ZANU's first—and only—Congress held in Gwelo on 21-23 May 1964. It was no longer a question of civil rights but of majority rule.

The two parties, ZANU and ZAPU (functioning as Peoples' Caretaker Council (PCC)) sought to eliminate each other; physical thuggery and party clashes became the order of the day.

When both parties were banned in August 1964 most of the leaders were detained. The two parties began recruiting their followers for military training in order to bring down the minority regime by force, especially after UDI in 1965. ZANU in exile was led by Herbert Chitepo, Nathan Shamuyarira, Hamadziripi and Simpson Mtambanengwe, while ZAPU was led by James Chikerema, George Nyandoro, George Silundika and Jason Moyo.

The war of liberation—Chimurenga—began in April 1966 with the Sinoia Battle waged by ZANLA forces and this period was one of experimentation in the various tactics of guerrilla warfare.

Towards the end of this period a new political movement—the Front for the Liberation of Zimbabwe (FROLIZI)—was formed.

CHAPTER FOUR

TOWARDS UDI

15 Zimbabwe African National Union: presidential address at the Zanu inaugural congress by Rev Ndabaningi Sithole. Gwelo, 12–13 May 1964

Sons and daughters of Zimbabwe—
I am delighted to see so many of you here. I fully realize the sacrifice you have made in order that you might be here. Here we meet for the first time as ZANU supporters from over 40 districts. Here we shall elect our own leaders freely, and here we shall make important decisions which will affect this country for a long time to come.

ZANU which was formed on 8 August 1963, stands for democracy, socialism, nationalism, **one man one vote**, freedom, Pan-Africanism, non-racism and republicanism. Those who care to know more about our programme are advised to read our policy statement.

All of you, I am sure, know that since the birth of ZANU, The People's Caretaker Council has tried its best to liquidate us physically. They had hoped that with a regular supply of money from the United Arab Republic, and by employing thugs to intimidate us, they would carry the day; but to their amazement and dismay they have completely and hopelessly failed. Today ZANU can boast of over 100,000 card-bearing members. Let alone general sympathisers. ZANU is destined to liberate this country because it acts from a deep and sacred sense of devotion, dedication and humanity, unlike PCC which has thoroughly antagonized the people because of their intimidation and thuggery—the alpha and omega of PCC leadership.

The white settler government has been very ruthless with us. They have raided our offices and homes quite regularly. Most of our members of the national executive have been sentenced, for political reasons, to periods ranging from six to 18 months. Let alone the ordinary supporters who are serving sentences ranging from one year to 20 years.

The white settler government is terribly afraid of ZANU. Its growing strength has so scared it that for no apparent reason they decided to cancel our first national rally which was due to be held on 23 May 1964, after this congress. You all know the most stringent conditions under which the congress is being held. All our sessions are required to be open to the police and to allow the police to record everything. Only a fear-ridden government can do this. As long as this government continues to be in power based on the will of the white settler minority, freedom of assembly and freedom of speech will continue to be denied to the majority of the people.

ZANU has had to walk a tight rope between the PCC and the white settler government both of which, though for different reasons, have been determined to kill it in the cradle. But we are happy that our party which began as a toothless baby has now teeth. It can bite and bite hard. In fact, ZANU is now ready to bite hard after thorough organization during the last ten months.

Now, I wish to turn to the explosive situation in this country:

1. BAN ON POLITICAL MEETINGS IN THE RESERVES

There are 4,000,000 Africans in Southern Rhodesia. 42% of these people live in the reserves and no political meetings may be held in these reserves. This is to say that 1,680,000 (almost 2,000,000) people are denied the simple right of political assembly and therefore political expression in areas which are legally theirs. This iniquitous set up is caused by the fact that the Africans do not have an effective vote. It should be remembered that these people are refused political gatherings in their own areas purely to entrench white minority rule. This is why it is the duty of everyone in Zimbabwe to destroy minority rule—root, stem and branch.

2. BAN ON POLITICAL MEETINGS IN THE BIG CITIES AND TOWNS

The fear-ridden white settler government has virtually banned all political gatherings in Salisbury, Bulawayo and other towns. The whole idea is to weaken and destroy the African nationalist movement in this country. But, of course, they won't succeed in this. We have our plans.

3. BAN ON THE *DAILY NEWS*

The fear-ridden white settler government has banned the circulation of the *Daily News* in jail and in detention so that the African prisoners and detainees may be completely cut off from the outside world. They seem terribly keen to starve our people of mental food.

4. BAN ON AFRICAN LEADERS TO ENTER RESERVES

African nationalist leaders are not allowed by the white minority laws to enter any of the reserves. Many of these leaders who have relatives and friends in these areas have been forced to enter the reserves and have been fined or sentenced to imprisonment. They may not remain in the reserves and they may not remain in European areas as this would be against the spirit of the notorious Land Apportionment Act.

5. DETENTIONS

Wha Wha and Gonakudzingwa have become notorious places where African nationalist leaders may be detained without trial. To detain a man without trial is to do him gross injustice. At Gonakudzingwa the African nationalist leaders are cut off from any contact with the outside world. Nothing could be worse than this. It is indeed the worst mental torture of its kind. At Wha Wha men and women and even babies are confined to an area of five acres of land. Nothing could be more brutalizing and de-humanizing than this.

Another restriction camp at Matetsi, near Binga, is ready to receive the ZANU leaders any day. Again another restriction camp is being built near Marandellas for African women and girls. I suppose the whole idea of restricting these men and women is to teach them to accept white minority rule, and to forget all about majority rule which is inevitable in any case. It should be remembered that detentions were tried elsewhere in Africa, but they failed; but majority rule triumphed.

We must not forget that these restrictions and these white minority imposed bans have resulted in the loss of bread winners of many families. A good number of children today go hungry, scantily clothed and cannot afford school fees because their parents are in restriction. These restrictions have disrupted more African homes, and more social problems have been created. Many of these restrictees have lost their employment and their businesses. It is therefore important that this congress gives this matter its serious consideration.

6. WHITE MINORITY—MADE LAWS

There are now hundreds and hundreds of African political prisoners in Southern Rhodesia. Their major crime is that they oppose the highly oppressive white settler regime. The white minority-made laws are indeed inherently unjust in relation to the majority who do not have the vote, and since the so-called courts administer such laws, it is not wrong to say that such courts are in fact rubber stamps of injustice. This is why many of our people cannot find justice in these courts. The legislature and the courts reflect minority and not majority interests. This is why we insist without any reservation that only majority rule is good for our country. The worst curse to this country is minority rule which has been responsible for most of the oppression which has gone on in this country.

What has been the result of these politically oppressive measures? Has law and order been maintained? Has security come to this country? The answer, of course, is 'no'. Everywhere I have gone people express deep concern and they demand a showdown now. 'We cannot go on like this. We cannot go on accepting these oppressive conditions. Action! Action! is the only answer,' they say. Some put it this way, 'We have talked enough. It's high time we acted like men.'

It is clear from the measures that the white settler government is taking against African nationalists that it is determined to silence their voices and therefore the voice of the people. It is desperate to neutralize them politically so that white minority rule may continue indefinitely. Mr Ian Smith, the *apartheid*-oriented Premier, has clearly stated that he does not hope to see an African government in his lifetime. This means that he will do everything in his power to prevent the birth of an African government in this country. Mr Winston Field was overthrown from his premiership because he was considered by the disciples of white supremacy or *apartheid* as a stumbling block in their determination to create another South Africa here. The racist politicians of the Rhodesian Front are dreaming of unilateral independence regardless of the disastrous consequences which are bound to follow such an irresponsible act. No realistic observer can fail to see that a head-on-collision between the Rhodesian Front government and the African nationalists is inevitable, and when this comes to pass a racial war would have begun, and this is bound to involve the entire continent of Africa, and hence the international world.

The question today is not: Are the African people ready to go into country-wide action? But it is: Can the African leaders hold back their followers from taking desperate country-wide action? For the last ten months I have counselled patience, and up to a point I have succeeded in holding back the rising wave of desperate acts. Can I continue to hold back this wave? The answer is clearly no. No leader can continue, under the present nationalist tempo, to ask his followers to be patient. Impatience is bound to have its way. The people must have an outlet or else country-wide violence and disruption overtake us.

I shall return to this aspect later, but now I wish to draw the attention of this congress to the various factors that influence the present situation in this country:

1. THE UNITED NATIONS

This international body has played an important part in the Southern Rhodesia issue by championing majority rule as the only solution to the present problems that face us. Their moral support is much to be appreciated.

2. THE INDEPENDENT AFRICAN STATES

These have also played a very significant part by condemning the oppressive white minority set-up, and by advocating majority rule as the only sensible solution to the present problem. Their moral and practical support is inestimable.

3. THE UNITED KINGDOM

The United Kingdom is the only power that can grant Southern Rhodesia legal independence. It has power to intervene in the affairs of this country if it is so desired. At present Britain which holds the constitutional key to the problem facing us is unwilling to use that key. She is more inclined to side with her kith and kin than with us. With her tongue she supports majority rule, but with her actions she supports the *status quo.*

4. THE COMMONWEALTH COUNTRIES

While many Commonwealth countries share in general the view that majority rule is the only answer to the present problem, their help just ends there. They have not gone beyond the moral support they give us.

5. THE AFRO-ASIAN BLOC

We enjoy tremendous moral support from the Afro-Asian bloc; but it should be clearly noted that this support, like other moral support we get elsewhere, is limited to the moral sphere and does not seem to affect the practical facts of the political situation here.

6. THE WHITE SETTLER FACTOR

There was a time when European liberalism was regarded as the only hope for this country, but events have shown that European liberalism is only sugar-coated white supremacy. European liberals do not subscribe to the doctrine of one man one vote. They still believe that the white man must rule the African, but he must do so justly. They might as well say the African must be oppressed justly!

The white settlers are determined, as I have already stated, to hold on to political power indefinitely. They do not have the solution to the present problem since they champion the cause of white minority rule.

7. THE PEOPLE'S CARETAKER COUNCIL FACTOR

The PCC as a political factor that would help solve the problem facing this country is equally a negative factor since all its efforts are directed against its rival party. The country-wide intimidation and thuggery promoted by PCC against ZANU supporters only shows the incapacity of the PCC to solve the national problem that faces us. Indeed, the problem is beyond their comprehension and vision. PCC tends to cloud the national issues.

8. THE ZANU FACTOR

ZANU is a positive political factor, and it will not be long before its carefully laid plans begin unfolding in a determined effort to bring about the right solution which can only be majority rule.

I have deliberately recounted to you the various factors which influence the situation here one way or another. Those who believe that the United Nations will bring us independence are greatly mistaken. Only PCC believes that. Those who believe that the Afro-Asian bloc will bring us independence are greatly mistaken. Only PCC believes that. These countries can only help us up to a point, but independence can only be brought to this country by us. No one can liberate another. Independence is not ours unless we liberate ourselves. There is no such thing as being liberated by others. Others can only help us to liberate ourselves.

This has been our great mistake in our nationalist movement. People were taught to expect to be liberated, instead of being taught to liberate themselves. As Mr Enos Nkala eloquently expressed it, 'The people's determination to liberate themselves was transformed into expectation to be liberated.' I am, however, very glad to see that our ZANU supporters and sympathizers have grasped this central point of liberating ourselves, and with this new outlook Zimbabwe should soon be free. We are our own liberators.

The Zimbabwe African National Union, of which I am proud to be President, has been ideologically distorted, and it is right and proper that I put right the ZANU ideological picture.

Some white settler politicians here accuse us of being adherents of Communism, and so the Rhodesian Front government can have the impunity to say that in fighting the African nationalists they are fighting Communism! What hypocrisy! They cry Communism to uphold white supremacy! Any African nationalist who visits any Communist country becomes, in their hysterical machinations, a Communist. They might as well say an African who visits England becomes an Englishman. We are not going to have our friends or enemies chosen for us by others. We reserve the right, in spite of the white settler squeals, to visit any country we like. Let the entire world know that we are not going to be carbon copies of the West or the East. We believe it is impossible to transport what has been perfected in one set of historical circumstances and transplant it in an entirely new environment. This is why we are unwilling to be rubber-stamps of either American capitalism or Communism. We shall pursue our own ideology of socialism best suited to Zimbabwe conditions. The history of one people is not that of another, and this is why it is so revolting to us when we are asked to choose between the West and the East. We don't want to choose to be like anybody else. We just want to be ourselves. True freedom is not being like the West of the East, but in being like ourselves. Any help given by either the West or the East must help us to be like ourselves and to be ourselves, or else that help is worse than useless. We refuse to be used as pawns in the international power struggle between the West and the East.

Now I wish to return to the issues facing us. I am sure this congress is more keenly interested in the issues facing us here at home than outside borders of our country.

The question has been asked: What method is ZANU going to use in liberating this country? Is it going to use the constitutional or the unconstitutional method; in other words, is ZANU going to resort to violence or non-violence? Or is it going to use both? These are questions which are being asked earnestly by all those who are determined to see that this country is brought under majority rule in the shortest possible space of time. It is my duty, as your President, to answer these questions as honestly as I can.

First, I want you to note this important general observation on human behaviour. No leader however clever can dictate to his followers what method to use in liberating their country. The particular circumstances prevailing in a particular country dictate the kind of method to be used in any freedom struggle.

As a rule human beings everywhere first try the method of non-violence, but if circumstances are such that non-violence cannot work, the same human beings have not hesitated to use violence to achieve certain practical ends which would be denied to them if they pursued only the path of non-violence.

For instance, in the former French African colonies in the West and Equatorial Africa, non-violence was resorted to as a method of gaining independence for these countries. The constitutional machinery was there, and it was used and hence the method of non-violence succeeded. Tanganyika is another good case in point. Their method was one of non-violence. Their particular circumstances dictated this kind of method.

But in such countries as Algeria, Congo (Leopoldville), Kenya and the United Arab Republic, independence was preceded by bloodshed, violence and disruption because the particular circumstances in those countries did not allow the use of the method of non-violence. Violence had to be used in order to shake the powers that existed out of their political complacency. This is how human beings have behaved everywhere in the world. This has nothing to do with the colour of one's skin.

Southern Rhodesia is not an exception. If non-violence fails, then its counterpart becomes the only hope for the majority of the people. This is where we have to do more thinking. Many white settler politicians in this country will praise non-violence to the sky, but support grossly oppressive measures against Africans which only encourage solution by violence. No government can create impossible conditions without promoting at one and the same time country-wide violence.

The white settlers here have the constitutional answer to the problem facing this country. By using their right to vote they can save this country from an imminent disaster. They can help the method of non-violence to work. But by refusing to extend the right to vote to the majority of the people they only promote conditions of violence. The white voters· are equally responsible for most of the violence that has taken place in this country, and they will be equally responsible for the violence that will take place. Any oppressive set-up can only create conditions of violence and those who support such a set-up are morally responsible. It's sheer nonsense and hypocrisy to blame only the African for the present wave of violence. The white settlers who have the vote are equally responsible for it. The tension between minority rule as supported by the white settlers, and majority rule as supported by the African people is the fundamental cause of the present unrest and violence. Unless this tension is resolved soon Southern Rhodesia is heading for real trouble.

Make no mistake about this. The tension cannot be resolved by banning political meetings from the Reserves; it cannot be resolved by banning African political meetings in the cities; it cannot be resolved by imprisoning more and more African nationalists; it cannot be resolved by creating an army of African nationalist detainees. It can only be resolved by acceding to the legitimate demands for majority rule. Anything short of this is naive, unrealistic and only leading this country to a long period of anarchy, chaos, disruption and fiasco.

There are tentative solutions which have been put down for the consideration of the public here. I wish to say a few words about each of these solutions so that you may all be quite clear as to where ZANU stands on these great issues of the moment:

1. FIGHTING WITHIN THE PRESENT PARLIAMENT

ZANU can never fight elections under the present constitution. We boycotted the 1962 elections under the 1961 constitution and we cannot go back on our word. Our opposition to the present constitution still stands. In a country that is 96% African and only 4% European, it is wrong to have a legislature 77% European and only 23% African.

2. BLOCKING-THIRD

Another mad solution that has been put forward is the so-called blocking-third which we reject out of hand. There is no earthly reason whatever why we should be denied independence now when our friends in Zambia and Malawi now enjoy it. We cannot be a party to a scheme that purports to deny us the independence that rightly belongs to us.

3. PARITY

There has been a great deal of talk about parity. The problem that faces us is one of disparity, e.g. 15 African MP's as against 50 European MPs in a House of 65. It is suggested that the solution to this disparity is parity, i.e. 50-50. But an examination of the facts shows that the so-called parity in a country that is 96% African and only 4% European is in fact disparity. There cannot be parity between 4,000,000 Africans and only 250,000 whites. Hence the suggested solution to the present problem of disparity is superficially parity but in fact disparity. In other words, you solve disparity with disparity which of course does not make sense.

4. NO CHANGE DURING THE LIFE-TIME OF THE PRESENT PARLIAMENT

As those in power are interested in their monthly cheques for salaries they have lost sight of national interests, and are not interested in any constitutional changes regardless of what happens to the country. They would like to see no change until 1967. This, of course, does not solve anything except that it is an attempt to maintain the *status quo.*

5. UNILATERAL INDEPENDENCE

A rapidly growing number of white settlers here believe that the only solution to the present problem is unilateral independence. 'Create another South Africa here, and the problem is solved right away,' they say.

If the white settlers declare themselves independent, we will also declare ourselves independent. Once this happens, we shall have two states within the same territory—a white state and a black state. This would mean war, meeting force with force, but eventually the black man is destined to win since the country is his by birth, and therefore, by right, and the white man is destined to lose since the country is not his by right. The best the white man can do is to accommodate himself to the idea of African majority rule. His security lies in African majority rule, not in white settler minority rule which is on the way out in any case.

6. MAJORITY RULE

This is the only true solution to the present problem. This solution is supported by the majority of the inhabitants in our country. Most members of the white settler minority group, however, do not support this approach, but time is on the side of majority rule everywhere in Africa, and the white settlers here should re-adjust themselves to this fact.

Time for fine speeches has gone. This is now time for action in order to solve the problem facing us. This congress must direct its attention to the following problems:

1. What steps must we take in the event of unilateral independence?
2. What steps must we take now in order that we may effectively oppose legislative measures at present designed to weaken and silence the African nationalist movement in this country?
3. What steps must we take immediately in order to bring about favourable constitutional changes?

We have the power in our hands. We must all be prepared to suffer. In the words of Ben Bella, we must be prepared 'to die a little' if need be. Other people have done it when the need arose, and we also can do it as the need arises. We have now come to the point when we must act now or never. There are now serious plans under way to deprive us of our independence, and we must prevent this with our very blood or else we are not worthy of our beloved Zimbabwe.

I do not promise any of you that you will not suffer if you champion our cause. I do not promise any of you comfort. You will be imprisoned. You will be deprived of your employment. You will be detained. You will be torn away from your families. In some cases some of us may be shot dead. But this is the price all human beings must pay for their freedom. We must pay the price or remain unfree.

May the spirit of our ancestors give you the wisdom, the strength and the courage you need as we face the onerous task of reversing the wheel of history in this our beloved Zimbabwe. The white settlers will lose because they believe might is right. We are destined to win because we believe right is might. This congress is the turning point and Southern Rhodesia will never be the same.

16 Zimbabwe African Peoples Union: Political Situation in Zimbabwe. Statement to the Committee of Nine by James Chikerema, acting President. Dar-es-Salaam, Tanzania, 5 June, 1964

The political situation in Zimbabwe (Southern Rhodesia) has terribly deteriorated since the arrest of our leader, Mr Joshua Nkomo and top officials of the PCC (ZAPU). The Smith regime has detained over 3,000 patriots since Mr Nkomo was arrested. This includes about 900 women who are presently detained in Marandellas prison, 50 miles from Salisbury. Other freedom fighters are restricted at Wha Wha Restriction Camp, Gwelo.

The white settler police and army are terrorizing our people in the towns and country. They are making regular day and night raids on the homes of our supporters.

In spite of the brutal treatment being inflicted on them by these ruthless power-hungry white settlers our people continue to wage a relentless struggle against minority rule.

The Smith regime is trying its best to cripple our liberatory movement by all the means at its disposal. These include the restriction of nearly all the ZAPU executive and branch leaders, mass arrests and the use of Government radio and press propaganda to discredit us and demoralize our followers.

The plight of the freedom fighters in Zimbabwe is indeed very critical and only outside assistance can retrieve the position. We ask the

Committee of Nine to give us financial and material assistance immediately. This will enable us to keep the fight going on in Zimbabwe.

We have absolutely no money at the moment, and if the Committee of Nine is there to aid those genuinely fighting against colonialism then this is the time for it to come to our aid.

We still abide by our stand that the Committee of Nine has either to recognize us as the sole liberatory movement in Zimbabwe or have nothing to do with us. We are sick and tired of being told to make a united front with a party that was rejected by the people right on the day it was launched. The people in ZANU, a handful of misguided and power-hungry so-called intellectuals, are the ones who must come back to the people and not us to make a united front with such a discredited group. The Committee of Nine has either to recognize us, the people's party or ZANU, which stinks to the ordinary man and woman, boy and girl in Zimbabwe. There can be no two ways about it.

The Committee of Nine has had an ample opportunity to know which party enjoys the support of the majority. Dr Kaunda has shown the way and we expect the Committee to follow suit if at all it is genuinely interested in the overthrowing of white supremacy in Zimbabwe. . . .

17 Zimbabwe African Peoples Union: memorandum submitted to the Rt Hon Harold Wilson, MP, Prime Minister of the UK, on the recent political and constitutional position in Rhodesia. 12 November 1964

On 9 September 1964, conversations concerning independence for Southern Rhodesia under exclusive settler minority rule were concluded between the British Prime Minister, Sir Alec Douglas Home and the Southern Rhodesia Prime Minister, Mr Ian Smith.

These conversations were embodied in a communiqué released for publication to the press on 11 September 1964. The text of this communiqué, which was the subject of some considerable haggling between the two Prime Ministers, is as follows:

> There was a full discussion of all aspects of the problem of independence for Southern Rhodesia. *The Prime Minister of Southern Rhodesia expanded his case for the grant of independence on the basis of the present constitution.* The British Prime Minister restated and explained the position of the British government as already stated in Parliament.

The British Prime Minister conveyed to the Prime Minister of Southern Rhodesia the views expressed at the meeting of the Commonwealth Prime Ministers conference in July as set out in their final communiqué; the Prime Minister of Southern Rhodesia for his part made it clear that he did not feel bound by any of the statements made at the Prime Ministers meeting to which he had not been invited.

The British Prime Minister told the Prime Minister of Southern Rhodesia that the British government looked forward to the day when Southern Rhodesia would take her place as an independent sovereign state within the Commonwealth.

For their part they were anxious that this should come about as soon as practicable.

The British Prime Minister said that the *British government must be satisfied that any basis on which it was proposed that independence should be granted was acceptable to the people of the country as a whole.*

The Prime Minister of Southern Rhodesia accepted that independence must be based on general consent and stated that he was convinced that the majority of the population supported his request for independence on the basis of the present constitution and franchise. The British Prime Minister took note of this statement but said that *the British government had as yet no evidence that this was the case. The Prime Minister of Southern Rhodesia recognized that the British Government were entitled to be satisfied about this and said that he would consider how best it could be demonstrated so that independence could be granted.*

The British Prime Minister said that *the British government would take account of any views which might be freely expressed by the population on the issues involved;* but he must make it plain that the British government reserved their position.

Certain very obvious conditions emerge as fundamental pre-requisites of the referendum in terms of this communiqué.

1. Independence can be granted only on the basis of acceptance by the country as a whole.

2. The majority of the population has to be consulted.

3. The consultation of the majority of the population should be conducted in conditions and circumstances which permit of freedom of expression, freedom of communication and movement.

4. The British government had as yet no evidence in support of Mr Ian Smith's claim that the majority of the population supported his request for independence on the basis of the present constitution and franchise.

5. Mr Ian Smith recognized that the British government were entitled to be satisfied about this claim. In other words evidence must be forthcoming that the majority, i.e. Africans, support the Rhodesia government's request for independence on the basis of the present

constitution, that the referendum was conducted in such manner and in such circumstances that the Africans, the majority, were given a free and untrammelled opportunity to say, and to record their 'Ayes' or 'Noes'.

6. That when the referendum is over, and Mr Smith presents his results to the British government, the British government reserves its position. It is perfectly reasonable to postulate that it is necessarily inherent in the nature of this reservation that should the British government be not satisfied that the majority of the population were not properly consulted, i.e. that the referendum was a fake, elementary justice would require that the British government turn down Mr Smith's request for independence. Not only that, Mr Smith's government would have been proved to employ cheating practices in order to achieve its declared objective; the perpetual maintenance of a system of serfdom over the majority of the indigenous population by a minority foreign settler regime.

CHAPTER 2

Let us now examine how, and the circumstances in which, the referendum was conducted.

A resumé of the background to the referendum will assist to put the matter in clearer perspective. We cannot take it for granted that the world knows about the Southern Rhodesia problem. But no doubt informed people will be aware that it is one of the most agitated colonial political issues of the contemporary era, and, indeed up to now the highest world council, the UN, stands seized of this issue. It will be recalled that the matter of Southern Rhodesia is presently under the consideration of the UN Committee on Colonialism.

1. The 1961 Southern Rhodesia constitution was overwhelmingly rejected by the African people of Southern Rhodesia almost to a man. It is not unusual that in the circumstances of a popular national movement, a few quislings can be found ready and willing to co-operate with the oppressor. Most countries do, and have experienced this. But in Southern Rhodesia it would be quite fair to say that that forlorn class of people, however well-intentioned they might be in co-operating with the oppressor to work the 1961 constitution, constitute the exception that proves the rule, i.e. the 1961 constitution was overwhelmingly rejected.

The reasons for its rejections are basically these:

(a)   Out of a total of 65 seats in the Legislative Assembly the European minority has 50 seats, the Africans 15 seats.

(b)   The Europeans are elected on one Roll, the A Roll, the Africans on a separate Roll, the B Roll.

The franchise is based on income and property qualification, the qualifications for the A Roll being very high, the maximum requirement being income £720 pa, or immovable property valued £1,500 plus literacy.

The qualifications for the B Roll maximum being income of not less than £240 pa or ownership of immovable property valued at £450.

There are other pettifogging details of the franchise qualifications, but the principle of the system is to exclude Africans in any effective numbers from the A Roll and to retain the majority of the Europeans on that roll. It was estimated that in 1962 only 564(!) Africans qualified for the A Roll whereas the Europeans were 87,000. The natural order of things is thus reversed and an absurdly oppressive situation obtains in which the minority becomes the majority. Moreover, the fact that these qualifications are enacted by reference to income and property and that there is an accompanying provision whereby the income and property qualifications can be raised without reference to the people by decree makes the franchise arrangements a durable instrument of oppression, freely at the disposal of the Southern Rhodesia Government. As a matter of fact, the history of the denial of political rights to the majority of the people in Southern Rhodesia, is the history of the raising of the franchise property qualifications.

The average annual earnings of Africans in Southern Rhodesia are £114; whereas the average annual earning of Europeans are £1,217.

In fact, these income and property qualifications were raised recently in September this year, a subject which shall be dealt with later in its proper place.

The constitution contains a Bill of Rights which in terms of the actual operation of this constitution, is now proved to be illusory. While it purports to declare and confer rights on the one hand, life, liberty, security of the person, the enjoyment of property and the protection of the law, freedom of expression, of assembly and association, freedom of conscience, respect for private and family life, on the other hand, these purported rights can be taken away at any time, should the government consider it necessary to do so in the interests of the so-called defence, public safety or public order.

Our own experience of the application of this purported Bill of Rights is that in so far as the powers of government are exclusively in the hands of a minority and the majority is for effective and practical purposes virtually disenfranchised, the provisions relating to the interests of defence, public safety, public order, have been used as means to choke the popular national movement, by banishments, prescriptions and detentions. ZAPU is banned under these pretexts.

Concentration camps, Wha Wha and Gonakudzingwa have been

erected to which the leaders of ZAPU have been rusticated.

It is perfectly true to say at no other time in the history of this country and directly as a result of this constitution (with its Bill of Rights!) has there been a greater number of political prisoners, opponents of the minority regime, in gaols and concentration camps.

There are innumerable examples, two of which we give as typical, graphic, yet melancholy refutations of any claim that this constitution protects or guarantees any of the rights that it is supposed to confer.

1. In terms of this constitution, a Constitutional Council exists which is charged specifically with the task of watchdog of the Bill of Rights and to make adverse reports to the government of the day on legislation which is inconsistent with the Bill of Rights.

Among the chief props for the deprivation of the African population of land and reduction to serfdom is a piece of legislation entitled the Land Apportionment Act. This nomenclature is a misnomer because in actual fact the purpose of the measure is to deprive Africans of land and to assign such land for European settlement. It was passed in 1930 and considerable tracts of land were taken over the years from Africans. To mention only a few specific instances of ejection of Africans from their traditional homes and the settlement of Europeans therein: Rhodesdale Estate, Lancashire Estates and Matopos. In 1960 the Southern Rhodesia government was bound to make a shamefaced admission of the results of this Act in these words:

'The division of land under the Act is completely unfair to Africans in that 42 million acres are reserved for $2\frac{1}{2}$ million Africans, whereas 48 million acres are reserved for about 200,000 Europeans.'

(Southern Rhodesia Legislative Assembly, second report of the Select Committee on Resettlement of Natives, 1960 at page 49.)

The land, both urban and farmland, is zoned completely into separate European and African areas.

In March 1964, the Constitutional Council examined this legislation and made its adverse report to the government of the day to the effect that the measure is inconsistent with the Bill of Rights.

As the Act is a cornerstone of the government's principles and policies, its reply to the Constitutional Council's report was to the effect that the Land Apportionment Act will remain as intact as ever before.

The provision regarding freedom of speech was made a complete mockery of when the only paper in the colony which up to a point catered for the views of the African national movement was banned 'in the interests of public security and safety'.

Thus in the name of this very Bill of Rights, the majority of the population of Southern Rhodesia today are without a political party, without a public vehicle of opinion, and all political leaders incarcerated in jails and concentration camps.

Past British governments vaunted this constitution as the solvent of a multi-racial society in Southern Rhodesia. The greater majority of the African population rejected it for what it truly is in substance—an instrument for the perpetuation of serfdom. We have no more rights and liberties under this constitution than serfs had in the baronial society of the Middle Ages. It is clear now beyond a peradventure from our perilous experience that the harshness of the Southern Rhodesia political system indicates the old established maxim that the true support for constitutional guarantees and rights is universal adult suffrage, the only way of ensuring that government rests on the consent of the governed. The future security of the minority settlers lies in an honourable transference of power now instead of prolonging a foundation on which they are bound to crash with irretrievable losses in correspondence to the prolongation.

It is no wonder that the Ian Smith government of Southern Rhodesia desires independence on the basis of this constitution.

As is public knowledge the rejection of this constitution was followed by a sustained campaign at the United Nations. Only as recently as 25 April 1964, Mr G. Nyandoro, General Secretary, ZAPU, urging the rejection of this Constitution recommended to the Committee of 24 at UN as follows:

1. Obtain immediately from the UK Government the release of Mr Joshua Nkomo and all the nationalist political prisoners.
2. Demand from Britain the repeal of the present constitution.
3. Demand from Britain the implementation of all the past UN resolutions calling for an immediate constitutional conference with the specific purpose of transferring power to the majority under one man, one vote.
4. Call for a convention of the Security Council to implement the resolutions of the UN.

In response to a series of resolutions and recommendations of the United Nations, which established the responsibility of Great Britain in and over Southern Rhodesia and urging Great Britain as the sovereign power to take steps to effect constitutional arrangements acceptable to the majority of the population, previous British governments not only offered tenacious resistance, but took the position that Britain cannot intervene in the internal affairs of Southern Rhodesia, thus indicating to the latter that they had complete licence to deal with the Africans as they liked.

The issue was seriously canvassed in the capitals of Commonwealth countries, and as a result, at the Commonwealth Prime Ministers conference in July 1964, the problem was discussed. The Commonwealth Prime Ministers were concerned to find ways and means to hasten constitutional progress within Southern Rhodesia toward majority rule. They recognized that responsibility for the constitutional progress towards independence of Southern Rhodesia must remain with Great Britain and the grant of independence would not be made before Southern Rhodesia had achieved majority rule. They recommended that constitutional progress should be worked out by early agreement between representatives of the various political parties in Southern Rhodesia which would naturally include the African party. They were also concerned that the Southern Rhodesia government might try to avoid a solution of its internal problems by making a unilateral declaration of independence.

Mr Ian Smith, the Southern Rhodesia Prime Minister was not invited to the conference. This was properly so, because the majority of the Commonwealth Prime Ministers objected to his presence.

The conference is a conference of heads of sovereign states. And as they recognized that Great Britain as the sovereign power has the ultimate responsibility for constitutional matters in and over the colony; and as the Southern Rhodesia government by their treasonable utterances of a unilateral declaration of independence were not in a frame of mind to contribute anything constructive at this conference, we think it was only right that Mr Ian Smith should be put in his proper place inasmuch for example as the head of a local authority would be presumptiously arrogant by threatening not to co-operate with the sovereign authority in order to achieve illegal objectives. It is rather ironical that a man whose government rests on the very negation of consent and consultation of the majority should be heard to complain that he was not invited to put his views to the Commonwealth Prime Ministers conference. Perhaps we might be excused for expressing what we consider in all the circumstances to be perfectly fair comment that it is in the habit of people who have long been exercised in the hearts of tyranny to think that only their views matter, and to act that way.

Subsequent to the Commonwealth Prime Ministers conference, Mr Ian Smith was invited to go to London in order that the British government might communicate its views to Mr Smith as leader of the local settlers.

CHAPTER 3 THE REFERENDUM

Having sketched this background the referendum falls to be seen in its clear though sordid perspective. *Firstly,* it will have been evident from the foregoing that in so far as Mr Smith's claim that the majority of the population desire independence under the present constitution, we cannot be accused of using unduly intemperate language if we dismiss this claim as we do now without any further repetition in the most appropriate words—a fantastic lie.

Secondly, the Southern Rhodesia government repudiated any suggestion of consulting the majority of the population.

In the very constitution under which his government is seeking independence, there is a provision, Section 108, which specifically provides for the participation of Africans in a referendum in circumstances in which it is sought to bring about fundamental changes in the constitution.

On 8 October 1964, the Southern Rhodesia Government initiated a measure, the Referendum Bill, which specified that only those who were enrolled on the A and B Rolls would be entitled to vote in this referendum.

Prior to this, in the week ending 12 September 1964, the income qualifications for the franchise were raised. The minimum qualifications for the A Roll are now £330 per annum for an individual with four years secondary schooling. For the B Roll a minimum of £132 per annum plus two years secondary schooling. The average annual wage of the Africans is £114 and the Europeans £1,217. Even the *Rhodesia Herald,* itself the powerful votary of settler minority interests was moved to comment:

> Both increases are more than 10 per cent by which the means qualifications for the vote have been raised. There is, however, one difference. The average European wage is still above, and the average African wage is still below, the minimum needed to qualify for the vote on either roll.

In rather euphemistic undertones the paper went on: 'Mr Smith has pledged that he would not try to "pull a fast one". Naturally not. The Prime Minister could not lend himself to any constitutional fraud, and in any case he is content to have British observers.'

When it is realized that (1) only a handful of Africans are registered voters; (2) the referendum Bill barred the rest of the African majority from participating in the referendum, by whatever words you describe it, the Southern Rhodesia government's method of conducting the referendum revealed itself for what it substantially was—a constitutional fraud.

In the course of enacting the Referendum Bill which became an Act on 5 October 1964, Dr Arhn Palley, one of the European independents in this legislature, had this to say during one of the debates on this measure: 'Under no circumstances did the government wish the true and effective opinion of the African people to be known.'

Even Mr C. Hlabangana, one of the African MPs of the Whitehead-Welensky party (a well-known supporter of white minority rule) decried the moves of the present Government in no uncertain terms: 'No African will support independence under the present constitution.'

Thirdly, having excluded the majority from the normal referendum machinery, how did the Southern Rhodesia government go about the task of testing their opinion?

Mr Smith declared that he would test African opinion through chiefs and he would seek the opinions of anthropologists.

As regards the chiefs, whichever way you look at their position, are in effect an arm of the civil service. By the provisions of the Native Affairs Act, they come directly under the Ministry of Internal Affairs. They are confirmed in office by the Governor in Council, and may be dismissed by the same. (There are several instances of chiefs who were dismissed from office for refusing to be pliable instruments of the government in the implementation of its oppressive measures of which the most gallant is Chief Mangwende. Because of their refusal to co-operate Chiefs Musana, Makope and Mangwende were deposed and placed under restriction at Gonakudzingwa.)

Their salaries are paid directly by Government.

From May, 1964, the Southern Rhodesia Government began to lay emphasis on the policy of currying favour with the chiefs. A selected group was sent on a world tour, ostensibly to study agricultural methods. In Southern Rhodesia the chiefs have little or nothing to do with the administration of agriculture which in fact in African areas comes under the day to day supervision of Land Development Officers. It is therefore, perfectly reasonable to draw the inference that this 'agricultural study tour' was planned by the government in the light of anticipation of the referendum scheme from their exchange of correspondence with the British government. Clearly enough, the chiefs were being prepared in advance. The tour having been finished and upon Mr Smith's return from London, their basic wage was increased from £16 to £60 per month with not considerable perks in the bargain; a Land Rover, petrol allowance, and the enjoyment of proceeds from fines in the Chiefs' Court.

Were this ordinary corruption one would condemn it by analogy perhaps to the 'rotten borough system' in England in the eighteenth and nineteenth centuries. But, this is only part of a vast sinister system to deprive permanently four million people of the prospects ever of attaining majority rule.

By any standard of fairness, this method could not, ought not, to have been within the contemplation of the communiqué.

In any case, do the chiefs represent the majority of the people? The anthropologists whom Mr Smith had declared he would consult—a declaration which it now appears was made without prior consultation with them—promptly answered him. Headed by Professor J. C. Mitchell, a group of anthropologists and sociologists and lecturers of the University College at Salisbury issued the following statement as reported in the press (*Northern News* 22.9.64):

> In their professional opinion, the only way to test the African viewpoint on the question of Southern Rhodesia's independence was to give every man the opportunity to express his own views by vote. No other method could give valid results.
>
> The Prime Minister, Mr Ian Smith, has said he hoped to consult anthropologists and other experts as to how African opinion on the independence issue can be tested.
>
> In African society—of the past as well as the present—decisions have been, and are made by processes which involve all adult members of the community.
>
> In Southern Rhodesia, Africans are no longer organized solely on a basis of a tribal system. Therefore, African opinion on the national issue of independence cannot be tested within the framework of this system.
>
> Approximately half of the adult men in the population live and work outside tribal areas at any one time. Most of these do not qualify for the B Roll vote and it appears that the full expression of their opinion is to be ignored.
>
> Furthermore, on this issue, no one individual can pretend to speak for all members of his community as he may be mistaken, misguided or self-interested.
>
> It is therefore our professional opinion as sociologists and social anthropologists that the only way to test the African viewpoint on this issue is to give at least every man the opportunity to express his view by vote. No other method can give valid results.
>
> We are utterly opposed to the idea that there is something peculiar to Africans which makes it impossible to test their opinions by other than normal procedures.

The expression of this view led to quite a curious episode. Its publication on the Southern Rhodesia broadcasting station, a government controlled organ, was banned on the direction of Mr J. M. Helliwell, Chairman of the Broadcasting Station. In consequence top men of the station's news department resigned (*Sunday Mail*, 27 September 1964).

The Southern Rhodesia government planned to use chiefs and chiefs only as the means of testing African opinion. They set up a committee comprising the government and opposition members (i.e. Edgar Whitehead's Party). This committee was charged with the task of meeting chiefs and persuading them to accept the government's proposals of independence on the basis of the present constitution.

Speaking in the Southern Rhodesia Parliament on the move to set up this committee, Mr Ian Smith said, 'We believe we should tell the chiefs and headmen to consult their people in the traditional manner. We know there are different systems among tribes. There is no universal pattern.'

Fourthly, what of the communiqué's requirement that the opinions must be freely expressed?

It is vital to appreciate that the basic principle of Southern Rhodesia security legislation, as it is embodied in the Law and Order Maintenance Act and the Preventive Detention Act, is to suppress the African nationalist movement. ZAPU is banned, its leader Joshua Nkomo languishes in Gwelo jail. The result is that the entire African population is without their normal political party. The banning was followed by wholesale imprisonment of individual members of the banned political party.

Following the declaration of states of emergency in Highfield in August, 1964 and Harare in September 1964, thousands of men, women and juveniles were ruthlessly herded into jails.

The concentration camps at Wha Wha, Gonakudzingwa, and the jails at Gwelo, Bulawayo, Nkai, Gwanda, Marandellas and Sinoia hold between them 6,000 political prisoners.

We say little about the deleterious social effects of mass imprisonments which leave children and women bereft of their breadwinners. The hideous cruelty with which the arrests and imprisonments were carried out has become a by-word among the African population. We narrate briefly the experience of a member of ZAPU who escaped from police arrest in Mrewa District. Having been arrested by the police for being a member of ZAPU he was buried in the ground, being covered by earth up to the shoulders. While in that position, he was subjected to several hard smacks in the face, dug out and then asked to recant and to say where other wanted members were hiding.

At the time of organizing the so-called referendum, the whole colony was crawling with armed police and heavily equipped troops to round up the African population.

In the process of interrogation, the African population was subjected to brutal and severe intimidation. People's cattle, goats, chickens were wantonly destroyed. Police and the Army helped themselves of the loot. We have it on record that the Army said this was better food than the rations they got from the government.

Nothing could be more evident than the fact that in the given legal system of Southern Rhodesia, the banning of the African political party, the wholesale imprisonment of members of this party, the resort by the government to cheating in order to ram its own propaganda down the throats of the people, it is a cardinal travesty of the truth to talk of 'African views freely expressed'.

How remote the situation in Southern Rhodesia is from the elementary requirements of freedom of expression and freedom of consent is starkly revealed in the evidence of Miss Judith Garfield Todd. Miss Todd, a daughter of the famous former Prime Minister of Southern Rhodesia was charged and convicted before the courts under one of the many encompassing provisions of the draconic Law and Order Maintenance Act. On 14 October 1964, appearing before Salisbury Magistrate, E. J. Hamilton, she said:

> I demonstrated not to embarrass or disobey the police, but as a protest against the system of government which we are under . . . I demonstrated because the parties I support have all in turn been banned, because the people I recognize as my political leaders have been restricted or imprisoned, and because the only newspaper in this country that was courageous enough to effectively oppose the government has been silenced . . . My wish was to protest peacefully and in silence. I was denied this right. For the government finds any form of opposition increasingly intolerable. Even justice which a citizen might expect to find in these courts has been governed by the legislature and my friends are restricted or imprisoned without trial.'

Miss Todd is a member of the African nationalist movement. The Party she is referring to here is ZAPU.

The reverberations of the Nazi system are still echoing and have not yet died down. Surely, is not the system in Southern Rhodesia reminiscent of what the Nazi system was, and is it not the same as the South African system?

In view of the overwhelming evidence that the Rhodesia government departed diametrically from the terms of the communiqué to which they were party, pronouncements of momentous significance were made by the British government.

1. In the last week of October the British government rejected the method of consulting Africans through chiefs. They refused to send

observers to the Indaba which was staged at Domboshawa. In the refusal to send observers, the British government was followed by the United States government.

2. On 27 October 1964, the British government issued a public warning as to the consequences of a unilateral declaration of independence.

In the face of these two developments the Southern Rhodesia government proceeded with the so-called referendum. We do not think that the referendum exercise having been rejected by the British government scarcely deserves to be considered as worthwhile to put forward to the British government as a standpoint by the Rhodesia government in any future discussions on new constitutional developments.

But no doubt the referendum exercise can be considered only as frightful evidence of the fraudulent designs of the Southern Rhodesia government.

With due respect to the British Labour government, we note the stand they have taken by these two pronouncements. But this stand does not take the matter any further. Assuming that Mr Smith will heed the warning on the consequences of a unilateral declaration of independence, the stand now taken by the British government merely brings the position to rest at the very situation which is the source of unrest, the 1961 constitution. The British government might be prevailed upon that they have made their point, the Rhodesia government has obeyed and matters should be left at that. We consider that nothing could be more dangerous than to leave the position where it started.

In view of all the circumstances, the case could not be stronger for calling a constitutional conference SOON. Mr Ian Smith has indicated that he would not be prepared to sit at a round table conference with the African people's leader, Mr Joshua Nkomo, who is in jail. Since the leader is Mr Smith's political prisoner, and since the British government has sovereign powers in and over Rhodesia, the fundamental merit of the case of calling for a constitutional conference wholly demands the presence of the African people's leader at any such conference. It would be inconceivable that the jailer, Mr Smith, should refuse to deliver a prisoner in the face of the writ of demand by the British government for the freeing of the prisoner for the purpose of discussing the very cause of his imprisonment. Any such objections by the Rhodesia government ought, within right, and in view of the seriousness of the situation, to be rejected as subterfuges and pettifogging.

ZAPU demands the presence of Mr Joshua Nkomo at any constitutional conference. We therefore demand from the British government to convene immediately a constitutional conference in

Britain of major parties concerned for the purpose of working out a constitution to provide for majority rule in Rhodesia (Zimbabwe) based on 'one man one vote'.

18 Joshua Nkomo: The case for majority rule in Rhodesia. Gonakudzingwa Camp, 1964

As we inevitably move towards majority rule in Southern Rhodesia, a lot of questions are being asked by a number of people, both here and abroad. Not only are questions being asked, but also statements of facts and intentions are being advanced. Not all of these questions and statements of facts and intentions are being made with an undoubted honesty of purpose. Others are so.

Being, as I am, an ardent exponent of majority rule, as the only and natural solution to the political, social and economic problems that beset the country, let me give a picture of the majority rule that we are struggling for, as I see it. . . .

I am well aware of the fact that there are many well-meaning European men and women who have spent their lifetime working for and with the African people.

Some of them have contributed very important services; others have quietly worked to bring human equality in the country; others still have altruistically worked to improve the lot of the Africans; and still others are working quietly to bring about majority rule in the country, sincerely believing that it is the only and best way to secure peace and prosperity in the country.

All this is true; all this I know. But it is too little, ineffectual and incapable of changing the wrong course and direction followed by those who want a destination only known to themselves, and by people who are bent on destroying the country and themselves.

During this period the African has contributed to the overall progress of the country just like anyone else.

During the last two World Wars, he fought on the battle-fields as well as on the home front.

He was told that the world was in danger of domination and oppression of man by man.

He willingly came forward to play his part to save mankind from that evil.

But, alas, this same evil showed its ugly head in his own country. Parliament in Southern Rhodesia remained exclusively white. More and more discriminatory laws were passed. The whole machinery of administration was set at his disadvantage.

The African was told that he would take part in the Government and administration of the country when he was more educated and civilized.

Unfortunately he believed this political humbug. But as years went by he was disillusioned. As he moved towards those requirements (set standards), he saw the line being pushed further and further away from him.

Each time the requirements to qualify for voting were raised higher and higher and beyond his reach. The vote remained the preserve of a chosen few and almost 100 per cent white.

Of course, a few Africans managed to cross the 'holy line'.

But the masses could not and have not been able to reach it. This 'select group of people' became the sole guardian of the destiny of the country. They are known as the 'electorate'. They number between 80,000 and 90,000 in a country of over 4,000,000 people.

They are made of a small number of the early European settlers, a big number of whites who settled in the country after World War II and less than five per cent of the indigenous African people.

This small 'select group of people' has become the sole deciding factor in any change that has to be made in the country. No government dare make any change that does not comply with the wishes of the 'electorate'.

Any changes in education, wages, system of property-ownership and all those factors that enable one to qualify membership of the 'electoral clubs' are strictly controlled and jealously guarded by the club.

When people in the country speak of preserving 'our Rhodesian way of life', they mean this system of control by the 'exclusive club', and the way of life as viewed by it.

This is exactly what Ian Smith meant when, addressing a Rhodesian Front meeting at Sinoia on 22 May 1964, he said: 'Our independence will maintain the standards we have enjoyed for the last 40 years. The independence will be a civilized one.'

As far as we are concerned, the whole thing is inhuman, uncivilized, uncultured, stupid, selfish and above all un-Christian.

It must be remembered that the official religion of this country is Christianity.

It is therefore essential that the standards of the affairs of the state must measure up to Christian ethics and values.

Britain also has Christianity as her official religion. But this is what

Smith said at his Sinoia meeting: 'There was a time when the British and Rhodesian moral codes were the same. It is obvious today that our moral codes are different.'

The pertinent question is: 'Who has gone off the rail—Sir Alec Douglas-Home or Mr Smith?'. . .

EDUCATION

Up to this day, the church still shoulders more than 90 per cent of African education.

The churches have played no small part in the provision of medical services, particularly in the outlying districts. Of course, the Africans themselves played an important part in providing these services.

Lest I be misunderstood, let me hasten to add that the church has not been spotless regarding the wrong things that have been perpetuated in this country. As a matter of fact, I am at variance with the Church on a number of issues. However, these do not call for comment here.

I point out these things because it seems that many people do not understand the position of the church in our society. I am not at all suggesting that the church should take part in party politics. But I do say that the church, as the conscience of the people, has a right and duty to make its voice heard on such a definite question of right and wrong as the one that confronts us in this country.

FICTION

Smith and Dupont have said that 'international Communism' is the cause of the troubles in this country. Others say that if the United Nations did not interfere in our affairs all would be well. Smith told a cheering crowd at Banket that he had facts and figures to prove his allegation about international communism.

I hope he did not mean the fiction told by his Minister of Law and Order. One thing that must be clearly understood is that one does not have to be a 'Communist' to recognize the political imbecility of such statements as 'I do not expect an African government in my lifetime', or 'if we were foolish enough to allow more African representation in Parliament, we would be guilty of the greatest folly'.

The manifestation of this type of thinking among the European population of our country became clear to us after the Second World War. It was obvious that the intention of the settler minority government was to stiffen the rules and conditions of gaining membership of the 'electoral club'. It was shouted: 'We cannot lower standards!' What was meant was that the country must remain under European minority control for the foreseeable future.

THE MASKS

It was on 12 September 1957, when we decided to do what was done all over the world to free the masses from domination by the minority. That is, to organize the masses into one powerful force to fight for this basic human right—the right to vote.

There was no question of outside influence. None of us at that time had been outside the country. We set ourselves on a course to fight a wrong and bring about a new order where a person's skin colour was treated as the accident that it was, and not a passport to a privileged life. We set ourselves on a course to fight for the establishment of a Zimbabwe where human rights and dignity would be respected irrespective of skin pigmentation.

DOMINATION

When in 1959 our organization (the ANC) was banned and its leaders imprisoned without trial, there was no question of our having turned red, or having been influenced by the Afro-Asians.

The truth is that the ban was a reaction by very conservative white supremacists who had realized that we were no longer prepared to be led up the garden path or tolerate, as we had done hitherto, any more domination.

Following the ban of the ANC, a number of harsh laws was passed, laws such as the Unlawful Organizations Act, the Preventive Detention Act, and the Law and Order (Maintenance) Act, as well as several other acts designed to suppress the genuine aspirations of the African people.

THE ENEMY

During the last five years thousands of Africans have been sent for detention, restriction and prisons for political reasons—all in a bid to frustrate African political and economic emancipation.

Those who, for self-interest, want to maintain the status quo, and are resorting to harsh legislation to achieve their ends, are at pains to tell the world that they are fighting 'Communism', which wants to see Europeans out of Africa.

What we are fighting to crush in Zimbabwe is not the white man, but white domination. And we can easily draw the line between the white man and white domination. We suffer no amount of confusion whatsoever on the matter. Our enemy in Zimbabwe is not the white man but political, economic and social domination of a majority by a very small minority.

We rejected the 1961 constitution in no uncertain terms. We rejected it for two reasons: one was political and the other was moral.

Politically, we could not accept a constitution and sit in a parliament created by that constitution and justifiably reject a motion by the House requesting Britain to grant a Smith-type of independence. If we had done that, we would have committed national political suicide. Present events have substantiated and justified our wisdom in rejecting that constitution.

Morally, we could not have accepted a constitution which implied that the white minority section of our population was superior to the African majority.

FRUSTRATION

There are those who say that I accepted this piece of constitution. This, of course, is just a lot of nonsense. If I had, then those concerned should have been able to produce a document bearing my signature.

Apart from our rejection of the constitution at the conference table, we rejected it again at our congress held in Bulawayo in 1961.

We also rejected it concretely by our referendum, in which over 500,000 Africans voted against it and about 800 for it. So, the new constitution was agreed to by Sir Edgar Whitehead and confirmed by the exclusive 'electoral club'. Here again, a major decision in the affairs of our country was made without the consent of the African people, and against their will. This has resulted in a serious dispute between those who believe in minority rule and us.

Because the white minority supremacists wield political power, they have used these powers against those who represent majority aspirations. A political crisis has been created in this country.

The courts, through the harsh laws that they have to administer, have passed all sorts of sentences against those who found themselves accused of contravening one act or another.

One has to be an African to know and to feel what is going on. I do hope that some people among us will be spared to write the history of this dismal period that we are passing through.

As I write this article, I and six of my colleagues are restricted, or rather detained, here at Gonakudzingwa ('where the banished ones sleep') in the Gona-Rezhou ('where elephants sleep') Forest Area.

It is not for me to describe the area, and the bathos and pathos of people who find themselves thrown into a strange area (teeming with wild animals) for opening their mouths to demand that which is right, just and proper. Not right and just only for those whom we represent, but for all the people in this country.

Unlike Smith, who believes in a settlement that lasts only for his lifetime, we believe in a settlement that lasts for ever—for the good of all. The settlement is majority rule and then independence.

We are quite aware that many new problems will arise. But we shall have achieved a condition that will bring about the working together of the majority of our people, which will make the solution of our problems an easy operation.

The working together of all our people is a prerequisite to national progress.

It has been said in certain quarters that I and my colleagues want to destroy industries in this country. Nothing could be farther from the truth.

In actual fact, we are battling to bring about just the opposite of this.

We want to see, created in this country, favourable conditions that will provide security for both public and private enterprise for national progress.

The main ingredient of the 'favourable conditions' is majority rule—a *sine qua non* of political stability and, therefore, economic and social progress.

There is talk by some people that 'majority rule' means rule by Africans only; that Africanization will deprive Europeans of their jobs and that there will be a general lowering of standards.

To us majority rule means the extension of political rights to all people so that they are able to elect a Government of their own choice, irrespective of race, colour or creed of the individuals forming such a Government.

All that matters is that a Government must consist of the majority party elected by the majority of the country's voters.

'Africanization' means the opening of all those jobs and the extension of the ceiling which had been closed to Africans, without necessarily eliminating those who at present hold such jobs, unless they choose to do so on their own accord, or are proved to be disloyal to the administration.

There should be no fear of anyone losing his job, because ours will be an ever-expanding economy and administration.

With regard to the question of maintaining standards, if by that is meant what Mr Smith and his kind imply—white domination at the expense of the masses—then those 'standards' must go.

If, on the other hand, they (the Smiths) are referring to standards as known throughout the world, then nobody need fear majority rule.

Our intention is not to lower standards of any kind or anybody.

We have planned to raise standards and expand opportunities for all our people without prejudice to anybody and to any section of the community.

We believe this is the only way to create a massive buying power for our people. This will, in turn, increase the internal consumption of our products and thereby stimulate our industrial and commercial activities.

We believe that with the existence here of an administration acceptable to all the African countries, we should be able to intensify and increase tremendously our export trade within Africa itself.

The fact that we are a comparatively industrialized country, coupled with our 'acceptability', should place us in a position to be the chief exporting country in Africa.

The question now is how to get this majority rule which is indispensable for the creation of conditions that will bring us the Zimbabwe that I have described in the preceding paragraphs.

Mr Smith and his Rhodesian farmers believe that if they obtain independence, that will confer all powers upon the minority without any check, and all will be rosy in the Rhodesian garden.

He believes that once all ties with Britain are cut, African representatives of the majority of our African population will then take orders from him, and they will no longer look to Britain for help.

This, of course, is a comfortable political dream. If Mr Smith honestly believes in it, then I can only say: 'May the Lord have mercy on his political soul.'

Imposition of independence by such a minority will not change us even by one iota in our determined struggle against minority domination.

Instead, there will be perpetual resistance and rebellion against arbitrary action.

The country will be rejected by the entire world, except South Africa and Portugal, and it will be a bad financial risk.

The overall effect will be that the present political and economic ills of the country will become a permanent feature, and it will be the white man, accustomed to a luxurious life, who will be hard hit.

The talk of a unilateral declaration of independence is similar to the well-known talk about the 'Boston Tea-Party' of the days of Sir Roy Welensky and his now defunct Federation.

I hope the Europeans in this country will not allow themselves to be taken for another ride. The original 'Boston Tea-Party' succeeded, because the political, economic and international environment at that time favoured it.

Those who believe it can succeed in the present context of the international situation, and particularly here in Southern Rhodesia, where at least 95 per cent of the people are prepared to fight it tooth and nail, are living in a cloud-cuckoo-land of make-believe.

Mr Smith with, I suppose, the advice of 'Father Morris', is further deceiving himself or trying to deceive the world that he has African support.

He has taken about 30 African chiefs on a grand tour of some parts of the world.

Mr Smith should know that this once-important and dignified traditional institution of the African people has been reduced by legislation to almost nothingness.

Under the Native Affairs Act the chief was reduced to the status of the Native Commissioner's messenger.

This has undermined the position of the chief among the African people to such an extent that the chief no longer enjoys the prestige of a traditional leader that he once was.

He can only hope to regain his lost dignity and prestige when majority rule is achieved.

Mr Smith also talks glibly of 'loyalty to the Queen, but not to the British government'.

This is an irresponsible talk by men who are supposed to be civilized and to know better and who claim to be up-holders of standards.

It does not seem to be known that the Queen is a constitutional monarch.

That being the case, one cannot be loyal to the Queen and not to her government. All these things are aimed at confusing and thus delaying an early settlement of our problem.

We, the leaders of the PEOPLE, want a settlement, and we want it now. There are two ways by which this can be achieved.

(a) By a constitutional conference which will hammer out a constitution granting immediate majority rule. The conference must be presided over by Britain and attended by leaders of all effective political groups in the country.

(b) By the British government using its powers over Southern Rhodesia and legislating for the necessary change that will bring about peace and prosperity in the country. It is common knowledge that Britain has undoubted inherent powers to legislate for Southern Rhodesia.

We regard statements by the British government that she cannot interfere in the internal affairs of Southern Rhodesia as racial, unfair, timid and an intention to shirk her responsibilities. The interests of 95 per cent of the country's population cannot be rightly regarded as an 'internal affair' of five per cent of the country's population.

The assertion that Britain is prevented by a convention of long standing from intervening in the affairs of Southern Rhodesia is erroneous.

First, a convention that fails to protect the interests of the majority as against those of the minority is null and void.

Second, this convention is supposed to prevent Britain from intervening in those matters that are within the legislative competence, of Southern Rhodesia; but a change in constitution is not within the legislative competence of Southern Rhodesia.

Third, a convention has no legal validity. It is just an expedient device which can never transcend that which is legal.

That being so, we demand action by Britain now. She must do to Southern Rhodesia what she has done to her former colonies.

We want to be afforded the opportunity to develop our country and to improve the economic and social lot of all our people.

Any further delay on the part of Britain will destroy the country.

Since this is our country, and the onus to build and develop it will always lie with us, we feel obliged to press Britain to take action NOW to prevent any further drain and destruction of our country.

19 Zimbabwe African National Union: supplementary memorandum presented to the Commonwealth Prime Ministers conference. London, 17 June 1965

A catalogue of events in Southern Rhodesia since the last Commonwealth Prime Ministers Conference in July 1964 will demonstrate the trend of things, the gravity and explosiveness of the political situation in Southern Rhodesia.

1. In a bid to muzzle the expression of the legitimate aspirations for majority rule, Smith's regime banned the only African mouthpiece—the two nationalist parties—the Zimbabwe African National Union (ZANU) led by Rev Ndabaningi Sithole and the People's Caretaker Council (PCC) led by Mr Joshua Nkomo. Leaders and followers were either imprisoned, detained or restricted. Restriction camps were built in remote and dangerous places of

Gonakudzingwa, Wha Wha and Marandellas. Old disused mines were turned into prisons and detention camps. In purported maintenance of laws designed to protect white rule well over 10,000 men, women and youths are today languishing in these prisons, detention and restriction camps.

2.   Draconic laws have been scuttled through the minority parliament investing the fascist settler police with sweeping powers to conduct arbitrary searches, raids and arrests on Africans at any place, even in bedrooms, and at any time under the guise of checking on 'subversive activities' and maintaining 'law and order'. The discretion of the court in regard to the punishment of offenders has been taken away. More is promised. Any expression of the legitimate aspirations of the African majority is ruthlessly crushed. The borders have been sealed off and immigration officers have assumed arbitrary powers. Police and soldiers' posts have been erected along the borders and armed soldiers patrol the borders daily. Innocent African men, women and youths and even children have been tortured and flogged into making false confessions to suit the whims and convenience of the fascist police and soldiers. Men have been shot at close range by blood-thirsty police and women have been raped.

3.   The army and the air force given by Britain to Southern Rhodesia at the break of the Federation with the promise that they will not be used to suppress Africans, are currently being intensified and used to suppress and oppress Africans. Fascist experts have been employed to train the army in guerilla warfare.

4.   About 23 Africans, 17 of whom are ZANU supporters, have been sentenced to death under the Mandatory Hanging Clause of the diabolic Law and Order (Maintenance) Act and are awaiting hanging. To mention but a few of those sentenced to death are: Lloyd Gundu, Herbert Sambo, Samson Majengwa, Victor Mlambo and James Dhlamini.

Two of those, Lloyd Gundu and Herbert Sambo, were due to be hanged on 11 May 1965.

5.   A 17-year-old ZANU supporter, Alexander Mashawira, was battered to death on 25 January 1965 in Salisbury Main Police Station by Smith's fascist police in a bid to extract information about ZANU's plans to liberate the country. At Nyanyadzi, 70 miles south of Umtali, ZANU supporters, men, women and youths were tortured and brutally flogged and some gunned at close range by the settler police; at Mtambara also south of Umtali two defenceless men were shot dead in cold blood by a senior ranking

white settler police officer. At Khami prison, near Bulawayo, some African prisoners were also shot dead in cold blood by white prison warders. At Nuanetsi, an African labourer was brutally murdered by a European settler farmer. On his release in February from prison, Mr Leopold Takawira, ZANU deputy president, was tortured and flogged unconscious in Salisbury Central Police Station before being sent to restriction at Wha Wha for four years. Only very recently Mr Ndabaningi Sithole, President of ZANU, while serving his prison sentence in Salisbury Main Prison, was barbarously assaulted by the white prison warders. He has since been restricted for five years—the longest period ever given to any nationalist leader in the country to date.

6.   In a much more intensified bid to usurp the country, declare UDI and entrench white supremacy Ian Smith

(a)   declared a state of emergency in Highfield and Harare African townships in Salisbury and only about two weeks ago states of emergency were declared in two rural areas Nuanetsi and Lupani, accompanied by mass arrests. Wha Wha restriction camp is completely barricaded by armed soldiers and has been so ever since December last year.

(b)   assumed direct control of news media—radio, TV and is now producing a Government-controlled mass-circulation newspaper with specific purpose of indoctrinating the masses. Government propaganda vans fitted with loud speakers are sent to all rural areas in a bid to undermine the nationalist resolve of the masses. News is heavily censored and police are given the powers to decide what news to release.

(c)   deceived, bribed and intimidated an overwhelming number of chiefs to sing his tune of UDI under the iniquitous, wholly rejected 1961 constitution. In his hurried preparations to clear the ground for the creation of Bantustans—*apartheid* in disguise—Smith consigned a bunch of 30 chiefs last year and only recently another 50 to countries in Europe including Britain and finally to Transkei in South Africa for the sole purpose of indoctrinating them to appreciate apartheid. He has had the audacity to parade these chiefs abroad in his campaign to dupe the world into believing that he enjoys African support.

(d)   After the bogus 7 May settler elections he has threatened wildly that if Britain imposes economic sanctions he would as a retaliatory measure forcefully repatriate approximately half a million Zambians and Malawians now working in Southern

Rhodesia, unilaterally abrogate the Kariba agreements and the joint use of air, railway and power services.

7. Despite the serious warning issued in October last year by the British Prime Minister that an unilateral declaration of independence would be treasonable and would be answered by economic and diplomatic sanctions; despite the visit to Southern Rhodesia of Mr Bottomley, Commonwealth Relations Secretary and Lord Gardiner, Lord Chancellor; despite a renewed warning of economic and diplomatic sanctions issued shortly before 7 May settler elections, the minority government led by blinkered Ian Smith has strengthened its position and become increasingly more defiant and intransigent.

8. In the process, final and irreversible racial polarization has been accomplished. Ian Smith is now clearly the leader of only the whites, who have clearly voted for exclusively white political power. He has the mandate of the majority of the whites to use the whole machinery of the Government created under the rejected 1961 constitution imposed by Britain against the will of the vast majority of the African population for the maintenance of white supremacy and perpetual suppression and oppression of the African majority.

9. He has threatened to use this mandate to declare Southern Rhodesia independent. He has used his position as Prime Minister under the 1961 constitution to enter into secret agreements with South Africa, Spain and Portugal in preparation for a unilateral declaration of independence. The warnings on unilateral declaration of independence have fallen on deaf ears.

10. The reason why British warnings on unilateral declaration of independence have failed to make an impression on Smith is that they have been wholly negative. Britain has said that she will not recognize a government of Southern Rhodesia based on unilateral declaration of independence. It will not support such government in any of the international organizations. It will impose economic sanctions by which is meant that it will cut off both aid and all trade preferences to Southern Rhodesia, as well as all exports and imports to and from Southern Rhodesia, if Southern Rhodesia should declare itself independent. In Salisbury the British warning is seen as empty and ineffective because in a similar situation over South Africa Britain itself has said that diplomatic and economic sanctions are ineffective. Some go so far as to say that Britain would not against her kith and kin impose sanctions which would bring disaster upon them. Britain, they say, would never let her soldiers take up arms against her kith and kin in Southern

Rhodesia. They see British warnings as a bluff, a sham, a mask to conceal her true intentions which are that she will let her kith and kin do as they will with the Africans in what is after all a back door re-entry into the lost British African Empire.

11. The prospects of unilateral declaration of independence are staggering. But the prospect of a minority of under a quarter of a million people wielding for an indefinite period the entire machinery of government and using it to keep itself in power and exclude four million Africans from political power is simply appalling. Nor is this reaction unwarranted. Immigration Officers and other in like position of authority. Laws that are already draconic are to be made even more drastic. Over twenty people await hanging after conviction on political charges. The discretion of the court in regard to the punishment of offenders has been taken away. More is promised. Any expression of the legitimate aspirations of the African majority is ruthlessly crushed. Every one of their leaders is in detention, restriction or prison. The borders have been sealed off and every Rhodesian African who returns from abroad is automatically suspect. He is fortunate if he is released without first being subjected to brutal assaults and utter humiliation as explained earlier. It is not simply a Police State that has been created, a reign of terror has come to be the order of the day in Rhodesia.

12. The attitude of the British Government to the Rhodesian situation has been stated from time to time. Britain acknowledges herself as the sovereign authority over Southern Rhodesia. She says, however, that she is powerless to act to prevent the humiliation, brutality and human degradation perpetrated against the Africans by Smith so long as he is acting in terms of powers granted to him under the constitution of 1961. It was Britain which gave that constitution. She has promised to take action only if Smith acts illegally in order to increase his control over the Africans. The action she has promised to take is wholly negative. Did Britain forsee that the 1961 constitution which it imposed would make it possible for the White minority legally to perpetrate acts of racial aggression against the Africans in the way which they have done? If this is so then the British position must be embarrassing to the African members of the Commonwealth. Britain is saying that Smith may use the 1961 constitution which she gave to Southern Rhodesia against the clearly expressed wishes of the Africans to entrench White supremacy. So long as he does not violate the 1961 constitution he may introduce legislative measures whose only aim is to protect

White positions and to degrade the Africans. He may use that constitution in fact for the purpose of establishing a racial oligarchy in Southern Rhodesia. Britain will not interfere—she will say simply 'this is legal, it is covered by the provisions of the 1961 constitution. Britain is powerless to intervene'.

13. It is impossible not to construe this attitude as implying that Britain envisaged from the beginning that this constitution would be used for this purpose and was prepared to let it be imposed with that aim in view.

14. The African members of the Commonwealth cannot be expected to share this legalist approach to the problems of Southern Rhodesia involving as it does an assault on the African personality as such. For this reason a call is made by the Zimbabwe African National Union to the African members of the Commonwealth to make it clear to Britain that this view of the Southern Rhodesian constitution is wholly inacceptable to them. They must call on Britain to intervene not only when the constitution is legally violated but also when it is prostituted. To use the 1961 constitution for perpetrating and entrenching white rule is nothing less than prostituting it!

15. The failure or refusal by Britain to intervene even when it is clear that the constitution is being prostituted for the creation of a racial oligarchy must cast doubts on Britain's belief in any principles governing the Commonwealth. TO US THE COMMONWEALTH HAS TWO PRINCIPLES—RACIAL EQUALITY AND THE RIGHT OF COMMUNITIES TO SELF-DETERMINATION. THE BRITISH ATTITUDE ON THIS ISSUE IS A REPUDIATION OF THESE PRINCIPLES. A COM-MONWEALTH which involves this repudiation by one of its senior members lacks foundation or faith. THERE CAN BE NO SENSE IN ITS CONTINUED EXISTENCE. It is appreciated that the present Labour government with a small majority in the House of Commons might find it difficult to take strong action. We think she must, to her friends in the Commonwealth, at least indicate what steps she would be willing to take in defence of the principles of the Commonwealth. She is entitled if she does so indicate to the support of the remainder of the Commonwealth. The practical effect of this would be to mitigate the unpopularity in Britain of action on Southern Rhodesia. EACH OF THE COMMONWEALTH COUNTRIES SHOULD COMMIT A CERTAIN PART OF THEIR ARMIES OR MILITARY FORCES TO A COM-MONWEALTH FORCE UNDER A BRITISH COMMANDER

TO TAKE ACTION AGAINST SOUTHERN RHODESIA, if there is military resistance by Southern Rhodesia to the suspension of the constitution.

16. Smith in his bid for unilateral declaration of independence has openly asserted his willingness to take aggressive action against both Zambia and Malawi for the purpose of advancing the interests of the quarter million Europeans in Southern Rhodesia. He has threatened to deport half a million citizens of these two neighbouring countries, to cut off trade with them, to cut off power which is generated on the southern bank of the Kariba dam and to deprive Zambia of rail communication and coal supply from Southern Rhodesia. This is a clear threat to international peace. By his threats Smith has put Britain into the position in which she may legitimately, as one of the members of the Security Council of the United Nations, support a resolution of the Security Council that the situation in Southern Rhodesia constitutes a threat to international peace and warrants the invocation of UN Charter Articles 39, 40, 41, 42. Britain should act now at the United Nations to prevent the inevitable mess and immediately implement the resolutions passed by the Commonwealth Prime Ministers and UN to solve the problem once and for all, and support the Commonwealth to take action in Southern Rhodesia.

CHAPTER FIVE

FROM UDI TO HMS *FEARLESS*

20 Zimbabwe African Peoples Union: statement by James Chikerema, acting-President. Lusaka, March 1966

. . . The difficulties facing Rhodesia today are artificial, arising as they do from a system which had made a section of the community base judgement of all issues on the rails of colour and race. We have long declared, I wish to repeat, that racialism in any form or guise has no room whatsoever in Zimbabwe. Our objective, among other things, is to rid the country of this detrimental system of prejudice in order to usher in an era of sober approach in tackling the fundamental problem of our country.

That the fight must continue is definite. There can be no question of relaxation on this because our cause is right and just. As this is understood, I thought today I should begin, in a small way, to unfold to you the direction towards which we are fighting. You know very well that apart from our country living under delicate and dangerous political framework, it is also dragging absurdly along a false economy. What are the features of this false economy? This is first of all a system of so-called maintenance of civilized standards. Under this system the white population has created an inflated structure of privileged wages for themselves quite unrelated to their productive capacity. This involves the exploitation of African labour and land. Naturally the Africans are no longer prepared to tolerate the continuance of this system. In fact, the weakness of the system has been exposed by the recent bill which coerces African labour force to stick to jobs against its will. This can hardly be called a healthy relationship between job and labour.

There is a belief emanating from the system of false economic privileges accruing to the white community that every one of its members is on the short-cut road to possessing a piece of land in Rhodesia and of becoming a millionaire. This false impression accounts for the resistance most white fanatics have, in Rhodesia, towards the establishment of a popular African government. Hence the Rhodesian Front slogan—'What we have we hold.' It is vital for the ordinary European follower to realize that his receiving of inflated wages at the expense of the African worker is something completely different from setting him on the road towards the dream-land of being a millionaire or possessing vast extents of land. This system is just a conspiracy by large property owners, most of whom are absentees, to set into conflict the majority of the white community who are also workers, against the African worker, whilst luring them to a dreamland they will never reach. Quite clearly, the greatest victim of this kind of bluff in Rhodesia is the ordinary white worker. The time is fast approaching when it will no longer be possible to use the exploitation of the African as a bluff—and at this point the rank and file of the white community is bound to be extremely disillusioned.

My appeal to day is that if those people concerned cannot take heed of our timely advice, they should know precisely where the blame lies when resentment sets in. The individuals who are running the present minority regime are so conscious of the ultimate fate of their regime that they for themselves are amassing what wealth they can and taking advantage of government facilities to arrange other homes elsewhere to escape to when the situation is no longer tenable, thus leaving the larger part of the white population they deceived to bear the brunt. The choice is therefore quite clear.

The problem extends far wider than that. Presently, the minority rule regime is busy destroying the country out of the international market for all its essential products—chrome, sugar, lithium, tobacco, etc. The regime is completely unable to negotiate for the wider market in the African continent, which is its initial and natural field for economic interdependence.

Economic trends today are that within individual countries small business or industrial concerns are melting away into larger enterprises, whether private or state directed; individual countries themselves all over the world are finding their economic survival in wider economic association. Asian, European and American trade enterprises are bound to find greater attractions to widely co-ordinated markets on the African scene. We have to move along these historical trends. Tragically, however, the minority regime is drifting the country into isolation. With the entire world totally hostile to Rhodesia; with the international markets drying out for our essential products; with productivity and business in existing establishments dropping to the lowest level; with the complete lack of capital to tap the other potential resources of the country and the drift towards internal war, it is tragic that some people in Rhodesia could continue to deceive themselves to believe that we are heading for peace and prosperity. How can the economy of a country hang upon the adventures of pirate oil tankers? We cannot allow our country to be handed over to a clique which is sustained by international pirates.

What is essential is to create conditions of freedom for every individual in the country, so that each can give full expression to his natural capacities without hindrance in the task of providing for his livelihood and consequently that of the state. It should be obvious that the system of privileges in wages, possessions and before the law, for any individuals will have to disappear. There is no question on our part of holding any piece of land for prestige and speculation purposes, as it is for the livelihood and benefit of the entire country, since the land belongs to the people.

Since, however, it is fundamental and a well demonstrated principle that a country must have a sound political basis before it can face any other tasks of re-construction, it is vital that all in Zimbabwe must rally behind the majority inhabitants under the leadership of Mr Nkomo to ensure the accomplishment of this initial task . . .

21 Zimbabwe African Peoples Union: memorandum to the UN Ad Hoc Human Rights Commission by George Nyandoro, Secretary-General. 27 August 1968

Your Excellencies,
ZAPU is fully aware of the inadequacy and limitations of the United Nations in the implementation of its decisions particularly when in direct confrontation with the racist forces of Southern Africa.

In spite of this impotence, we have decided it judicious to briefly spell out to you the atrocities which, by and large, are not new to those who have witnessed the brutalities of fascists in the two World Wars and many wars of liberation waged in Africa—and at present in Vietnam, Zimbabwe, South Africa, Mozambique, Guinea-Bissau and Angola.

1. SOUTHERN RHODESIA

It is pointless to begin this Memorandum by a discussion of the status of Southern Rhodesia at international law. It is a well established fact that Southern Rhodesia is a colony of the United Kingdom. The very existence of the British regime in Zimbabwe and all its complex laws is a violation of human rights *per se*.

The controversies surrounding Southern Rhodesia are a direct consequence of the United Kingdom Government's aggression against the people of Zimbabwe. The usurpation of the so-called independence by the British settlers flows from this British act . . .

As from 11 November 1965, the British settlers in Southern Rhodesia have not only committed aggression against the indigenous population but also against the international community as represented by the United Nations, its organs and other non-members of this Organization. In an article *Rhodesia and the United Nations: the lawfulness of international concern*, Myers S. McDougal and W. Michael Reisman in the *American Journal of International Law*, Volume 62, No 1, 1968, had this to say:

> . . . Moreover, the promulgation and application of policies of racism in a context as volatile as that of Rhodesia and South Central Africa must give rise to expectations of violence and constitute, if not aggression of the classic type, at least the creation of circumstances under which states have been customarily regarded as justified in unilaterally resorting to the coercive strategies of humanitarian intervention.
>
> . . . In point of fact, however, the list of indictments of Rhodesian transgressions against international law is alarmingly long. As far as conventional international law is concerned, the Rhodesian authorities have repudiated a number of Security Council decisions, which, under Article 25 of the Charter, are binding upon all Member States and which, according to Article 2(6), may be applied to non-members 'so far as may be necessary for the maintenance of international peace and security'. They have also repudiated the human rights provisions of the Charter, as authoritatively interpreted by the competent UN organs, and the prescriptions of the increasingly authoritative Universal Declaration. As far as international customary law is concerned, they have violated the more traditional human rights policies in a degree which, as we have noted, would have in the past served to justify 'humanitarian intervention' by individual nation states. It scarcely need be added that circumstances which would justify coercive action undertaken unilaterally by one state must surely be regarded as sufficient to justify organized international actions.

Africans have therefore, intensified their resistance against the settler regime and are waging a war of liberation.

3. ARMED STRUGGLE

In this war of resistance well trained and disciplined fellow partisans are carrying out a guerrilla warfare against the British settlers' regime. In the prosecution of the war, the partisans conform with the requirements of Article 4 of the Geneva Convention of 1949.

Article 4 A(1)(2) which reads as follows:

Prisoners of war   A. Prisoners of war, in the sense of the present Convention, are persons belonging to one of the following categories, who have fallen into the power of the enemy:

(1) Members of the armed forces of a Party to the conflict as well as members of militias or volunteer corps forming part of such armed forces.

(2) Members of other militias and members of other volunteer corps, including those of organized resistance movements, belonging to a Party to the conflict and operating in or outside their own territory, even if this territory is occupied, provided that such militias or volunteer corps, including such organized resistance movements, fulfil the following conditions:

(a) that of being commanded by a person responsible for his subordinates;

(b) that of having a fixed distinctive sign recognizable at a distance;

(c) that of carrying arms openly;

(d) that of conducting their operations in accordance with the laws and customs of war.

The question that the United Nations has not appreciated is the extent and magnitude of the armed conflict which has through the participation of the South African armed forces assumed a greater international character. It is therefore imperative that the parties to the conflict should be bound to apply Article 3 of the Geneva Convention.

Article 3 which reads as follows:

'. . . In the case of armed conflict not of an international character occurring in the territory of one of the High Contracting Parties, each Party to the conflict shall be bound to apply, as a minimum, the following provisions:

(1)Persons taking no active part in the hostilities, including members of armed forces who have laid down their arms and those placed hors du combat by sickness, wounds, detention, or any other cause, shall in all circumstances be treated humanely, without any adverse distinction founded on race, colour, religion or faith, sex, birth or wealth, or any other similar criteria.

To this end, the following acts are and shall remain prohibited at any time and in any place whatsoever with respect to the above-mentioned persons:

(a) violence to life and person, in particular murder of all kinds, mutilation, cruel treatment and torture;

(b) outrages upon personal dignity, in particular, humiliating and degrading treatment;

(c) taking of hostages.

At present those of our fellow freedom fighters who are captured by the aggressors are not treated according to the provisions of Geneva Convention on the treatment of prisoners of war.

Confessions are enlisted from those captured by the use of one or a combination of the following methods of torture:

(i)   Forcing through the penis a bicycle spoke;

(ii)   Using a pair of pincers on testicles or on finger-nails;

(iii) Throwing live snakes into detention cells;

(iv)   Beating to death of persons under interrogation or in detention. (The case of Mashawira who was beaten to death by the Police, and whose case was abandoned because the prosecution refused to adduce sufficient evidence);

(v)   The use of captured cadres to dig their own graves before being shot dead;

(vi)   The laying of injured freedom fighters in nets which are then hooked to helicopters which are flown while the freedom fighters are dangling in the air and while in this position the freedom fighters are swung against trees and are dropped into camps—the seriously injured die in the process;

(vii) Electric shocks;

(viii) The shooting and killing of wounded and captured partisans indiscriminately;

(ix)   Killing of African civilians in the area of battle;

(x)   The tying of a person to a rope connected to a Land Rover which is then driven off;

(xi)   Tying the arm and leg of a person under interrogation to a rafter and assaults with a stick on the testicles;

(xii) Mass trials of captured freedom fighters who sit in court in leg irons;

(xiii) Exposing the captured freedom fighters to ridicule by inviting the white public who come to jeer and sometimes spit at them;

(xiv) Forcing the freedom fighters to drink their own urine;

(xv)   150 partisans awaiting execution.

Our fellow partisans should be treated as prisoners of war in accordance with the provisions of the Geneva Convention.

4. The Southern Rhodesian Courts have rejected judicial impartiality in order to identify themselves with the aspirations of the racist regime and to further the aims of that regime.

In deciding whether an accused person has a civil or political right against the racist government, the judges in Southern Rhodesia have decided that the first question for them to answer is, 'Who pays them their monthly salaries'. All the judges left in Southern Rhodesia have agreed that it is the regime which pays them and that therefore any constitutional question must be decided in its favour.

No freedom fighter who appears before the Rhodesian judges can expect impartial justice and it is wrong that freedom fighters engaged in a war should be tried as criminals. The Courts in Rhodesia today are used as slaughter houses as the judges feel duty bound to defend the interests of the minority British settlers.

Those the bullets miss in the battle field, the judges quickly dispatch to the gallows.

5. The United Nations and the world at large is aware of the recent murders committed by the regime and the hundreds of thousands of Africans in detention, restriction and in interrogation centres all over the country.

The President of ZAPU Comrade Joshua Nkomo has since 1964 been detained at Gonakudzingwa incommunicado.

6. The burden of this Memorandum is

(a)   That a state of war exists in Zimbabwe;

(b)   That the freedom fighters should be treated as Prisoners of War in terms of Geneva Convention.

(c)   We cannot feel ourselves bound by these Conventions in our treatment of captured oppressors when these Conventions are being flagrantly violated by the British settlers in the conduct of the current war in Zimbabwe.

22 Zimbabwe African Peoples Union: statement on the ZAPU-ANC alliance. December 1968

The whole country bristled with military and police personnel and informers. The Smith regime was acting exactly according to rules of all police states. The African people were brutalized, terrorized and tyrannized. African chiefs were turned into worse craven stooges and messengers of the regime than the 1928 Native Affairs Act had even made them. They no longer acted as their people's spokesmen, not even on such matters as affected the seemingly insignificant daily lives of the African peasants. They were. converted into messengers of the white dictatorship. Their despicable duty it was to carry orders from the regime to the African masses without a single question, let alone opposition. Those who showed signs of opposition to this state of affairs were deposed and sent to places like Gonakudzingwa where they joined their fellow Zimbabweans. Such was the fate of Chief Munuwepayi

Mangwende who had been deposed earlier; such was the fate of Chief Mathema who spent a quite long spell with national leader Joshua Nkomo at Gonakudzingwa. Other chiefs, like Ndabakayena Mpini Ndiweni of the Nata Reserve of the Bulilimamangwe District of Plumtree, expressed reservations about and against the dirty role the regime wanted them to play against their own people. Chief Mpini died under very suspicious circumstances at Plumtree after spending a spell under interrogation by the local armed police.

While this atmosphere was seeping through, deeper into the daily lives of the African people, freedom-fighters of the Zimbabwe African People's Union and those of the African National Congress of South Africa clashed with combined forces of Rhodesia and South Africa in the Wankie, Karoi, Sinoia, Binga and Tjolotjo areas of Zimbabwe. Pitched and running battles raged on for many weeks from August 1967 off and on till 1968, while South Africa poured more and more of its troops into Rhodesia. The Smith regime depended largely on bombers which it had inherited from the defunct Federation of Rhodesia and Nyasaland. These war-planes had been handed over to Rhodesia amidst strong opposition from Zambia and Malawi (formerly Northern Rhodesia and Nyasaland) when the factitious federation was dismantled on 31 December 1963. Britain, however, gave the protests a very racialistically deaf ear and handed the planes over to Salisbury.

While the fighting between ZAPU-ANC freedom-fighters on one side against Rhodesian-South African forces on the other went on, grumblings and rumblings were heard from near and far about the alliance between the two organizations. Some bodies and states openly welcomed the move and described it as a sign of what the whole of Africa ought to do and what the OAU had in fact been meant to achieve. Some organizations and states claimed that had South African freedom-fighters not set foot on Rhodesian soil, South African racist forces would not have been dispatched to fight side by side with those of Smith against ZAPU and the South African ANC on Rhodesian soil. Some governments and organizations called on the British Government to act to kick out the South African forces from Rhodesia which is, they argued, basically a British colony.

The British Government was reminded by these people of its statement that it would intervene militarily in Rhodesia only if there were a breakdown of law and order. 'Could there be a worse breakdown of law and order than the presence of foreign troops in one's territory?' they asked. Britain, however, made no reply worth remembering. As for the South African Boers, Vorster stated publicly that according to their customs, one does not wait to be invited to help when one's neighbour's house is on fire. What he meant was that Smith's house was on fire and he (Vorster) had acted customarily by sending his troops to put out the fire in the old Boers' good neighbourly spirit!

But critics of the way Africans were waging their armed struggle in Zimbabwe continued to condemn the ZAPU-ANC alliance. Here it is worthwhile to clarify briefly why it was a very wise move for ZAPU and the ANC of South Africa to forge an alliance against the Salisbury-Pretoria axis. Historically, the first settlers led by Cecil John Rhodes to establish themselves in Zimbabwe came from South Africa where Rhodes was both a powerful diamond tycoon and political giant. Economically, Rhodesia is linked very strongly with South Africa. The big mining and industrial companies found in Rhodesia have their regional and main bases in South Africa. Politically the South African regime and the Rhodesian settlers had made it known that they would work in unity to curb the flow of freedom from the north by stemming it along the Zambezi River. This undertaking had been made as early as 1960 when it had become clear that the Federation of Rhodesia and Nyasaland would be wound up following its vehement rejection by the African majority. It must also be borne in mind that Smith made his UDI only after he had been assured of military, economic and political support by South Africa. This much Smith himself revealed to the whole world. To prove it, there were South African troops in Rhodesia months before ZAPU and ANC cadres clashed with the fascists. So much about the racists and their own alliance, co-operation and connections.

On the side of ZAPU and the ANC, there has always been a spirit of co-operation between Zimbabweans and South Africans dating back to the days when a few lucky Zimbabweans went down to the south to study (or to work) and joined the ANC which has always been regarded as the traditional political fold of the African people of South Africa. In addition to this fact, both the ANC and ZAPU feel very strongly that a defeat of a minority regime in Mozambique, or Angola, or Zimbabwe, or Guinea-Bissau, or in Namibia has a very demoralizing effect on all minority regimes which may still be clinging to power elsewhere. It is an absurd belief that if Mozambique's FRELIMO is left to fight the Lisbon fascists by itself, Rhodesia, South Africa and even international mercenaries will stand idly by and watch Caetano's forces being torn to pieces. There is too much at stake for the exploiting oppressors to adopt such an attitude, and, in any case, oppression knows no territorial boundaries. A South African racist driving through Angola travels with his eyes wide open for signs of freedom-fighters in Angola and reports such signs to the nearest Portuguese military or police camp. The same applies to Rhodesians and the Portuguese.

The moving spirit of the ZAPU-ANC alliance was (and still is) the universality of the struggle against oppression and deprivation of human rights. If the ANC cadres had succeeded in passing through Zimbabwe undetected and had crossed the Limpopo River into South Africa, that would have been best for the oppressed masses of both Zimbabwe and South Africa; if they had failed to pass through and were intercepted by the enemy (Rhodesian, South African or Portuguese) inside Zimbabwe and had to fight, the better for the struggle as a whole; if, however, they had not met a single enemy troop and had established themselves solely in Zimbabwe and later managed to overthrow the Rhodesian regime, that would have been good for the liberation of Southern Africa as a whole.

Those who criticized the alliance on the basis of tribes cannot be spared from the condemnation under which the British Government is placed on Rhodesia for its rancid racialism. Both ZAPU and the ANC were not formed for tribes and have never at any time claimed to work for the liberation of only a single tribe. Both are national organizations whose aims and functions are national. To have formed an alliance on the basis of tribal considerations or reasons would have been baser than the aims and objectives of both ZAPU and the ANC. The argument that alliances should be formed only by people from one and the same colonial area, whose borders were drawn by colonials, is a misnomer for a call for tribalism. This brings to mind the sensitive question of whether free nations ought to support the fight for majority rule all over the oppressed world by supporting liberation movements with majority support, or by supporting every movement that claims to speak for an oppressed people. It also brings to mind the basic question of whether national unity can and should be achieved from within and by the people concerned, or can and should be achieved through persuasion (which at times borders on the realms of imposition) by external supporters and well-wishers whose material and moral support may be supplementary to what the oppressed masses themselves can and should do within their own borders. Upon an honest and thoroughly analytical answer to these two questions may depend the efficacy or otherwise of international support and sympathies for the struggling peoples whose material needs during the early stages of the struggle may depend on the attitudes of the international world towards liberation movements.

Criticism of the ZAPU-ANC alliance based on what actually occurred in the battlefield in the Wankie, Sinoia, Sipolilo and Binga areas is a completely different kettle of fish from criticism of the alliance itself. It is different because it involves tactics and not the broad base of the ZAPU-ANC strategy revolving on the two parties' alliance founded by and sealed with the patriotic blood and lives of freedom-fighters battling against common oppression.

It is not logical to condemn similarly the joint oppressive practices of the Smith-Vorster-Caetano regimes which are motivated by and based on common interests and criticize an alliance whose sole aim is to destroy those regimes. It is not logical to belong to and support an international body (or bodies) whose aims and objectives are to forge unity among nations against oppression, deprivation, denial of basic and inalienable human rights, and criticize an alliance whose avowed goal it is to fight against forces of oppression, deprivation and denial. It is in like manner a deplorable sign of lack of mental maturity to attach great sentiments and deep loyalty and emotions to one's tribe and in the same breath condemn racialism. Whereas racialism is an odious form of active malevolence of one race against another (or others), tribalism is exactly the same feeling by one tribe against another (or others). Both are base and despicable human sentiments which militate actively.against genuine patriotism and nationalism. It was with that spirit that ZAPU and the South African ANC forged their alliance which caused the ding-dong battles fought in Zimbabwe's Sipolilo forests, the Wankie Game Reserve, the Sinoia and Lomagundi regions from August 1967 up to and including the greater part of 1968.

23 Zimbabwe African Peoples Union: memorandum to Commonwealth Heads of States conference on the Fearless proposals. 7 January 1969

The vicious machinery of oppression and exploitation of the African people by the British settlers in Rhodesia is an established evil. We could not possibly submit ourselves to this form of dehumanizing evil. We have exposed, condemned and fought this evil from its inception. There is no question of adjustment to it. The battle must continue.

The majority of nations in the world support our stand and method of struggle. The Organization for African Unity, the socialist countries and the progressive organizations all over the world have declared openly their concrete material support for our struggle. Spearheaded by African and Asian members, the majority of countries in the Commonwealth extracted a reluctant undertaking from Britain not to grant independence to Rhodesia before African majority rule. The United Nations has stood firmly on measures to remove the oppressor settler regime and for the establishment of majority rule. The recent United Nations Assembly resolution calling for the extension of sanctions to cover Portugal and South Africa for their breach of previous resolutions against the Smith regime is evidence of the continuing and growing anxiety of the international community to the grave turn of events in Rhodesia.

It has been the hope of the international community that Britain would heed the anxiety of the world over her policies in Rhodesia and respond accordingly. We have never had any illusions about the direction of British policy in Rhodesia because she has never been anything else but the creator of the vicious system of which we are victims today. There is the famous saying that 'You can take a horse to the river but you cannot make him drink.' This is how Britain has behaved on the Rhodesian question since the Commonwealth and the United Nations regarded the situation a threat to international peace. She launched the Rhodesian regime on to a course of unilateral declaration of independence in the full consciousness of both the uncompromising opposition of the Africans and the hostility of the world to the move. She then gave herself time to study the progress of her UDI experiment whilst at the same time devising plans of containing opposition to it. In this event she embarked upon a policy of 'join them and lead them towards blind alleys, exhaust them and abandon them at a point and proceed to legalize the unilateral declaration of independence'.

Britain, after giving the go-ahead sign to Ian Smith for the UDI adventure by assuring him of 'no force' to prevent it, proceeded to be at the forefront of world opposition to it for no other reason than to foil any possible radical measures that would result in the destruction of the regime. She has blunted the effect of the whole exercise of sanctions and is now bolting out carefully and completely, to proceed with her original plans. Britain, as stated earlier, gave a categorical undertaking to the Commonwealth that she would not grant independence to Rhodesia before African majority rule. Her present conduct demonstrates that this undertaking was not sincere. It was an act of appeasing and blunting sharp opposition within the Commonwealth. She has unilaterally altered the conditions of this undertaking and has, today, completely reversed (and reverted) to her original policy of seeking recognition for her legalization of Smith's UDI. Like the horse taken to the river, Britain did not and could not fulfil the obligations of dismantling her colonial system in Rhodesia as expected of her by the world because it is never the policy of a colonizer to decolonize.

Of course the British Prime Minister, Harold Wilson, boasts of Britain having granted independence to millions comprising 27 Commonwealth countries. The fact is that Britain never withdrew voluntarily from any of her colonial territories except perhaps from Australia and New Zealand. She was pressured out. So the former colonial countries whether under Britain or some other colonizer, achieved their independence and were not granted it. But even if 'granted' were the word, the many millions would not be the bargain for allowing Britain to surrender the four million Africans of Zimbabwe to oppressive rule by her settler kith and kin in Rhodesia. The safe grant of independence to other territories does not become a basis for granting Britain a blank cheque of trust that she will do the same in Rhodesia.

The position, fortunately, is clear enough. Everything Britain has done in Rhodesia has confirmed a single course of policy, that of entrenching the monopoly of power in the hands of the British settler oppressors. Everything which the British government states to the contrary is diversionary.

On 15 October 1968, the British government published constitutional proposals supposed to be for the granting of independence to Rhodesia. These were worked out between the British Prime Minister, Harold Wilson, and the British agent in Rhodesia, Ian Smith, on the British ship, *Fearless*, in Gibraltar. The exclusion of the Africans from these talks can only mean that a conspiracy against the African people was being worked out. The terms of the document substantiate this point fully. What, then, of what was agreed upon was not disclosed? The technique of containing hostility in the process of selling the *Fearless* proposals has been to speak of fake 'deep differences' without making any significant change in the actual terms in subsequent discussions held by Thomson. This is understandable because the tactic seems to be to announce agreement only when dangers to the Commonwealth have been fully assessed. And, of course, to speak of 'deep differences' is to draw an image of a Wilson government struggling to the last drop, to secure the rights of the African people. The attempt to lend this impression is tragic because it is naked deceit as exposed by the nature of the proposals themselves.

The proposals are said to satisfy the six principles put forward by Britain and accepted by the Commonwealth. It should be noted, of course, that it is the British government which claims that her proposals satisfy the six principles.

Briefly, the so-called principles are: guarantee of the principle and intention of unimpeded progress to majority rule; guarantees against retrogressive amendments to the Constitution; immediate improvement in the political status of the African population; progress towards ending racial discrimination; British government to be satisfied that the basis for independence is acceptable to the people of Rhodesia as a whole; regardless of race no oppression of majority by minority or minority by majority.

The summary of these so-called principles is that majority rule ought to remain a distant ideal objective the progress towards which will be guaranteed by minority rule. How can a minority which for next to a century has established an unprecedented record of a colossal machinery of oppression of the natural owners of the country, be entrusted with the task of bringing about what it sought to frustrate over the years? Minority rule is the direct impediment to majority rule. We never considered the so-called six principles to be principles at all. They are calculated vague statements capable of all sorts of wide stretches of interpretation, set for the precise purpose of dodging the specific solution—majority rule. The *Fearless* terms bear us out:

THE *FEARLESS* FRANCHISE

'The B Roll franchise to be extended to include all Africans over 30 years who satisfy the citizenship and residence qualifications. Reserved European seats—to be elected by the European electorate. Cross voting to be retained at 25% and applying to all seats in the legislative Assembly filled by A and B Roll elections.'

The question here is not how many Africans can qualify for the vote but—Why should those who are excluded by these provisions be excluded at all, whatever their number? If they are as much of citizens and residents as those who are provided for why should they be denied their rights? The negative principle being applied here is that of qualified franchise. The legislation providing for this franchise determines the qualifications on educational and income levels. These are known to coincide with the racial line of demarcation as between whites and Africans, with the whites on the side of privilege. This was brought about by the corruption of manipulating the economy and education to give the whites an irreversible, decided advantage.

The issue in Rhodesia is to break down these artificially and racially created differences and reposit the power in the hands of every citizen, by birthright, and thereby secure confidence in everyone that there can never be a recurrence of the same evil. But the *Fearless* proposals set out a franchise which does not only take into account these differences but retains and maintains them as a means of differentiating voting privileges. There is, of course, what is fearlessly called an 'European electorate' in addition to the educational and economic establishments used as instruments to achieve the same racial purpose. How can constitutionally engraved discriminatory instruments be a means of ending discrimination? This is like trying to convince people with the argument that because petrol is a liquid like water, it can be used to extinguish a veld-fire. Listening to such an argument is not only a waste of time but is being as foolish as the argument itself. So it is to listen to the British argument that discrimination can be ended by a discriminatory franchise.

The 25 per cent voting influence for both the A and B rolls is supposed to be the mechanism for bringing about racial harmony in politics. How can the harmony and national identity of a people be brought about by, first of all, dividing them into racial camps and then generating racial mistrust by providing that each spy and check on the other by voting influences such as is the 25 per cent cross voting? In any case to what avail is the exercise because, in the event, the controlling party will, as it has always done, either indulge in intrigue or straight away eliminate any threat to its plans. Why has the settler regime taken so violently to any provision which derogates, even theoretically, as it can only be, on its sovereign exercise of power through the legislature which it is being given absolute control? This is not a case for the so-called safeguards as devised by Britain. It is, rather, to demonstrate their uselessness. However, the argument to substantiate this will come under the appropriate heading.

From the franchise principles we must then assess the practical nature of the *Fearless* franchise proposals. The idea of a qualified franchise, as we pointed out earlier, is to exclude a class of citizens from exercising the right to vote. Even in the attempt to create a class of voters on educational and income grounds this trick gets caught up. The idea of extending the B roll franchise to include Africans from 30 years of age is well calculated to disable a larger number of Africans who, under the provisions would otherwise enrol. Africans below 30 are of the greatest number which would qualify under the educational provisions since it is the group that is being produced by the schools. But they do not, as yet, have the income to make up the required combination to qualify for this type of franchise. For them to accumulate or reach the fixed income they have to go well beyond 30 years working in employment under the settlers who may, if they deem, refuse to give them either the employment or the income that would enable them to qualify for the franchise. Africans beyond 30 years, in the main, never had the extent and kind of education required for this type of franchise. This automatically eliminates the majority from qualifying under the franchise stipulations, though it is from this group that some are the more likely to have a bit of income or property after years of toil. It should be obvious that 30 years is the critical point at which for a long time those below will be disqualified from the vote by property and income provisions and those beyond will be disqualified by educational provisions and indeed property as the economic state of the Africans is known. In summary, if the Africans fell for the trap no more than ten per cent of the Africans would go through the sieve to qualify under the franchise provisions.

It is pointless to waste time and energy describing the A roll franchise. In all practicality it is a European franchise and any Africans that may qualify under it constitute a totally negligible number.

The implications to the franchise, of the fifty million pounds offer by the British for African education are obvious. The scheme lends the impression that it would be an investment for turning out large numbers of voters, thereby quickening the pace towards majority rule. This is utterly false. Ninety per cent of African education is sponsored by religious denominations. This underlines the negative attitude of the regime towards African education. Looking backwards to the years of utter neglect, and taking today as the starting point for jacking up African education, it would not be less than 40 years before the Africans would be the majority on the franchise rolls. This is on the assumption that the settler regime would work towards this objective and that the Africans would submit themselves to this prospect, both of which are impossible courses for diametrically opposed reasons. The whole exercise is tantamount to asking the present generation of four million Zimbabweans to submit itself to continuing oppression under the faith that when everyone of the present generation is dead the prospect of majority rule would then begin to be real. Naturally, this is out of the question. We know that the whole attempt to make a vote a privilege when it is a right, is for the express purpose of frustrating African political power. Can anyone then seriously expect us to fall for the trap?

In his broadcast on 19 October 1968, Ian Smith unwittingly confessed that in the last Rhodesian elections only one thousand Africans voted. Could anything define the unrelenting opposition of the African people to qualified franchise than the fact that now, after 50 years of its application, only one thousand Africans fell for its use out of a total population of four million people? This spells the doom of the *Fearless* franchise proposals.

When the British government, in October 1968, was on the one hand fixing a minimum of 30 years of age for an African voter in Rhodesia, plus, of course, the income and educational blockages, she was, on the other, drawing legislation that the minimum age for universal suffrage in Britain should be lowered to 18 years. Could there be any basis for the

British government distinguishing an 18 year old Zimbabwean from an 18 year old Britisher other than sheer racism? There is no other qualification for being a voter than being human and a member of the given society.

THE LEGISLATURE

In their *Fearless* document the British and their Rhodesian settler agents propose the following composition:

    33 A Roll seats
    17 B Roll seats
    17 Reserved European seats

Each block of seats is to cover the whole country.

The Assembly is, of course, a reflection of the franchise we have just analysed. The 33 so-called A seats are, like the franchise which produces them, straight European seats. It is the A Roll franchise which has since 1962 produced the all-white 50 seats in the present structure of the Rhodesian Assembly of 65 seats. To the 33 seats one should add the 17 fearlessly reserved European seats. This retains the 50 strong European control of the legislative Assembly. Since the legislative Assembly is the seat of a country's sovereignty, it then means the whites are in absolute control. This is what Britain is scheming to perpetuate by legalizing the settler regime's UDI under the *Fearless* terms. The 17 B Roll seats are not African seats in the strict sense. They are set for a class of an economic and educational level to which, conceivably, some Africans can qualify. However, it is these seats which add up to the 50 European seats to constitute a legislature of 67 seats. Note that this is an addition of only two seats to the present composition of 65 seats.

All business of the legislature initiated by the white racists will go through without any hindrance of any kind in the 50 to 17 structure. Conversely any business initiated by the African representatives can never go through under any circumstances.

> '. . . provided that there is at all times a "blocking quarter" of directly and popularly elected Africans as a safeguard against retrogressive amendment of the constitution, the British government do not insist on any particular composition for the legislature.'
> (Wilson, House of Commons, 15 October 1968)

An amendment to the entrenched clauses in the proposed constitution can be carried out only at a joint session of the legislature and the senate. It is only at such sessions that the blocking quarter takes effect. The supposed usefulness of the elected Africans can only be at such sessions which the settlers could choose not to convene. Even then, if the settler representatives thought the speeches of the elected Africans were causing irritation in the ordinary business of the legislature, the regime could, with ease, transfer the seats of the elected Africans to the senate and replace them with chiefs because, after all, 'the British Government do not insist on any particular composition for the legislature' since the mechanism of the blocking quarter would not have been affected.

The body of laws in Rhodesia, built up by the successive settler regimes, amounts to a comprehensive constitution which in itself could be a basis for running oppressive rule without need for a formal constitution. In this sense, the settlers could well continue to implement their policies without recourse to the so-called independence constitution, thus making it remain a monument to the foolishness of 'safeguards' without power.

THE SENATE

Composition:

12 Europeans	Six to represent Mashonaland and six to represent Matebeleland
8 Africans	to be elected by African registered voters. Four to represent Mashonaland and four to represent Matebeleland
6 Chiefs	elected by the Council of Chiefs, three to represent Mashonaland and three to represent Matebeleland.

The total composition of the senate then becomes 26 members. We are not concerned with whether there should be a senate or not. We are concerned with its construction, the method of the election of its members and the grave implications of this to the Zimbabwe society. We have just seen that for the legislature each block of seats is supposed to cover the whole country. Why, then, should senate seats represent the regional blocks of Mashonaland and Matebeleland? To understand the evil motive behind this it is essential to understand the African society of Zimbabwe first. There are two main African language groups in Zimbabwe—the Shona and the Ndebele. These, roughly, coincide with the tribal structures. The practical understanding of Mashonaland and Matebeleland is that one region represents the one tribal and the other region the other tribal group. It is the British colonialists who, of course, imposed the regional demarcation. African political organization is, and has always been, national, ignoring completely the provocation explicit in the regional demarcation line. Now that the British are desperate to surrender sovereignty to their kith and kin and are eager to frustrate any possibility of the Africans, later, seizing control of power, they are offering African political participation on a tribal basis. Naturally the British have studied African society sufficiently well to know that the surest method of destroying African unity is to encourage tribal attitudes by making Africans sort out their political interests on a tribal basis. It is this poison of tribalism which Britain seeks to inject into the African society by suggesting regional representation of Mashonaland and Matebeleland in the proposed senate.

One can see the British attempting to argue that the white settlers will also elect their representatives to the senate on the same regional basis. This would be patent absurdity because the settlers are neither part of the African traditional social structure nor are they affected by the trends within it. On the contrary the white representatives in the senate are set to fan tribalism by inclining one way or the other on different issues depending on their interests. So what is the envisaged practical working of the proposed senate?

The main business of the senate is to discuss tribal issues:

Seven tribal representatives on the one hand (three chiefs and four elected) for the Mashona;

Seven tribal representatives on the other (similarly three chiefs and four elected) for the Ndebele;

Then, in between, there are:

Twelve elected representatives of the white settlers to steer the course of discussions by falling one way or the other depending on their interests. These settler representatives can only maintain their influence by generating tribal differences and conflicts.

Of course the senate has no effective powers but for being a cooling chamber.

It is true that through employment in industries and resettlements there is an overlap of Shona and Ndebele speaking peoples in all areas of Zimbabwe. By introducing political activity on suggestively tribal basis the British are trying to reverse the stream of national unity and force a regrouping of tribal entities through negative tribal attitudes. If the A and B roll African voters are to elect tribal representatives to the senate, as proposed, how does one avoid the highly inflammable negative tribalist attitudes from poisoning the entire fabric of African society during campaigns? This is very much like throwing a meatless bone to two dogs and forcing them thereby to quarrel over nothing.

It is pretty obvious that this mischievous construction of the senate is intended to dissipate African energies in empty quarrels to enable the settler regime to pursue its oppressive rule without serious challenge.

SAFEGUARDS

The protection of African 'rights' is the British government's sing-song camouflage for smuggling a formula to legalize the Rhodesian regime's unilateral declaration of independence. But what are these safeguards?

> A Bill to amend one of the specially entrenched provisions of the Constitution will require a vote of at least three-quarters of the total membership of both Houses voting together. In addition there will be a system of appeal against such amendment . . . by the Constitutional Council (or by a Rhodesian citizen who has obtained a certificate from the Constitutional Council) to the Judicial Committee of the Privy Council. (*Fearless*)

Sitting together the senate and legislature under the proposals make out a total of 93 members—62 elected Europeans, six chiefs, and 25 elected Africans. The necessary three-quarters to amend an entrenched clause in the constitution would be 70 votes. The European elected members and the chiefs, who are civil servants of the regime, are automatic allies. All they need, to make up the three-quarters, is to win over two of the elected Africans.

To regard the 25 B roll elected members as Africans is, in the strict sense, to take a chance on a probability. Whilst, from the educational and economic angle, it is just out of question that an African could be elected under the A Roll, precisely on the same basis every other race (except Africans) in the country has unlimited access to B roll seats because of the lowered qualifications. Further sweeping assumptions suggested by the British are that the Africans so elected will be of one party, and of one mind. Suppose in two largely mixed sections of the city, plus the 25 per cent European A Roll influence in the area, two black puppets are returned to these B roll seats, what is the fate of the so-called blocking quarter? It ceases to have effect forever. Add to this the reality of administrative harassment of the elected Africans by the regime through trumped up cases and, very much indeed, pressures of bribery. For this all they need is to concentrate on two elected Africans.

It would not be strange, of course, to encounter an argument that the Europeans are subject to the same probabilities. This would be spurious. The whole Rhodesian problem hinges on the fact that the British settlers have acted as a clique for the last 70 years and created the present vicious problem. They cannot, therefore, behave in the direction of any other probability than this proven one as long as power is left to them. What objectionable encouragement to racialism could there be than a constitutional provision calling upon elected members to take racial positions over an issue?

The extension of this so called blocking-quarter-safeguard is the provision for an appeal to the Judicial Committee of the Privy Council. The Constitutional Council, the body supposed to make or certify the appeals, is appointed and approved by the settler regime. Evidence of its performance since its institution under the 1961 Constitution is that it has been totally ineffective. It is just a scarecrow. In any case the whole concept of appeal through the courts for a politically defeated case has absolutely no political advantage. If the political power which the British are handing over to their kith and kin cannot bring about the political advantage to the Africans what can any court, however impartial, do in issues of this kind? If the settlers defy and refuse to conform to the decisions of the Judicial Committee of the Privy Council (as in the recent case of Stella Madzimbamuto on the release of her detained husband) now when Britain has both the political and legal authority over the Rhodesian regime, by what stretch of logic could these very settlers be expected to submit to the rulings of the Privy Council when Rhodesia has been accorded independence status under the regime?

Any political issue must be solved in the chamber where it belongs, and this is in the legislature. The sovereign decisions of any state are made in the legislature and it is there that the power of the majority inhabitants must be expressed. The courts are there to maintain and protect the decisions of parliament. Who then can be deceived to believe that the Judicial Committee of the Privy Council is there to protect political rights? The whole fuss about a so-called external safeguard is absolute nonsense.

DISCRIMINATION

> . . . a Commission . . . will be set up under existing Rhodesian legislation . . . to study and make recommendations on the problems of racial discrimination including the Land Apportionment Act, and the possibility of extending the competence of the Constitutional Council to embrace pre-1961 legislation.

Firstly, this commission will be appointed by the Rhodesian regime in consultation with the British government. This alone rules out the commission because the oppression we suffer today results from this form of partnership between the United Kingdom government and its kith and kin in Rhodesia. Secondly, it is absurd to suggest a commission for the 'study' of the obvious. The crisis in Rhodesia is due to long-established forms of discrimination, over decades, and not to some obscure cause requiring a commission 'to study and recommend'.

Solution of the Rhodesian problem means the immediate and total eradication of all forms of discrimination which have plagued the country in its administration and statutes. These are known. What is the point, therefore, of setting up a research body?

These forms of discrimination were brought about by an ill-constructed legislature and an administrative machinery set for the purpose. The legislative powers must be in the hands of the majority to end this evil. The solution cannot lie in some token and sentimental body called a commission. The solution must tackle the cause and not the effects.

TEST OF ACCEPTABILITY

Again on this the British propose establishing a Royal Commission to test the acceptability of their Rhodesian constitution. Of course by this the British would like to satisfy *themselves* and not the African people. The British settlers are not material in this test because their leaders are part of the agreement since the proposals are framed and finalized with them. The wild assumption of the British government in making this proposal is that the Africans will be attracted and led to a false confidence by the word 'Royal' and that it is a British commission as against that bearing the label of the Rhodesian regime. Any such belief is a plain delusion. The British government must know from the fact that the African people's stand is majority rule, that the *Fearless* proposals are automatically out of the question. To proceed with a so-called Royal Commission is a pointless exercise. We are not interested in political tricks. In any case any test of acceptability, whether by referendum or otherwise, can only be a test of the performance of the leaders of a people over a task with which they are entrusted. The *Fearless* proposals are British proposals with the Rhodesian settlers and, as such, have nothing to do with the African people because we have not been a part in their framing. So, the test of acceptability proposed by the British on the Africans is irrelevant.

It is under this section that all sorts of tantalizing suggestions are made about the release of the detainees. Of course this is playing on the plight of families that have long been separated by detention. To begin with, people in detention were detained for a cause for which they will stand whether detained or released as long as that cause is not realized. The device of tribunals for the clearance of political detainees is not anything new in Rhodesia. The present Chief Justice of Rhodesia, Sir Hugh Beadle, was appointed by Sir Edgar Whitehead in 1959 to review the cases of detainees at the time. We all know that this man condemned a number of detainees for an indefinite period of detention. The motivation behind this decision was nothing but political. There is therefore no element of progress whatever in the elaborate arrangements for the so-called release of detainees.

The appointment of the reviewing judge is by the settler regime; even if an appeal is made by the detainee, via the Royal Commission, this commission still has to present this appeal to the so-called Rhodesian authorities for their decision. The Royal Commission is supposed to do the same if applied to by an African living abroad.

Right through these arrangements, one sees the continuing dominance of the settler regime, the very evil which must be removed from the Rhodesian scene. Once a popular government is established then all these commissions and tribunals fall off and the release of the detainees will no longer be an issue for political gimmicks since their cause will have been achieved.

AFRICAN EDUCATION

> Vigorous . . . action will be taken to provide such additional facilities for the education and training of Africans . . . as will enable them to develop their capabilities. This will equip them to take up the greater employment opportunities that will raise their earning capacities and standards of living, and will enable them to play an increased part in the life and progress of their country.

If this were a genuine solution of an educational problem in the country, then it would not be part of a constitutional agreement. This problem, like many others, would be left to be the business of a popular government to negotiate on, with Britain or with any other country. This offer is made by Britain in order to meet the objection of the settlers that Africans cannot participate fully in the life of the country because they are not civilized and would lower the so-called settler standards. In short, this educational programme is acknowledgement of and concession to the settler outlook. This means the educational plan is a form of investment to manufacture the type of African acceptable to the settlers. The concept running through the *Fearless* proposals is that a citizen's right to participate in the affairs of his state must depend on his educational and economic level and NOT on his human value as such. This educational plan is intended to serve this concept. In practical terms it means the African masses of Zimbabwe who were denied educational facilities by these very same settler oppressors will not exercise their rights of self-determination until and unless the settlers deem it so. We do not think this educational offer is genuine; it is intended to serve a totally objectionable concept whose insinuations on the dignity of the African we cannot tolerate.

OUR STANDPOINT

It is of course obvious that our stand is for immediate, and unconditional majority rule. It is the correct solution and it is the only solution. There can be no reasonable argument whatever to justify why it should not be introduced. Neither can there be any sensible argument to prove why it should be delayed if conceded. The evil of minority rule is established and known. Anyone who says the right solution should wait for a known evil to continue in one form or another would have to submit himself for mental examination. Who does he expect to be the victim of evil during the period of waiting? For freedom to take its full meaning every Zimbabwean must be free. There is no such thing as rights for some and none for others. No one enjoys freedom for another. There is no gradualism in freedom. One is either free or oppressed; that is all.

There is no room whatever for all constitutional proposals put forward by the British so far, whether they are *Tiger*, *Fearless* or the 1923 Letters Patent. They are all a continuation of minority rule one way or another. Minority rule has had its day and must just go and give way to majority rule. Seventy years of suffering oppression is enough. There can be no point in letting it even for the smallest scale of gradualism. Evil is evil and has no acceptable form. It must be resisted without the slightest accommodation.

The British settlers of Rhodesia argue that concession to majority rule means that they, as a group, are expendable. Are we to conclude that their insistence on minority rule means the majority, the Africans, are expendable? Alongside this is the stock argument that acceding to African rule would mean the dropping of civilized standards and the breakdown of economic progress. From this develops the British policy that majority rule must wait in Rhodesia until the Africans are educated to standards acceptable to the British settlers. In practical terms, this means the minority must rule and admit Africans into public life at its pleasure. Conscious of the wickedness of their policy, the British then proceed to devise a system of what is called safeguards in the hope of containing African hostility. Hence the construction of a train of shock-absorbing bodies like Royal Commissions; commissions; tribunals and constitutional councils, and so-called blocking quarters. What people can surrender themselves to such makeshift bodies whilst leaving the actual substance of power in the legislature to their oppressors and exploiters? It is totally and completely out of the question that we can tolerate being presented a *fait accompli* on a matter affecting our country and our destiny.

Britain will not concede majority rule in Rhodesia for the simple reason that its kith and kin reject it. We reject minority rule. This leaves Britain without justification for its approach but sheer racialism. There is the usual cunning argument for a transition. This is virtually a plea for giving a chance to oppression to continue in some disguised form. There was no transition to the introduction of minority rule. It was just imposed and we suffered. Minority rule must go out with the same speed with which it came in, if not faster.

The pressure of industrialists in Salisbury for a settlement on the *Fearless* terms is given prominence. They are worried about the effect of sanctions on their economy. Like the British government and the Rhodesian regime they are not interested at all in the genuine freedom of the African people of Zimbabwe. The British government's role is to contain international opposition by all manner of tricks; the role of the settler regime is to carry out internal repression of the African people; the role of the industrialists is to exploit the African people economically and the three organs combine to reap the profits. The problems of the industrialists are not the problems of the African people. The attitude which shows concern for the welfare of the economy when the issue is human freedom, is very degenerate. The economy is there to serve the people and not the other way round. Human freedom is, therefore, a priority unconditioned by the state of the economy. The argument of trying to project the welfare of the economy against or alongside the demand for African rights is a mark of selfishness just as insistence on minority rule is born out of racialism. It is an attempt to mar the real issue.

The solution of the Rhodesian problem must be complete and total. It cannot be in bits or gradual. We are facing a single solid system of oppression and not phases of it. The police, the army, the administration, the legislature are all constructed in a manner to serve oppression and exploitation of the African people. These must be dismantled and reconstructed to serve justice and freedom. The statutes must then be expunged of all laws born out of racism and the economy adjusted for the benefit of the entire people in the country and not just a few.

The country is plagued by white racialism. It is mischievous to then draw a constitution which acknowledges and gives expression to racial differences, creates classes, degenerates further to provoke tribalism and worse still retains the monopoly of power in the hands of an already condemned racist minority. The whole construction of the *Fearless* constitution is direct incitement to class, tribal and racial conflict.

We do not accept the proposed constitutional safeguards. The entire people of Zimbabwe must have the power, be sovereign in themselves and in this way safeguard themselves without any external device. We never accepted British rule over our country. The reserved clauses of 1923 were an external so-called safeguard whose results are the plight we are in today. What better lesson could there be than this? In any case, the very conception of a safeguard results from recognition of a danger. Once the danger is recognized why not eliminate the danger and forget about the safeguard? It is an obvious case of prevention being better than cure. What is worse in this issue is that Britain herself has created the danger.

The most ridiculous feature of the *Fearless* is the arrangement to appoint Ian Smith as leader of the interim administration with, virtually, all the ultimate powers of the state. What is the basis of this? Nothing but a guarantee to the British settlers of the continuity of their minority racist rule.

In our view the British government is no longer solving the Rhodesian problem. She is solving her own problems resulting from it. She finds herself now able to win the support or recognition by a nucleus of states for her legislation of the racist regime's UDI. She is concerned with the consequences of this step on the harmony of the Commonwealth, a fact she has more or less assured herself in relation to the internal problems of individual Commonwealth members. As we pointed out earlier, uppermost in Britain's mind is not the freedom of the African people but the freedom of the economy for the benefit of the industrialists and for the welfare of the white settlers. As usual, it is the hope of Britain to get a few African collaborators who can be used as the excuse for justifying the granting of independence to the white oppressors. All these calculations of the British government are terribly and tragically off the mark. The African people of Zimbabwe will not participate in anything but the correct solution—immediate and unqualified majority rule.

Inevitably, of course, there are views that would suggest that the African people of Zimbabwe should see what best use they could make of the proposals even if objectionable because Britain will not bring about the solution desired. First of all, as is evident from our views, we have never and do not expect Britain to bring about a political solution in our favour for the obvious fact that she is the creator of the oppression we suffer today. Secondly, we are in a life and death struggle and, as such, we have no intention of responding to the British game of political gambles and constitutional riddles when this game is for no other purpose than to frustrate out just cause.

Propaganda is being put out that the British *Fearless* proposals are the only hope of preventing Rhodesia from drifting to *apartheid*. What trash! *Apartheid* exists in Rhodesia in law and practise as in South Africa but in name. The Land Apportionment Act is one example. By its distribution of voting rights and seats in the legislature and the senate on racial, class and tribal grounds the *Fearless* proposals are the very cradle of *apartheid*. The very granting of independence to a racist minority is as much an act of *apartheid* as was the granting of independence to the Boer racists in South Africa by this very Britain in 1910. Who can seriously believe that a legislature loaded 50 to 17 in favour of *apartheid* assisted by a research commission into discrimination can prevent the process of *apartheid* already set in motion?

In the absence of a peaceful solution, what is the hope for the African people of Zimbabwe? We must fight at all levels, at every front, by all means and at all times. There are only two choices in Rhodesia. African majority rule or war. We have no illusions about the military organization of the settler oppressors and their extent of material and financial support. But they have already lost half the war morally and psychologically by the very fact that they know that they are defending an empty case of injustice opposed by the whole world. What remains of the war is skill and determination in the battlefield and not the quantity of arms—a war which the settlers know they will eventually lose whatever their temporary advantages.

It is clear the Rhodesian problem is only an aspect of the racialist complex of Southern Africa. It is equally clear that the solution of the problem is inextricably linked with the solution of the related problems in South Africa and Mozambique as the failure of the sanctions programme has so demonstratively proved. Not only that, every step Britain and Smith take on Rhodesia is always in prior consultation and concurrence with the South African and Portuguese regimes. South African troops are in Rhodesia today with the acquiescence of Britain.

We have taken account of these realities in our determination to fight it out to the bitter end.

A peaceful solution of the Rhodesian problem will have to fulfil, simultaneously, all of the following conditions:

1. immediate and unconditional release of all freedom fighters condemned to death; all freedom fighters in imprisonment and all those under detention and restriction; dropping of all charges and release of any freedom fighters under arrest;

2. free and unfettered conditions for Mr Joshua Nkomo, leader of the African people of Zimbabwe, to take full charge and conduct of all the affairs of the African people in order to bring about immediate

and unqualified majority rule;

3.   dissolution of the minority regime and all its institutions;

4.   drawing of an unqualified majority rule independence constitution with no elements whatsoever of class, racial, or tribal distinctions or differentiations;

5.   immediate, total and radical reconstruction of the army, police and administration so that these correspond with the principles and purposes of majority rule;

6.   all racist and reactionary laws must cease to have effect immediately and be expunged from the statutes.

Majority rule must take immediate effect with no transition whatever. There can be no bargaining on any of the above conditions. They are correct and just.

We are demanding and insisting on no more than what is ours by right. In this regard the question as to whether the British settlers in Rhodesia accept our position or not is irrelevant. It is not for the settlers to determine whether or not we should have or exercise our full rights in our country.

It is not our objective to deny any other rightful citizen of our country's rights which belong to and are exercised by every other citizen. It is by reason of this principle that we condemn minority racist rule and are determined to crush it without conceding it the slightest lease of life. The consequences of the looming racial conflagration in Southern Africa must be laid squarely on the doorsteps of Britain because she has bred the conflict through deliberate policies on her part.

Whilst it is absolutely clear that we are the decisive factor in the liberation of our country, it is, nonetheless, our hope that the international community for its part, in all its forums, will continue to stand resolutely behind our struggle because it is for justice, freedom and peace in Southern Africa—and, indeed, in the whole world.

CHAPTER SIX

THE SECOND INTERNAL CRISIS

24 Zimbabwe African Peoples Union: Observations on our struggle by J. Z. Moyo, National Treasurer. Lusaka, 25 February 1970

For the pursuance of an armed struggle in Zimbabwe the organization established a War Council. This body which was preceded by the Special Affairs Department was formed because it was felt that prosecuting an armed struggle would be a tall order for one person. Hence it comprised five (5) members of the national executive, and it was made responsible to the national executive and the Peoples' Council. It planned activities throughout the whole country and took major decisions in consultation with the national executive.

In 1964, during the construction of our army, there was an element of passiveness on the part of the War Council—i.e., no participation in the spade work; in the camps their participation was lukewarm. The day to day administration of the camps was done by the Military Command administration to whom credit for maintaining discipline under difficult conditions should be given.

It was not until towards the end of 1967 that the War Council began to take an active interest in army administration. The military administration held regular meetings and from time to time joint meetings between the administration and the War Council were held to plan the strategy of the struggle. Occasional meetings were also held together with Umkonto comrades. Everything seemed to be improving and some progress was realized. The whole army administrative structure had the backing of the War Council at all levels. Strict discipline was enforced in all camps including our town residence—Zimbabwe House. Offenders were duly punished. Military procedures in the processing of reports, execution of orders were, although with faltering here and there, observed.

Mid-1969 brought in its train an unfortunate decline in our army. A small unit under the command of Comrade Musa who were, to all intents and purposes, set on a calculated course of disengagement and disruption of the army, succeeded in their demands to meet the War Council.

Discussions with this unit at Camp C2 were conducted in a thoroughly un-military fashion. In the presence of the War Council scathing attacks were made on the Military Command. Cases of corruption involving some members of the Military Command were cited. Accusations of a sordid and scandalous nature were levelled against the administration. Cases of cruelty on the part of the administration were enumerated. Cases of tribal incitement were also cited. A great deal of what was said, although denied by members of the Military Command, was true. But the intention of the showdown was never an attempt to make a correction. It was an open rejection of authority and a bid to justify demobilization of the army.

Following the meeting referred to above in which the cadres of C2 emerged victorious over the Military Command, there was an exodus from that camp into the city ostensibly for medical treatment. Five out of the nine comrades who were in that camp have since deserted. Others have committed worse crimes than those they levelled against the administration. Bent on their ill intentions the disruptive clique spread their gospel to other camps. This totally failed in the west but succeeded in the east where there was an unfortunate repetition of what happened at Camp C2.

Since mid-1969 there has been a steady decline of a serious nature in our military administration and army. Military rules have been cast overboard. Relations between some members of the War Council and the military administration are strained. Attitudes are cooked. Accusations of a serious nature have been made. Military administration and War Council meetings are no longer being held. Planning of strategy is seriously lacking. There is no co-ordination in the deployment of cadres in Zimbabwe.

This unhealthy atmosphere now prevalent in our military organ would easily trigger a dangerous situation similar to what befell some of our friends in the past.

The prevailing situation wherein there is no effective controlling machinery marks a notable stage of decay in our military organization. It is precisely what the fracas at the Musa Camp C2 was intended for. Some time in September last year Camp C2 staged a mutiny when the Chief of Staff and Headquarters officers were detained pending the arrival at C2 of the Vice-President. This was a despicable case of mutiny and could have happened to anyone.

Indiscipline is fast approaching dangerous proportions in our army. Apart from an alarming number of deserters, loose forces are increasing—cadres live anywhere they choose.

It has become optional for the military and administration personnel to sleep at the Zimbabwe House when in town. A great many cadres now live out. When questioned they make references to some members of the executive and Military Command who sleep or live out. The whole business makes administration at the house impossible. There is an urgent need for a definite policy in this connexion.

Loose forces are dead against authority. Their next target is the War Council. I have experienced several cases of indiscipline wherein cadres have refused to take orders from me. I have also witnessed a case of a cadre I referred to the Chief of Staff—Comrade Manyika. This cadre said to me, 'What animal is this called Chief of Staff?'. He refused to go to Manyika as I had told him to and also refused to take orders from me before many cadres.

Our military organ is dismally lacking in specification of duties. People do not know their duties and their rights. For instance, I do not know the scope of my functions as a member of the War Council. I do not know what I may or may not do. I do not know what I am entitled to know. Sometimes it is embarrassing and frustrating in the extreme to be in such a situation.

On a number of times beer and spirits collected from private sources have been carried for comrades in the camps in order to afford them happy occasions. I have no quarrel with the idea as such, but I am concerned with the problems which I have personally encountered when I visited camps without beers and spirits. If so and so can manage to bring us something, why is it not possible with you? Implications of lesser concern on my part in this respect have been made. I therefore suggest that, to avoid this embarrassment, from time to time beer be purchased for cadres from public funds.

The recent filming of ZAPU cadres involved what I consider to be a major party policy. A unilateral decision in this connection was most unfair to say the least. Personally, when I read about the film in the newspapers, I was astonished. I strongly felt and still feel that the security of cadres was compromised. Speaking for myself as a member of the national executive, high command and War Council, I find it hard to conceive how on earth a film taken by a white—Angus MacDonald—could be concealed from me. I wish to confess that I regard this concealment of the film which was known to cadres and a selected group of military headquarters personnel an expression of no confidence in me.

Whilst there is need for some relationship between our movement and the Zambian intelligence, I contend that an arrangement wherein top leaders of our organization or intelligence officers have direct contact with local intelligence is inimical to our present and future interests.

I strongly feel that direct contact with the local intelligence opens the leadership to closer study and in the case of our intelligence officers it renders our intelligence system, at its embryonic stage, liable to penetration.

I feel that our connexion with the local intelligence should be at a political level.

Other suggested measures:

To curb deterioration of discipline among cadres and the unhealthy atmosphere in our military organ it is imperative that military regulations should be implemented forthwith. Military rules must be observed and followed at all levels.

On conflicts between War Council and military headquarters, and cadres, I feel that all concerned should know their rights and the scope of their functions. People's rights must be respected from top to bottom at all levels of the army.

All involved in the administration of the army—the high command, War Council, military command and camp administration, must show the spirit of oneness in order to be able to exercise effective control over the personnel.

The headquarters Military Command should be charged with the task of planning regularly the strategy of the armed struggle in Zimbabwe, working out programmes for the camps and implementing them. They should meet to review progress as regularly as possible.

The War Council and the high command should meet to review the struggle regularly. In fact planning of strategy must be a full time occupation of the high command, War Council and military command. The War Council should consult on all issues affecting the Zimbabwe Peoples Revolutionary Army.

The War Council should be expanded by inclusion of three comrades from the military command (acting on behalf of the three War Council members at Gonakudzingwa) and each member of the War Council should have special supervisory functions to perform, e.g.

1. Army administration
2. Recruitment, training and personnel
3. Operations
4. Logistics and supplies
5. Intelligence and reconnaissance

There must be no dislikes and likes in the administration of the army from top to bottom. Nobody should be caused to feel he is playing the

ZIMBABWE AFRICAN PEOPLES UNION
1970 Programme of Recruitement, Training and Deployment

	BULAWAYO	F/VICTORIA	GWANDA	GWELO	NKAI	SALISBURY	SINOIA	UMTALI	EXTERNAL	TOTAL
Combatants	150	50	25	50	25	150	25	25	20	520
Demolition experts	4	2	2	2	2	4	2	2	6	26
Intelligence	6	2	2	2	2	6	2	2	10	34
Communication operators	4	2	2	2	2	4	2	2	10	30
Medical orderlies/nurses	2	1	1	1	1	2	1	1	8	18
Couriers	6	2	2	2	2	6	2	2		24
Doctors	2	1	1	1	1	2	1	1	2	12
People's commissars	6	2	2	2	2	6	2	2	3	27
Combatants (locally trained)	20	10	10	10	10	20	10	10		100
Instructors	4	2	2	2	2	4	2	2		20
Functionaries (non-combatants)	10	5	5	5	5	10	5	5		50
ARMS (weapons and ammunitions etc.)	100	50	50	50	50	100	50	50		500

role of a pawn—being at the mercy of other person/s. Principles of the army must be seen to prevail over personal wishes.

Liaison officers should fall within the established system of our army—that is, in issues of a military and intelligence nature they should report direct to the department concerned.

Due to the irregularities within our military organ the administration and cadres in the Morogoro Camp entertain a mistaken notion, resultant from a rather juggled system of administration, that they fall under East African administration. We have one army based on the principle of singleness of command.

As it is becoming almost impossible to recruit personnel from Zambia, I suggest that we draw a programme of recruitment, training, which should cover the whole country—Zimbabwe. Preference for training must, as much as possible, be given to personnel who shall be utilized immediately after completion of their course.

Attached is a suggested programme for 1970-71.

25 Zimbabwe African Peoples Union: Reply to 'Observations on our struggle' by James Chikerema, acting-President. Lusaka, 17 March 1970

I must from the very outset correct the impressions given in the first paragraph of this document of *Observations on our Struggle* whose theme permeates throughout this whole document. It is not true that the organization established a 'War Council'. It is also not true that the organization established a 'National Executive' or a Peoples' Council.

The Cold Comfort peoples' conference dissolved all previous arrangements in the party on 10 August 1963. The revolutionary people of Zimbabwe decided in very clear unambiguous language and resolutions that they had had enough of power-hungry leadership and elected one man to lead the whole struggle for their emancipation. Full and complete mandate was given to only one man, our President Comrade Joshua Nkomo.

The department of special affairs, like any other department in the organization, has a head or secretary, responsible to the head of the organization, the President of ZAPU, Comrade Joshua Nkomo. Appointments to any positions in the organizations of ZAPU as it stands today is the prerogative of the President, in his absence his deputy or acting-President. The President's executive functions, together with all departmental functions of the organization of ZAPU are presidential affairs. They are not controlled by a committee or through a committee, although the execution of these functions may in practice be delegated to committees or to individual officers of the party appointed by the President.

In early 1964, the President of ZAPU, Comrade Joshua Nkomo, requested me to remain abroad and directed that Comrade National Secretary, Comrade National Secretary for publicity and information and Comrade National Secretary for the Treasury would join me, and under my leadership, in my capacity as his deputy-President, to lead the struggle of the liberation of Zimbabwe abroad and within Zimbabwe by whatever material forces I can command.

The national executive of the Zimbabwe African Peoples Union is not represented in its full capacity in the mandate of the conduct of the liberation struggle. It is only represented by an emergency arrangement directed by the President to me and to nobody else. If the President of ZAPU, Comrade Joshua Nkomo, was present in person here abroad, he and he alone through the agencies he may deem fit to create has the sole and absolute right to conduct the liberation struggle . . .

It is suggested in the document in circulation that the 'War Council' was established because it was felt that 'prosecuting an armed struggle would be a tall order for one person'. I reject this view entirely. The people of Zimbabwe rejected this view completely . . .

What were the underlying reasons which led the whole nation of Zimbabwe to place their entire trust in the hands of one man? Is the decision of the people of Zimbabwe now being questioned that the entire emancipation of the people of Zimbabwe and the liberation of the whole country is a 'tall order for one person'? Who of us stood up to challenge this mandate given to our national leader by the people? None!

The people of Zimbabwe, after a long period of finding themselves placed in a mess of confusion by power-hungry individuals, by regional parochial elements, by tribalists and political bases' seekers, decided to place only one hand on the trigger and not more than one hand. Matters had gone completely out of hand. The doctrine of collective responsibility had been stretched too far in order to suit individuals' prestige with the people, playing politics with the destiny of the people. Decisions were taken, disastrous courses followed sometimes without the knowledge of the President, the leader of the people.

It is for these reasons the people decided that positions and functions of the national executive of ZAPU (with the exception of three posts) must not be subjects for canvas but that all officers to serve in these posts will be appointed by the leader of ZAPU who is elected President.

In accordance with the emergency powers given to the President at Cold Comfort, the President appointed me to serve as his vice-President. I accepted but advised him not to make the position of the vice-President prominent in the structure; I feared that divisive elements in our society may exploit this rank and erode on the mandate and prerogative specifically assigned to the President by the Zimbabwe people. For this reason I was designated Secretary for Presidential Affairs.

The President and I constructed the whole structure of the People's Caretaker Council, appointed all its office bearers comprising of all member of the national executive, all members of the Peoples' Council, all regional and district officers. This whole structure and body is directly responsible to the President of ZAPU Comrade Joshua Nkomo, or to his agent specifically delegated authority to exercise his mandate. In this case, the man so specifically delegated by the President to exercise his authority and mandate is me. I will exercise this authority and mandate in the interest of the struggle for the liberation of our country.

The document of *Observations on our Struggle* endeavours to separate and isolate the political and party authority of the armed struggle over the army; to place this authority in the hands of five men, create a leaderless 'War Council', and by implication remove my authority over my departments and have them run for me; to expand my departments to include representatives (in Lusaka) to act on behalf of the three 'War Council' members at Gonakudzingwa. But because it is in line with destructive, unrevolutionary activities that have been set free to erode and sap the whole spirit of ZAPU, thereby setting in convoys of political conclusions throughout our whole membership here, and abroad, I shall return and deal with this subject quite at length.

It is observed in the document of *Observations on our Struggle* that during the construction of the army wing of the Party 'there was an element of passiveness'. I am not aware of this. The idea to resort to the armed struggle did not start in 1964. It started very soon after constitutional conferences had failed. The revolutionary people of Zimbabwe rejected the unequal treaties embodied in that constitution. Cadres were sent out for military training in preparation for an armed struggle. If there was any element of passiveness as early as 1960, when the first cadres were sent abroad, I for one knew nothing about this passivity on the part of those who were responsible for this department at the time.

What I know of 1964, are simple details of facts. The President ordered me to visit socialist countries, to negotiate for a bigger intake of our cadres for military training. To negotiate for the training of the branch of special affairs and to seek financial and material support. I reported my finding to the President. The nucleus from the cadres we sent for training at the end of 1963 and during 1964 and from then onwards up to this day, compose what we now call the Zimbabwe Revolutionary Peoples Army.

The objectives of this army when it was created (not in 1964, but as far back as 1960) were not for the purposes of waging guerilla warfare but for the purpose of carrying out acts of sabotage which were considered relevant to bring forth fear and despondency to the settlers in Rhodesia in order to influence the British government and the foreign settlers in Rhodesia to accede to the popular revolutionary demands of the people of Zimbabwe. Who of us—*including the authors of this document*—did not believe at that time that that was the proper course to follow in our struggle? Were cadres not sent out abroad for training for the purposes of achieving the above objectives?

Comrades, I find myself having to state as matters of facts, certain historical facts of our struggle relevant to the answers I have been called upon to reply as a result of this document of *Observations on our Struggle*—by the authors of this—the most unfortunate piece of work ever brought in ZAPU.

The whole of this document, from beginning to end, states a position of calculated hypocrisy, calculated manoeuvres for positions and influence in the party and the army. It is intended to protect clans, and tribal corruption in the party and the army. It is not a truthful analysis, it is not a revolutionary heart searching of the ills that have befallen the Party and the army.

Yes comrades, the party and the army is in dismay. It has no commander. It has no administration. It has no team spirit. It is corrupt, and therefore not sincere to its objectives. But who is responsible for this state of affairs in the party and the army? Who has set in this present chaotic state of affairs, in the party and the army? I find it is a section of certain officers appointed by the President and me to run their present offices in ZAPU. In two cases on the subject of appointments, I had to prevail on the President, Comrade Joshua Nkomo, to appoint them to their present offices. He had utterly refused to do so.

The reasons he had advanced to me for his unwillingness to include them in his team of officers to run departments of the organization under his new mandate given to him by the people of Zimbabwe were that:

1.   They had committed in the past gross acts of irresponsibility.

2.   They had pursued policies inimical to the unity of the people of Zimbabwe.

3.   They had done things in his name as leader of the organization without consulting him and without his permission.

4.   Their whole general behaviour of irresponsibilities were known throughout Zimbabwe and were completely unacceptable to the people of Zimbabwe.

But, because I insisted that the country wanted unity and that the mandate given to him was sufficient in itself to allow him to let bygones elapse into the past and move forward with all the people under his leadership—only did the President agree to appoint these two comrades.

In 1964, one of these comrades decided unilaterally to abandon his post in Zimbabwe, left the country without permission of the President and without his knowledge for purposes only perhaps known to this comrade. The President reacted very sharply and sent messages to me, ordering me to have this comrade return to Zimbabwe. Some of these messages on these subjects came through channels of a head of state. Most came through emissaries sent by the President at that time.

You will recall, comrades, that in the period covering 1964–5 certain emissaries were sent by the President to *report to me and to no one else* his instructions concerning how he wanted certain things to be run. You will also recall the pressures you subjected these emissaries to disclose the subjects of their missions to some of you, especially when these emissaries arrived in Lusaka in my absence. You will recall, comrades, that some of you expressed displeasure to them when they showed reluctance on their part to disclose the substance of their missions to you but not to me.

The President was ordering me to dismiss outright the head of a certain department because this comrade was indulging in immoral irresponsibilities with the President's niece in Dar-es-Salaam, and here in Lusaka.

In one instance, I was ordered to shift a whole department and place it under, and in the office of the Secretariat and to appoint the head of this particular department to run a diplomatic post overseas. There were reasons the President had received which I cannot reveal in this document.

In all these cases, I put forward my representations to the President, pleading with him that the magnitude of the task of our liberation struggle was now too big. That the presence of our comrade who had joined us abroad without—his, the President's,—instructions was to me a small matter and that I would require his services and contribution.

As for the cases concerning outright dismissal, and the case concerning a diplomatic appointment overseas, I argued that the party was beginning to acquire a strong image in all the quarters we imagine favourable to us, and the struggle. I pointed out to the President that the party had just emerged from the convulsions which have led to the formation of ZANU, and that any such drastic steps as he had ordered me to effect would affect the Party outside in a very serious manner. I pleaded that in the interest of the struggle, he must close his eyes and ears, and let me run these matters with the co-operation of all my colleagues here abroad. I have led this path to this day.

I have earlier on agreed with some observations cited in the document of observations in our military situation. I will now go into details which have destroyed the whole moral structure of the party and the army.

First, the ills of the party: I am responsible for allowing and bringing in certain individual officers—appointed to their own departments—and, together with me, run my departments. I took their advice even in my appointments of certain heads of my departments. Hence the party is now divided. There was no *War Council* appointed by the President of ZAPU under the mandate given to him by the people on 10 August 1963. There had been a special affairs department for which I was appointed leader. Because I had been out of touch with the day to day situation throughout Zimbabwe for a period covering four years, I requested the President to give me four comrades to help me to appraise the situation. This committee was not a War Council in any sense. It was not responsible to the national executive as such. There was no Peoples' Council, appointed by then. I was responsible to the President directly. It was not by any stretch of imagination controlled by this committee. Some members of this committee went ZANU.

The Cold Comfort resolutions dissolved the whole party set-up including all positions held by all of us at that time. A completely new revolutionary approach was taken, from which we, today holding top administrative offices, are subjected under.

If this War Council still existed in the President's mind, why did he not appoint other names in place of those members who went ZANU? Why did the President not send these War Council members out and direct me to carry my task with their permission and consent?

My acts of omission are: I stretched our revolutionary democracy far in excess as to be completely misunderstood. I delegated my authority in a manner now being completely misunderstood by some of us here abroad. Now, I will stand this no more. I am a leader of this organization—a leader among equals—but my authority and mandate is above that of all my colleagues. My authority has been undermined in the party. Decisions and deliberations of the exile officers here have been leaked to relations and tribal groups. People have been confused. The district of Lusaka and the regional office have been made a tool for promotions of tribalism and sectionalism.

Some members of this executive have taken part in destructive tribal small meetings in the dark, all aimed at promoting tribal interests and dominance in the party. The whole spirit of comradeship known to all of us whilst inside the country is not there any longer. Our Zimbabwe society here abroad has become a hot-bed of tribal intrigue, nepotism and corruption. I have let this ship drift far too long in the interest of revolutionary democracy and the sharing of power and authority. I had prevailed upon my leader, Comrade Joshua Nkomo, not to insist on the changes he had in mind. I will still preserve the present arrangements. But I will effect a national balance for responsibilities in every department of the party and the army.

It has been observed that the (War Council) began taking active interest in the army only towards the end of 1967. Comrades, I am not aware of this. The correct position must be stated clearly here and now.

When we created the military command as early as the first military group of cadres came back from training, it was decided that the high command, as much as possible, must refrain from dealing with questions of discipline of the army and the cadres in general. The present military command requested to deal with these matters. I agreed. But I did not know that the delegation of full powers to the military command to deal with all questions of discipline meant abdication on my part from listening to and accepting complaints from the army concerning maladministration, cruelty, nepotism and corruption in the army . . .

Comrades, no military commander, let alone the Chief Commander of a guerilla revolutionary army, has the right to use party property and personnel in the army to undertake work for him. Party property and our personnel were used by the Commander-in-Chief to build his girl friend's house somewhere around Lusaka. According to this document, I should not have listened to this complaint from the army personnel some of whom had taken part in the construction of this corrupt house at the order of the Commander-in-Chief.

Is it the policy of the party to incite tribal divisions in the party and the revolutionary army? Is it right for anyone of us to object to the free comradeship association of all the sons and daughters of Zimbabwe whether from east, west, north or south of Zimbabwe? I pose these questions because it has been alleged that I acted unmilitarily by allowing these allegations to be discussed publicly by the army.

A guerilla revolutionary army is a politically conscious army. It is an army of the people, founded by the people. Its affairs must be discussed freely irrespective of rank or any other consideration when matters of principles and behaviour affect it. I saw no victory of the army over the military administration in all the two meetings I held in the east, and the one I held in the west. What I found was a shocking state of affairs, the depth and height of decay, corruption, nepotism, tribalism, selfishness, and gross irresponsibility on the part of the military administration from top to bottom. These meetings were an eye opener for me and for any honest leader.

It is not the matters that were revealed by the army which have caused decay in the relationship between the army command and revolutionary army. *It is the practice by this military administration of all the* above evils I have clearly stated. All these evils and irresponsibilities had to be corrected.

I ordered the military administration to leave Lusaka, to stay with the comrades they command in their various camps, and share with them all their day to day problems. The security of the army was at stake in that the stay of members of the military administration in Lusaka, and not at the camps was now being subjected to suspicion by the army. Evidence had been brought forward alleging that girl friends of members of the military administration were well versed with the movements of the army and some of its personnel. These girl friends had discussed some subjects with some comrades in the army at a period these comrades were around Lusaka. They had been left in no doubt that these girl friends could only have got this information from their boy friends who were members of the military administration.

The order to move the military administration out of Lusaka to the camps was very unpopular. It was resisted by all sorts of stratagems. After making some short appearances in the camps, Chona and Livingstone became the headquarters of the tribal section of the military administration.

The other tribal section in the east used all methods to find a reason to return to Lusaka. At one time they were all detained by the army in the camp for wanting to leave the camp, and return to Lusaka for no reason whatever. Finally, they all found their way back into Lusaka and are now beating their chests in Kanyama, Kamwala, Matero, Chilenje, etc., boasting of what wonderful generals they are. Must I be made to protect, and cover such a rotten state of affairs? No! Never, comrades.

In this document of *Observations on our Struggle* we are told that 'there must be no dislikes and likes in the administration of the army from top to bottom. Nobody should be caused to feel he is playing the role of a pawn—being at the mercy of other person/s. Principles of the army must be seen to prevail over personal wishes'. Yes, comrades, I find the above quotation a fair assessment of how matters should be, not only in the army but in the party as well.

But do the authors of this document seriously believe in and practise these dictates and principles? Why do they confer privileges on themselves, exploit the party, and the revolutionary army? Who authorized party property to serve individual corrupt interests? Who in the army, in the party, is blind to what is going on? Does our day to day living show in any way that we have even attempted to live and act according to the principle cited above?

The army has been divided into tribal factions. The party is divided into tribal factions and clannish empires. There are cadres that are more equal than others in both the party and the army. There are cadres who are given special treatment on tribal and clan considerations in both the party and the army. They have places rented for meeting and sleeping with their girl friends. They are the most smartly dressed. They never run short of money, and, in fact, some of them have boasted that as long as so and so still holds the position he holds, they will never suffer.

The document of *Observations on our Struggle* is to me a very curious piece of work. It has observed only these matters that touch the prestige of the military command whose headquarters are Lusaka, Kanyama, Choma and Livingstone. Has it failed to observe such clear symptoms of the disease affecting the party and the army here and abroad? How do players in the field of sports suddenly turn observers of their own game? This is beyond my understanding and knowledge.

That there is demoralization in the party and in the army has reached gigantic heights. The reasons for all this is that the public has known our personal ambitions, our treacherous activities in the public and our irresponsible disregard of the feelings of those we purport to lead. Some officers (those who refer to themselves as members of the national executive) have taken it as their hobby to destroy the homes of our most dedicated officers and cadres. These cases are known to the public, they are known to practically all members of the party. They are known at every level of the army. There have been cases during the recruitment of cadres when certain individual officers ordered conscription of certain people—our party members—so as to make room for these officers to remain having love affairs with their wives or girl friends. The home of one of our most dedicated army officers was destroyed by one of the members of this mafiaso. That very man persuaded the President to appoint him to his present post against the President's better judgement. The Party, the public and the army know by names all these culprits. Why do we now observe and wonder that the discipline of the party and the army is in a state of decay when some of us have committed the most irresponsible acts which have resulted in the loss of confidence in our leadership in the party and the army?

It is strongly suggested that some authority of the party descend, crush, and control the situation in the army by drastic military codes, to cover and protect the authority of this corrupt, irresponsible, present military command. I am not carrying any such measure aimed at covering and protecting individual vested interests in the party and in the revolutionary army. I am going to shoulder fully and completely all my responsibilities in the party and in the revolutionary army.

I am appointing officers to run my department in the party and in the army who will be responsible to me directly and to no one else. I will have no intruders in my departments. I will have no poachers in and over my authority in the running of the party and the liberation army. I am the captain of this ship.

I reject completely all the observations made in this document of *Observations on our Struggle* save those which I consider quite relevant to the causes of this dismay in the party and the army. I have dealt with most of them in my document of reply.

I will now refer to the suggestion that the so-called 'War Council' should be expanded to include three members from the military command to act on behalf of those War Council members at Gonakudzingwa. I shall return to deal with the mentality behind all these suggestions.

I have knowledge of meetings held in the dark by some of the authors of this document in conjunction with a tribal group of the District Council of Lusaka. These meetings have been going on for a long time in and around Lusaka. Matters discussed were and are as follows:

1. That our President's prestige and image is now dying in and outside Zimbabwe. That the prestige and image of his vice-President has grown by leaps and bounds in and outside Zimbabwe and that therefore, if the struggle in Zimbabwe is won with this state of affairs unchecked, if the vice-President chooses to challenge the President in free elections in Zimbabwe the President will lose to his vice-President.

2. That the vice-President is by nature a capitalist. His origin is not that of the working class in Zimbabwe; his father owns a farm and is not therefore a true revolutionary.

3. That the socialist countries trust the vice-President more than any other members in the national executive and know him better than our President Comrade Joshua Nkomo and that therefore, the leadership of the national leader is being undermined by the vice-President.

4. That all our diplomatic missions with the exception of one are manned by cadres loyal to the vice-President and not to the authors of the document of *Observations on our Struggle*.

5. That because the vice-President comes from the Shona speaking

group—a group considered the largest in terms of the population of Zimbabwe—he will use this group to dominate all other tribes in Zimbabwe.

6. In some of these dark tribal meetings in and around Lusaka, methods of dealing with the vice-President were discussed and conclusions arrived at and decisions taken, which form the substance and foundation of the document of *Observations on our Struggle.*

I have noted the above six points in order to expose the depth of ideological decay, the loss of revolutionary direction in the party and the army, the heights of tribal tensions and plotting for tribal positions and stakes in a future Zimbabwe.

I, for one, have never thought of challenging my leader Comrade Joshua Nkomo in a future Zimbabwe. If I were a threat to his leadership, why did he shoulder me with his mandate and responsibilities? He knew and still knows that I would never be a threat to him in any shape or form. But this does not mean that I will just stand by and allow tribal empires in a future Zimbabwe—like the ones which are being built around us here and abroad. I will challenge them.

Who is a capitalist and who is socialist in Zimbabwe?

A discussion was held on the roof garden bar of the New Metropole Hotel in Dar-es-Salaam. Present were the signatory of the document of *Observations on our Struggle,* party officials in Dar and cadres from Cuba, and my brother among them. The whole discussion was reported to me as follows:

1. The national leader, Comrade Joshua Nkomo, was a well known bourgeois throughout Zimbabwe. He, therefore, cannot be trusted to lead revolutionary socialism in a free Zimbabwe.

2. The vice-President was worse than the President. He is a capitalist because his father owns a farm. He, too, because of his capitalist background cannot be trusted to lead the Zimbabwe socialist revolution.

3. When my brother cited Fidel Castro as an example of a revolutionary leader—who originated from capitalist environment in that his father had bought an estate in Cuba and Fidel, his brother and sisters were brought up on this estate—this point was dismissed as irrelevant to the Zimbabwe situation. In any case he was told that I was such a capitalist reactionary so much that my brother would quarrel with me first over all issues of socialism.

4. All other leaders in ZAPU were analysed, none was found suitable.

But the signatory of the document of *Observations on our Struggle* volunteered his opinion that he was the only man suitable to lead the socialist revolution in a free Zimbabwe. All people present were astonished.

The chief speaker at this small gathering of Zimbabweans in a bar in Dar es Salaam was the comrade whose signature is attached to the document of *Observations on our Struggle.*

I have cited this discussion to show any reader the origin of discussions now being conducted by a tribal group in the party district of Lusaka.

Point four of the matters being discussed in dark tribal secret meetings in and around Lusaka is directed against a number of our officers in our diplomatic offices abroad. It is specifically directed to the liaison officers who have persistently refused to bow to the demands by the present military command and administration, that they be controlled by the military command and not by the high command through the East African offices as has been the case up to now. To beat them to submission all types of methods have been used. Some have been insulted, others brow-beaten and referred to as those who caught the Zimbabwe revolution train at a siding. They are despised and hated because they have refused to submit reports of their work and activities direct to the heads or leaders of the tribal mafiaso in the party and the army. Hence, the attempt to bring them under the present military administrative structure—the same military structure that has proved beyond any doubt that it is corrupt, selfish, not dedicated to carry the day to day activities in the army in general and in the camps in particular. For some of them the social life in Lusaka and other townships in Zambia is their number one priority. They cannot face the day to day hazards of living in the bush and in the camps. They are always keen to subject others to face these hazards. They are white collared townships' social guerillas. The army and the cadres have lost confidence in them.

Comrades, the party and the army are the backbone and spear-heads of the Zimbabwe revolution. Nobody will be allowed to stand in the path of this revolution. No one is allowed to exploit the party and the army to further his or her personal interests. Our party and army have been subjected to these evils here and abroad. I have decided to put a stop to these rackets.

The question of the film I authorized to be shot has been made the springboard from which to launch a wholesale attack on my authority and leadership of the party and the army. I must hasten to state that I take full and complete responsibility of the shooting of this film. You have all and rightly exonerated yourselves from the repercussions you thought may follow. If then, in the final analysis, I am responsible not only for my own errors and omissions but for the errors and omissions of others in the party and the army, I have every right to authorize certain things to be done—which I think are in the best interest of the struggle—without consulting anyone in the party and the army.

The Zambia government has rightly taken exception to my authorizing the taking of the film in question without consulting them and without their knowledge. I have apologized to the President of Zambia. As far as I am concerned the matter is over. It is no longer the subject for celebrations in the townships to mark the downfall of the vice-President of ZAPU.

It is said the film exposed the cadres and was, therefore, quite uncalled for. This was to my knowledge not the first film of this kind. I am aware of a film unit that took some of our cadres not very long ago.

I do not intend to deal with the suggestion that our party should not work closely with the Zambian intelligence, for I find these suggestions equally inimical to our present and future interests and cynical to the common security problems which face Zambia and Zimbabwe. It is a very wrong advice and merits no intelligent discussion.

The programme of recruitment, training and deployment surprises me with its degree of unreality regarding the population distribution of the eight regions cited in the document of *Observations on our Struggle*. It reveals clearly the kind of thinking the authors have in mind. Tribal parity is stretched to try and overshadow the reality and facts concerning true population distribution in these regions.

I find that deployment of combatants and arms is put at par in some regions, disregarding the population content of these regions. Has the Bulawayo region the same population content as the Salisbury region? Has the Fort Victoria region the same population content as the Gwelo region? Is the Umtali region bigger or smaller than the Gwanda region? Is the population of Nkai region the same as the population content of the Sinoia region?

Through what kind of spectacles do some of us view the liberation armed struggle in Zimbabwe? It appears to me, we have become so parochial and are fast losing the true homogeneity so clearly prevalent in our Zimbabwe people. Some of us have very unfortunately become victims of parochial selfishness.

No revolutionary can ignore the true facts of any given situation, let alone our Zimbabwe situation. I reject this scheme totally. It is parochial and very unrealistic. It attempts to ignore all the material revolutionary facts necessary to carry out and win our armed struggle.

The programme of recruitment and the deployment and the supply of arms in the eight regions cited points a very ludicrous armed struggle situation whereby a region with a population of about 30,000 people is compared equally to another holding a population of 100,000 people.

That a regional city with a population content of 200,000 is compared equally to another regional city with population content of over 800,000 people. Deployment of combatants, recruitment, and training of cadres and supply of arms in all the eight regions must follow a programme which disregards the capacity of all our revolutionary masses in their regions, in order to tie them to tribal and regional unrealistic parities.

What a revolutionary programme is this?

What are the fears this programme intends to guard against, by reducing the role of our Zimbabwe masses in their thousands and in their different regions and cities, by tying them to a programme based on parity of infiltration of combatants to every region, and regional training of combatants (locally trained) who must be limited in number in every region?

Is this not an attempt to limit the participation of the masses in the armed struggle? If not, I do not understand the aims and objects of the programme of recruitment, training and deployment, attached to the document of *Observations on our Struggle*.

Finally, I must now come to the reconstruction and redistribution of functions in the Party and the army. I have earlier on stated, in very clear terms, the responsibilities and the authority of the presidential powers given to the President of ZAPU in terms of the peoples' resolutions adopted at Cold Comfort on 10 August 1963. I have also stated the mandate and authority conferred on me by the national leader, Comrade Joshua Nkomo, to direct the struggle in and outside Zimbabwe in accordance with the mandate and authority given to him by the people of Zimbabwe.

I have, therefore, dissolved the whole military command as presently constituted. I have substituted it with a new military administration and a new command structure directly responsible to me and to nobody else. I have prepared for all the cadres who hold administrative posts in the present military command and administration to go for further military studies and refresher courses in military studies for one year. I have taken direct control of certain party departmental functions, previously exercised by heads of departments here and abroad.

I am taking direct control of all foreign affairs matters, and the administration of all our foreign offices from Comrade G. B. Nyandoro, the National Secretary.

I am taking direct control of all matters concerning education of our ZAPU cadres and people from Comrade T. G. Silundika. I have taken direct control of all external accounts of the party funds from the National Treasurer, Comrade J. Z. Moyo.

I have taken direct control of the administration of transport and all vehicles of ZAPU from the Department of the Treasury.

I have divided the ZAPU funds into two sections:

1. There will be the revolutionary armed struggle fund. All OAU and all funds from external sources will be deposited into this account. This account will cater for all requirements of the armed struggle under my direct control assisted by two other secretaries I have appointed.

2. I am leaving Zambia regional administrative funds in the Treasury control. But I have appointed an accounts clerk who is a trained accountant to handle all the accounts in the Treasury. He shall be responsible for keeping both sets of books.

In the Zambian Region, the Lusaka District Council has been the centre of tribal intrigues, conspiracy and the promotion of personality cult for a long time.

I have, therefore, decided to dissolve the whole Lusaka District Council because of some of its members' involvement in the general disruption of the party and their complicity in some of the sordid acts committed by officials in the Head Office and in the branches.

I have in the same vein suspended from holding office in the Party for three years, the following District Council members: 1) D. Khupe, 2) Chihoro, 3) Mlotshwa, 4) John Makiwa, 5) Msimanga, 6) E. Madyara, 7) M'guni.

The above District Councillors jointly and severally committed an offence in that they conspired to attempt to assault Comrade National Secretary.

In view of the fact that this document of *Observations on our Struggle* was cyclostyled and I have knowledge that copies of it were circulated to a tribal group within the Lusaka District Council, I have accordingly cyclostyled both copies for circulation not only to Lusaka but also to those concerned in the party and army.

26 Zimbabwe African Peoples Union: On the coup crisis precipitated by J. Chikerema. Statement issued by J. Z. Moyo, Edward Ndhlovu and T. G. Silundika. Lusaka, 21 March 1970

To Comrades Zimbabwe fellow revolutionaries,

1.   On 17 March, the occasion of Zimbabwe Day when we should have been free to reflect on and rededicate ourselves to the struggle for our liberation, the party was plunged into a crisis sadly enough, by the man holding the office of Secretary to the President in the Party, Mr J. Chikerema. It is a sad crisis of the same inconsiderate dimensions to the struggle as that caused by the ZANU elements in 1963. Mr Chikerema declared at 2.30 p.m. that forthwith he was seizing all powers of the Party to himself and was going to be the beginning and end of the organization and the struggle. It was a coup of Jonathan Leabua's style for a man who has no country, plunging the only hope of the people, the party, into the sorry mess of his personal power ambitions.

2.   Mr Chikerema entitles his paper, declaring the coup, *Reply to 'Observations on our Struggle'*. If his reply, like J. Z. Moyo's observations, had been a list of his own observations about the state of the party, short of the jump to seize power we would have been pleased to have his document also as a valuable basis for assessing problems and enabling the national executive to solve problems in the interest of progress in the struggle. But to attempt to seize power and run the organization on the basis of 'I' as an individual like the Malawi Congress Party is attacking the very foundation of the party. This we cannot allow.

3.   We must point out at once that Mr Chikerema's document and moves were worked out jointly with Mr George Nyandoro. Chikerema's name is a front for power which they hoped to share in running the organization as two people imposing themselves on the whole nation of Zimbabwe. This seems to stem from a tragic myth that they are the organization and struggle in Zimbabwe.

4.   We have no intention to descend to the irrelevance of petty personal attacks which Chikerema has dragged in in order to make up for his poor case, nor do we wish to deal with what appears to be genuine observations and opinions. But because his document abounds with exaggerations, fabrications and distortions in the desperate hope of creating a credible case for a coup we feel obliged

to put the record straight to save the party from being cheated.

5.   Right through the document Chikerema creates the impression that all other officers and people of the party are wrong, have made mistakes, practise tribalism and nepotism, manoeuvres and so on except himself, Nyandoro and their tribe. If this on its own is not tribal bias then there is no tribalism. Could it be that Chikerema and Nyandoro are trying to battle against the predominant number of persons that is presently coming forward to fight for their country Zimbabwe or is it that they are victims of tribal pressure from elsewhere or both? This seems to be the case. Most reactionary and unrevolutionary.

6.   Mr Chikerema makes several references to the decisions of the Cold Comfort Farm, 10 August 1963, as justification for his seizure of power. There is not a single decision of the Cold Comfort Farm which authorized the President or anyone to effect a coup of the powers of the party. In fact the entrustment of Cold Comfort Farm was to take precautions against this very tendency whether by a group of persons like ZANU or by an individual like Chikerema. The entrustment was not a licence. The Cold Comfort Congress reinforced only the Executive powers of the President but did not surrender the authority of the Peoples Congress and the Peoples Council of which we are members as well.

7.   Mr Chikerema is struggling to make the point that he alone was sent out by the President to carry the onerous task of the struggle and we, his colleagues, were sent to him to be his appendages. Tragic. The original nucleus of the national executive of ZAPU of four (subsequently five) was sent by the People's Council, which is the standing authority of the party in between congress, at its plenary session at Gwelo in February 1964. The President and all executive officers are members of the Peoples' Council. The decision and directives of the Peoples' Council to this nucleus of its members was that it should seek a base in a friendly country from which to carry out the responsibilities of the party and the struggle, in an increasing role in relation to the deterioration of the situation in the country. It was to liaise with external support including forming a government-in-exile when circumstances justified.

We were directed to act, we have acted for the last six years and will continue to act in exercise of the powers of the Party above our normal executive duties. In short, we shall continue to exercise the powers of the People's Council according to its mandate.

Perhaps the confusion which seems to prevail in Chikerema over the mandate lies in that he did not attend this session of the Peoples'

Council. He, however got the message; that he is tailoring these directives to his personal wishes is a tragedy of his own ambitions.

8. To plunge the organization into a crisis at this stage of the struggle on the issue of powers after six years of working under the correct mandate of collective responsibility, without fear or favour to anybody is total lack of seriousness and suggests preoccupation with totally different issues than the sacrifices of the struggle.

9. Mr Chikerema battles hard but in vain to dismiss the institution of the War Council in the party. The only reason why he is against it, is because he thinks it compromises his sense of personal power in running the affairs of the army. The War Council was established in recognition of the enormous tasks in organizing and suggesting strategy for a violent struggle. It existed before the ZANU elements reneged. It was subsequently confirmed at the Gwelo session of the Peoples' Council of February 1964. Here the War Council was directed to launch the armed struggle on the basis of zones set out by the Peoples' Council. In the country comrades Chikerema and Moyo were members of this War Council and as such they have acted as its nucleus in running the army for all these years outside.

Only last September, 1969 did the national executive unanimously draw a far-reaching document defining and setting out regulations and relationships of the War Council with other organs in the party because of expanded work. We, the national executive, adopted this historic document without the slightest resistance or dissension from any member. The basis of these regulations were those drawn by army and training officers. Why should Chikerema today destroy all this work? Just to substitute unbridled personal power.

10. Mr Chikerema quotes his trip in 1963 to socialist countries to negotiate for training which took place between 1963 and 1964. He then says from then onwards to this day was constituted what 'we now call the Zimbabwe Revolutionary Peoples' Army'. The implication here is that the 'Zimbabwe Revolutionary Peoples' Army' is the product of his work to be counted on a personal score more significant than any other. Mr Chikerema's trip on this type of mission was one of several undertaken by other colleagues even before Chikerema's.

11. Mr Chikerema claims that he delegated authority to us his colleagues and that now his authority is being undermined through his omissions. None of us was appointed by Chikerema in the first instance. In the last six years that we have worked together, Chikerema has *never* raised complaints or produced one example

before us his colleagues of us undermining his authority. It is obvious that on this question he is just fabricating an excuse for the precipitous step he adventured.

The only omissions of Chikerema we know are those of taking decisions behind the backs of us his colleagues and the rightful officers on questions he shouldn't, like taking Europeans to our secret military positions to shoot films.

12.   'The President and I constructed . . . appointed'
'I accepted but advised him . . .'
'In two cases I had to prevail on the President to appoint them'
'I insisted (to the President) . . .'
'I pointed out to the President . . .'
This is how Chikerema portrays his role behind the President—Joshua Nkomo.

We take strong exception to this deceptive and fawny posture of Chikerema to the President Joshua Nkomo. It is not difficult to read through, that Chikerema is holding the President high only to prove him a caricature whose decisions are in error except those on the advice of Chikerema himself.

Virtually what Chikerema is saying is that members of the Party's national executive owe their positions to him and not so much to the President behind whom he presents himself as a decisive force. What we know is that the President, in making his appointments, consulted his colleagues including the post Chikerema holds.

It is wrong for Chikerema to use the name of the President as a cover for furthering his ambitions.

13.   In addition to accusing everyone else of corruption, manoeuvres and tribalism except himself and Nyandoro who are spotless, he accuses his colleagues and other officers, further, of nepotism; yet in the next breath in the same document Chikerema raises his own brother to the status of a diplomatic representative of the party in Nigeria and implicates this young man in his (James') own quarrels with his executive colleagues by quoting Chikerema junior as an authentic witness on an issue.

14.   One of the immediate causes of this crisis is that the party's District Council of Lusaka discovered that Chikerema himself was holding a series of private meetings behind the back of the District Council with groups of his own tribe who are members under the charge of this very District Council. The District Council obtained direct evidence of the tribal disaffection he was sowing among ordinary members of the Party and his calculated undermining of us his colleagues by spreading rumours that people of a certain section

wanted to kill him for the film.

This adventure of Chikerema was a desperate effort to exploit tribal sympathy as a base to salvage his image in anticipation of drastic criticism over the film. His unconstitutional action of trying to suspend the District Council is just jumping the gun as a defensive mechanism or anticipatory action. It is abuse of power.

We must point out that the anticipations of Chikerema were just imaginary because none of us ever had in mind to take advantage or exaggerate his blunder over the film. It was a matter for national executive treatment, and that is all.

But now Chikerema has confronted us with an accumulation of a series of irresponsible, precipitous and incompetent decisions and actions whose consequences of dividing the nation at this critical moment he does not seem to care about. What are his motives?

15.   On the question of the abuse of party property and transport we agree that this should not be done but Chikerema himself is not an exception to the abuses of party transport for personal purposes. Instances can be quoted.

16.   We agree with Chikerema that no one will be allowed to stand on the way of the peoples' revolution and, we must add, including Chikerema himself through his incompetent and precipitous actions of a personal revolution within the party.

17.   As we indicated earlier on, we would have no quarrel with Chikerema if he had presented his worries about the state of the party and made his proposals, which he has never done before, for consideration and solution by the national executive, but for him to emerge from his recluse and out of the blue to say:

(i)   'I have dissolved the whole military command.'

(ii)   'I have taken control of certain party departmental functions . . . here and abroad.'

(iii)   'I am taking control of all foreign affairs matters.'

(iv)   'I am taking control of all . . . education.'

(v)   'I have taken control of all external accounts'

(vi)   'I have taken direct control of the administration of transport.'

(vii)   'I have decided to dissolve the whole Lusaka District Council.'

(viii) Verbally he says 'I will report information about the Party and struggle to my colleagues only so much as and when I feel like.'

—and crowning it all with an administrative structure which he has worked out with Nyandoro to impose on the party—all this is blatant nonsense.

Chikerema is quite aware that by this action he cannot achieve any more than dividing the nation and destroying the struggle. No one has ever queried or contested Chikerema's post in the party and no one intends to. Why all this desperation? It is a calculated bid for absolute power with no consideration of the struggle but the self—only.

18.   No one can be deceived by the claim that the proposed show-case structure achieves a tribal balance even against Chikerema's own tribe. This is not the issue. The fact that it was constructed with tribal manipulations reveals a pretentious, reactionary, unrevolutionary and indeed an underlying attitude dictated to by tribalistic considerations. Where tribalism exists it cannot be solved by striking tribal balances; these are methods of arch-tribalists who see shadows of tribalism at every turn. The only basis for selected officers in an army is soldierly merit.

But the more dangerous aspect is that no military administration can be secure which is subject to the fancy of an individual wielding personal and not party power. The officers in the show-case administration can be sacked and collapse like a pack of cards at any time Chikerema has a flash in his mind and since tribal consideration is his basis couldn't he, tomorrow morning, set up a structure of his own tribe?

What guarantee could there be for the security of party officers against such a demonstrably power hungry man with more than 40 'I's and 'me's in his document and advised by Nyandoro for all his decisions?

The guarantee is the party machinery on the principle of collective responsibility of the national executive. We will not have ZAPU run the way Banda runs the Malawi Congress Party as a personal estate.

19.   In fulfilment of our national obligation, we declare, without fear or favour, that Comrade Chikerema's reckless bid for personal power in the party as contained in his document abounding in falsities called *Reply to 'Observations on our Struggle'* and as uttered by him in blasphemy of Zimbabwe Day on 17 March 1970, is null and void.

20.   We assert that:

(a)   The authority of the party is central in the national executive and not in an individual.

(b)   All policy decisions, in our circumstances, are the responsibility of the national executive which carries collective responsibility for progress or blame.

(c)   The security of the organization, the cadres and officers of the party is the responsibility of the national executive and not an individual whose vindictiveness in undermining other officers sometimes for personal differences (particularly defenceless junior officers) could cause confusion in the party.

(d) No individual in the party, whatever rank, can be allowed to try to corrupt dedicated cadres by baiting them into a puppet administrative structure under which they will be serving the power caprices of an individual and not the national.

(e) At no time can any officer of the party be allowed to stretch or confuse executive power, which is purely for implementing decisions, with the AUTHORITY or POWER to take those decisions which is the exclusive responsibility of the national executive acting on its behalf, the Peoples' Council and the people.

(g) The Cold Comfort congress of 10 August 1963 merely reinforced the executive duties of the President but did not surrender either its power or that of the People's Council. The Cold Comfort congress did not dissolve any office as provided under the party constitution, except giving the President the allowance to increase those offices when justified.

(h) The fundamental purpose of Cold Comfort Farm decisions was not only to curb power-hungry tendencies of the ZANU elements but to prevent in particular such reckless lust for power and incompetence in judgement of situations as comrade Chikerema has revealed of himself.

(i) We cannot stand idly by and allow members of the party to be cheated by fabrications and exaggerations.

(j) Any difficulties confronting the party and the struggle at the present moment, be they of tribalism, nepotism, corruption, and manoeuvres are the collective responsibility of us all in the national executive including Chikerema and Nyandoro who are trying to jump and pass the buck to others. None of us can escape management or mismanagement of the party by the simple trick of pointing fingers at others and then descending to use and involve junior officers of the party by baiting them into a pseudo-military structure. We have to pick up our problems, sort them out coolly and solve them as a national executive in fulfilment of our responsibility without involving cadres, officers and members as has already been done by Chikerema.

(k) There is no question of us taking advantage of the grave blunders of our colleagues for any other motive than to make him realize his mistake and correct them to enable our comradeship to harmonize and prosecute the armed struggle in an atmosphere of no spite whatever.

(l)   The reinforcement of the executive powers of the President (national leader) by 10 August 1963, Cold Comfort resolutions was specifically limited to the 'Cabinet' (national executive) only and no further. The exercise of these powers is conditional on considerations of efficiency and reliability in serving the national interests to prevent arbitrary use or abuse. Appointments already made by the President, Joshua Nkomo himself cannot be reversed by any other officer, except by the Peoples' Congress or the Peoples' Council which, outside here, we also represent since we are its members and are on its mandate.

(m)   No constitutional provision of ZAPU or any resolution of the Cold Comfort Congress places the President or any other officer above the authority of the party. Section (C) of the Cold Comfort asks: 'the National Leader and/or the People's Caretaker Council to convene a People's Caretaker Convention, whenever any issue of national concern arises.'

No national issue of importance therefore is left to the President alone. In short there is no constitutional provision or resolution which gives the President, and certainly never any other officer, a blank cheque in the conduct of national matters as Chikerema wants to establish of himself.

(n)   The mandate of the Cold Comfort Farm on the conduct of the liberation struggle is quite explicit and unambiguous in defining that the National Leader cannot act without or outside of the Cabinet and Peoples' Council.

RESOLUTION VIII

The Conference EMPOWERS the national leader, the cabinet, and the Peoples' Council to engage in any efforts, in Zimbabwe or abroad, which contribute towards the liberation of Zimbabwe and its people.

In short these three organs have to act together. No one is or can be the beginning and end of a people's struggle in Zimbabwe.

(o)   Mr Chikerema seems to be in an undue hurry to assume power and status without leaving this initiative to the Party by already signing himself Acting President when the President is still alive and when Chikerema's actual technical designation is that of Secretary to the President, a post he shares with William Mukarati.

(p)   The honour of a leader always begins at the point of realizing, admitting and correcting one's mistakes. The fall begins at being stubbornly blind to one's mistakes.

The above principles and on our obligations in the commitment to the armed struggle of a united Zimbabwe people under ZAPU, we shall neither shake nor be shifted.

27 Zimbabwe African National Union: press statement issued by the Supreme Council (Dare) on behalf of the Rev N. Sithole, ZANU President. Lusaka, 19 April 1971

On or about 10 December 1970, the press published an AFP report from Salisbury alleging that an agreement had been reached between Ndabaningi Sithole, President of ZANU, and Joshua Nkomo, President of ZAPU, as follows: That as a result of correspondence in the preceding four months between the two leaders, and in the interest of national unity, both Sithole and Nkomo had agreed to the formation of a new party to supersede both ZANU and ZAPU. The report further alleged that they had agreed to stand down in favour of Robert Mugabe, the Secretary-General of ZANU, presently detained in Salisbury jail.

We have now received a direct communication from our President, N. Sithole, in which he says this press report was false and groundless. There has been no correspondence between him and Mr Nkomo; there was never any agreement that he would stand down; and that he has no intention whatsoever to give up the struggle as implied in the report.

Our President says he supports the formation of a new party. This has been his consistent stand since 1964. He has not veered from it. He feels that the formation of a new party to forge national unity is a must for Zimbabwe. But he stresses that the new party to be formed should be led by persons who are free to organize the people, and raise their morale, and not be led by those in prison, detention or restriction like himself.

He has advised the ZANU Supreme Council that, if a new party is to be formed, serious consideration should be given to the practical purposes it would serve, and how it could help to raise the morale of the five million Africans inside the country.

Although President Sithole is in solitary confinement and is allowed to come out of his cell four times a day for exercises for a period of 30 minutes each time, he is in good health and considers his imprisonment a blessing in disguise. He has been able to think deeply about the strategy for liberation, and consider plans for national development after victory has been won. During his long detention and imprisonment he has been able to write several books, one of which, *Obed Mutezo,* (a biography of a fellow detainee) has just been published by the Oxford University Press in Nairobi, Kenya.

28 Shamuyarira: explanation of why FROLIZI was formed

WHY EXPLANATION NECESSARY

Many people have been asking, and rightly so, for the reasons behind the formation of the new Front for the Liberation of Zimbabwe (FROLIZI). As people deeply concerned about the total liberation of Southern Africa; committed to the unity of all Africans within and across boundaries; and contributing as heavily as you do to the liberation struggle from your scarce resources, you have a *right* to know. Those of us identified with this new organization have a duty to explain our action to those peoples and organizations who support our just cause for national independence and freedom. As members of the old ZAPU and ZANU, we have a particularly urgent responsibility to explain to you why we have identified ourselves with the new organization.

THREE MAIN REASONS

There are three main reasons for the formation of FROLIZI which are clearly stated in its preamble to the interim constitution. This interim constitution will be submitted to the peoples of Zimbabwe living in Zambia, Malawi, Tanzania and other countries, and to the militants, later this year.

1. *The imperative national unity*
The first reason is 'the imperative for national unity among all

Zimbabweans', and to bring to an end the 'shameful chapter in the history of our struggle, in which ZAPU and ZANU were more often at each other's throats than they cared to fight the real enemy'. The split occurred in mid-1963 at a time when the nationalist movement was faced with the decision of either continuing constitutional politics, or launching the armed struggle. Differences of method and strategy existed then. But these have been removed progressively by the rapid advance and consolidation of white settler oppression since the 1965 UDI. At present, all sections of the peoples' nationalist movement, both inside and outside Zimbabwe, completely support the method and strategy of the armed struggle. If ZAPU and ZANU, the masses of the people of Zimbabwe, and the revolutionary forces are agreed on this fundamental issue—as indeed they are—there is absolutely no need to perpetuate the split. The clear duty of national leadership is to forge unity by all possible means.

With few exceptions, the national leadership of both ZAPU and ZANU did not accept this imperative. Instead, some of them started building tribal blocs and alliances within the peoples' nationalist movement for the sole purpose of maintaining their positions of leadership at the expense of the national revolution and the national interest. In ZANU, this started in 1967, and in ZAPU in 1969. Indeed, what proved to be the main stumbling block to the unity talks throughout 1970 was the regionalism prevalent in ZANU, and tribalism in ZAPU. Each leader feared that a united movement might shift the little power he had to persons from other regions.

In his famous document that has now been made public by ZAPU, written on 25 February 1970, under the title *Observations on our Struggle,* J. Z. Moyo, Treasurer of ZAPU, produced a tribal table of recruitment, training, and deployment of ZAPU, which shocked us all. It was only matched by the constitutional plan of racist Ian Smith which divided our people into similar tribal regions. H. W. Chitepo, ZANU Chairman, in a statement handed in at the TANU bi-annual Conference in Dar-es-Salaam last month, admits that unity talks foundered on the 'side issues' of regionalism and tribalism, which he equally encouraged. In the same statement, he takes the negative position that 'ZANU is now the only vehicle of the revolution', and that 'all those who wish to pursue the struggle can do so through ZANU'. *This was the position held by ZAPU for the last six years.* It argued that ZAPU was the only vehicle of the revolution, and that ZANU members must join it individually. At that time Chitepo regarded the ZAPU position as unrealistic, reactionary and divisive. When it became clear to us that the national leadership was not seriously seeking to unite the toiling masses of Zimbabwe, and that while they were vociferous in condemning regionalism and tribalism, they, in fact, practised it and used it in the organization, we were forced to question seriously the whole direction of our national struggle.

2. Revolutionary inadequacies of ZANU and ZAPU

The second reason for the formation of FROLIZI is the revolutionary inadequacies of ZANU and ZAPU, both of which have failed the revolution because 'they were created not for protracted armed struggle but for reformist platform politics'. In the last few years there has been growing disappointment among the rank and file members and the masses of Zimbabwe with the performance of the two 'defunct' parties or movements. Membership and subscriptions have dropped from your figures to naught in most cases.

The two parties have not been able to sustain the spirit of a confrontation with the white settlers that had characterized the struggle in the early years of armed conflict, 1964-8. There is no doubt that the four major battles which were fought during this period shook the confidence and morale of white settlers in their ability to maintain the oppressive system of white domination. Furthermore, a revolutionary spirit was created among the peasants and workers of Zimbabwe. This revolutionary spirit has remained, and has been shown in the heroic stand of Chief Rekayi Tangwena and his people, and other chiefs, who have refused to be moved from their traditional homes, and the university and secondary school students who fought pitched battles with the police in June, during the Goodman talks. There is ample evidence that the objective and subjective conditions are ripe for a massive confrontation between the indigenous owners of the land—the five million Africans—and the foreign agents of British imperialism—the 200,000 racist white settlers.

Although these favourable conditions exist, as exemplified by the successes scored by FRELIMO in recent years just across the borders of Zimbabwe, our parties did not seem able to create a revolutionary base within the country, or generally a revolutionary situation. Moyo admits in his public document that 'since mid-1969 there has been a steady decline of a serious nature in our Military Administration and Army'. ZANU has publicly reported a decline in membership and subscriptions only.

Credit must be given to the people inside Zimbabwe who have continued to struggle against the oppressors. This year thousands of African peasants who were to be shifted from the Lower Gwelo, Sanyati, and Mhondoro areas to the dry and waterless Gokwe area in the Zambezi valley, refused to move, even at the point of guns. The whole scheme of moving no less than 30,000 families into the Gokwe area had to be abandoned. South African and Rhodesian armed police and army units could not move a determined peasantry.

But why do these peasants not link up with the liberation movements in a firm and effective manner, and in an organization capable of creating a revolutionary situation in general? We came to the conclusion that the continuing division was one of the major stumbling blocks. Spokesmen for peasants and workers from Zimbabwe have cried loudly and clearly for unity. They have condemned the inter-party fights of 1963-4, and demanded that unity be forged. In press statements published in *Moto*—the Roman Catholic weekly newspaper circulating inside Zimbabwe—in February 1971, even former ZANU-ZAPU detainees said continuing division was hampering the struggle. Evidence collected independently by certain African Governments and made available to the OAU shows clearly that the five million Zimbabwe people want a united front. Furthermore, they want battles aimed at a progressive, even if gradual, seizure of power rather than those aimed at provoking international or British constitutional action.

One of the distinguishing marks of truly revolutionary movement is the *correct identification of the 'enemy'*. In our case, the enemy has clearly identified himself. He is foreign, capitalist and white. There are agents among us who are used by these forces, but essentially we know, or should know, who the enemy is. Because ZAPU and ZANU were essentially reformist movements whose leaders sought to replace the white masters, they incorrectly identified each other as the enemies of the revolution, largely because they were competing for the same positions. If they were seeking to make fundamental changes in the whole society and system, their priorities would be different and they would identify the common enemy and join in common struggle.

3. *Ideological bankruptcy of ZANU and ZAPU*

This brings us to the third and last reason that has motivated the formation of FROLIZI. ZAPU and ZANU were not motivated by a clearly defined socialist ideology. We believe that ideology is very important to guide the revolution, as well as to give the leaders a frame of reference within which to make policy, or react to new situations in which they have to take a position. Furthermore, and even more important, the Zimbabwe people who are struggling for their freedom want to be certain that their own regime or government will indeed govern for their own benefit. There are many situations in independent Africa where the peasants and workers are as oppressed as they were during the colonial era. The Republic of Malawi is a case in point. There are others. If our people are going to shed their blood for their country as the liberation movement is calling upon them to do, they want to know, and are entitled to know, what they are dying for. They want to know what their children will inherit in the way of rights and privileges in a free, independent, democratic and socialist Zimbabwe.

Neither ZANU nor ZAPU have spelled out their socialist goals for a free Zimbabwe. ZANU's policy statement *Mwenje* (meaning Light) simply says in the operative ideological paragraph: 'ZANU is a mass movement of all the people of Zimbabwe who share in a common belief in the African character of Zimbabwe and the democratic rule by the majority. ZANU means the people—all the people of Zimbabwe. ZANU regards every man, woman and child of Zimbabwe as an important unit of our people's struggle against foreign domination. Each individual counts and each has an obligation to fulfil; that is to play an effective part in the struggle. To join ZANU is to join the forces of liberation. It is to claim that dignity, self-respect and honour which the settlers took away from us. Our cause or aim is of the highest' (*Mwenje*, p. 4). *Mwenje* further emphasizes the need for communal ownership of land, and makes passing references to African socialism, and to fighting colonialism, settlerism and imperialism in that connexion. ZAPU's policy statement condemns in very strong language the present oppressive settler system of government, and says it will be replaced by a 'socialist system of government', but it is not spelled out.

We believe that if ZANU and ZAPU had developed a strong ideological base as we see other parties and the more successful movements have done, *regionalism and tribalism would have been averted*. Without a clear ideology that challenges in practice every tenet of capitalism and imperialism, it is no surprise that the movements have now turned inwards on themselves.

It may now be asked why these issues could not be discussed and resolved within ZANU and ZAPU? Once ZANU decided at its congress held at Kafue, Zambia, on 8 August 1971, that all negotiations for unity with ZAPU must be abandoned completely and forthwith the die was cast. Furthermore, that decision was taken in an atmosphere of intense hostility for those who wanted unity talks to continue. Once the ZANU bureaucracy had achieved that objective which it sought it was impossible for anyone seeking the unity of the people of Zimbabwe to continue working within ZANU effectively. In ZAPU the tribal split—Shonas versus Ndebeles—ran so deep that the acting-President, Mr J. R. D. Chikerema, could no longer commit the entire organization as in the past. In fact, the Zimbabwe movement now had four groups—the Shona-Ndebele factions in ZAPU, and the pro- and anti-unity factions in ZANU. Admittedly, the issues of ideological orientation and 'revolutionary inadequacies' could be tackled by discussion within the existing organization—although some of us had tried hard, and had been stampeded by the bureaucracy. But the issue of unity was so fundamental that once it had been thrown completely out of court by ZANU, the parting of the ways had been reached. It is against this background of fragmentation of two ineffective guerilla movements that the formation of FROLIZI must be viewed.

SOLUTIONS AS SEEN BY FROLIZI

Frolizi's political bureau, headed by Comrade Shelton Siwela, states in its political programme that it intends to intensify the class struggle in Zimbabwe by 'mobilizing the oppressed workers and peasants' and engaging them in a common struggle for the ultimate victory of socialism over capitalism in Zimbabwe. It will endeavour to 'unite all the people of Zimbabwe in order to resolutely overthrow British colonial-capitalism in our country'; 'establish and build an independent self-reliant, socialist economy'; 'establish and build an independent socialist Zimbabwe'; 'give back land to the peasants and guarantee their right to it'; 'guarantee and safeguard the interests of the workers'; 'to improve the living conditions of the toiling masses'; 'ensure and strengthen the equality, unity and fraternity of all Zimbabweans without regard to ethnic origin, or region'; 'establish a revolutionary peoples' army that would defend the people's gains'; 'develop and strengthen solidarity with revolutionary movements, organizations and governments in Africa, Asia, South America and elsewhere' etc. etc. This political programme will be elaborated on soon. The constitution, the political programme, and a document on democratic centralism, will form the ideological base of FROLIZI's organs.

1. *FROLIZI an historical turning point*
The birth of FROLIZI could provide a turning point in the history of the liberation movement of Zimbabwe in particular and Southern Africa as a whole. It is clearly a progressive movement in the sense that it is committed to the essential principles of a revolution—the unity of the people who are oppressed, correct leadership, the correct identification of the enemy and the social forces behind him, and, of course, the complete social transformation of the society, the economy, and the system. The words 'reactionary' and 'progressive', 'commitment' and 'non-commitment' are used so loosely by ZANU and ZAPU spokesmen that they have lost meaning in that context. Often they just throw them

at political opponents. In actual fact, a reactionary movement or personality is one opposed to the unity of the people, and tries to identify fellow Africans by regions and tribes in order to keep them divided. Commitment must mean commitment to these basic principles, not just commitment to sitting in an office in Lusaka or Dar-es-Salaam, while pursuing reactionary policies. In this sense, FROLIZI is the only Zimbabwe organization that can rightly be called 'progressive' and 'committed' to the essential and basic principles of a revolution.

2. *The Leadership*

FROLIZI leadership is drawn from the revolutionary fighting forces themselves. *Shelton Siwela,* Chairman of FROLIZI, has both university and military training, and has already engaged the enemy in two battles inside Zimbabwe. He lives in the camp and in the field where the peasants and workers are, sharing their joys and sorrows. *Godfrey Savanhu,* the Secretary, has a similar background. FROLIZI has shifted the leadership of the armed struggle to the place where it belongs—to the political comrades-in-arms. This fact has removed a major contradiction where civilian politicians have been trying to direct and lead an armed struggle. Although these young men have been described as 'nonentities' and 'unknown' in political circles in Dar-es-Salaam, they have the qualities which the editorial of *The Nationalist* on Tuesday, 5 October 1971, called for: 'determination, singleness of purpose, and above all actual capability to fight for the liberation of Zimbabwe'. As politicians so often say things they do not mean, I agree with the part of your editorial which says FROLIZI must demonstrate its adherence to the idea of unity of all the people of Zimbabwe, and must demonstrate its actual capability. The seven members of its political bureau are drawn from all tribes, and regions in Zimbabwe. No other existing party can claim this spread of representation in the leadership. The remaining ZAPU leaders are all drawn from one tribe, and ZANU leaders are all from two regions only.

It is not the birthplace of the leaders that matters, but their national or parochial outlook.

Obviously, the continuing task of the FROLIZI leadership is to ensure that the Front embraces all the people of Zimbabwe, and especially the militants. There are many young militants both in ZAPU and in ZANU who have the determination, the singleness of purpose, and the ability and capability to fight. At their extraordinary meeting of ZAPU militants held in Zambia early this year, the leadership was castigated by militants for ideological bankruptcy, corruption and maladministration. Several of these young militants had a clear vision of the kind of revolutionary organization they wanted to see, and sound ideas on how to tackle the task ahead. ZANU has several militants who also have this clear conception of the machinery they need and the task ahead. All these young militants will follow those who have gone into the Front, and fight together against a common enemy. It should be stressed that behind the regionalism and tribalism which is being used by the present civilian politicians either to keep or seize power, there is a titanic class struggle between the bourgeois nationalists and the young socialists. FROLIZI's leadership is the first tip of a socialist iceberg. Even if the bourgeois nationalists were able to keep ZAPU and ZANU going, they cannot suppress the young militants within their ranks, nor can they quench their desire for a socialist programme and for unity. Already T. G. Silundika of ZAPU has said publicly the answer to ZAPU's problems lies with young militants scattered in different parts of Zambia. FROLIZI has provided the framework for the co-operation of these young militants determined and capable of fighting a common oppressor. It is the beginning of the process of unifying our people, and consolidating their gains.

3. *Main Direction of FROLIZI*

The fact that FROLIZI expresses a basic aspiration of our people will be demonstrated soon in all the places where exiled Zimbabweans live, study or work. Expressions of solidarity and support have been received from Zimbabwe itself. It is also significant that FROLIZI has been supported by so many militants already, and by two or three men who founded modern nationalism in Zimbabwe—James Chikerema and George Nyandoro. They still represent the main tree-trunk of the resistance movement in Zimbabwe. *The main emphasis of the activities of the new front will be directed homewards. It is intended to create a 'revolutionary situation' within the country as quickly as possible.* Only a minimum of external diplomatic work will be undertaken to enable the movement to operate effectively. Once our case has been explained to supporters of liberation movements, no more time or energy will be spent on attacking or trying to discredit other Zimbabwe peoples or organizations. The main focus of our attention with the very limited resources we may be able to get from progressive and revolutionary governments and organizations, will be Zimbabwe.

4. *The OAU*

The assistant executive secretary of the OAU's Liberation Committee, Mr O. O. Adesola, has said that unity should 'not only be true and genuine, but should also be complete and embrace the support of the majority of the rank and file of the two movements, as well as the masses inside Zimbabwe'. It will and can be demonstrated that FROLIZI enjoys the support of the rank and file members of both movements, inside and outside Zimbabwe. But it is clear that if genuineness and completeness means bringing in all bureaucrats from the party offices in Lusaka and Dar-es-Salaam, the answer is in the negative—for reasons that have already been stated. No united movement can ever be complete. Mr Adesola also told a BBC interviewer that he would like to know the views of Joshua Nkomo and Ndabaningi Sithole, who are in detention in Zimbabwe. He should know the insuperable difficulty of consulting with these men from their present detention cells. Sithole's last letter to ZANU denied that he had ever agreed with Nkomo to stand down as had been published in December 1970, but he stressed that the unity of the people of Zimbabwe was a must, and even suggested the formation of a united party inside the country. It is impossible to consult them fully and discuss any communications they may be able to get out from time to time. *Their names have been used for many purposes, but one thing they would not like is a continuing state of inactivity and division that delays their own release.*

5. *Solidarity with anti-imperialist forces*
Finally, our international relations will be guided by our desire to oppose imperialism and capitalism in every part of the globe as we are doing in Zimbabwe, and to promote solidarity with all oppressed peoples in the three continents of Asia, Latin America and Africa, and all anti-imperialist and anti-colonial Governments and organizations.

In South-east Asia this means solidarity with the four Indo-Chinese peoples, and especially the provisional government of Vietnam, in their just struggle against USA aggression and imperialism; in the Middle East solidarity with all progressive Arab governments and especially the Palestine liberation movements in their just struggle against Israeli Zionists; in Latin America solidarity with those Governments and movements opposing American exploitation; in North America solidarity with our brothers and sisters, and all oppressed groups. Our solidarity with the socialist countries of Eastern Europe, and especially the Peoples' Republic of China, and the Soviet Union, as we try to forge our own socialist revolution is self-evident.

We share a common purpose. But we in Zimbabwe can neither share nor shift from our primary responsibility to create a revolutionary situation in Zimbabwe. We will also collaborate fully with progressive organizations and persons in Western Europe who are as opposed to colonial and imperial-capitalism as we are!

29 FROLIZI: draft constitution

PREAMBLE

The Front for the Liberation of Zimbabwe (FROLIZI), uniting ZANU and ZAPU, is the people's political and military instrument for national liberation.

FROLIZI is today born of the imperative for national unity among all Zimbabweans, and of the revolutionary inadequacies of ZANU and ZAPU, both of which have failed the revolution because they were created not for protracted armed struggle but for reformist platform policies.

The need for a progressive revolutionary movement, uniting not only ZAPU and ZANU but the masses of the people and all the revolutionary forces of Zimbabwe behind a single banner, has for a long time been urged by the rank and file of both parties, by the broad masses of the people, by dedicated militants and by all serious supporters of the Zimbabwe struggle, including the Organization of African Unity.

However, a strange combination of the enemy of our struggle and certain misguided elements among our brothers within the leadership of ZANU and ZAPU had until today succeeded in perpetuating the divisive politics of the past seven years—a shameful chapter in the history of our struggle, in which ZAPU and ZANU were more often after each other's throat than they cared to fight the real enemy!

The formation today of FROLIZI puts an end to this sordid and self-destructive state of affairs. The struggle will from now on be waged against the enemy and oppressor, not against the Zimbabwe people.

POLITICAL PROGRAMME OF FROLIZI

1. To unite all the people of Zimbabwe in order to resolutely struggle to overthrow British colonial-capitalism in our country.
2. To establish and build an independent, socialist Zimbabwe.
3. To guarantee human democratic rights for the people—free speech, freedom of assembly, freedom of the press, etc, etc.
4. To establish and develop an independent, self-reliant, socialist economy.
5. To give back land to the peasants and guarantee their right to it.
6. To guarantee and safeguard the interests of the workers.
7. To improve the living conditions of all the toiling masses.
8. To provide free education and health services for all.

9. To build and develop our national culture.
10. To ensure and strengthen the equality, unity and fraternity of all Zimbabweans without regard to ethnic origin, sex or race.
11. To establish a revolutionary people's army that would defend the people's gains.
12. To develop and strengthen solidarity with revolutionary movements, organizations and governments in Africa, Asia, South America and elsewhere.

SECTION (I) MEMBERSHIP

1. Any Zimbabwean above the age of 15, who accepts the objectives of the FRONT FOR THE LIBERATION OF ZIMBABWE (FROLIZI), its discipline, and works actively in one capacity or another for the cause of national liberation, shall be eligible to membership of the Front.

2. An applicant or recruit for membership in a FROLIZI branch must fill out an application form, obtain the recommendation of no less than two activist Front members in addition to being examined for suitability by the branch, which shall accept or reject the application at a general membership meeting of the branch.

In cases where the Front must function clandestinely, a cell of no more than seven members will constitute the Front's basic organizational unit.

3. Front for the Liberation of Zimbabwe members shall be required to:

(i)   consult regularly with the masses, both within and outside the Front, in order to keep in close touch with the thinking of the masses and to learn from them in a practical way;

(ii) work tirelessly to promote the unity of the masses by resolutely exposing and defeating any factionalistic, tribalistic, regionalistic, opportunistic and adventuristic tendencies within and outside the Front;

(iii) practise criticism and self-criticism in a revolutionary spirit.

4. Within their function at various levels, organs of the Front shall take necessary disciplinary measures aimed at protecting the organization and the revolution from the machinations of the enemy and his agents. Such disciplinary measures shall include, depending on the seriousness of a particular case, WARNING, SEVERE WARNING, SUSPENSION and EXPULSION from membership.

No member shall be expelled from the Front until his case has been heard before the various disciplinary bodies which shall try his case in accordance with the constitution, other rules of the organization and the general interests of the revolution.

A member shall be suspended for a period not exceeding one year, during which he or she will not be allowed to vote or be voted into office.

Appropriate organs of FROLIZI at the various levels shall discipline or expel members who become apathetic or inactive, provided, however, that all efforts aimed at political re-education have failed.

SECTION (II) DEMOCRATIC CENTRALISM—ORGANIZATIONAL PRINCIPLES OF FROLIZI

Leading bodies of the Front at the various levels shall be elected through revolutionary democratic consultation. The principle of democratic centralism, which aims at ensuring the existence in a revolutionary organization of both centralism and democracy, both discipline and freedom, shall be observed strictly by all Front organs. This principle means simply that 'the individual is subordinate to the organization, the minority is subordinate to the majority, the lower level is subordinate to the higher level, and the entire organization is subordinate to the Central Committee'.

Members of the Front shall have the right to criticize the Organization and its leadership at all levels, provided that the criticisms are constructive and aimed at building the organization and advancing the revolution. Members who criticize must come forward with concrete proposals.

Decisions of the Front involving policy and other important issues shall at all levels be reached *collectively,* so as to facilitate in the organization the practice of revolutionary democracy and to prevent the emergence of any personality conflicts. A quorum shall be formed by 17 members for all Central Committee meetings.

The CENTRAL COMMITTEE shall function as the policy-making body of the Front. The Central Committee, composed of functionaries from all levels of FROLIZI, shall meet at least twice a year. A Revolutionary Command Council shall be responsible for the implementation of decisions of the Central Committee. It shall also make and implement the day-to-day policies of the Front.

The Chairman and Secretary of the Revolutionary Command Council shall also function in that capacity in the Central Committee and, together, shall be responsible for the supervision and co-ordination of the departments of the Front.

The Chairman and Secretary of the Revolutionary Command Council (RCC), in consultation with all members of the RCC, shall be responsible for the convening of meetings of the Central Committee.

SECTION (III) ORGANIZATIONAL STRUCTURE OF FROLIZI

1. THE CENTRAL COMMITTEE

The Central Committee shall be the policy body of FROLIZI in between Congresses, as well as the last court of appeal for all cases of discipline.

The Central Committee shall be composed of the following:

(i)   All seven (7) members of the Revolutionary Command Council
(ii) Five (5) combatants from the various units of FROLIZI
(iii) Seven (7) senior military officers of FROLIZI
(iv) Eight (8) leading militants of the various departments of FROLIZI
(v)   Two (2) women militants of FROLIZI
(vi) One (1) militant from the Zimbabwean community in exile.

Total membership of the Central Committee: Thirty (30)

Emergency meetings of the Central Committee shall be convened by its Chairman after democratic consultation with the Secretary and all members of the Revolutionary Command Council.

2. REVOLUTIONARY COMMAND COUNCIL

The Revolutionary Command Council shall be the executive arm of the Front for the Liberation of Zimbabwe responsible for implementing the policies of the Central Committee, running the Front and giving directives to the various organs of the Front.

The RCC shall be presided over by a Chairman, who shall also be the Chairman of the Central Committee. In his absence meetings of the Central Committee and the RCC shall be chaired by the Secretary.

The following shall constitute the membership of the Revolutionary Command Council:

1. *Chairman,* whose duties shall include the following:
   (i)   Chief Executive of FROLIZI
   (ii) Commander-in-Chief of all the armed forces of FROLIZI
   (iii) Chairman of the Central Committee and Revolutionary Command Council.

2. *Secretary*, whose duties shall include the following:
   (i)   Taking and keeping of the records of the Revolutionary Command Council
   (ii) To co-ordinate together with the Chairman the activities of the various departments of the Front
   (iii) To serve as the chief political commissar of the Front, responsible for political and ideological education.

3. *Secretary for Military Affairs,* responsible for the day-to-day administration of the army; supervising the implementation of the

Front's military programme as decided by the Revolutionary Command Council.

4. *Secretary for Organization, Information and Publicity,* who shall be responsible for the creation and consolidation of FROLIZI cells and branches inside Zimbabwe; to encourage and co-ordinate the participation in the work of the Front of patriotic mass organizations in Zimbabwe.

5. *Secretary for Research, Finance and Foreign Relations,* who shall be responsible for the gathering and documentation of all information relevant to the struggle on behalf of the Revolutionary Command Council; collecting, receiving and keeping of all financial records of the Front; to develop and strengthen international solidarity (i.e. to develop, promote and maintain friendly and comradely relations with all progressive national liberation movements, organizations and states on the basis of equality and mutual respect).

6. *Secretary for Communications,* who shall be responsible for relaying of all military and related communications of the Front.

7. *Secretary for Administration and Transport.*

Four members of the Revolutionary Command Council shall constitute a quorum for all Revolutionary Command Council meetings.

SECTION III

THE PERIOD OF ARMED STRUGGLE
1971–4

This period was marked by the Anglo-Rhodesian Settlement Proposals, the emergence of the African National Council and the intensification of armed struggle.

On 24 November 1971, the British government concluded an agreement with the Smith regime in Salisbury aimed at settling the constitutional crisis. The Pearce Commission was sent out to test the acceptability of the proposals by the people of Rhodesia *as a whole*. For the first time since 1890 Africans were to be masters of their own fate. This led to the formation of the African National Council (ANC) on 16 December 1971 in order to oppose the proposed settlement.

The ANC was chaired by Bishop Abel Tendekayi Muzorewa, head of the United Methodist Church in Rhodesia. Other leaders included the Rev Canaan Banana, Dr Edson Sithole, Edson Zvobgo, Michael Mawema, Josiah Chinamano and C. C. Ngcebetsha.

Meanwhile, armed struggle was taking on a new course. From December 1972 a new wave of attacks was launched. A new front of operation was opened in the north and north-eastern regions of Zimbabwe.

CHAPTER SEVEN

THE ANGLO-RHODESIAN SETTLEMENT PROPOSALS

30 Rhodesia Settlement Forum: Why settlement is vital for Rhodesia. Salisbury, 21 November 1971.

1. THE PROBABLE CONSEQUENCES OF NON-SETTLEMENT

(i) *Political*

(a) Internal

There is no possibility of a resumption of normal political activity and evolution whilst the present conflict between Rhodesia and the rest of the world is maintained. The erosion of traditional non-racial policies will proceed unchecked, and the present racial division in Parliament will crystallize, leading to general polarization between the races and perhaps, eventually, confrontation.

There will be little or no prospect of political advancement for Africans, except possibly at the low level of provincial administration.

Race relations, and the mutual trust and respect between the races on which Rhodesians have justifiably prided themselves in the past, could deteriorate rapidly if some progress is not made fairly soon towards a reduction of discrimination—still more so if new forms of discrimination and petty *apartheid* are introduced.

There would be a probable hardening of European attitudes if a settlement is not obtained, the white electorate feeling that nothing could be gained from further attempts to compromise with African aspirations; intransigence begets intransigence. A defensive attitude on the part of the whites who hold power is likely to result in a further diminution of the rights and freedoms of all Rhodesians.

Ultimately rejection of the settlement proposals could lead to the elimination of modern opinion, white and black, a move towards extreme right-wing policies of *apartheid*, the end of true democratic opposition in Parliament, and the entrenchment of all power—military, constitutional and economic—in white hands; and there would be nothing that the African people could do about it.

On the other hand, if Africans, who rejected the settlement proposals not on their merits but out of mistrust of government intentions, were now to accept them, European respect for and consideration of the African sector of the community would be enhanced, and a new era of co-operation between the races for the advancement of the interests of all Rhodesians would be ushered in. The effect of this on Rhodesia's future would be immeasurable, far transcending in the long term the immediate practical advantages of a settlement.

(b)   External
In the external field, if there is no settlement with Britain, Rhodesia will become increasingly isolated from the rest of the world and is likely to lean more and more towards South African policies of separation, without South Africa's opportunities of contacts and dialogue with other nations, derived from its vastly greater size and strength.

Membership of international organizations, from so many of which so much is to be gained if we are to keep abreast of economic, scientific, educational and other developments in the rest of the world, will continue to be barred to Rhodesia, which could only decline into a small impoverished backwater.

(ii) *Economic*
Although a reasonable economic growth rate may be maintained, possibly for a number of years, the lack of foreign capital and expertise to exploit our resources to the full must ultimately have a depressive effect. Already the infra-structure is under strain—e.g. the country is short of electric generating capacity, and Air Rhodesia is long overdue to take off into the jet age—and can be developed only by starving the industrial and commercial sectors of the foreign exchange requirements they themselves need for growth.

The explosive growth rate of the African population springs largely from insecurity, economic and political; and it is extremely doubtful whether government, with the best will in the world, can maintain a rate of development in the Tribal Trust Lands sufficient to keep pace with the natural growth rate of the population, the higher proportion of young men resident therein for lack of job opportunities elsewhere, and the consequent deterioration of the land. More Africans would be reduced to a (probably declining) subsistence standard of living. These factors involve grave problems, not which *ought* to be solved, but which *must* be solved if there is to be any future for succeeding generations of Africans, whatever the system of government may then be.

Therefore sooner or later economic depression is almost inevitable, regardless of world conditions. A hungry man is a dangerous man, and likely concomitants of depression are harsh security controls, repressive discriminatory legislation which in turn could lead to disorders and suffering for all races.

Introducing the settlement proposals in Parliament on 25 November 1971, the Prime Minister himself said: 'Rhodesia could have gone on without a settlement and her position would not have been prejudiced this year or next. But it is our' (i.e. the government's) 'assessment that in 10 or 20 years' time the position would not be so good for our children'.

With the population growing as it is, higher African unemployment is inevitable without major expansion of the economy which is not possible without injections of foreign capital and expertise; and the unemployed will not all be able to find a reasonable living in the Tribal Trust Lands, even with maximal development there.

It is all very well to describe the British government's offer of £5 million per annum, and the Rhodesian government's matching contribution, as a mess of pottage to be exchanged for the Africans' birthright; but without such aid, and indeed far more, and without the joint co-operation of all Rhodesians, black and white, in planning and executing development projects, the 'birthright' of the type of majority rule which those who speak in these terms envisage could well prove to be the inheritance of an economic desert.

(iii) *Social consequences of non-settlement*

The Pearce Commission observed that amongst Africans who favoured the settlement proposals the desire for better educational facilities often outweighed political considerations. But the Minister of Education has recently stated that it is becoming a practical impossibility to provide from the resources of the country for the expansion which is desirable in the African education system. Therefore without a settlement and the accompanying grant of £50 million from the British government, educational facilities will become progressively more inadequate, and the proportion of children able to obtain any form of secondary or higher education will decline.

The introduction of any form of state-sponsored social security for Africans, particularly in old age, will be indefinitely deferred, and meanwhile African methods of providing for this by means of large families will increase the problems of over-population.

The diminishing ratio of European in proportion to total population is likely to engender more defensive attitudes amongst Europeans, to provoke them to concentrate on holding what they have and strengthening their own economic, social and political position; and to this end repressive and discriminatory rules and regulations are likely to be increased, and all forms of communication between the races, so necessary in our country, to become more and more difficult.

2. SOME IMMEDIATE AND PRACTICAL ADVANTAGES OF A SETTLEMENT

The positive benefits likely to flow from a settlement have often been stated, and in most cases the reasons why they are advantageous are so obvious and widely accepted that it is not necessary to enlarge on them.

Using the same categories of definition they may be stated as follows:

(i) *Political—Internal*

(a) The political proposals contained in the settlement agreement, whilst probably *wholly* acceptable to very few Rhodesians, black or white, are the only hope for breaking the existing deadlock. Once that is broken, further evolution may be possible in the new climate of co-operation which will ensue.

(b) The constitutional proposals ensure the maintenance of government in responsible hands, and remove the fear, shared by many Africans, of premature majority rule. On the other hand they ensure that 'responsible hands' cannot be equated with 'white hands'—a concept to which, it should be noted, the Prime Minister has never committed himself, although some of his party have.

(c) Looked at from the African viewpoint, the constitutional proposals provide an assurance of some progress and satisfaction of African political aspirations, of which there is little prospect under the present constitution.

(d) They provide for eventual parity of representation in the legislature, and approximately equal number of voters at that stage on the African Higher and European Rolls. Thereafter provision is made for the restoration of a Common Roll—always until 1969 a feature of Rhodesian constitutions—or of 'any alternative arrangements which command general support', to be determined by an independent commission. The possibility exists that, thenceforward, in terms of numbers, there might be more African than European members of the legislature; but the vital feature would be that they could, and it is hoped would be divided on party political and not on racial grounds, thus providing stable non-racial government.

(e) The proposals contain adequate safeguards against retrogressive amendments of the constitution; but far more important in the long term than any paper safeguards, however strong and binding they may be, would be the spirit of mutual goodwill and tolerance between the races which may be expected to flow from the achievement of a settlement, and the influence of the electorate, which has overwhelmingly demonstrated its acceptance of the constitutional terms as a pre-requisite for settlement. In this connexion it should be recalled that the Prime Minister, in introducing the proposals to Parliament, commended them to members as 'a fair and practical instrument, one which I believe will meet the needs of all fair-minded Rhodesians and . . . deliberately aims at fairness and justice'. The sincerity of the government's intentions is also indicated by the Prime Minister's statement in the House that 'if only Rhodesians could be apprised of the facts and predictions available to government—our economic requirements and anticipated development difficulties; the security problems which loom before us—then they would more readily understand our position'. For those who have expressed distrust of the government's intentions to honour a settlement agreement, and see inconsistency between the principles of the agreement and some of the actions of the government, it should be remembered that the settlement agreement was an act of state carried out by the government (i.e. the Cabinet) on behalf of Rhodesia as a whole, whereas government measures to which many Rhodesians, white and black, take conformity with the ideology of the political party now in power (the membership of which it was disclosed not long ago amounts to only about one eighth of the total electorate).

If by any chance government were to go back on the undertakings implicit in the settlement proposals, a watching world would be quick to deny them the material advantages to be gained from a settlement.

(f) Acceptance of the settlement proposals would lead to more effective opposition in Parliament, and in general they offer a better opportunity to achieve good government than has been possible for many years.

(g) Settlement would gradually lead to the restoration of rights and freedoms of all Rhodesians which have been diminished by the persistence of present tensions, internal and external.

External—The political dividends of settlement on the external side include—

(h)   International recognition and the restoration of contacts with the rest of the world, thus ending the introspective isolation of the past seven years.

(i)   Our near-total dependence on South Africa would be terminated, and Rhodesia would be exposed to ideas and influence from, as well as benefiting from, trade with other parts of the world.

(j)   Conversely Rhodesia would again be free to give to the world at large, and especially to Africa, the benefits of its sophisticated knowledge, experience and research in many fields relevant to the common problems of this continent.

In more general politico-economic and socio-political terms—

(k)   Settlement would promote racial co-operation, enabling the different races of Rhodesia to move closer together once more (without ignoring their differences) and live in greater harmony. It is axiomatic that only by working together for the future can the maximum progress and stability for our country be assured; neither the Africans nor Europeans alone can effectively promote the long-term development of Rhodesia, especially the advancement of the African people, which calls for a joint effort and understanding by *all* sectors of the population.

(l)   The proposals prevent the passing of any future racial legislation, and also provide for the examination of existing legislation of a racially discriminatory character, whilst at the same time providing recognition of the different levels of development of different races.

(ii) *Economic advantages of settlement*

(a)   *The withdrawal of sanctions*

There is no need to emphasize the advantages to Rhodesia of the removal of sanctions with all their wide ramifications, and particularly the benefit to the country if we could again sell our products on world markets in open competition and buy our requirements in the same way, instead of, as at present, trading 'under the counter' and selling at a discount, buying at a premium.

Some people are sceptical of the extent to which sanctions, having been imposed by the Security Council of the United Nations, could be removed in practice. However, it is a safe assumption that, once settlement is achieved, formal recognition is given to Rhodesia and sanctions are withdrawn by the United Kingdom, all the western powers and the major trading nations of the world would follow suit. So far as the UN is concerned, the British are adept at devising formulas and devious diplomatic means of achieving objectives which could never be attained by a frontal approach; even if the Security Council could not be induced (e.g. in over-simplified terms, by veto of a resolution for continuance of sanctions) formally to abandon them, it is probable that they would only be maintained, as a facade, by countries with whom we have little or no trade anyhow.

(b) *The restoration of foreign investment*
Whilst giving due recognition to the difficulties which may persist for some time arising from shortages of foreign exchange and other internal factors, there are strong grounds for believing that the influx of foreign capital which would follow a settlement would generate a surge of industrial and commercial expansion.

(c) Foreign investment would also promote general development, and especially of the African areas on which commerce and industry must rely for expansion of their internal markets.

As an indication of the sort of investment and aid which Rhodesia is 'missing out on' at present in the public sector alone, it is of interest that Kenya and Uganda have recently received loans (a few interest-free) totalling EA £19,400,000 and grants totalling EA £6,807,000 from sources such as FAO, CDC, foreign banks, and British, Canadian, German and other governments' international aid programmes, for such diverse purposes as housing, roads, tourism, fisheries, education and agricultural development etc; Malawi has received loans of K2,000,000 from CDC and the British government for development of its tea industry, and part of K1,000,000 from the World Bank for improvement of Lake ports; loans of US $3,300,000 have come to Botswana and R2,000,000 (interest free) to Lesotho for development of their livestock industries. (Figures culled from *Standard Bank Review*, August 1972.) This is the type of aid which, given a settlement, Rhodesia would no doubt be able to draw on if it wished.

(d) There would be a substantial improvement in job opportunities for Africans, not only in terms of numbers, but also of better openings at higher levels. The experience of South Africa has proved that, in times of prosperity and an expanding economy, even legalized job reservation has broken down and more use has had to be made of indigenous labour and skills in the higher levels of industry. The settlement proposals specifically provide that 'as vacancies occur in the public service they will be filled according to the criteria of merit and suitability, regardless of race', and record the Rhodesian government's undertaking 'to take steps to enable an increasing number of Africans to fit themselves to compete on equal terms with candidates of other races so far as appointments or promotions are concerned'. And there can be no doubt that if government gives a lead in pursuing such an employment policy the private sector would follow suit.

(e)   Better wages and conditions of service would become available to Africans. This is particularly the case in the agricultural industry, which recognizes the inadequacy of its African wage rates and the room for improvement of housing and other conditions of service, but under present conditions just cannot afford it.

(f)   To quote from the settlement proposals, 'there will be a development programme to increase *significantly* educational and job opportunities for Africans to enable them to play a growing part in the country's future development'. The governments agreed that a proportion of this aid would be devoted immediately to the improvement of African areas. The development programme is to be financed by a grant of £5 million a year for 10 years from the British government, with a matching contribution from the Rhodesian government, additional to development expenditure currently planned by them. Thus, apart from the immediate material benefits to be derived from this programme, it also gives assurance to Africans of opportunities to play a more active and constructive part in the development of our country, in which they will be able to assume a role commensurate with their qualifications and abilities.

The infusion of money into this development programme will have not only the direct effect of stimulating the productivity of the Tribal Trust Lands, but also a ripple effect on the general economy, increasing demand and creating employment. It should also go a long way towards satisfying the educational needs of Africans for some time to come—needs which otherwise the country would scarcely be able to meet.

(g)   The conditions created by a settlement and the ensuing development, by giving Africans a larger stake in the economic life of the country, will create a stable middle class; and also, indirectly, they will be assisted in ever greater numbers towards acquiring the qualifications for the franchise, and thus to play a greater part in its political life.

(iii) *Some social advantages of settlement*

(a)   The Declaration of Rights annexed to the constitution will become justifiable, i.e. any aggrieved person who considers his rights or freedoms are unjustifiably infringed by the state will be able to have recourse to the courts.

(b) The Declaration further provides that no more discriminatory legislation may be enacted save within the limitations defined by it. Whilst existing legislation is not affected by the Declaration, the settlement proposals provide for the establishment of an independent commission (whose three members, one of whom will be an African, must be approved by the British government) 'to examine the question of racial discrimination, to consider existing legislation and to make recommendations on ways of making progress towards ending any racial discrimination', with which objective the Rhodesian government has expressed its firm agreement. It has undertaken to commend to Parliament legislative changes required to give effect to the Commission's findings, 'subject only to considerations that any government would be obliged to regard as of an overriding character'.

This last proviso should not be interpreted as providing 'an easy let-out' for ignoring the Commission's recommendations: for firstly they are to be made public; and secondly the government might, indeed almost certainly would be called to account, both within and outside Rhodesia, to justify its rejection of any of the Commission's findings. On the other hand, the proviso does give a degree of latitude for the retention of certain forms of 'protective' discrimination to take account of cultural and economic differences while they last, e.g. the recognition of African customary law, reduced charges for services, and other aspects which are advantageous or acceptable to all.

In general terms, the settlement proposals do give Africans an assurance of the ending of the more degrading aspects of racial discrimination—which might otherwise be intensified—and represent a positive move away from it. A re-orientation of outlook must inevitably follow, which would lead to each race accepting the other with dignity and respect, and to increasing understanding.

(c) A settlement would increase the rights and freedoms of all Rhodesians. For example, they will again be able to move freely around the world with Rhodesian passports and resume social, cultural, sporting and other contacts with peoples of other countries which are now denied to them. Internally, the state of emergency under which we have lived for seven years will be revoked (in the absence of unforeseen circumstances) as soon as sanctions are lifted.

(d) The commission on racial discrimination to be set up as one of the pre-conditions of settlement is to be charged with a special duty of scrutinizing the provisions of the Land Tenure Act and the possible creation of a permanent and independent Land Board 'to preside over the long-term resolution of the problems involved'.

One of the greatest though least tangible of the benefits to be derived from a settlement is that it would create an atmosphere in which such long-range thought, and flexibility of ideas, can again prevail to replace the rigid and doctrinaire attitudes now prevalent among people of both races.

3. NOTES ON SOME OF THE MORE COMMON OBJECTIONS TO SETTLEMENT

1. Amongst the small minority of Europeans who voiced objection to the settlement proposals before the Pearce Commission, some held that they did *not* in fact ensure the permanent retention of government in civilized and responsible hands.

But, as the Commission's report itself observed, those of this persuasion for the most part equated responsible government with white government (which, it is worth repeating, the Prime Minister himself has never done) and saw 'majority rule' as meaning all-black government to the exclusion of white interests, with the probable concomitant of universal suffrage. They either did not see, or did not believe in the opportunities offered by the proposals for the inter-play of party politics across the colour line, and apparently accepted the idea (more commonly emanating from the United Kingdom) that increased African representation, all the way to the parity stage and beyond, can mean only a hard and fast division on racial lines in the legislature.

It rests largely with the Europeans whether this happens or not, but there is no question that it need not happen if government is conducted in the interests of all the people and without an appearance of sectional or racial partiality.

It is the qualified franchise—widely accepted by modern political thought as a legitimate instrument in any non-homogeneous society—which provides the guarantee of responsible government, by confining the vote mainly to those who have a stake in the country and in stability.

But the ultimate answer is that all governments can rest only on one of two bases—force or the consent of the governed. A dictatorial system of government has no appeal to any Rhodesians, especially those imbued with the long traditions of western democracy; and force in the physical sense, apart from being distasteful, is clearly impossible in Rhodesia as an instrument to maintain European domination in view of the population ratio of the main races.

It follows that consent of the people as a whole (which is *not* synonymous with participation by all the people) is the only true foundation on which government can rest in Rhodesia; and, again because of the population ratios of the races, and the existence of a qualitative franchise, the consent of the electorate alone—even when it becomes fairly evenly divided between the races—is not sufficient if at least passive acquiescence does not exist amongst the unenfranchised.

2. Some Europeans and many Africans rejected the proposals because they did not concede enough to African aspirations. This is an understandable point of view; but morality and politics are not necessarily synonymous, the first being concerned with ideals and ultimate truth, and the latter being the art of the possible, taking account of human frailties.

The settlement agreement is a compromise reached by concession on both sides after hard bargaining, and it is unrealistic to suppose that further negotiations could produce a substantially different agreement, unless there was a radical alteration in the bargaining position and strength of either side which is not in prospect.

The main point is that the proposals represent a major reversal of direction on the Rhodesian side, ensuring evolutionary political progress for Africans; they provide a launching platform or jumping-off point from which many developments will follow in time. It cannot be gainsaid that, from the African's point of view, the proposals offer far better prospects in every field than exist under the 1969 constitution.

3. It is believed that many Africans said No to a settlement as a means of expressing their opposition to the present government, without regard to the intrinsic merits or demerits of the proposals.

The point has been made, and continued rejection for this reason alone can serve no further purpose.

4. Others told the Pearce Commission that they did not trust the government to carry out the agreement, largely because its terms seemed so inconsistent with the past policies and practice of the Rhodesian Front.

The proponents of this argument fail to draw a distinction between the government, whose duty it is to rule in the national interest, and the governing party of the moment, whose policies and ideology will provide the normal guidelines for a government but must sometimes be subordinated to the national interest. There is no doubt that the

Conservative government in Britain has pushed through its decision to join the Common Market against the wishes of the majority of the electorate and of its own supporters, and with barely a majority of its own MPs (having had to rely on some Labour and Liberal Party support), the reason being that, with the specialized advice and information available only to governments, it believes this course to be the best in the national interest. Those who read between the lines of the Rhodesian Prime Minister's statement in Parliament on 25 November 1971, and especially his remarks that 'If only Rhodesians could be· apprised of the facts and predictions available to government then they would more readily understand our position', will appreciate that the settlement agreement was an act of state done by the Rhodesian government in the national interest and not an act of the Rhodesian Front. If and when the settlement proposals go forward, no doubt those members of the ruling party who feel they cannot accommodate themselves to them will leave the party or, if they are in a majority within it, throw out the government and put the issue to the electorate—whose verdict has already been made abundantly clear.

This distinction between government action taken in the national interest and that dictated only by party politics is of the utmost importance, and not only in Rhodesia. Whilst it is of course the duty of all governments to rule in the national interest, it is usual for them to interpret this in terms of their own party policy and ideology, which may often lean towards a sectional viewpoint (as does the Labour Party in the United Kingdom by its very name). But there are times for all governments when statesmanship must supersede party politics and they they must make major decisions in the over-all national interest (which they are in the best position to assess), even possibly against the policy or wishes of their own party or without a mandate from the electorate. Such a decision was that of General Smuts in 1939 to take South Africa into the Second World War—which split his country and his party down the middle; and such a decision too was that of the Rhodesian government to conclude an agreement with the British government in 1971, the full effects of which on domestic party politics have been deferred by the Pearce Commission's Report, and may only be seen when a change in African views makes settlement a live issue again. It is noteworthy that in this instance (as is usual in such circumstances) the Rhodesian government did *not* consult the ruling party about the terms of the agreement until it was an accomplished fact. The final verdict on such major acts of statesmanship rests, not with the ruling party, but with the electorate.

An understanding in these terms of the nature of the settlement agreement may help to allay suspicions that the Rhodesian government would not carry it out. The whole basis of international relations rests on the sanctity of solemn agreements reached between governments, and no responsible government could ignore them without irreparable damage to its country's standing in the world. Rhodesia has over the years acquired an enviable reputation for strictly honouring its agreements, even at times against its own interests. Had the Rhodesian government had any thought of not honouring an agreement it had entered into, it could easily have accepted the *Tiger* or *Fearless* settlement proposals (neither of which left a very wide gap between the Rhodesian and British positions) and then defaulted on them.

Thus there is no reason to suppose that the present Rhodesian government, or its successors, would fail to honour the settlement agreement, once it was committed; what it does before commitment of course is entirely another matter, of domestic party politics; and even the pursuit of policies directly opposed to the terms of the settlement—before commitment to it—is not an indication that they would not be honoured. Indeed the pursuit of such policies (in view of suggestions that if Africans rejected these terms they must therefore prefer the 1969 constitution) could be interpreted as designed to influence them to change their minds and acknowledge a preference for the settlement proposals.

Apart from the extreme improbability, on grounds of international morality, that a Rhodesian government would fail to observe the terms of a settlement agreement, there are so many emotional pressures on Rhodesia today from outside that international scrutiny would inevitably be concentrated on its performance, and demands made for the restoration of sanctions and the denial of other benefits of a settlement, if it failed to live up to the terms of the agreement. The Rhodesian electorate too would not wish a settlement, once arrived at, to be put at risk.

The following words of the Prime Minister to Parliament on 25 November 1971, also indicate a sincere and genuine belief in the terms of settlement which should not be obscured by the smoke of party political manoeuvring either before or after the agreement was reached. He said:

'I hope all Rhodesians will join me in looking forward to a period in our history which will be marked by its economic development and expansion; an improvement in standards of living—especially that of the lower income groups; a continuing improvement in race relations, with the acknowledgement of personal feelings and human dignity; a belief in trying to assess people on merit, ensuring that they have the opportunity to advance in life, according to their ability. Let us dedicate ourselves to these ideals, and if we do so, then I believe that we, the people, will match up to Rhodesia, the land . . .'

It is therefore suggested that, whilst suspicion of government's intentions was understandable, there is in fact no justification for believing that the settlement agreement, once finalized, would not be fully honoured.

5. A common objection raised by Africans to the settlement agreement is that the African people were not consulted about it beforehand, which of course is undeniably true. But it should be remembered that neither was the Rhodesian Front nor any other section of the electorate consulted about its terms before the agreement was reached. As explained in the preceding section, the settlement agreement was concluded by the Rhodesian government as an act of state in the light of its own understanding of the national interest, and this is the normal procedure in the case of all inter-governmental negotiations, which are ultimately subject to ratification by Parliament.

Governments are elected to govern, and are presumed to know and understand what is in the best interests of the people—as a whole. It is an unfortunate feature of the present political set-up in Rhodesia that the governing party, so far as is known, has no African membership, and that there is not perhaps the degree of contact there should be between it and the opposition. There may, therefore, be some validity in questioning the government's ability to comprehend the feelings and aspirations of the African sector of the community. But the national interest is not divisible on racial lines, and it is not normal practice for any government, in conducting negotiations with other governments, to seek the views, still less the prior approval of sectional interests.

6. It was argued by some Africans before the Pearce Commission that the issues involved were essentially ones between Europeans or the Rhodesian government and the Africans in Rhodesia, not between the British and Rhodesian governments, and must be settled in Rhodesia. This is a very important and fundemental truth; and it has always been an argument of white Rhodesians against solutions to our problems sought to be imposed from outside that it is we, black and white, who live and have our roots in the country who will have to live with the solutions, a fact which ensures that they must be practicable and broadly acceptable to both races.

But this is in fact a strong argument in favour of the settlement proposals, not in the sense that they fully satisfy African aspirations or provide an immutable long-term solution of all Rhodesia's race problems, but that they represent a reversal of some of the government's previous policies and, going as far in the way of concessions to the African viewpoint as the government believes the electorate will at present accept, establish a starting point, facing in the right direction, from which both races may get closer together in the future to co-operate in the further development and evolution of our country. Sir Alec Douglas Home himself said that he was not attempting to solve the Rhodesian problem, but to put Rhodesians on the right road towards solving their own problems.

The need for more dialogue and communication between the races remains as great as ever; but completion of the agreement would create a more favourable atmosphere in which this could take place, and assist fulfilment of the wish expressed to the Pearce Commission by a 'leading African' that 'The two races should work as a team in restoring peace and make the country a shop-window in the world, where races can live harmoniously'.

> There is a tide in the affairs of men,
> Which taken at the flood, leads on to fortune;
> Omitted, all the voyage of their life
> Is bound in shallows and in miseries.
> On such a full sea are we now afloat,
> And we must take the current when it serves,
> Or lose our ventures.

31a   Rev Ndabaningi Sithole: letter to the Rt Hon Edward Heath, MP, Prime Minister of the UK, on the settlement proposals. Salisbury Prison, November 1971

Dear Prime Minister Heath,

I wish to write to you this letter in order to point out to you the serious implications of the Anglo-Rhodesian proposals which have now been endorsed by the House of Commons and the House of Lords, and the serious implications of your attitude towards the five and a half millions people of Zimbabwe. It is only right and proper that even from my present circumstances, I should not refrain from rendering this service to my people who are entitled to self-determination in the land of their birth like any other people elsewhere in the world. I would like to speak directly to your conscience, if I can, because I honestly believe that what you intend doing is not only evil but basically dishonest, and only 25 years ago mankind has had to pay very dearly to put an end to such evil schemes that deliberately maintain political repression on grounds of colour, culture or race.

First, Mr Prime Minister, I wish to draw to your attention to the glaring fact that the Anglo-Rhodesian proposals, from start to finish, desert the Five Principles enunciated by your own Conservative government. The first principle of unimpeded progress towards majority rule is nullified by your own intention to grant legal independence to 240,000 Rhodesian whites at the expense of 5,500,000 people of Zimbabwe. The second principle of guarantees against retrogressive amendment of the constitution is neutralized by the very fact that all effective political power is left in the hands of a fear-ridden white government and an equally fear-ridden white electorate both of which can never be impartial in their own cause. The third principle of immediate improvement in the political status of the African population is repudiated by the fact that it takes at least 60 years before even parity is reached. The fourth principle of progress towards ending racial discrimination is firmly contradicted by the fact that the proposals contain explicitly and implicitly racialism, white supremacy, white minority rule, and white paternalism. The fifth principle of testing the acceptability of the proposals by the people of Rhodesia as a whole is negated by the fact that this test is not going to be done by referendum but by a commission which at the outside cannot test more than 0.2 per cent of the people of Rhodesia as a whole. Testing only 0.2 per cent of the people of Rhodesia gives a lie to your principle of testing the people of Rhodesia as a whole. In other words, Mr Prime Minister, your Anglo-Rhodesian proposals run false to your Five Principles, and this is why I have not the slightest hesitation in saying that not only are they evil, but they are also basically dishonest.

Secondly, Mr Prime Minister, I wish to remind you that your claim that among Britain's rights is included the right to grant independence to Rhodesia is not only cynical of the rights of the black majority of Zimbabwe, but is also basically false. The grant of legal independence to 240,000 whites means in effect the denial of independence to Zimbabwe's 5,500,000 blacks. Surely, Mr Prime Minister, you do not mean to tell us and the world that it is Britain's right to deprive 5,500,000 people of Zimbabwe of this freedom and independence. No nation on earth has any right whatsoever to consummate a political act the effect of which automatically disinherits a whole people of their rights in the land of their birth. We refuse strenuously to allow your Conservative government to disinherit us of majority rule now, and we reject without reservation your colonial snobbery that it is your nation's right to grant legal independence to your kith and kin at the expense of the overwhelming majority of the indigenous people of Zimbabwe. Furthermore, I wish to draw your attention to the fact that the grant of legal independence to your 240,000 Rhodesian kith and kin at the expense of five and a half million blacks of Zimbabwe will have disastrous consequences for the future of this country. Such a grant will inevitably divide the two races here into armed camps, one always seeking to defend minority rule with the selfish privileges that go with it, and the other seeking to subvert by hook and crook such a rule that denies majority rule now. While you may feel that your nation has right to deny legal independence to the black majority, you should bear in mind that it is naive on the part of your Conservative government to expect the indigenous people of Zimbabwe to accept a political arrangement so replete with political repression without taking matters into their own hands. The grant of legal independence to a white minority at the expense of the vast black majority is a clear invitation to that majority to *take to arms* to make good their claim.

Thirdly, Mr Prime Minister, I would remind you that you are being naive and unrealistic when you regard the Anglo-Rhodesian proposals as a settlement and as a cause of great relief to you. The proposals may be a settlement between the Conservative government and the Rhodesian Front government, and they may temporarily serve the interests of British trade, but they are far from constituting a settlement between black and white. The crucial problem between black and white is yet to be solved. You have no good reason to feel relieved as a result of the Anglo-Rhodesian proposals because these by-pass altogether the heart of the problem facing Rhodesia, and no man in touch with the realities of the African determination to establish in Zimbabwe majority rule now can derive any sense of relief from these Proposals. It is not farfetched to say legal independence to a white minority rule is equal to a time bomb in Rhodesia and the only factor remaining is when it will go.

Fourthly, Mr Prime Minister, I wish to remind you that in spite of your claim to be a model of democracy it is self evident that in drawing up the Anglo-Rhodesian proposals as basis for granting independence to Rhodesia, you followed other standards. You were not led by democratic considerations, that is by considerations of government of the people, by the people, for the people, but rather by purely arbitrary and dictatorial considerations. You are going to grant legal independence to your Rhodesian kith and kin not because right but might is on their side. You intend robbing us of legal independence not because we are bereft of right but of might. You could not have demonstrated worse than this the bottomless depth of the Conservative government's hypocrisy and double standards. Today, when the issue facing Rhodesia involves your kith and kin, you desert your traditional tune 'Right is might' with which you sent millions of British youth and men and African colonial soldiers to their death to prove that rule by might was evil. But you now, after millions have paid the supreme price to uphold 'Right is might', invent a new tune: 'Might is right'. Even the Nazis must be smiling in their graves and saying to themselves: 'Might is all right when advocated by the Conservative Party, but wrong when advocated by the Nazi Party!'.

You cannot, Mr Prime Minister, run away from the fact that you intend granting legal independence to your kith and kin because they have physical force with which a mere 240,000 can impose their will upon the 5,500,000 indigenous people of Zimbabwe. The type of legal independence you intend granting is one based on might, and it will have to be maintained from year to year by the same means until independence based on right is established in Zimbabwe. Like the Nazi regime, the legal independence you intend granting will have to resort to brute force all the time and like the Nazi regime, it must eventually and abruptly give way to an independence backed by right and not might.

Fifthly, Mr Prime Minister, I wish to make it clear to you that the Conservative government's assertion that the African stands to benefit economically and educationally from the Anglo-Rhodesian Proposals misses the crucial point either deliberately or because they are ignorant of the true realities of the African situation in Zimbabwe. We are not interested in your promise to finance us educationally; we are interested above all in majority rule—the same thing that Zambia, Malawi, Kenya, Tanzania, Uganda and all other independent African countries have. You can keep your £5,000,000 and it will not bother us in the least. We are not interested in your buying our independence at that figure for the next ten years. We are aware that this amount the Conservative government is offering is merely to sweeten the bitterness which will be caused by your disinheriting us of our legitimate claim to majority rule now. This goes without saying. Cunningly, the Conservative government has concluded a deal of unashamed political repression couched in terms of economic and educational development. No, Mr Prime Minister, we cannot be satisfied by anything less than majority rule now. Your Conservative government so boastful of democracy must concede the legitimate demands of the majority here.

Finally, Mr Prime Minister, in the name of democracy, ordinary human decency and justice, I wish to appeal to you and to your Conservative government to desist altogether from granting legal independence to 240,000 Rhodesian whites at the expense of the 5,500,000 people of Zimbabwe. You don't seem to be aware of the enormous harm that the grant of independence to a minority at the expense of the majority will cause not only to us as a people but also to your kith and kin whom you seek to protect by hook or by crook, and also to the image of your own country. I cannot see how you can escape the disastrous consequences which logically flow from legalizing independence under minority rule to the exclusion of majority rule.

Yours sincerely,

NDABANINGI SITHOLE

31b Rev Ndabaningi Sithole: letter to the British Foreign Secretary on the Pearce Commission. Salisbury Prison, January 1972

Dear Sir Alec,

Greetings to you.

Because of the swiftness with which events here are moving since your announcement of the Anglo-Rhodesian proposals on 25 November 1971, I feel compelled to draw your attention to the following points.

1. The Pearce Commission

When the Commission was set up, we felt it would be a 'Stooge Commission'. Your refusal to include an African on it also strengthened our fears which have been further justified by events which have taken place here since 11 January. Upon its arrival in Rhodesia, the Commission issued 'Yes' and 'No' forms, and when the African 'Noes' rapidly rose, Lord Pearce held his second meeting with Mr Ian Smith, and after that meeting the forms were withdrawn! This does not look like the work of an independent Commission. It is working at the dictation of Mr Smith, an interested party.

Some of your Commissioners say to the African interviewers: 'These are the proposals, and there is no alternative.' The implied suggestion is that the interviewees might as well accept them. A statement like this clearly shows that your Commissioners are not neutral but interested parties. Obviously, there are two alternatives to the proposals, and the interviewees are expected to say 'Yes' or 'No'. Your Commissioners are therefore, going out of their way when they cleverly suggest that there is no alternative to the proposals. In terms of your own Commission the people of Rhodesia are to make a choice between 'Yes' and 'No' to the Anglo-Rhodesian Proposals. Your Commissioners are therefore, guilty of giving their own opinion to the interviewees, and a wrong one at that. They have come here to get our opinion, and not us to get theirs.

Your Commissioners have already recited to some of the interviewees the benefits that will flow from the acceptance of the proposals and the ills that will flow from non-acceptance. By doing this they have, beyond any shadow of doubt, demonstrated that they are a 'Yes Commission' when they should be neither a 'Yes' nor a 'No' Commission'.

Your Commissioners have already said to some of the interviewees: 'This is your last chance.' Not only is this an absurd and unwarranted statement by a Commission which claims to be neutral, but this gives the impression that it is a 'canvassing Commission' which cannot therefore, be credited with any high degree of impartiality.

One of your Commissioners said to some African interviewees: 'How do you expect 16 people to speak to 5,500,000 people.' Clearly, your Commissioner admits the inadequacy of testing Rhodesian opinion by means of a Commission. I have already pointed out to you in my memorandum this fact. Your Commission now realizes that it can only test at the outside one per cent of the people, and this is not the people of Rhodesia as a whole. Why not switch to a referendum which is a more honest and adequate method of securing a 'Yes' or 'No' from the people of Rhodesia as a whole?

2. Good faith assurances

According to the Anglo-Rhodesian proposals, the honouring of the agreement rests entirely on the good faith of the white Rhodesian government, but since the test of acceptability began the fickleness and unreliability of that good faith have been clearly demonstrated. In terms of the Anglo-Rhodesian proposals we were assured that normal political activities will be allowed. But what has happened since the arrival of the Commission on 11 January 1972?

(a)   Many African political leaders are still not allowed to enter Tribal Trust Lands where the bulk of the African people live.

(b)   Both the ANC (African National Council) and the CP (Centre Party) cannot hold public meetings in the Tribal Trust Lands. The bulk of the people here are regarded as the political monopoly of the government, and this is grossly unfair to other parties.

(c)   Many influential ex-detainees may not have their names mentioned in the newspapers or have their pictures appear in any newspaper in this country. This does not look like normal political activities assured by the Anglo-Rhodesian proposals.

(d) The Chairman of the ANC, Bishop Abel Muzorewa, made a written complaint to Lord Pearce on 11 January regarding his difficulties in holding meetings in Tribal Trust Lands, and Lord Pearce drew the attention of the Government to this matter, but up to now he has not received a reply from the Government which guaranteed normal political activities.

(e) According to the Anglo-Rhodesian proposals radio time was to be alloted for all political parties represented in Parliament to express their views on the Proposals, but up to now that has not been done. This is a clear violation of the agreement.

(f) Since your announcement of the Anglo-Rhodesian proposals the only European members of Parliament who have taken the trouble to assure the Rhodesian public that there will be no going back on the proposals are Mr Smith and Mr Howman, the rest—48 of them—have not done so. They seem to have other ideas on the matter.

(g) Prominent and influential Rhodesian Front members make no bones about it that once they can secure 'Yes', and therefore legal independence, they will tear up the agreement and do as they have always wanted to do—i.e. follow South Africa's apartheid.

It is clear, Sir Alec, that the solemn undertaking that there shall be normal political activities during the test of acceptability has already been dishonoured even before the Anglo-Rhodesian proposals have been ratified by both the Rhodesian and British Governments. The solemn undertaking that radio time will be allotted for the various political parties has also been already dishonoured. The solemn undertaking that no further removals of African communities from their present areas until after the test of acceptability, has also been already dishonoured. 831 familees at Stapleford, Umtali, are to be removed. In other words, Sir Alec, before the ink in which the proposals are written is dry, the Anglo-Rhodesian agreement has already been dishonoured. If the dishonouring of solemn undertakings is taking place now when the Government is desperately looking for 'Yes' to the proposals to legalize UDI, it does not require a brilliant imagination to see that the solemn agreements will be dishonoured after legal independence has been granted to your kith and kin here by your Conservative government.

3. *Pressurization of Africans*

Great pressure is being brought to bear on the African people to induce them to say 'Yes' to the proposals, and those who say 'No' are being subjected to all sorts of threats by the various categories of Europeans. To counteract the mounting African 'Noes' various European businessmen, industrialists and farmers have thrown in their lot with the Government which is desperately seeking 'Yes' to the proposals. The following examples will illustrate the point more clearly.

(a) Various European farmers have threatened to evict their African tenants if they do not toe the Yes line. Many African farm labourers have already had their forms filled in 'Yes' by the European farmers who got them to sign before the labourers knew what it was all about.

(b) European businessmen and industrialists in Salisbury, Bulawayo, Gwelo, Umtali and other centres have already warned their African employees that if they want to retain their jobs, they must say 'Yes' or lose them.

(c) Various mining officials have adopted the same tactics to induce the African miners to say 'Yes' and they have threatened to dismiss those who say 'No'.

(d) African soldiers have already been told by their white superiors that they need not appear before the Commission. They have been assured that they will be adequately represented by these superiors.

(e) African policemen have been made to sign 'Yes' or 'No' in the presence of their superiors, and to save their job and rank, some of these policemen have signed 'Yes' much against their conviction.

(f) African prison warders have been assured that they need not appear before the Commission since they would be adequately represented by their European superiors.

(g) African chiefs, sub-chiefs and headmen are being threatened by the District Commissioners that unless they co-operate with the Government in this matter, they will be in serious trouble. Ordinary peasants are being threatened in turn by these African authorities to side with the government or face the loss of their fields.

(h) A good number of African nationalists who go around explaining these proposals are needlessly arrested, locked up for several days and then released by the police without any explanation. The purpose of these arrests is to warn other Africans that they will get into trouble with the police if they associate with these African nationalists. This is a good example of police intimidation going on to secure 'Yes' and to prevent 'No' to the proposals.

As a result of this behaviour on the part of the Europeans and the government, strong resentment has come up to the surface right across the country, let alone the resentment caused by the proposals themselves which deny the African people self-determination in the land of their birth. The European intimidatory behaviour coupled with the iniquitousness of the proposals has left the people of Zimbabwe in no doubt that the white people are determined to get 'Yes' from the African people by hook or by crook so that they can have their illegal independence legalized, and then after that they can do as they please with the African. The African people, realizing what is in stock for them, and that what is being sought from them is not a vote of confidence in the illegal regime, are saying massively right across the country, 'No' and yet 'No' a million times. Too much is at stake for them.

4. *The present proposals*
The proposals have sparked off the present wave of violence because, as I indicated to you, Mr Heath, and to the Security Council, they do not attempt to solve the problem facing black and white in Rhodesia. They deny the African self-determination *now*. They enshrine racialism and white supremacy which have victimized the African since 1890. They cut across basic African political beliefs and aspirations. They force five and a half million African people to hold the thin end of the wedge while a mere 240,000 whites hold the fat end. My grand-parents on both sides were victims of racialism and white supremacy. My parents were. I am. My six children are. My grand-children and my great grand-children will be if these proposals are implemented. This is briefly how the people of Zimbabwe feel on the proposals. They hate them with perfect hatred.

Your Conservative government is to blame for what is now happening in Zimbabwe. Elsewhere in ex-British colonies independence was granted on the basis of majority rule, but in the case of Rhodesia you want to grant independence on the basis of minority rule. It is this naked, unashamed distortion and reversal of democratic values and procedures which have created in the people of Zimbabwe a frightening and deep sense of being British-cheated and white-cheated of their rights in the land of their birth. It is this double standard that has now poisoned the African people against these proposals which you describe as an honourable settlement, but which only show how out of touch you are with the depth of African feeling on the question of majority rule *now*. You must, Sir Alec, recognize the crucial fact that nothing short of majority rule *now* can solve the problem facing black and white in this country.

Your Conservative government cannot escape the blame that, by making the undertaking that it is prepared to grant Rhodesia independence before majority rule, has caused the white minority here to feel that they are entitled to legal independence at the expense of the black majority. To make good their claim to minority rule, backed by your Conservative government, they are opening fire on African demonstrators who show strong feeling against the proposals—the Magna Carta of your kith and kin here—and the legalized humiliation of my people. Already the forces of racialism and white supremacy have shot dead one African in Shabani, one in Gwelo, four in Salisbury and eight in Umtali. How many more are to be shot as the African 'Noes' soar, I leave that to your imagination.

The fundamental point you should bear in mind, Sir Alec, is that the problem facing this country is basically a political one. But your kith and kin, with your support, hope to solve it by police and military action. The Anglo-Rhodesian proposals cannot be implemented without military and police action over many years, because they lack one fundamental thing, and that is majority rule *now*. The black man is not asking for the white man's favours. He demands self-determination now, and it is he who will decide what favours he will apportion to himself. He wants effective power in his own hands so that he does not remain the victim of racialism and white supremacy which he has been since 1890. That is the crux of the matter. Forget about your £5,000,000 per year for the next ten years. Money is not our problem but self-determination *now*.

I sincerely hope that you will give this matter a further rethink so that a realistic solution to the present problem may be hammered out for good, for the good of the black and white, and this can only be done if all interested parties meet together, at a conference table on a basis of give-and-take.

Yours sincerely,
NDABANINGI SITHOLE

32 African National Council: Why the ANC says No to the settlement proposals. Statement to the Pearce Commission in Salisbury, 3 January 1972

WHY THE ANC REJECTS THE PROPOSALS

Both before and after UDI the British Government has carried on a dialogue with the Rhodesian authorities to the complete exclusion of the recognized African leaders. The basic demand of the ANC is that no settlement of the Rhodesian problem can be achieved without the active participation by the African people, through the leaders of their choice, in the actual process of negotiation leading to any settlement to be approved by them. The ANC accordingly rejects these proposals which have been arrived at without any consultation with the people of Rhodesia. Further, the ANC believes that after the cynical disregard for law represented by UDI, the 1969 so-called 'Republican Constitution' is a high water mark in such lawlessness and can never be made the basis for any settlement. The ANC, on behalf of the overwhelming majority of people in Rhodesia, cannot, in any circumstances accept a settlement whose result, directly or indirectly, is the legalization of UDI and the Republican Constitution. The ANC believes that the present proposals do not amount to any significant amendment of the 1969 Constitution. Unlike previous occasions when the fate of the country was being considered the African people can at least say 'No' to these proposals and attempt to block them even though they have not been consulted during the stages of their negotiation. This is the first and last chance of the African people to pass a verdict on white minority rule. Our rejection of these proposals is unanimous.

THE SETTLEMENT TERMS

The Test of Acceptability

The ANC has serious misgivings about the method now adopted for the testing of public opinion. We believe that the only democratic method of testing such opinion is on the basis of one man one vote and universal adult suffrage as we made clear in our published preliminary reaction to the Settlement Proposals. We are sceptical of the present test, not because we question the impartiality and integrity of the British Commission but because we believe that no Commission can function properly in the present atmosphere where a minority regime would never permit a testing of public opinion.

Our fears in this regard have now been confirmed. Some ANC officials have been arrested and detained shortly before the Commission visited certain areas. This was because the regime is determined to crush the ANC campaign. Acting on instructions from above, District Commissioners have refused us permission to hold public meetings in Tribal Trust Areas. Our local organizers have been harassed, intimidated and threatened by public officials and certain District Commissioners have gone out of their way to distort the import of the proposals, to conceal the fact that the Pearce Commission hearings were being held in their areas and to attempt to ensure a 'Yes' decision from tribesmen within their jurisdiction. Fortunately these methods have not worked.

The continuation of a state of Emergency with the plethora of Emergency Regulations makes it difficult if not impossible that a fair and just testing of opinion can be made by a Commission as now presently constituted. The immunities promised in the White Paper for witnesses appearing before the Commission have not been legislated for and this will leave persons possibly open to prosecution at a later stage. Consequently, we only give evidence to the Commission on the basis that it is the only method available to us at this time.

The Constitution
These proposals represent an acceptance of the illegal 1969 Constitution, a document specifically designed to entrench white minority domination. Sir Alec Douglas-Home has himself denounced that constitution as illegal and unacceptable. The ANC on behalf of the African people are not prepared to assent to anything which would appear to legalize UDI.

Parliament: The House of Assembly
These proposals create three voters rolls which will have the effect of entrenching and perpetuating racialism. Apart from this, the franchise system is both unjust and undemocratic. The African Higher Roll qualifications are so unfair, taking into account the legal disabilities the African people are subjected to in this country that no sane and fair minded person could accept them. All African soldiers, most African policemen, most teachers, nurses, agricultural demonstrators, ministers of religion and the mass of African workers would never hope to qualify. It is nonsensical to require the possession of immovable property of the value now proposed from the African when, in the terms of the Land Tenure Act and related discriminatory legislation, Africans are debarred from owning land on the same basis as Europeans in more than 90 per cent of Rhodesia.

As to the African Lower Roll, the ANC rejects the qualified franchise thus enshrined, as unjust and undemocratic, especially, no matter how many Africans qualify for inclusion on the Roll the number of seats that they can elect remains constant at 16 seats. The allocation of parliamentary seats in the House of Assembly is unacceptable to the ANC since we cannot accept any arrangements whereby 5,200,000 Africans are granted 16 seats while a mere 250,000 whites are given 50 seats. Nor are the ANC prepared to accept an arrangement which is designated in its proposals for increases in the number of African seats, to postpone indefinitely the Africans' right to govern themselves. It has been calculated by some experts that majority rule cannot come any earlier than 2035, if then.

The Senate

The ANC adheres to the view that the Senate, as presently constituted, is undemocratic and racial. Why, for example, should the European members of the House of Assembly enjoy the privilege of constituting themselves as a separate electorate for the purpose of electing the Senate when African members are denied the same right? In any event, the ANC finds it impossible to accept the tribalism and racialism that the present system entrenches.

The Declaration of Rights

In principle, the ANC thinks that inclusion of a Declaration of Rights a good thing as is the decision to make it justifiable. But the existing oppressive Statute Law is saved by the proposals and will not be affected by the provisions of the Declaration. In view of the limitations which have been imposed as regard the scope and justiciability of the Declaration the ANC is forced to reject this proposal as well.

Renewal of the State of Emergency

The ANC believes that the proposal to reduce the period within which a State of Emergency requires renewal misses the point since such an emergency invariably affects the safeguards which the Bill of Rights contains.

Other Proposed Safeguards

The ANC does not regard the safeguards on amendment of the Constitution or review of existing legislation as satisfactory. In particular, the proposed Commission on Racial Discrimination will not be set up until after the test of acceptability is complete. It will not therefore be able to report until long after independence has been granted by the British Parliament. The Commission itself will be nominated by the regime and responsible to it. In these circumstances we think that the proposed Commission will be valueless. This is especially as the Commission will only have advisory powers and will be similar if not identical to the ill-fated Constitutional Council established under the 1961 Constitution.

Detainees and Persons under Sentence of Death

The ANC considers it astonishing that the British Government should have agreed with the Smith regime that only 31 of the then 93 detainees should be released (as soon as the necessary arrangements could be made). The ANC are not prepared to accept a situation where many of our leaders are kept in gaol without trial.

Since the arrival of the Pearce Commission more than 100 people have been detained and 14 killed by security forces. The Government have been particularly repressive towards ANC supporters. In some areas, the whole area Executive Committee of our organization have been arrested and detained. The Treasurer of the ANC, Mr Josiah Chinamano, and his wife, have been detained as have many others.

No mention is made in the proposals as to the fact of those under sentence of death for acts committed against an illegal Government. Our fear is that the regime, armed with the legality which could be conferred by the acceptance of these proposals will execute those persons now under sentence of death. Nor do the proposals provide for an amnesty for those people who were forced to leave the country as a result of UDI.

Land

The settlement proposals accept the basic provision of the Land Tenure Act. The Commission on Discrimination to be appointed after the granting of legal independence cannot recommend the repeal of the Land Tenure Act. The ANC rejects unreservedly the Land Tenure Act as embodied in the Settlement Proposals because it is blatantly discriminatory, unfair and incitement to racial animosity among the peoples of this country.

Development Programme

The amount of aid is uncertain. All that is clear is that it will not be more than £5 million per year and will be applied to purposes and projects to be agreed with the Rhodesian Government. The strings attached to the aid are questionable. The principal beneficiaries of the proposed £50 million British aid will be the Rhodesian Government in terms of foreign exchange and the stimulus to white industry. The ANC believes that much of this money will be used on the promotion of 'provincialization' which is the regime's euphemism for bantustans, and thus reject these proposals as perpetuating and extending an already unjust system.

The Rhodesian Public Service

The undertaking by the Rhodesian Government (to take steps to enable an increasing number of Africans to fit themselves to compete on equal terms with candidates of other races so far as appointments or promotions are concerned) is vague and unsatisfactory. It does not spell out what steps are to be taken in pursuance of the undertaking. It implies that at present Africans have neither the qualifications nor the experience of appointment or promotion in the Public Service. This is not true.

In spite of the regime's claim that promotion is on the basis of merit only, the ANC would especially point out the failure to promote African inspectors of schools to positions of Provincial Education Officers in spite of their high qualifications and long experience; the appointment of young Europeans as District Officers with only Form IV education instead of African graduates with university degrees; the refusal to amend the Education Act so that all teachers regardless of race can become members of the Public Service; the refusal to allow African nurses to take up appointments in so-called European hospitals in spite of the shortage of nurses in these hospitals. This story is repeated in every Government Department. The ANC cannot trust the Rhodesian Front Government to apply criteria of merit and suitability in filing vacancies in the Public Service. The ANC therefore rejects this section of the proposals as vague and illusory.

Conclusion
It is clear that the proposals as they now stand do not provide a satisfactory arrangement acceptable to the vast majority of people in the country. On behalf of these people, the ANC calls for the Pearce Commission to report the rejection of these terms, which, if accepted, can only serve to perpetuate the existing divisions and injustice in Rhodesia.

33 Joshua Nkomo: memorandum on the settlement proposals submitted to the Pearce Commission. February 1972

Southern Rhodesia has a population of about five and three-quarter million people. Of these, five and a half million are black indigenous people. The rest of the population is made up of people of European and Asian descent, as well as the coloured people. All the African people and some of the other sections of the population are citizens of this country by birth, and the rest by registration.

We maintain that any decisions that affect the present and future of this country must be made by all the citizens, irrespective of their colour, creed or station in life. But, as we observe, since the occupation of this country by Europeans in the mid 1890s, all political, economic, financial, administrative and military control has remained an exclusive preserve of the European section of our population, so that the direction of the affairs of the country took since then, was, and is still being determined by this section of the population.

This position has been, and is still being maintained by ingeniously worded legislation and various legal instruments, and has effectively kept Africans and other non-European people of this country out of full participation in the affairs of the country. The rate and spate of this type of legislation, which became much more discriminatory and oppressive, increased with the granting of responsible government in 1923. The electoral Act was changed each time it was realized an appreciable number of Africans would satisfy the required qualifications for the vote (property, income and some knowledge of English). The Land Apportionment Act and other related legislation were used to place impediments in the way of African advancement.

It was when the African people realized that their fellow white citizens did not intend playing fair with them under existing constitutional arrangements that they called on Britain to make new arrangements that would place political power in the hands of all the citizens (one man, one vote) and then grant independence to the country. It was during this constitutional dispute between the people of this country and the British government that the minority Rhodesia Front government declared illegal independence. This was regarded by the African people of this country not just as a rebellious act against the Queen, but as an affront to them as well. It was plain to them that UDI was aimed at thwarting their legitimate political aspirations permanently.

It has also to be remembered that in preparing for their treasonous act, the Rhodesian Front government arrested and detained, without trial, all their opponents and also extracted, from the then Governor, a state of emergency by falsehood.

The British government, under Mr Harold Wilson, declared to the world that the Rhodesia Front government had rebelled against the Queen and that the rebellion had to be brought to an end; this was supported by the Conservatives in the House of Commons. The people in this country, on their part, did all they could to oppose the rebellion. Others left the country to stage their opposition from abroad. As a result of this, many were arrested and sentenced to death, and others to long terms of imprisonment. Many are today still in the death-cells, others are serving their long terms of imprisonment and yet others are exiles in foreign countries.

All these people, according to these proposals, are to be left to the mercy of those who took an illegal act (and rebelled against the Queen) to do what they please with them. It is the African people who are today treated as if it were they who committed the rebellion and not the Rhodesia Front. The way negotiations for these proposals were carried out, with complete exclusion of the African people, makes them feel slighted by the British government. They will have to be excused, therefore, if they regard this to be a question of 'my brother, wrong or right'.

These proposals must be viewed with the background in the preceding paragraphs firmly in people's minds. The question to be asked is this: 'Do these proposals attempt to solve all or any of the above basic problems of this country?' To us the answer is an emphatic 'NO!'. These proposals are a superficial modification of the 1969 illegal republican constitution, whose main purpose is to entrench, maintain and enforce oppressive and discriminatory practices in this country permanently. Are the African people of this country expected to accept a constitution whose purpose is to entrench half the country (44,948,300 acres) for use by 249,000 people of European descent (including Asian and coloured people) while $5\frac{1}{2}$ million of them (said to stand a chance of doubling in 20 years) are to share the other half? Are they expected to accept that all the towns in their country that they, together with the other sections of the population, built are to be European areas permanently? NO! This we cannot accept.

We are more than convinced that to allow entrenchment of racial division of land in the constitution of our country in the manner suggested in these proposals is to allow entrenchment of mistrust and conflict. How can we hope to build a united people and nation on a divided foundation?

As we have stated above, UDI intervened while there was a constitutional dispute between the African people on the one hand and the British and Rhodesian government on the other. These proposals do not attempt to solve this basic constitutional dispute. If anything, they aggravate the situation. The aim of these proposals, as we see it, is to end the derived dispute between the Rhodesian rebel government and the British government, leaving the constitutional problem as it affects the majority of the people in a worse position than it was before the declaration of illegal independence. The proposals are an attempt by the British government to recognize UDI and to get the African people, against whose interests UDI was taken, to endorse it. We cannot agree to this, Lord Pearce. Our answer is an emphatic 'NO!' We reject these proposals in the strongest of terms.

Sir Alec Douglas-Home is reported as saying, if the answer is 'no', there will be no further negotiations. This to us is a fatalistic attitude. The African people are not saying 'no' to a genuine settlement of the real problem of their country; they are saying 'no' to proposals which, if accepted, are bound to make their country a permanent area of conflict. The African people want a settlement that will bring about a reconciliation between our peoples; not one that is aimed at only reconciling Britain and the Smith regime as these proposals do. We expect Britain to respect our stand and call a constitutional conference to discuss the future of our country. No matter how long it may take, Britain, together with white and black citizens, must find the right answer for the sake of our country. . . .

The so much talked about unimpeded progress to parity and majority rule by Africans is so impeded by this legislation that one cannot see how it can ever be achieved.

It is suggested in the proposals that Africans can move towards this goal by increasing their numbers on the African Higher Roll. This can be done by a big number of Africans satisfying voters' qualifications as contained in Appendix I of the proposals (Appendix A of this document).

This they can do by either acquiring immovable property of a specified value, or income at a specified rate per annum, or a combination of four years of secondary education of prescribed standard and a lesser value or rate of the other two.

Let us examine each of these requirements and the prospects of Africans acquiring them in sufficiently large numbers for the purposes of the African Higher Roll under existing legislation and administrative arrangements.

1. *Ownership of farm or land*

African *per capita* land is about nine acres. Approximately 95 per cent of this is communal land and therefore cannot be used for qualification purposes. Even if this land was turned to individual ownership its value would be too low for the requirements.

The remaining five per cent of African land is made up of purchase areas, parks and wild life areas and specially designated land. Of this, land open to individual ownership, i.e. purchase area, amounts to only 3½ million acres as against 38,671,232 acres for Europeans. If divided into 300 acre plots (as many African holdings are), only about 12,000 people would own land. The value of these small farms is far below the required value for the vote unless heavily developed. Those Africans who own some of these small farms have found it almost impossible to raise development funds. The nature and constitution of the Agricultural Finance Corporation is such that small African farmers stand very little chance of financial assistance, if at all.

2. Ownership of house or building

Ownership of houses or buildings in appreciable numbers can only be achieved in urban areas for obvious reasons. As shown in Appendix C all urban areas in this country, according to the Land Tenure Act, are in the European area, and entrenched in the constitution. This being the case, whatever house or building that the African may own in these areas, is dependent on what European-controlled municipal councils may provide under strict government supervision.

It is generally accepted that commerce and industry in any country grow in urban areas: as these areas are European-owned, whatever commercial or industrial undertakings Africans may carry out are those that individual European municipal councils may allow, and because of the nature of land tenure in these European-owned African townships, it has been found to be almost impossible for financial institutions to extend credit to African businessmen and for building societies to give loans for either dwelling or business premises.

As the position is as stated above, we cannot see how Africans can increase their numbers on the African Higher Roll appreciably by ownership of immovable property of any kind.

3. Education

Educational qualification required for combination with either income or immovable property is 'four years secondary education of prescribed standard'. In the first place, European education is free and compulsory; African education is not. Only 12½ per cent of African children passing through primary schools may proceed to four years' secondary education, irrespective of the availability of funds for secondary education. In this way the number of Africans with a four-year secondary education is kept in check each year as against that of Europeans. (See Appendix D).

Further, African education is plagued by a number of restrictive regulations and gradings that do not apply to European education. Different examinations, certificates and nomenclature between African and European education, has in many ways militated against the African school-leaver. The fact that there are two education departments in one country has been used, and will continue to be used, to devalue African education for career purposes and hence political purposes. Under the present educational set up Africans have no chance of following an accepted technical or commercial career. Junior secondary schools, as provided by the African Education Department for Africans only, are a very poor substitute; and if money promised by Britain in the proposals is given, most of it will be spent on this type of secondary education (which is regarded safe for voting purposes).

4. *Income*

The difference between the annual average earnings of Africans and Europeans as shown in Appendix E for the year 1970, shows that the number of Africans earning the required income for the purpose of registering on the African Higher Roll must be very low indeed. The African earning capacity cannot be expected to increase appreciably for a very long time to come for various reasons. Rhodesian traditional prejudice and discrimination, undeclared job reservation, differential educational qualifications which militate against the African school-leaver, European skilled workers' refusal to train African apprentices and different racial pay scales for people doing the same type of work are examples of this discriminatory practice which permeate all sectors of employment in the country, public or private.

In the teaching service, conditions of service, pay, leave, pension schemes etc., for African teachers are far below those of their European counterpart of similar qualifications. In the uniformed services, army, police and prisons, there are two racial streams, with the African occupying the lower stream with its inferior conditions of service, accompanied by promotional prospects of not higher than non-commissioned officer.

In the civil service, the racially-orientated and constituted civil service Board has kept employment in all branches of the service a complete preserve for people of European descent; except in one or two professional branches where a few Africans are employed. This exclusion of Africans in the public service extends to the judiciary.

Under these circumstances there are no prospects for Africans increasing their numbers on the African Higher Voters' Roll sufficiently to bring about political change or parity, within a period less than a century.

It may be possible that at the time of the implementation of the proposals initial numbers registered on the African Higher Roll may gain them two seats; but thereafter the increase on the European roll will outpace the increase on the African roll because of the bigger number of European school-leavers, who, because of their colour, will earn the required income. Added to this will be numbers of European immigrants who qualify for the vote after only two years' stay in the country. It is estimated that within two years of settlement there will be 30,000 immigrants, this number increasing to between 25,000 and 35,000 per year thereafter. The chances of Africans increasing their numbers in proportions that will swell the African Higher Roll are very bleak indeed.

We know that it will be said that some of the points we have raised in the preceding paragraphs may be alleviated by the implementation of Section III and VII (1) of the proposals. To this we would like to say the institution of the commission as proposed in Section III of the proposals is irrelevant in that it is based on the acceptance of a constitution that entrenches separation and discrimination. The most that this commission can do is to find ways of cushioning discriminatory practices sanctioned by the constitution. The terms of reference of this commission (Appendix IV) support our conclusions on it.

Section VII (1) is to us meaningless as we have heard similar words before. Such important issues as these cannot be left in such vague and nebulous terms as has been done in Section VII (1) of the proposals.

5. *Declaration of Rights*
Much has been said about the protection of individual rights by the Declaration of Rights as contained in the proposals. But, looking through them, we have discovered that the nature and extent of exceptions in the Declaration of Rights render it ineffectual and of little value to the citizen. It cannot escape our attention that, under the Declaration as it stands in these proposals, courts would not be able to exercise any powers if measures taken against any individual or group of individuals were taken under legislation passed more than ten years before the Declaration of Rights came into force, or any law that was part of the law of Rhodesia before the fixed date. It is quite plain that these provisions are aimed at protecting all oppressive and discriminatory legislation.

We submit that with powers contained in, for instance, the Law and Order (Maintenance) Act, the Unlawful Organizations Act, etc., an unscrupulous ruling party dedicated to white supremacy, can render the working of a genuine representative African party impossible in a number of ways and courts would be powerless to intervene.

It is not impossible for such a ruling party to restrict or detain its African opponents a few years or days or even weeks before an election in order to render them ineligible for election to parliament under the provisions of the Electoral Act or to African Councils under the African Councils Act; here again courts would be powerless to intervene.

One would have thought that the Declaration of Rights would have been made to protest effectively the election of people to Parliament, African Councils and to the Council of Chiefs. The two last mentioned bodies are electoral colleges and yet the manner of election to them under the respective Acts is so appallingly open to abuse by the ruling party and the courts are unable to mediate.

Last, but not by any means least, in these proposals, the House of Assembly can renew a state of emergency at intervals of nine months. During this period the Declaration of Rights would be, in a way, suspended. As we have experienced in the last seven years, a government bent on suppressing normal African political activity can declare a state of emergency on the section of the country where its opponents reside and thereby keep them in detention indefinitely. This was done by the Rhodesia Front government in 1964/5 when emergencies were declared in Highfields African Township, Gonakudzingwa and Nkai District, before the country-wide emergency of 25 November 1965.

Finally, we would like to emphasize to the commission that we unreservedly reject these proposals because they do not satisfy universally accepted conditions of independence and self-determination for all our people; they are racial and discriminatory, and we believe that if implemented they will engender feelings of hostility between black and white citizens of our country and bring about bloodshed and untold human suffering. This must not be allowed to happen. We, therefore, appeal to you, Lord Pearce, to impress upon the British government to abandon these proposals and summon a constitutional conference at which leaders of all sections of our population will take part. We know there are formidable problems to be encountered but we believe that with goodwill by all of us they can be overcome.

We on our part are prepared to work resolutely for a constitutional settlement that will give peace and security to all citizens of our country irrespective of colour.

APPENDIX A

European roll and African higher roll qualifications

(a) Income at the rate of not less than $1,800 per annum during the two years preceding date of claim for enrolment, or ownership of immovable property of value of not less than $3,600.

or

(b) (i) Income at the rate of not less than $1,200 per annum during the two years preceding date of claim for enrolment, or ownership of immovable property of the value of not less than $2,400; and

(ii) Four years secondary education of prescribed standard.

APPENDIX B

(1) European Land: 44,948,300 acres. *Per capita* European land 168 acres.
(2) African Land: 44,949,100 acres. *Per capita* African land 9 acres.

APPENDIX C

Population in country:	
1. African:	5,220,000
2. European:	249,000
3. Asian:	9,000
4. Coloured:	16,000

Urban population:	
1. African:	752,000
2. European:	198,000
3. Asian:	8,480
4. Coloured:	14,040

Number of Urban Areas in the whole country	
1. European Areas:	12
2. African Areas:	NIL

APPENDIX D

Four years secondary education of prescribed standard for 1970

1. African school leavers:	2,545
2. European school leavers:	4,329
3. Asian and Coloured leavers:	599

APPENDIX E

Annual average earnings for Africans and Europeans for the year 1970

	Africans $	Europeans $
Agriculture and Forestry	153	2,437
Mining and Quarrying	343	4,456
Manufacturing	478	3,606
Electricity and Water	448	3,840
Construction	428	3,273
Finance and Insurance	714	3,280
Distribution	454	2,654
Transport	626	3,000

Services	Africans	Europeans
	$	$
Public Administration	409	3,120
Education	590	2,709
Health	579	2,383

34 FROLIZI: memorandum to the Liberation Committee of the Organization of African Unity. January 1972

The Zimbabwe liberation question is a matter which must be very familiar to you all now. A lot of memoranda are lined up in your files. These express the old content and forms of our struggle against the British ruling circles and the racist colonial-settler regime in our country. They must also in a way outline the history of the hostile conflict between the people of Zimbabwe and their colonial enemy. To date, this conflict is marked by the recent Anglo-Rhodesian settlement, an act which not only affects us adversely but also has far-reaching harmful consequences on the whole of Africa in terms of the designs of imperialism on the entire continent.

2. The African people of Zimbabwe have rejected the designs of British imperialism on their country:

(a) they rejected the whole settler-colonial regime a long time ago;

(b) they rejected the 1961 constitution;

(c) they rejected the 1965 unilateral declaration of independence;

(d) and down in their hearts they reject the 1971 Anglo-Rhodesian 'Independence' settlement—the so-called test of acceptability is a face-saving and deceptive imperialist strategem on the part of the British ruling circles and their Rhodesian kith and kin.

In this light, it is very important to look into the conditions of the Zimbabwe National Liberation Movement.

3. First we have to consider briefly some of the objective conditions. There is little doubt that there is a mature revolutionary situation in our country:

(a) poverty and disgusting suffering have been aggravated to extreme proportions as a result of the exploitative land, educational and industrial policies of the oppressive racist settler-colonial Rhodesian regime and the imperialist British ruling circles;

(b) the African people on the whole do not want to live in the old way, i.e. under settler-colonial domination and exploitation; and it is increasingly becoming impossible for the colonial rulers to rule in the old way, i.e. without increasingly resorting to exclusive dependence on the use of their military-police machine to maintain settler-colonial law and order;

(c) there is considerable increase in independent action on the part of the Zimbabwe masses themselves. The Tangwena type struggles, the economic struggles of the workers and the protest actions of the students and other social sectors demonstrate this.

4. But it is the subjective conditions that have proved inadequate, not a hopeless mess altogether. We all know that for a revolutionary liberation struggle to turn into an effective and victorious reality the people must be ready and able to undertake systematic revolutionary mass action, the people must be organized against the common enemy. In fact, the decisive factors of the victory of a struggle like ours are:

(a) mobilization of the whole people for the revolutionary struggle for liberation by organizing them into the framework of a single united front against the common enemy;

(b) ensuring clear-sighted leadership for the national liberation movement;

(c) building up and developing a revolutionary army of the people.

These three factors have not obtained on the Zimbabwe scene and this is why the rate of advance of our liberation struggle has been such a big disappointment, not only to our reliable supporters such as the Organization of African Unity but also to us the people of Zimbabwe themselves.

5. This the people of Zimbabwe have of late realized. Precisely, they have at last settled the basic subjective condition of victory in their national liberation struggle. They have called for total national unity at home and abroad, concretely under the banners of the African National Council (ANC) and the Front for the Liberation of Zimbabwe (FROLIZI). These have ushered in the end of the ZAPU/ZANU split and [personality clashes] and shall ensure that there is clear-sighted leadership.

As the young militants in Zimbabwe have said in a note to the African governments and other interested bodies, dated 11 November 1971, 'The Front for the Liberation of Zimbabwe represents a genuine landmark in the freedom struggle: it demonstrates that personality, principles (so-called, party or faction) should be subordinate to the need of revolutionary action . . . The young generation here . . . is not interested in the division's squabbles of people concerned with the future of their political positions. To them, ZAPU and ZANU are episodes of the freedom struggle, and as such should be side-stepped at this crucial moment . . .'

6. Of course, one cannot at this stage overlook the relation of the old to the new in the qualitative change that has taken place on the Zimbabwe National Liberation scene. The birth of FROLIZI and the ANC is in fact a resolution of contradictions; it is a negation of the old and the obsolete by the new and progressive elements of the Zimbabwe Liberation Movement. It is evident that such a birth could not have been and has not been a simple struggle.

7. In line with expectations, when the idea of total national unity was seriously launched the old and obsolete elements in both ZAPU and ZANU sprang up against it. And up to this day, they continue in their desperate struggle against it, using of course, all sorts of cheap opportunistic tactics to hoodwink the world.

8. In negotiations and detailed talks that were strictly limited to us Zimbabweans, the anti-unity elements came out openly against merging ZAPU and ZANU into a single united front of all Zimbabweans; but of course in international circles they preached that they were not against unity, that all they wanted was to be consulted and presented with an acceptable formula by the pro-unity people—that kind of double talk. This sing-song has been going on for almost two years now and it should be clear to anybody interested in the liberation of Zimbabwe who exactly is for Unity and who is against.

Mister President,

Your Excellencies,

9. The real point at issue is that the old and absolute elements are bent on continuing with their old unproductive ways and safeguarding the future of their political positions—personally and ethnically, while the new and progressive elements have resolutely undertaken to give a new and productive content and form to the Zimbabwe liberation struggle. *This is the point; this is the basic contradiction.* And here it is certain which side will win in the end; the main direction of the Zimbabwe liberation struggle is the irrepressible advance of the new and progressive. There may be setbacks on the way, but this will not alter the triumph of the new progressive forces.

10. Therefore, it is our submission that the Organization of African Unity should dump the effete relics of the past phases of the Zimbabwe liberation struggle and give full support to the new and progressive forces who are determined to wage a resolute people's armed struggle for national liberation.

11. Briefly and to conclude, there are two central issues before us at this meeting:

(a)   to finally settle the question of the united front;

(b)   to obtain a recommendation for the recognition of the united front.

We have come here to give concrete substance to the central requirement of our situation—that is, the unity of all the oppressed people of Zimbabwe.

12. Unity has been given concrete and practical meaning in the form of FROLIZI and the ANC.

13. The task of the Committee today, as we see it, is not to set up more reconciliation commissions, but to lend support to and consolidate the unity already achieved.

14. The militants and members of FROLIZI are prepared at this meeting of the OAU Liberation Committee to unite immediately with any party, group or individuals that are prepared to unite in a national united front with one structure and centre of command; they are prepared to unite now; they are against any further debates or formal negotiations and talks; what is needed now is concrete action.

15. If this unity that Zimbabwe so much needs, and that so many have worked for so assiduously cannot be arrived at by, or forced on all of us at this meeting, then we and the fighters we represent shall count on our own efforts to consolidate the united front we have already concretized.

16. If the Liberation Committee is unable to unite all of us at this meeting, then we would request the Committee to play its part in consolidating the existing forces of unity by resolutely recommending the recognition of the united forces of FROLIZI.

17. Such a firm recommendation would greatly assist us in many ways.

— It would help in the movement of our militants across certain national boundaries, which is virtually impossible now.

— It would enable us to use radio facilities in friendly neighbour states, aimed at mobilizing our people for the liberation struggle.

— It would help to make available military material and supplies now barred to us.

— It would enable governments to deal officially with the united front and provide information and diplomatic facilities.

Mister President,

Your Excellencies,

18. We can tell you from our experience during the last three months that it is very difficult to operate without OAU recognition.

It embarrasses the host governments, making the work of the liberation movement extremely difficult. And at home, non-recognition to the pro-unity forces will demoralize the united masses.

19. Finally, as we see it, the broadened national united front that should emerge from Benghazi should have the specific task of reactivating the

armed struggle in our country.

20. FROLIZI's 'Programme of Action' has been presented before you. It shows our firm intention to increase recruitment into the guerilla ranks, and our resolute determination to heighten, qualitatively and quantitatively, the scope of our guerilla operations.

21. We are committed not to repeat the mistakes of the past when trained young men possessing all the attributes of excellent fighters:
— resolute determination
— singleness of purpose, and
— actual capability to fight
were left to idle for years in so-called transit camps.

22. We have outlined in our 'Programme of Action', on the basis of a thorough and scientific analysis of the enemy's characteristics and our own, and on the concrete conditions of the battlefield, the strategy of a long-term people's war of liberation.

Mister President, Your distinguished Excellencies, the armed struggle in Zimbabwe cannot be victoriously concluded in six months, nor in two years, nor in five years.

23. This unassailable truth imposes upon us who are charged with leading and directing this difficult and complex struggle, to rid ourselves of any and all illusions, to come down to earth, and to work out from theory, experience and concrete practice, the correct lines and methods for an effective and successful armed struggle.

24. As fighters, Mister President and Your Excellencies, we know that the penalty for a false military theory is military defeat, and the cost of military defeat is the butchery of tens, even hundreds of very good men of the people.

25. That is why we do not believe in sacrificing any of our fine comrades in futile and adventuristic harrassing actions calculated to force Whitehall to call for negotiations, or calculated to impress the OAU that FROLIZI is fighting.

26. We shall carry out our operational plans stage by stage, carefully and calculatedly, always conscious that spontaneity has never made revolution.

27. Mister President, and your Excellencies, in line with our commitment to a fighting united front, and not to another debating and welfare society, we have completely integrated the political and military aspects of the struggle.

28. In a serious armed struggle, we do not believe that you can have anything less.

29. In the Zimbabwe liberation movement, anyway, we cannot longer afford the luxury of arm-chair revolutionaries and tired politicians who

have little knowledge about the difficult and complex work of guerilla warfare to any longer plan operations and battles from the relative comfort of their offices in Lusaka.

30. Thus in our new front, the accent is on fighting, and the leadership and directions of this fighting has been placed firmly and securely in the hands of the revolutionary fighters—the men and women who bear the brunt of this struggle.

That is why also, Mister President and your Excellencies, our headquarters is at the front and there it shall stay.

31. We believe that the prime role of leadership in a struggle such as we are waging is to show an example in courage, self-sacrifice and self-abnegation.

32. The stationing of the headquarters at the front not only gives morale to the fighters, but also lessens the dangers of infiltration by the enemy, leakage of information etc. Above all, it ensures the effective and efficient execution of the war functions of the National United Front.

33. Mister President, and Your Excellencies, we believe that if we permanently re-activate the armed struggle in Zimbabwe, we shall also be simultaneously fulfilling our duty of solidarity with other fighting fronts in Southern Africa.

34. Particularly, a reactivation of combat in our sector shall, in our view, relieve the gallant fighters of FRELIMO who have now carried their heroic war south of the Zambezi in Tete Province, and are being met by two pressures from the Portuguese and the Rhodesians.

35. Mister President, Your Distinguished Excellencies, we believe that as a people fighting a just and popular war of liberation the masses and their participation are absolutely the most decisive force in our struggle.

36. Their participation, and the level of that participation is the determining factor of whether we succeed or fail.

37. That is why we have mapped our concrete plans, together with the activists at home, to arouse, educate, organize, mobilize and galvanize our people for a protracted national war of liberation.

38. Militarily, what little weaponry and equipment we had, and that we could lay our hands on, is being transferred to where it properly belongs, to where it can be the midwife of historical change.

39. Thus FROLIZI is busy laying the firm foundations for a long-term peoples war of liberation.

40. Our planning and preparation for those factors that we control and determine has been thorough.

41. However, there are other crucial factors that we do not, at present, control, factors that can hasten or delay the day of liberation.

42. Some of these factors are controlled by members of this committee,

singly or collectively.

43. We are convinced that without formal support to the forces of unity in the Zimbabwe national liberation movement from this august Committee, these factors beyond our control will, in effect slow down or frustrate our efforts for a more effective armed struggle.

44. It is our sincere hope, Mister President, Your Excellencies and brothers in the struggle, that members of this Committee, singly or collectively, will, in the Zimbabwe liberation movement, be on the side of those that are geared, or are prepared to gear themselves IN UNITY, to tackle the principal contradiction by fighting, and not by further debating.

I thank you, Mister President.

CHAPTER EIGHT

A NEW ERA

35 African National Council: aims and objects. Salisbury, 10 March 1972

On this tenth day of March 1972, at Highfield, Salisbury, we here assembled, claiming no more than to be heirs to the people's struggle which has ceaselessly been waged since the imposition of alien rule in 1890, in the name of Almighty God, who, in His love and mercy, created all people and races in His image, do hereby proclaim, constitute and declare the AFRICAN NATIONAL COUNCIL to be one sole voice and instrument of the African masses of Zimbabwe and all people of goodwill, in their just and normal struggle for national emancipation from the yoke of a racist and oppressive minority rule. Accordingly, the African National Council is born today as a result of the need and demands of primarily the African people and other racial groups of this country. And we here and now summon every African in this land, young or old, rich or poor, educated or uneducated, chief or subject, and those members of other races dedicated to the establishment of human brotherhood, to recognize the trumpet we here sound and to rally around us, so that together, we continue our arduous journey to Zimbabwe in a Christian and non-violent manner.

BELIEFS

1. This council believes in the power of the unity of the African masses in the imperative need for the opposition of those elements of forces which seek to sow the seeds of division among our people. Divided we will remain slaves and strangers in the land of our birth. United though we may suffer, we shall toil, but with dignity, until we are free. We should, therefore, be warned that our worst enemies are those who seek to divide us and those who labour to keep us in perpetual oppression, be they black or white.

2. We believe in the invincibility of numbers of the masses of men and women of goodwill in Rhodesia and that the African National Council is truly a grassroots organization in its very scope, membership and spirit.

3. We believe in a government that will establish and promote the sanctity and practice of the essential human freedoms of conscience, of expression, association, religion, assembly and movement of all people irrespective of colour, race or creed.

4. We believe in non-racialism, the universal brotherhood of man under the fatherhood of God. This means forced segregation and forced integration violate the principle of free choice of association.

5. We believe in a non-violent, peaceful, orderly but permanent and continuing struggle to be waged within the Law and for the establishment of a constitutional government.

6. We believe that true peace and harmony among all people and economic stability of this country can only be assured for all time by the establishment of 'the government of the people, by the people and for the people'.

7. We believe that the rights and property of the minority should be protected; we do not however believe in the minority's amassing of social, political and economic privileges at the expense of the freedom of the majority.

DECLARATION

The African National Council solemnly dedicates itself to strive for the realization of those universal human rights conceded to the citizens in all democratic and just societies. This being so,

1. We shall not waver or prevaricate in our demand for the creation, in this country, of a just social order; but shall strive to achieve this justice which is long overdue.

2. We shall not deviate from our just demand for universal adult suffrage.

3. We shall never concede to the fallacy that there is any justification for racial and other forms of discrimination as between one human being against another. Thus, we shall continue to oppose racial bigotry, racial intolerance, class arrogance, the idiocy of tribalism and undeserved economic privileges. And we shall strive to create a nation where black and white can live as children of the one almighty God.

4. We shall never compromise with the sin of greed which is the main characteristic of a minority controlled economy; but will continue to promote a fair and free participation of each and every citizen of this our mother land—rich in natural resources.

5. We shall forever abhor the continued denial, under the pretext of 'preservation of Western Christian civilization', of the masses' demand for legitimate self-determination.

6. We shall never support nor respect a system which lays emphasis on Law and Order at the expense of charity, justice and human dignity, but will continue to call upon the conscience of this country to influence the establishment of law and order with justice.
7. We shall require and desire nothing less than self determination. . . .

EXTERNAL RELATIONS

We declare our solidarity with those international organizations dedicated to the peaceful creation and preservation of the basic universal human rights and the brotherhood of man under the Fatherhood of God.

CHALLENGE TO THE NATION

Having stated our beliefs and declarations we now challenge all people of this country—Africans, Asians, Coloureds and Europeans who sincerely and honestly seek a genuine peace and mutual understanding to join us.

Only as we work together can we bring our country out of its present political deadlock.

We challenge the people of this country to come out of the current political dream-world by realizing that what has been called 'peace' and 'happiness' and 'good race relations' are, in face, repressed fear, restless silence, forced tolerance and hidden hatred of one another.

We call and call again to make people aware that our race relations are deteriorating and that they will continue to do so until all discriminatory legislation in this land has been removed.

We challenge our Rhodesian whites to realize the simple psychological fact that no one should expect love from a person he hates: or expect respect from a person he disrespects; or expect admiration from a person he despises, nor loyalty from a person whom he does not love.

We finally and particularly direct this challenge to the Europeans of Rhodesia that now is the day to sit down with us and, in peaceful negotiations, try and find a mutually agreeable formula for achieving racial harmony. This is absolutely necessary for social stability, economic growth and a secure future for all of us and our children.

Time for such negotiations is fast running out. Believe it! This is the day that circumstance and fate or, as we want to express it, God has led us all.

If we want to be blessed and not cursed by our children and children's children we have no time to lose.

We challengingly remind our African people that whatever position we hold, or status we enjoy we are all condemned as BLACK PEOPLE in this country. All are treated as second if not third class citizens. We therefore feel very sad when we see some of our people and hear about their behaviour which points out to the fact that they have lost the purpose and goal and are living and fighting for their own stomachs and self interests instead of liberation for all which should be every sane person's goal.

We have seen signs of these kinds of people who are bought to work out division, to work out frustration, to work out embarrassment and to work out perpetual slavery of the Africans. Shame!

We challenge our African people to stop fulfilling the accusation that 'The worst enemy of Africans are Africans themselves' and instead become our own liberators, by stopping all sorts of traitorous actions against the African United fronts for liberation and labour for the common goal of independence.

We call our African people to praise, and congratulate our fathers—the chiefs, for their courageous stand and true representation of their people which they displayed during the test of Acceptability of the Anglo-Rhodesian Settlement Proposals. We trust this is the beginning of a new day in Rhodesia for Africans.

We challenge the clergy of this country to stop preaching the useless and archaic doctrine of 'pie in the sky' and start vigorously to preach a 'whole gospel for the whole man'. To teach our people that politics is not a 'dirty game,' but that what makes politics dirty is the kind of people who play politics and how they participate in it. That the definition of politics is 'the science and art of governing people' and that there can never be any evil in that kind of science or art. There is no virtue in participating or not participating in politics, but Christians must be involved when the political system disturbs people and churches such as in the case of the Land Tenure Act.

We challenge our African people to be purpose-centred rather than personality-centred.

We challenge our African people to realize that, while we have chosen a peaceful and loving method of approach, in UNITY we have more than a bomb can achieve. Therefore, be UNITED, be UNITED until UNITY is strength and strength becomes POWER.

Your Servant
BISHOP ABEL T. MUZOREWA
President.
African National Council

36 Bishop Abel Muzorewa:
The role of the church in liberation.
Address to the General Conference of the
United Methodist Church, Atlanta, 22 April 1972

Africa is a wonderful land; Rhodesia is a beautiful country—at least the tourists tell us so. Whenever I hear this, I am reminded of the beautiful gate of the temple described in the Book of Acts, through which many people passed without seeing the cripple lying nearby. These travellers fail to see a crippled nation of $5\frac{1}{2}$ million Africans who live in misery in the land of their birth. Only a few, like Peter and John, see the suffering through Christian eyes and see the need for liberation in the name of Jesus Christ of Nazareth.

Rhodesia was enslaved as soon as she was colonized and her oppression was finalized by the Unilateral Declaration of Independence from Great Britain in 1965. Since that time black Rhodesians have been victims of violence, both bloody and bloodless.

The Rhodesian government proclaims to the world that it is 'preserving civilized standards'. It compares its declaration of independence in 1965 to that of the American colonies in 1776. But we all know that the difference is that America was seeking for freedom, but there the intention was to enslave the Africans.

What are the 'civilized standards' which are being preserved in Rhodesia today?

— The five per cent of the population which is white maintains political control over the 95 per cent of the population which is black.

— Whites elect 50 members of Parliament while Africans elect eight under highly restrictive franchise laws.

— Every African opposition party formed in the last 14 years has been banned.

— Hundreds of Africans have been arrested and placed indefinitely in detention centres under laws that allow for no trial, no statement of charges, and no appeal.

— Thousands have been imprisoned under a wide range of vague laws that are interpreted to cover almost any kind of behaviour. For example, Section 24 of the Law and Order Maintenance Act of 1962 states that any person who 'behaves in a manner which is likely to make some other person apprehensive as to what might happen . . .' can be imprisoned for up to ten years.

— A person is presumed guilty unless he can prove his innocence under these laws.

— Half the land, 45 million acres, is reserved for the use of the small number of white farmers, while Africans are assigned to the other half, located in dry or mountainous areas.

— During the seven-month dry season, when no rain falls, hunger, malnutrition, and disease are widespread.

— In urban areas, blacks must live in overcrowded townships where often two or three families must share one room.

— Thousands of unemployed compete for jobs that provide only a bare subsistence averaging $26 a month while whites average $300 a month.

— The government spends an average of $30 a year for the education of an African child while spending $300 for that of a white child.

— Rhodesia's segregation and discrimination legislation form 95 per cent of the prescription of *apartheid*. They do not have to form new laws to have perfect *apartheid*. All they need is money to implement it.

But the greatest tragedy of all is the crippling of human dignity by a system that constantly denies the sacred value of the individual. I ask you, are these the kinds of civilized standards that Christ calls us to preserve?

The Christian church in Rhodesia faced this question early in 1972. In January the British government began considering the recognition of Rhodesian independence. At this crucial hour, in the absence of African political parties, the church became the channel of expression for a voiceless, wounded, silent majority. Calling for no independence without firm guarantees of freedom and justice for all, the Christian Council of Rhodesia met and looked at the Anglo-Rhodesian settlement proposals 'with a Christian eye', and we all agreed that the proposals were not just. It was then that some clergymen made up their minds to reject the immorality. The five Roman Catholic bishops, the United Church of Christ, and the United Methodist Annual Conference spoke with conviction and rejected the proposals. The British Methodist Church did not either reject them or accept them. The will of the people became crystallized in the formation of the new African National Council, a grass-roots organization which I serve as President. It united people of all organizations, including ZAPU and ZANU. We are determined to achieve the rule of justice through non-violence, negotiation and reason. But the restraint of the people who look to us for leadership has its limits. Time is running out. Rhodesia is on a collision course with disaster. As a Christian, I ask myself, is there any way to avoid the slaughter of hundreds of Rhodesians, black and white? To whom can we turn for help?

I appeal to you, the members of this General Conference, from the developing and industrialized nations, to call upon your governments for renewed support for United Nations economic sanctions against Rhodesia as the strongest and last alternative to bloodshed. We are concerned particularly about the violations of these sanctions by West Germany, France, Italy and Japan. We know that these countries are trading with Rhodesia because of the presence there of large numbers of automobiles and electronic equipment that originate in these areas. We are especially hurt by the vital moral and economic support that the United States is giving the Rhodesian government through its purchase of chrome ore. I wonder if my American friends are aware of the implication of this in terms of our grave need of a freedom relationship in present and in future.

This is the plea of an oppressed and crippled people in the midst of a 'beautiful Rhodesia'. Can you see and hear what we say before it is too late? Would you please join us in building a Rhodesia commanded to rise up in the name of Jesus of Nazareth, where freedom and justice can rule?

The church should be complimented for the freedom which has come to other parts of Africa. Although some people give credit to Communism which should be given to Christ and His church, we know that 90 per cent of the educated people in Africa and its leadership are products of the church, and we understand that by the end of the century about two-thirds of the African population south of the Sahara will be Christian. We need you, the world church, to surround us with your ALL.

Our own United Methodist Church in Rhodesia is thriving under those oppressive conditions beginning in particular with the deportation of Bishop Dodge and other missionaries from Rhodesia as a result of their sacrificial and effective witness. The church is growing rapidly in membership. Ministerial training, stewardship and evangelism are strong. Relationship between missionaries and nationals is maturing. The church is very vital and alive.

Are you going to help us to continue to command Rhodesia to rise up in the name of Christ? I know you will, for I know that in spite of all our weaknesses and criticism, we are the best half of Christ on earth today.

I love the church. I love you all!

37 African National Council: policy after the Pearce report

The primary objective of the ANC, following the rejection by the African people of the settlement proposals put forward by Sir Alec Douglas Home and Ian Smith, is to ensure that full discussions between the various communities take place with a view to discovering the most effective means for a transition to majority rule in Zimbabwe. This process, we are aware, will be difficult, and will involve the deployment of political factors inside the country and outside. As an active political movement within the country, the ANC intends to pursue by the methods available within the limited political situation every means of awakening political awareness among the mass, and to demonstrate to the minorities that the majority rule is the alternative to the destitute policies of the Rhodesia Front, which are leading the country to ruin.

NATIONAL CONVENTION

The first step in this process has already been announced. The ANC has called for a National Convention of all interested groups to take place. This is intended to take place in four stages:

1. *A conference of representatives* of all political parties, all churches, all business interests, all trade unions, all civil service organizations, local authorities and, in fact, all the groups consulted by the Pearce Commission.

The purpose of the conference will be to:
(a) identify the precise conflict;
(b) demonstrate the advantages of a settlement which is based upon the interests of all the parties to the conflict;
(c) discuss, and thus dispel, the fears of each racial group by reference to possible general constitutional problems and protection.

2. *A national committee.*
Such a committee will be established with a view to its making an approach to the British government, the Rhodesia Front and the African political leaders. The British Foreign Secretary has already indicated his view that the initiative must now be taken by the people of the country itself. This the ANC takes to mean that the UK government will seriously consider proposals emanating from the 'people of Rhodesia as a whole'. The ANC initiative has already been welcomed by the white-led Centre

Party, but rejected by Smith on the grounds that it is 'political opportunism', though the reason is probably more accurately stated by Idensohn, the leader of the Rhodesia National Party, who refused to consider it as it would be 'political suicide' for anyone relying upon the white electorate. Until there are sufficient reasons for the minority to see advantages in talking to the majority, this will remain true. Reasons would include: (negatively) the increased deprivation and insecurity brought about by sanctions and diplomatic ostracism, insecurity resulting from external military action, potential intervention by the UK or the Security Council; (positively) such reasons could be found in the growing demonstration of African political organizations, independent of the existing racist structure, which the ANC will attempt to build.

3. *Meeting of officials*
Officers representing the UK government, the Rhodesia Front and the African mass will be appointed to work out an agenda for a constitutional conference, and to appoint a chairman and a venue.

4. *The constitutional conference*
After the above preliminaries have been worked out, which may well take a considerable period of time, a conference will be called.

INTERNATIONAL ACTION TO ASSIST THE ACHIEVEMENT OF MAJORITY RULE

A new basis for action
The OAU, the UN, and each individual member state of those organizations, have now a new obligation to assist the people of Zimbabwe, by all possible means, to achieve their freedom. The contradiction of the Pearce Commission is that it gave the African masses their first ever opportunity to express their feelings about the illegal seizure of power by the RF, and the form of government it has imposed on them since 1965. By this single, limited act of self-determination, recorded by Britain's own Commission (which was in no way partisan to the interests of the African people), they have rejected racist government. They accepted the invitation to participate in this experiment with their freedom at great risk to themselves. Many lost their lives, many more lost their liberty. Having made this stand, they are prepared to continue showing not only their rejection but their readiness to seek, at continued risk to themselves, for justice in their own country.

For this reason there are fresh grounds, provided by her own Commission, for the OAU to demand that Britain responds to the evidence and restores legal government to her subjects. She must not be allowed to escape the consequences of her own act.

The same fact provides a reason for the African states themselves to re-dedicate themselves, as the people of Zimbabwe have done, to the task of achieving freedom. The situation demands an imaginative initiative, for to allow the situation to remain would be an encouragement to the white minority to stick to their position.

A new objective

The objective of sanctions against Rhodesia was to bring Smith to the conference table. This they achieved but, as was obvious, this was too limited an objective. The objective now must be to achieve majority rule. Economic sanctions have thus far proved their limited effectiveness. What effect has been achieved is due largely to the efforts of a very few states, which include Zambia and, to some extent, Britain herself. This contribution must be admitted and worked from; there must be no going back upon the situation. The winding up of sanctions is hoped for by Smith, and even appears to be too easily foreseen by the British government. Blatant lack of support by allegedly law abiding states such as the USA does not help the position. But much more dangerous is that the surreptitious evasion of sanctions by states who pretend to apply them is allowed to continue.

An international blockade

The means whereby sanctions are evaded are well documented. They include false documentation relating to origin, and the establishment of false companies all over the world. South Africa and Mozambique are crucial to these techniques. Britain is now using this evasion as a potential reason for allowing sanctions to lapse. The Beira blockade has had total success within its limits. What is now suggested is that the OAU should press for the establishment of an international operation to be conducted on the high seas, to ensure that vessels trading out of ports from those two areas are not carrying goods which originate from Rhodesia. Such goods should be made subject to some form of seizure or identification which, if nothing else, would enable the UK to take action against the goods when they are identified. As with the Beira action, such action will require authority. The obvious choice would be for the Security Council, which, it must be remembered, has already characterized the situation as one which threatens international peace and security, to give such authority to act. In view of Britain's complaints that she alone bears the burden of such action, and despite the point that her burden is of her own making because she has not used force, it may now be opportune for other states to demonstrate their readiness to support justice by acting as participants in such an exercise to prevent the free trade in contraband from Rhodesia. Their willingness to do so would make it that much more difficult for Britain to use her veto against such a proposal. If however Britain did veto such an action, it would be worthwhile to seek a solution via the General Assembly. There is a majority in that body which should be able to give authority, if not mandatory authority, to states who wished to stop such trade. Such an exercise may well be conducted by states with some naval power, as India, Nigeria and Canada. It is suggested that for this purpose the Uniting for Peace formula be revived and used to authorize an international regime of 'visit and search' of all vessels suspected of carrying cargo from Rhodesia. In view of the critical importance of Rhodesia's export trade, it is suggested that the major effort be concentrated in that sector.

Equally, member states of the UN and the OAU have at their disposal weapons to discourage those nations which do not effectively stop their nationals from trading with with Smith. The object must be to prove that business with Smith is bad business.

Individual and joint action against sanction-breakers
Some states, including Japan, West Germany, Switzerland, France and Italy in the west, and Czechoslovakia in the eastern bloc, have been shown to continue their trade with Rhodesia. Britain quite fairly complains of this. What can African states do to stop it? It is suggested that *all* these states and the very companies which are guilty of this action, have greater interests in their trade with the rest of Africa than with Rhodesia. As long as they can have both without having to choose, they will do so. To this extent the burden is upon the African and other states to use the power they have as sovereign states, to show that business with Smith is bad business. It may be noted here that the African people in Rhodesia have made it clear that they are prepared to put up with the extra deprivation which effective sanctions may produce.

Assistance scheme for settlers who wish to leave
There should be a UN or Commonwealth scheme to assist, financially, whites who do not intend to stay in the country under majority rule to resettle in Europe or other countries of their choice. The effect of this will be to reduce support for Smith by the army, the police and the air force. It will also discourage immigrants from going into the country once they see others emigrating.

The above-mentioned points relate to a programme designed to involve Britain and all the communities in Zimbabwe in an eventual settlement based upon their joint interests. In return for a normal economic and diplomatic existence, the minority will realize that it must live in a democratic state. Such an agreement is known to be an outside possibility, but it is worth pursuing.

38 African National Council: Return to legality. Address by Bishop Abel Muzorewa, President. Harry Margolis Hall, Salisbury, 20 July 1972

Many of you will recall the Second World War and the years of agony we all experienced. Some of you still live with the impression that was conveyed to us daily through press, radio and by rumour—not the least about the cruelty and madness of the warfare of German people. I still remember very clearly the concept I had as a fourteen year old boy still in primary school. I was convinced, that if the Germans gained victory in the war, they would be here in no time at all, and we would be treated as animals. I developed a genuine fear and resentment of all Germans.

And how did I come to get rid of my fears of the German people? In 1958 I was studying at the Missouri School of Religion. During one long week-end one of my friends, who was a student pastor, invited me to go with him to his parish. An announcement was given to the parishioners that those who wanted to invite the African guest preacher from Rhodesia could do so. Five of the seven families that invited me for meals were German people. That came like a bombshell to destroy my fears of Germans. Today I love and respect them because I know they are human beings, full of feeling, love and grace.

Fears and resentments also plague us today within our own country. How vitally important it is for us to come together and come to know each other, rather than being misled by rumour and misunderstanding. Therefore I am deeply grateful that we have been given this privilege tonight to speak from the platform of the Harry Margolis Hall to people whom I assume would not normally have had much opportunity to lisen to us.

Early in my remarks let me state very sincerely how grateful many of us feel for the outstanding contributions that have been made to Rhodesia by the white citizens of this country, such as their skills, personal services, capital, but above all their wealth of good-will. There has been built-up over the years an interdependent relationship, which we feel is absolutely essential for a prosperous future.

I come to you as a citizen of Rhodesia by birth, concerned, and deeply so, as you are, about the sad state of affairs in which we find ourselves. My sole interest is to achieve the liberation of all of us. Mr Chairman, I have no personal ambition. I seek no office nor position for myself, only democratic rule for my country. I come also in my capacity as President of the African National Council.

Many of you sit with a question in your mind tonight as to what, in fact, is this ANC?

First, let me say what the African National Council is not. It is not the continuation of any previous organization. It is not a group of political agitators, dictating to five million Africans what they should think or do. It is not organized or controlled by anyone outside the country. It is not made up of hooligans, bent on destruction and violence. It is not responsible, as has been made out, for hostile acts that have occurred in recent months. It is not anti- any racial group.

What, then, is the ANC? It is a spontaneous grassroots movement, which came into being at the time of the settlement proposals, not merely to oppose the proposals but as a means to a greater end. It is the embodiment of the hopes and aspirations of the vast majority of the people of this country as a whole—farmers, trade unionists, teachers, ministers of religion, members of other professions, etc. It has the support of other prominent members of the country, such as a majority of Chiefs and African MPs.

The ANC champions the cause of the full rights of all peoples—Africans, Asians, Europeans, Coloureds. Its membership is wide open to all racial groups.

In terms of doctrine, as stated in the *ANC Manifesto,* 'We shall strive to create a nation where black and white can live as children of the one Almighty God.'

In terms of goals (I quote again from the *Manifesto*) we should 'try to find a mutually agreeable formula for achieving racial harmony. This is absolutely necessary for social stability, economic growth and a secure future for all of us and our children.'

In terms of method, we have pledged ourselves to work for the attainment of democratic rule by non-violent means.

Now, Mr Chairman, do you see any justification for the treatment the government has given this organization? First, the government sought to blame the ANC for all the rioting and intimidation which took place during the Pearce Commission's visit. However, after careful investigation, the Commission concluded 'that there is no real evidence to show that the African National Council Executive organized violence' (Para. 379, p. 101). On the other hand, the ANC was allowed to hold only ten public meetings during that time. At none of our meetings was there so much as a small traffic accident. Further the government has sought to strangle the ANC by banning its membership cards after printing, by threatening the printer if he produced any other ANC materials, by declaring us a political party which was not our wish, by prohibiting the receiving of funds and equipment from outside the country, by requiring banks and building societies to report on all receipt of funds by the ANC and by local harassment of ANC personnel. By such actions, the government succeeds in antagonizing the majority of the citizens of this country, and hence the distrust deepens. Now my fellow citizens, it is very dangerous for any government to threaten and treat over 90 per cent of its people in such a manner.

Let us now turn to examine the main reasons why the vast majority rejected the proposals, since this is one of the most burning questions of the day. First and foremost, we rejected the agreement because it was based on the 1969 Republican Constitution, commonly known as the UDI constitution. Africans know that UDI was meant to perpetuate white supremacy and frustrate democratic rule. Therefore, a settlement based on this constitution was nothing but a legalization of UDI which the majority regard as their number one enemy. How can we easily forget what Mr Smith said when he was advocating the acceptance of the 1969 constitution, that this constitution means 'the death-knell of African political advancement'?

Is this the constitution that any African in full control of his senses would want for himself and his children? The African who saw beyond his nose did not want to go down in history as having supported his own political assassination and that of his children.

The RF committed a treasonable act; rebelled against the Crown; treated our Governor as a toy; executed people who had been reprieved by the Queen, and reduced our country to being an international outcast. To accept the proposals would have been to condone such acts as these, which were not made by the majority.

Secondly, the proposals do not affect, with any significance, the racially segregatory and discriminatory legislation which constitutes the basic structure of *apartheid* in Rhodesia, which itself is the cornerstone of all our racial injustice. Here I want to say as a Christian, that such legislation is repugnant to the doctrine of the brotherhood of all men.

The majority of people know that this legislation is our greatest enemy to peace and harmony. For example, take the question of education—$20 per year is spent per one African child for $300 for one European child.

Consider the plight of the man in town who lives under the threat of the automatic loss of his house, if he loses his job. Or those thousands living on mission lands in areas now designated 'European' under the Land Tenure Act who face eviction, or from places they lived long before the white man came. If you had a son trained as a pilot, but was told he would not be allowed to fly because he was black, how would you feel?

Thirdly, we reject the proposals of because of our lack of confidence and trust in the RF government. At this point I believe it is not necessary to go into detail. I simply quote from the Pearce Report (p. 80), 'mistrust of the intentions and motives of the government transcended all other considerations' as the reason for African rejection.

Many have asked, 'Did not Africans realize they are losing 50 million pound sterling in aid?' Yes, they were fully aware of this token offer. Indeed, it is significant that those for whom this aid was intended, such as school leavers, were most vocal in their rejection. Why? These are intelligent African young people who know that 50 million pounds was just a temporary ten year ration. We would not need to look to Britain for 50 million if there were democratic rule and a fair distribution of wealth and opportunities. It was felt that to accept the proposals on the basis of this grant was like selling one's birthright for a mess of porridge. We would not be bought. The majority were clever enough to realize that by accepting this bait, their basic fundamental human rights would still be denied.

To summarize the whole spirit of the rejection of the proposals, let me quote from what one of the most prominent Africans, perhaps present here tonight, has said: 'I believe that when the verdict of history is given, posterity will ratify that the Smith-Home proposals were a political sell-out of the highest magnitude and that the Africans were justified in rejecting them.'

Following the publication of the Pearce Report, the government stated again that there would be no further negotiations and that the way forward is for Africans to repent and accept the proposals. It anticipates that the chiefs can be used towards this end. The trend now is for the government to go to the chiefs, informing them that they made a mistake in standing with their people in opposing the terms. By doing so, the government is continuing its practice of prostituting the traditional role of the chiefs, by making them a mouthpiece of the government instead of a spokesman for their people. Here is one instance where whites in this country are being taken for a ride by government propaganda, led to believe that the government have the support of the majority of Africans and their chiefs. This fallacy was clearly exposed by the evidence presented to the Pearce Commission. For although the Minister of

Internal Affairs announced that the Council of Chiefs 'unanimously accepted' the proposals, the Pearce Commissioners reported that the majority of chiefs, when interviewed in their own chiefly areas, rejected them. This is one reason why the majority of chiefs, since the test of acceptability, have received much praise from their people. In this case, they have acted traditionally in expressing the consensus of opinion in their area. According to African custom, the chief was a dictator. The people discussed and made a decision; the chief was the symbol of authority. When they reached agreement, they would then pass it on to the chief. He, in turn, would ask for re-assurance of their decision. The people would clap their hands, showing their approval. The chief was then bound by their decision.

Africans are very thankful for the opportunity which was given to them to express their opinion on the proposals. They have been sorely shocked and puzzled by the attitude, that because they exercised this democratic right in rejecting the terms, they were labelled 'mischievous, irresponsible, and destructive.' Indeed, they are viewed as enemies of progress. It may seem strange to you that those very people who are supposed to be suffering most from sanctions were strongest in rejecting this so-called 'hand of friendship'. But Africans rejected this offer because it was based on the 1969 constitution which Africans view as one of their worst enemies.

Mr Chairman and fellow Rhodesians, if Yes were the only response to be given, why was the No provided for? Why is it considered a crime for a citizen to vote against something he sincerely believes is not in his best interest? Why have men lost their jobs, houses, educational places for their children, just because they have exercised their democratic right in rejecting the proposals?

Now Africans are being blamed for the present impasse, as if they were the ones who drew up the proposals. Yet consider these questions—Was it the African electorate who brought in the RF who made UDI? Did they create the illegality from which the country suffers? Did Africans cause sanctions to be imposed on Rhodesia? Was it Africans who rejected the *Fearless* and *Tiger* talks?

Let me ask you, is there any responsible person in this country who would like to see us continue as at present? Our problems right now are not only numerous but deadly serious—a breakdown in communication between black and white; an *impasse* with the British government; the stifling atmosphere of being an isolated country, not accorded full recognition by a single nation; an exploding African population, not content to be treated as third-class citizens, never willing to turn back after being given the power of a veto as in the test of acceptability; a dangerous situation in which whites are often misled as to African thinking; the tendency of one race to think it can go it alone with the help of a handful of short-sighted Africans; the brain drain of our young men and women; the struggle along the Zambezi Valley where our young men, black and white, live as enemies instead of living side by side in the country, in the classroom, on the job, on the playground as citizens of the same community; and the exercise of invisible violence by the police and authorities within the country. Do you know what would change this unnecessary violence in a matter of hours? A just and honourable settlement.

Let there be no misunderstanding. The last proposals have been genuinely and spontaneously rejected, and there is no going back and accepting them. Let the next attempt be an inclusive effort, and one that will be workable. Mr Smith's so-called 'wind of change' must be recognized by the intelligent white Rhodesians for what it is—an ill and perilous gale that will drive the Rhodesian ship of state into uncharted and stormy seas where it will go aground. Provincialization and wider powers to the chiefs in order to muzzle and oppress their people is as futile as King Canute's attempt to stop the tide of the sea. We want all Rhodesian youth to know that their future, especially that of the whites, is at stake.

How can we possibly deal with the fears that haunt our people, the fears of Africans who live daily under the shadow of an oppressive state; or the fears of whites that once the majority is in control there will be no place for them? African fears can be cast out by the establishment of justice in this country.

My fellow white countrymen, I realize that this fear is very real with you. Perhaps this is due to your impressions of countries to the north of us, which has been over-played by government propaganda. But I want to assure you that Rhodesia is not a carbon copy of those countries. It is unique in a number of ways.

Many among the relatively privileged minority of this country look to Zaire or Burundi or Sudan saying, 'See what happens under African rule—it must not happen here!'

Yes, such hatred, hostilities and bloodshed must not happen here. I sincerely believe, ladies and gentlemen, that the people of this country possess qualities which can ensure an orderly transition to democratic rule with peace and prosperity for all. Let me briefly state some reasons.

First, we have the advantage of a greater educational advancement than that existing in most states to the north of us. Already we have 2,000 African university graduates, not to mention thousands with high school giving that basic education needed in a cash economy.

Second, we have achieved a level of economic development which means that an increasing number of our people have a stake in a growing economy in which an orderly transition to democratic rule is imperative for themselves and their children.

Third, a high percentage of our people has an understanding of and commitment to the Christian faith.

Fourth, there is a deep aversion to violence in the culture of the African people and a desire to solve the differences, no matter how great, through consultation rather than by bloodshed.

Fifth, the diversity of tribal groups which have accentuated the conflicts in some black states to the north is practically nil here.

Sixth, the whites there were mostly settlers, but here they are citizens by birth or otherwise. No sane, responsible leader would want to expel its citizens. Democratic rule will also provide for the protection of the minority and their property.

In the Bible we read of another time of national crisis. One of the greatest prophets of the day rose up and said to the people of Israel, 'O, come let us reason together.' I want to say tonight the invitation of Isaiah to his people is the same call which I am making to you as fellow citizens of this great country of great potentiality. 'Let us come and reason together.' These are not hollow words, but have been confirmed in the course of human history as the best way to settle one's differences.

The ANC believes in the necessity of a settlement. Despite having been called an anti-settlement faction, the ANC in fact earnestly desires a settlement, but it wants a just, honourable and democratic settlement. This has been, and still is its desire.

How can this be achieved? First, by accepting the wise, constructive suggestion of Sir Alec Douglas-Home for us Rhodesians to come together in order to iron out our differences. Secondly, by calling upon Mr Ian Smith to take the words of Lord Goodman seriously, to treat Africans as human beings and be willing to listen and to enter into constructive dialogue with them and all peoples. Thirdly, by recognizing the fact that the call of ANC to a national convention, leading to a constitutional conference is a genuine and honest call for the people of this great land to come and reason together for the common good. We appeal to government to take the lead in convening such a convention. Should they fail to do so, we call on any other enthusiastic responsible sector of the country to come forth and take the initiative. We accept the suggestion that has come to us from both black and white that no outsiders be invited to such a convention. Fourthly, by the white electorate's willingness to influence the government to accept such responsibility which could trigger a tremendous change in our present dilemma.

One of the leading objectives in such a convention would be to seek common ground for a just and honourable settlement.

It would be the responsibility of the convention to decide the basis of dialogue. Our number one question is, are we willing as a nation to take this step?

Now, Brethren, again the Bible says, 'Where there is no vision the people perish.' I call you to catch a vision that can save our country. I call you in the name of God, 'Let us come and reason together', return to legality and take our rightful place in the community of nations.

39 Zimbabwe African National Union: MWENJE No. 2. ZANU's political programme. Lusaka, Zambia, 1 August 1972

1. ZIMBABWE IN THE CONTEXT OF WORLD POLITICS

ZANU views the problem of the colony of Rhodesia (what we will call Zimbabwe) as a product and part of the world-wide conflict between the forces of imperialism, capitalism, colonialism and settlerism, on the one hand and the progressive forces of national independence socialism, self-determination and human equality on the other. Rhodesia was colonized and settled from South Africa under the aegis of British imperialism and capitalism. Imperial policies towards South Africa, especially the persistent desire to create a pro-British South African Federation, shaped the policy towards the colony of Rhodesia. Like other oppressed peoples we face three basic and fundamental contradictions in our country which must be removed and destroyed, root and branch. They are:

(a) The presence of a settler society of 234,000 white people who are an integral part of international capitalism that seeks to exploit and oppress the five million indigenous Africans and to prevent them establishing a truly socialist state. This is part of the global conflict of the forces of capitalism and socialism.

(b) The juxtaposition and consequent competition for power of the white settlers and the African people who differ in colour, social and cultural background, religion and civilization. These differences have been accentuated by the practice of the policy of separate development or *apartheid*. This is part of a global race conflict.

(c) The existence of a dual economy—a cash economy in which the settlers enjoy one of the highest standards of living in the world, and a subsistence economy in which the majority of the Africans, whether urban or rural residents, live in abject poverty on the verge of starvation. This too is part of the global conflict between the haves and the have-nots.

Since November 1965 the pretensions of the white settlers to establish an independent white state in the heart of Africa have sharpened these contradictions and brought the settlers into direct and sharp conflict with the five million indigenous Africans who wish to establish a truly socialist state of Zimbabwe, rid of all forms of capitalism, settlerism, racism and exploitation. The Zimbabwe African National Union has joined hands with other progressive forces in Africa, Asia, Latin America and in the socialist countries of Eastern Europe to confront and fight the forces of imperialism, capitalism, colonialism and settlerism in Zimbabwe. It has also sought and received the support of progressive organizations and individuals in Western Europe and North America.

2. THE PARTY AND THE UNITY OF THE PEOPLE

The party is the vanguard of the revolution. It is the machinery through which the revolution has to be planned, waged and prosecuted and finally consolidated. It is the main instrument in the hands of the people in their fight for national independence and national liberation. The party must unite all the people in a common struggle against a common enemy—the white settlers. All the African people of Zimbabwe must unite in the common struggle, irrespective of ideological, religious or regional differences. The unity of the people is absolutely necessary for the successful prosecution of 'Chimurenga' and the full co-operation of our people as brothers and sisters. Those Africans serving the interests of the settlers either directly or indirectly must be persuaded to see the folly of the course of action they have taken, as well as the need to place the national interest of Zimbabwe far beyond their own personal interests.

The party must involve all the oppressed people of Zimbabwe, not only in the common purpose of fighting against foreign rule and settler exploitation, but also in the detailed preparation for the new order. It is an instrument for determining the genuine grievances of the people, and not just the wishes of the leaders or of a few. Solutions to these problems must be found by the people themselves within the framework and through the machinery of the party. Where all the people are involved in the work of the party, their individual problems and grievances become common problems for the party as a whole.

ZANU policy seeks to unite all Zimbabwe people behind a clearly defined objective and not an individual. Policy takes precedence over personality. In 1963 confusion over policy and the personality cult of an Nkomo contributed to the split between ZANU and ZAPU (the Zimbabwe African People's Union). ZANU condemns utterly tendencies of tribalism, sectionalism and regionalism, as well as the personality cult prevalent among certain personalities and parochial organizations in Zimbabwe. ZANU was organized publicly in Zimbabwe for only one full year before it was banned by the settler regime on 26 August 1964. Although short of money and the means of transporting organizers and its leaders constantly harrassed and detained without trial, in that one year it penetrated all parts of the country, mobilized mass support and started underground work to challenge the impending settler unilateral declaration of independence and assert the African claim for real national independence. In the last six years ZANU has been transformed from a nationalist political party to a revolutionary movement with a growing military and paramilitary wing to spearhead the revolution. ZANU military cadres seek the maximum participation and involvement of the masses of our people in every phase of 'Chimurenga'. Their role is to guide and encourage and to be true friends of the people. The freedom-fighter must go in and out of every village with ease in the knowledge that he is among comrades-in-arms and with the self-confidence of a man whose good actions speak louder than his words.

Leadership
A committed and dedicated leadership is an important requirement in a revolutionary party. Leadership must spring from the workers and peasants themselves and those intellectuals fully committed to the task of national liberation, independence and reconstruction. The leadership must work on the basis of a clear set of principles and for clearly stated goals. It should lead and guide the people towards the attainment of these goals without fear or favour; it should show by good example the good living sought in a socialist society.

The leadership must show integrity, honesty and dedication all the time. From it must flow love of the fatherland and a clear design of the new society. Corruption of any kind betrays the revolution and must be punished. The leadership is answerable for all its actions to the masses of the people through the institutions of the party. Any differences of opinion over policy and administration must be placed before the representative and responsible organs of the party for their consideration, deliberation and decision. The leadership shall have full executive authority for the smooth-running of the party and the prosecution of the revolution. ZANU insists upon collective leadership and collective responsibility among and between those elected to office. However, the supreme legislative authority shall rest in the masses of the people who are members of the party. Usurpation of the powers of the people will not be permitted.

The role of the party

We must repeat that the party is the vanguard of the revolution. In addition it is the supreme authority whose every decision and objective has to be carried out by the various organs in the revolution. The party may:

(a) formulate policy and prepare programmes for action;
(b) maintain and enforce a clear revolutionary outlook;
(c) promote, guide and safeguard the integrity of the revolution;
(d) discipline all offenders after a full investigation;
(e) plan general strategy for attainment of declared objectives;
(f) foster political education and raise national consciousness;
(g) co-ordinate activities with progressive movements elsewhere;
(h) apply scientific socialism and Marxism-Leninism to the objective and subjective conditions in Zimbabwe.

The supreme authority of ZANU remains in the Central Committee, the majority of whom are in the enemy's prisons and detention camps in Zimbabwe. After 1965 (unilateral declaration of independence) those members of the Central Committee who were outside Zimbabwe established an external central authority of the party to carry on the task of revolution and to challenge UDI through 'Chimurenga'. A Revolutionary Council was created and it spearheaded 'Chimurenga' from the battle at Sinoia on 29 April 1966 to this day. Several heroic battles have been fought and brilliant victories won. Many plans for tactics and strategy have been made. On the whole groundwork has been firmly laid for forging ahead the struggle.

'Dare re Chimurenga' (Supreme Council)

In February 1969 a representative meeting was called in Lusaka in Zambia, at which the Revolutionary Council was replaced by a new body called 'Dare Re Chimurenga' of Supreme Council, as the supreme external authority of the party. The eight elected members of the 'Dare' have been charged with the responsibility of prosecuting the armed struggle and revolution started by ZANU at home and continued by the Revolutionary Council, uniting and liberating the masses of Zimbabwe and ultimately releasing the members of the Central Committee now in detention in Zimbabwe so that they can take their rightful places as leaders of the new nation.

Military affairs are organized by a specially appointed Military Council. It is responsible for the planning and execution of all military operations in accordance with the general strategy as laid down by the 'Dare' from time to time. It should be stressed that the struggle we are waging is primarily a political struggle. Every means we use is directed towards the attainment of political objectives. Consequently, at every stage political considerations must have a direct bearing on strategy, military programmes and operations. The party should direct the gun. Among the many duties of the Military Council is the political education of all cadres, and to ensure that political objectives of any military operations are understood and supported by all participants.

The party lays great store on political cadres who prepare the ground for mobilization, recruitment and for military operations. Their first task is to extend national political consciousness to every Zimbabwean. He should know why he is being oppressed, by whom, for what purpose, and what he can do to free himself. A major task of the party is to teach the people of Zimbabwe about the nature of their oppression, the character of the oppressor, his weaknesses and strength, and how and where decisive blows can be struck against the oppressor. Political cadres nurture a network of cells throughout the country for this purpose. They also prepare and initiate local revolutionary guards whose function is to sustain and safeguard the gains of any military campaign or operation. The homeguards protect the civilian population against enemy victimization and retaliation, and sustain the cell system.

The central unit of the military wing of the party are the freedom-fighters or guerillas. They spearhead the process towards democratic freedom and national independence in every way, especially by educating and orienting the people towards the new order, and carefully and systematically destroying the power bases of the settlers. They take every opportunity to demoralize and harrass the settlers. But they make it clear wherever possible that they are fighting against an unjust system and not against white people as white people. The freedom-fighters or guerillas are men of high calibre drawn from patriotic families in Zimbabwe; some of them have had an excellent formal education and held responsible jobs as teachers, clerks, orderlies, etc. in Zimbabwe before 'Chimurenga' started. Guerillas must fully understand party ideology, policy and programmes. As nation-builders they must conduct themselves in an exemplary way when they work among the people. They must always display qualities of leadership, discipline, obedience and love of the people.

ZANLA (Zimbabwe African National Liberation Army)

The ZANLA is the organization of the military wing of ZANU. All freedom-fighters, political cadres and members of the homeguard belong to ZANLA. The duties and functions of ZANLA have been indicated in the foregoing. At the head of ZANLA is the Military Council and the head of the Military Council is the 'Dare Re Chimurenga' (Supreme Council). The head of the Military Council is a member of the 'Dare'.

ZANLA will form the nucleus of the Zimbabwe African defence force. It will be a powerful force charged with the responsibility of defending the new nation and continuing the anti-imperialist struggle in Africa. It will also play a full part in mobilizing and educating the masses in the new tasks of economic development and nation-building. Unlike colonial armies that stood away and apart from the people, the Zimbabwe army will be part and parcel of the people and their social system; it will be part of the political system and process.

All disabled soldiers and freedom-fighters will be cared for by the state; those who will have fallen in battle will be honoured by the whole nation. Families of men who have served or are serving in the revolution will be cared for. Already ZANU finances an expanding welfare programme to support the families and dependants of freedom-fighters and full-time party workers. This work will continue and grow as the revolution intensifies. A special welfare trust fund has been estsblished for the purpose. Its accounts are inspected regularly by independent trustees and audited.

Throughout the revolution and more so after victory is won ZANU intends to protect the interests and rights of mothers and children wherever possible, especially the mothers and children of ZANLA men. Problems of refugees and freedom-fighters are well-known; but they will be minimized wherever funds and manpower permit.

ZANU insists upon full internal democracy within the party and the military wing. Its structure is designed to realize the revolutionary character and to give effect to the central aim of continuing participation by the people in decision-making and policy-formation at all levels of the party organization. The people have a right and a duty to take part in decision-making on policy or legislative matters. They do this by direct election of party leaders at branch, district and provincial levels and the indirect election of national leaders through delegates at a party congress. The national leaders consult with branch, district and provincial officials from time to time on policy issues and administrative problems, and take their views into account on major policy decisions.

Every official in all organs of the party and indeed every member must be acquainted with party policy, ideology and programme. In addition, he or she must be reliable, honest, dedicated and willing to implement directives of the party and accept the majority decisions of its organs. They are expected to be alert and to behave with the dignity and respect of others expected of every free Zimbabwean. Within the framework of the party a core of disciplined and dedicated men may be selected in each district and consulted from time to time by district officials and higher organs on party work or given special duties as the situation may demand.

3. THE TASK AT PRESENT

The most pressing task of the party, freedom-fighters and the people at present is to intensify the armed struggle in Zimbabwe in order to free our motherland within this decade. Work has to be intensified on three fronts opened in recent years: (a) the home political front; (b) the home military front; and (c) the international front. The work on these fronts is complementary but the home front is by far the most important.

As far back as 1964 President Sithole himself called upon all the people in Zimbabwe to prepare for a protracted struggle and use all the material and military resources they can find within their immediate surroundings—stones, axes, bows and arrows, spears and where possible home-made guns and explosives. Indeed, the first white victims killed in Melsetter in 1964 were killed with local village weapons, one by an arrow and another by a home-made knife. It is not necessary to wait for the modern automatic rifle in order to participate in 'Chimurenga'. The brave Mau Mau in Kenya did not use modern weapons.

Our people should learn to be self-reliant in their organization of the liberatory forces. They should not wait for a trained freedom-fighter or organizer to come and tell them what to do. They should act freely and independently in their locality. Zimbabweans must rely on their own efforts, resources and skills. Indeed the act of liberation and the attainment of national independence would be meaningless if it were not the result of determined efforts and organizing ability of Zimbabweans themselves. We have to compensate for the technological superiority of the settlers by using our advantages of numbers and knowledge of our country to build a superior guerilla organization. The people's war is invincible.

Existing organizations and party cells should join in the creation of a groundswell of resistance that will soon affect every corner of the country and involve every adult African. Resistance of this kind has begun everywhere, such as the refusal of the heroic Tangwena people to move from their traditional home, several strikes by Salisbury and

Bulawayo workers, the strike of African students at the University of Rhodesia, the decision of village councils throughout the country to close down their schools in protest against the Land Tenure Act, and several other incidents. Our task is to widen the scope and purpose of localized protest movements into a nation-wide resistance-movement.

The home military front opened in 1964 took a new turn with the Sinoia battle in 1966 when ZANU's armed guerillas used modern weapons in a clash with settler forces. The purpose of this front is to liquidate Rhodesian and South African military units which are stationed in Zimbabwe and especially along the Zambezi valley where they are poised to attack friendly African states.

On the international front ZANU has joined forces with all progressive movements and Governments in socialist countries of Eastern Europe, Asia and Africa and some progressive individuals and organizations in the capitalist countries in the West. In particular, ZANU has received generous and practical assistance from governments that are anti-imperialist and revolutionary in their outlook on international affairs. Diplomatic work on the international front is aimed at exposing our enemies by bringing to the attention of others the atrocities being committed against a part of humanity—five million people—in Zimbabwe. The party relies heavily on generous financial and material assistance it receives from time to time from friendly and progressive countries and organizations and especially the Organization of African Unity and its organs. A constant flow of factual information has to be provided to these organizations and governments.

4. POLITICAL OBJECTIVE

The main political objectives of our revolution are to create a free, democratic, independent and socialist Zimbabwe and remove the political domination of the foreign settler element in our society and its imperialistic and capitalistic tentacles. The goal is national independence. The Zimbabwe peoples have a long tradition of self-government and independence going as far back as the mighty and glorious kingdom of Monomotapa, the first great ruler of the Shona-speaking peoples in the sixteenth and seventeenth centuries. That freedom and independence which was filched by British colonialism and imperialism some 80 years ago must be restored and a new nation created.

Every citizen of Zimbabwe shall have the right to exercise a free vote to elect members of the national assembly and all other state institutions. The present national assembly will be abolished and all its discriminatory laws declared null and void. All citizens of Zimbabwe shall participate in decision-making and policy-formation through the party, referenda on major policy issues, and effective use of the people's power in all institutions of the state. Control of state power—the legislature, the administration, the judiciary, the army and police—shall be vested in the citizens of Zimbabwe as a whole and exercised by them on a continuous basis and in an effective manner at all times. It is not enough that every adult should cast a vote every five years for a candidate imposed upon him by party bosses and whom he may never see. Steps will have to be taken to make participation by all the people in the affairs of their own government real and continuous.

There shall be complete equality between all persons, men and women. Persons of all colours, cultures and backgrounds who identify themselves with a socialist Zimbabwe will have expanded opportunities to contribute fully towards the country's development and to fulfil their own aspirations as human beings. No-one will be permitted to exploit other free and equal citizens for his own benefit, or to receive material and financial benefits that do not derive from his own efforts.

Broad democratic freedoms—speech, press, assembly, association, movement—which have been taken away from the people of Zimbabwe by the settlers will be restored and guaranteed to all citizens of a free, democratic, independent and socialist Zimbabwe. All political detainees and restrictees will be released on the first possible occasion and re-united with their families. Existing concentration and detention camps will be closed and the buildings turned into adult education centres.

5. BUILDING A SOCIALIST ECONOMY

The economy of a free, democratic, independent and socialist Zimbabwe will be designed to meet the basic needs of each peasant and worker according to what he needs to live happily and to develop to the fullness of his ability. Zimbabwe is endowed with rich natural resources capable of supporting a large population and providing for their basic needs. All the means of production and distribution will be placed fully in the hands of the people of Zimbabwe as a whole. The present capitalist economic system which benefits a few settlers in Rhodesia and capitalists in South Africa, Britain and America, at the expense of the labouring masses will be abolished.

A truly socialist, self-supporting economy will be established and organized on broad principles enunciated by Marxism-Leninism. ZANU has been guided by these principles in its policies and in applying them to the concrete conditions obtainable in Zimbabwe, bearing in mind the need to put worker and peasant contributions to means of production and distribution beyond any reasonable doubt. There are many varieties of socialism practised in Africa today but nearest to the ideal are the ones that provide for the greatest dominance of worker-peasant interests in the entire economic system of Zimbabwe. It will be a self-supporting economy, not an extension or an enclave of the economies of Britain and South Africa or the West.

The greatest asset of the five million people of Zimbabwe are their bare hands of labour. Man's labour is an expression of his personality as much as it is a means of sustaining existence. Labour in our country must be used for the fulfilment of the personality of every Zimbabwean enabling him to lead a decent life. It must be employed in the production of goods in industrial and commercial enterprises in which the worker has a definite stake and interest. In the existing system, African labour is employed for the benefit of capitalist investors elsewhere and is therefore alienated. Such alienation destroys the human personality of the worker and does not always make it possible for him to live decently or develop his full capacity. Furthermore each individual worker is part of the community in which he lives and works. His labour contributes to the general welfare and well-being of the community as a whole. A socialist economy will enable every worker and peasant to make the greatest possible contribution to his own and the country's development. Labour recruiting agencies, labour gangs and all the oppressive labour laws will be abolished.

Exploitation and class privileges will not be allowed by and among free citizens of Zimbabwe. State power will be used to organize the economy for the greatest benefit of all citizens and to prevent the emergence of a privileged class of any kind. The present system is designed to create large gaps between the elite and the masses, one tribe and another, and to create the so-called middle-class African. A truly socialist Zimbabwe will remove these social and economic gaps, and, at the same time, take specific measures to prevent the emergence of new classes. An important factor in class formation is the ownership of property. Property values play a large role in politics and social values of capitalist societies. In the existing system in Zimbabwe ownership of property and the maintenance of high values is used as a major political, economic and social barrier between the settlers and the indigenous Africans. In a free, socialist, independent and democratic Zimbabwe, property as a commercial and exploitative factor will be abolished.

The participation of the people in all phases of the development of the national economy will be full and continuous. The people will participate by being owners and controllers of the means of production and distribution which are either owned by the state or by co-operatives. In addition, by their control of the government they also have a general control of the economy covering the state-owned enterprises, the co-operatives and even the private sector while it continues to any substantial degree.

In each industrial, commercial or agricultural undertaking joint worker-management committees will be created to give the workers full participation and obviate any tendencies towards labour alienation. Where possible, the principle of profit-sharing in the private sector will be introduced within a framework of industrial conciliation legislation.

6. THE LAND AND ITS PEOPLE

All the natural resources of Zimbabwe—the land, minerals, water, flora and fauna—belong to the citizens of Zimbabwe today and forever afterwards. Therefore there can be no private ownership of land and natural resources because they belong to the people as a whole. The state holds the land as administrator and trustee for the present and future generations.

Landlordism and estate farms owned by capitalists will be abolished. Landlordism is inconsistent with freedom and equality for all. Individuals and groups of peasants may lease land for a specified length of time under conditions which will ensure maximum utilization of the land. Chiefs and their followers who have been forced to leave their traditional homelands in order to give way to settler farmers can return to their homelands and the usurpers be expelled.

Each peasant will be alloted enough land to meet his requirements for food. The maximum 'land to the tillers' will be fully implemented. Where possible land will be made available to peasants who desire to engage in commercial farming. Extension and research services will be provided by the state. It will be the responsibility of peasants to organize themselves and to work together for their own good as they have always done in traditional society.

It should be stressed that the fertile land of Zimbabwe is a national asset given by Almighty God to succeeding generations of Zimbabweans. It is the bounden duty of every user of the land and every generation to hand it over to the next generation in the condition which they found it or even better. Soil erosion, indiscriminate cutting of trees, grass fires that destroy large tracts of bushlands, and overgrazing of cattle must be avoided at all costs. The nation must be taught to value this national asset and to preserve and protect the national game which abounds in our forests and rivers.

7. EDUCATING THE NATION

Every worker and peasant is entitled to a good education. In a free, democratic, independent and socialist Zimbabwe they will be given every opportunity to acquire education commensurate with their capacity and desire to learn, and consistent with the man-power needs and capacity of the nation. Adult and youth education centres will be established outside the school and where possible financed by the government. Stress will be laid on physical education both in and out of school.

The discriminatory practices in the present system of education in which schools and hospitals are segregated on racial grounds and where settlers spend only £9 on an African child for every £103 for a European child per year, African schools are run by voluntary mission bodies while European schools are state-run, technical education is denied African children and secondary school education severely restricted, will all be abolished, because it is only to produce cheap labour for European enterprises. Our aim is to educate the citizen for responsibility and participation in the economic, political, cultural and social life of the country.

In a free, socialist, independent and democratic Zimbabwe the state will take over the administration and financing of all education. Technical and science education will be stressed throughout the primary and secondary school system in order to provide skilled manpower for our state-owned industries and commercial undertakings for general development.

The education of a nation is a continuous and complex process. It means changing people's attitudes and outlook about beliefs they have held for many years or generations. In fact, a scheme of national education has already started in 'Chimurenga' itself. In camps, villages, caves, mountains, cornfields and cities, the guerillas and other members of ZANU and the Zimbabwe African National Liberation Army (ZANLA) have started re-educating themselves about the needs of the nation. As they come into contact with workers and peasants they endeavour to raise their national consciousness by example and education. The entire guerilla zone of operation is a vast school where the felt needs of the peasants and workers are discussed, analysed and solutions found. 'Chimurenga' is an educative project.

As soon as the settlers have been dislodged from an area, the guerillas assisted by the home guards and political cadres, establish a free and independent school which immediately admits all children of peasants and workers in the locality. Peasants and workers themselves are taught in their homes or at a central 'dare'. Several independent schools already exist in the home front. As the revolution succeeds the first schools of national education will also spread throughout the country and the continuous process of education and change started.

A University of Zimbabwe will be established to train men and women who will serve the peasants and workers by doing fundamental research and apply the results to the concrete situation in the village, town, mine and factory. It is not the aim of university education to laze and lounge in white-collar jobs, but to reach the village and the factory with technical advice for development.

8. THE NEW ZIMBABWE CULTURE

Eighty years of colonization have warped the minds of our people and shaken their confidence in themselves by a process of cultural alienation. The settler stage, screen, mass media, literature, school and church, have combined to create a false impression that a foreign culture was good and our own was bad. Consequently, our rich cultural heritage has been lost and at times despised by the young generation which has been indoctrinated and intoxicated with western cultural values.

In a free, democratic, independent and socialist Zimbabwe the people will be encouraged and assisted in building a new Zimbabwe culture, derived from the best in what our heritage and history has given, and developed to meet the needs of the new socialist society of the twentieth century. We are prepared to learn from the accumulated experience and refinement of mind, morals and tastes from other peoples and cultures in the world, especially those from other parts of Africa and use such knowledge to improve and enrich our own. But our culture must stem from our own creativeness and so remain African and indigenous.

The armed struggle will accelerate the liberation of our people from the colonial mentality imposed in the last 80 years of colonial and settler rule. Mental decolonization is as necessary a part of our struggle as the complete political and economic independence which we are fighting for. The armed struggle itself re-educates the participants, laying stress on the strength of their own value systems and the weakness of foreign ones. Many ingredients go into the making of a nation such as a common history and culture, but above all is a common striving for a common ideal against a common enemy. War trenches and ditches have made a nation out of diverse peoples. 'Chimurenga' forms an important part of our programme of re-educational mental de-colonization and nation-building. Killing of the white enemy in battle has a therapeutic value and gives confidence to the black participant in the struggle.

The emphasis of Zimbabwe's new culture will be on the community. The new screen, stage, mass media, literature and schools will project the richness of our community life and the role of the individual in it. While individual citizens must be self-reliant at the same time they must be active members of flourishing, self-contained communities to whose welfare and general security they must contribute generously. Individual and community self-reliance is a cornerstone of our struggle and our socialism.

9. STRENGTHEN UNITY, STRESS EQUALITY, END RACIAL DISCRIMINATION

A central feature of the present social system is the abhorrent policy of racial discrimination or *apartheid*. A large corpus of legislation separates Africans from Europeans socially and culturally. It sets the European element apart as a privileged economic and political ruling class and forbids any competition from the majority and indigenous Africans. The results of the policy have been political domination, economic stagnation and social degradation of the African for no reason other than that he is an African. Racial segregation has been the hallmark of settler policy since 1890 and was strengthened in 1930 when a Labour Party Government in Britain gave permission to the enactment of the Land Apportionment Act.

Racial discrimination may be consonant with capitalism but it is completely incompatible with true socialism. A free, democratic, independent and socialist Zimbabwe will treat every person residing in Zimbabwe as a human being entitled to full human rights and dignity. Racial segregation and discrimination will be outlawed and those who have practised it in the settler era will face trial in open court for their crimes against humanity as Nazi leaders did at Nuremburg.

In the urban areas the factory and office workers who have been subjected to slave labour conditions will have their position completely transformed. They will own directly and indirectly the factories for which they work. All discriminatory labour and trade union legislation will be repealed and all other exploitative practices terminated. An equitable system of wages and salaries will be introduced with pensions for aged workers and compensation for the disabled. Persons who cannot work because of old age or physical handicap will be the charge of the state. A social security system will be introduced to care for and assist all workers and labourers, and especially mothers during times of illness or child-birth. Emphasis will be on improving the living and working conditions of all workers and labourers, their families and children from 'the cradle to the grave'.

Zimbabwe cannot be free, socialist and democratic in the true sense of these words if it permitted or condoned any form of discrimination whether racial, ethnic or regional. Existing racial and ethnic divisions are the work of the oppressors—the settlers. They must be removed and measures taken to ensure the freedom and the full security of all tribal, regional and religious groups. Workers, civil servants and labourers in the cities will be promoted and paid according to their ability, without any reference to their tribal or regional origin. Tribal organizations and political parties based on tribalism will be banned. However national or tribal minorities will be free to engage in cultural pursuits and tribal celebrations provided they remain consistent with the goal of national unity.

Our national unity will be based on a common struggle and a common purpose to build a socialist, democratic, independent and free Zimbabwe; and to fight against exploiters of whatever colour and race, and imperialists and their supporters who have enslaved our people for the greater part of this century.

10. INTERNATIONAL AND PAN-AFRICAN AFFAIRS

ZANU's foreign policy is determined by two cardinal principles: to fight against imperialism and to unite with all other progressive forces in the world. The enemies we fight against are both local and international. There would be no logic in fighting imperialist tentacles in Southern Africa, then supporting or condoning them in the Middle East, South-East Africa or Latin America. Progressive forces are engaged in a titanic global conflict with imperialism and capitalism. ZANU has thrown its weight on the side of progressive forces and has to confront the opposing forces everywhere.

Our country and the problem it has faced have been the direct result of British imperialism. From the day Cecil John Rhodes—the leading British imperialist in the nineteenth century—sent the pioneer column to occupy the Rhodesias, to the declaration of independence by Ian Douglas Smith in 1965, the motive force behind European settlement has been the financial benefit—land, gold and other minerals. Britain has financed and supported these men—their kith and kin—to govern Rhodesia on their behalf. The farce about mandatory economic sanctions, and the talks-about-talks on the *Tiger* and *Fearless* were a smokescreen to cover up the true designs of British imperialism—to keep Rhodesian and Southern African riches in the British Treasury. The possible sale of arms to South Africa announced by Britain in July 1970 and the record investment of British capital in South Africa—it now stands at £1,000 million—is proof, if any was required, that Southern

Africa is an enclave of British capitalism and imperialism. Therefore ZANU has adopted a particularly hostile attitude to British imperialism as the central cause of the plight in which our people have been placed.

ZANU is a pan-Africanist party. It looks on the African continent and its people as one gigantic unit of oppressed peoples. The common element may not be colour, or customs, or the views of the 40 governments in the Organization of African Unity, but the state of collective oppression in which we have been placed since the centuries of organized slavery. ZANU pledges full support to the on-going search for genuine unity based on a clearly defined policy and ideology. ZANU supports the policy of African unity enshrined in the charter of the Organization of African Unity. A ZANU government would explore every opportunity for cultural and economic co-operation with other African states and would seek to join genuine political unions or regional groupings with other African states.

During the current struggle for national liberation it is necessary for party leaders, freedom-fighters and members to maintain the closest possible relationship with African states bordering Southern Africa and to collaborate with other liberation movements of Southern Africa. ZANU members and freedom-fighters who may find themselves in friendly African states must maintain cordial and friendly relations with all citizens of the host states and show respect for their institutions and customs. Zimbabweans living or studying overseas are encouraged to return home and join the struggle.

ZANU is committed to achieving national independence through the armed struggle. It disapproves of the policy of collaboration with the white racist states in Southern Africa advocated by the Republic of Malawi. While ZANU appreciates the motives and reasons behind the signatories to the Lusaka Manifesto, it completely rejects its approach to the problem and re-affirms its belief in the armed struggle.

Our aim is to establish a free, democratic, independent and socialist Zimbabwe. In the international field we will collaborate fully with progressive movements and governments in order to create peace as long as they recognize the independence and territorial integrity of Zimbabwe. ZANU will co-operate in general terms with other governments in Africa and elsewhere which may have different social systems but support the just struggle for our national independence and do not aid our enemies—the settlers—in any way.

Conclusion
It is the declared intention of ZANU to transform Rhodesia into a free, democratic, independent and socialist Zimbabwe in the decade that lies

ahead of us. The programme outlined above must be made a reality in the 1970s. The task of bringing about this glorious revolution has already started but it requires the combined efforts of every Zimbabwean to complete it with speed and efficiency. We have the means! We have the men! We have the organization! We only need the political will and the determination to succeed!

40 Zimbabwe African Peoples Union: The political direction of our party. *Issued by the ZAPU Directorate of the Political Commissariat. Lusaka, Zambia, 14 September 1972*

. . . Like all other peoples of the world, Zimbabweans passed in the course of their historical development through crises, accidents and misfortunes as well as periods of prosperity, victory and splendour. During the nineteenth century, just as other inhabitants of Africa, Zimbabweans suffered and are still suffering under the yoke of British colonialism. But, loyal to their long history of national pride and self-determination inspired by the heritage of Zimbabwe, the Zimbabweans never ceased to fight even at the darkest moments of their struggles in 1890–1903, now known in the imperialist world as the Matabele war and the Mashona and Matebele Rebellions. They carried on stubbornly against colonialist occupation and made supreme sacrifices to regain their national sovereignty. The history of Zimbabwe is filled with pages of glory and the lineage of our ancestors is rich in heroes. That is why today, guided by this noble tradition of our forefathers, and inspired by our rich national heritage, the entire people of Zimbabwe, united as one in the heroic struggle against the well calculated British colonialism, will in the end win complete national independence and establish a classless society.

With this rich experience, and the historical antagonism between the masses of Zimbabwe headed by ZAPU on one hand, and the British settlers financially and militarily backed by the Western imperialists and their monopolies on the other hand, colonialism is bound to fail in Zimbabwe as it has failed in other areas of the world. But the physical fighting is ours and ours alone, and whatever outside assistance we get is supplementary to our own efforts in the revolution.

THE FORMATION OF ZPRA AND ITS PRINCIPAL
OBJECTIVE TO THE HISTORICAL MISSION OF OUR
STRUGGLE

Our army, known as the Zimbabwe Peoples Revolutionary Army, was
born from years of experience and deep search under colonial oppression
for the last 80 years. Our army is, therefore, an ORGAN of our political
party, ZAPU, to fulfil the aspirations and demands of the landless and
rightless masses of Zimbabwe. The army is an instrument of ZAPU led
and directed by the party through its National Executive headed by the
only President Comrade Joshua Nkomo in and outside the country.

1. *Why have the people taken up arms at this stage?*
It must be borne in mind by every revolutionary that our struggle is a
political and military struggle against the systematization of British
colonialism in the land of our birth. We have taken up arms after all
avenues leading to self-determination have failed under successive British
settler regimes in our country. It is through their criminal legislations
that the existence of our very lives is being threatened. Thus our
revolution is for a complete change of the present political and economic
system.

2. *What kind of army does ZAPU have?*
The Zimbabwe Peoples Revolutionary Army is not and will never be a
colonial instrument for the suppression and plunder of our human and
natural resources for the benefit of colonialism and its monopolies, but
to serve the revolutionary future state of Zimbabwe. The army is,
therefore, not only an instrument of the nation but also is a part and
parcel of the whole nation. The purpose of our Revolutionary Army is to
attain a political objective which is freedom and independence of the
Zimbabwe nation. Our army is composed of dedicated freedom-fighters
who are imbued with revolutionary principles and who have refused to
submit to or be cowed down by bannings of our national movements of
the African National Congress (1957), the National Democratic Party
(1960) and, now, the Zimbabwe African Peoples Union. There has now
been a transformation of ZAPU, its leaders and rank file members into a
revolutionary party whose instrument is the revolutionary army. It must
be clearly understood that this is the most crucial stage of the struggle
against world imperialism and colonialism in Africa, Asia and Latin-
America. It is this historical and political development which has led
to revolutionary consciousness of the masses of Zimbabwe, and has,
therefore, become a base for the philosophical concept of our politi-

cal ideology. There has never been and shall never be any cordial relationship between an armed oppressor and an enslaved and downtrodden people unless and until the latter is politically and militarily in control.

3. *What is the guarantee for a successful revolution in Zimbabwe led by ZAPU?*

Our guarantee for final victory in Zimbabwe is the revolutionary masses whose history and tradition is that of struggle and without which our army would be like a fish out of water. The masses are makers of our history and, therefore, the soul and life of our revolutionary struggle. It is in these realities that our army must be politicized in order to equip itself politically and militarily for a successful peoples revolution in Zimbabwe. Once our army is politically aware of the principles, policy and objectives, it will know when, where and how to use its weapons. This will also help destroy position seekers, opportunists and reactionaries who would have liked to use the peoples army for personal glory. It would also be a revolutionary tactic to learn from the last two years (1970-1) of the ZAPU crisis which, in a way, has been a blessing in disguise in our struggle. It was after analysing all these problems and situations that the party embarked on the present revolutionary strategy of combating individualism, corruption and tribalism which were used by political prostitutes who have no love for their country and people. It must be clear to everybody in any organ of ZAPU that fortune seekers, rumour mongers and anti-revolutionary social elements can never be of any service in a revolution like ours.

It is therefore true that individuals in their masters' pockets will come and go, but the people, as builders of Zimbabwe, and their revolution will remain. One of the cardinal points to bear in mind is that no man, whatever his rank in any organ of the party, is above the party's authority and that of our Supreme Commander Comrade Joshua Nkomo, who has made tremendous sacrifices to further the Zimbabwe revolution.

It is beyond doubt that the real founders of our army have already laid down their lives and they are the basis of our political outlook and the only heroes and leaders of great example in our revolutionary development.

It is the duty of the commander and the political commissar in any camp or unit of ZPRA to face the challenge created by colonialism—to give confidence where there is despair, to give hope where there is doubt and to build the iron spirit of revolutionary brotherhood in the army. The whole political work in the peoples army will be carried by a commissar under the directorate of the Political Commissariat of ZAPU, to assist the army in every endeavour, to arm the fighters politically and ideologically so that when any member of the army is in battle he can solve without delay any political and military question. Ours is a protracted struggle, thus, we have to know our enemy, his sources of supply, his political and military strength in and outside Zimbabwe.

These are some of the basic ideas, the reasons why our party ZAPU had to be transformed and revolutionized in order to carry out its revolutionary tasks.

Our party, ZAPU, our people and our leadership, guided by revolutionary principle, would like rather to see Zimbabwe in ashes than surrender to slavery. Therefore, one of main guiding principles is: 'To die for one's country is to live forever.'

LONG LIVE THE SPIRIT OF REVOLUTION IN EVERY ORGAN OF ZAPU!

LONG LIVE THE FOUNDERS AND HEROES OF OUR ARMY!!

LONG LIVE OUR GREAT LEADER JOSHUA NKOMO!!!

CHAPTER NINE

TOWARDS LUSAKA

41 Zimbabwe African National Union: British plot uncovered. *Press statement, Dar-es-Salaam, Tanzania, 27 February 1973*

ZANU has observed with uttermost distaste the dirty manoeuvres and evil machinations being employed not only against the people of Zimbabwe, but also against the republic of Zambia by the British government.

ZANU has watched with sickening horror how Britaiñ, being the so-called administering power over Southern Rhodesia, sat by and idly watched the mad rebels indulge in unwarranted acts of aggression against the sovereign state of Zambia—an aggression which has resulted in the brutal butchering by the Smith forces of innocent civilians.

ZANU has seen Britain raise not a single murmur when Vorster first established his military presence in Rhodesia culminating in the recent further reinforcement of 4,000-plus South African troops now deployed on the border with Zambia to fight Zimbabwean people and ready to invade Zambia.

ZANU has watched Britain stay aloof when the minority settler dictatorship closed the border with Zambia, being an attempt calculated to force Zambia into submission. The British government's attitude over the Rhodesia/Zambia border crisis has been, to say the least, one of positive acquiescence of the rebels' action—as demonstrated by Britain's abstention in the Security Council when the Security Council was voting on the sending of a fact-finding mission to assess the border situation, and see how Zambia could be assisted in her problems brought about as a result of the rebels' action.

It has been established beyond doubt that:
(1) The British government is desperately involved in a full-fledged diplomatic campaign directed at dissuading other peace and justice loving people from coming to the aid of Zambia in her attempt to find alternative trade routes. This is an attempt by the British government to try to force Zambia to use the unreliable Rhodesian route. The British government is worried, like a mother of a sick child, lest Rhodesia should lose the revenue she used to get from the

use of that route by Zambia. She is worried the Rhodesian regime might fall to pieces.

(2) On the Zimbabwe front the British government is engaged in a conspiracy with Ian Smith's regime in a final desperate attempt to get Africans to 'accept' the unacceptable Anglo-Rhodesian proposals which were unreservedly rejected by the Africans of Zimbabwe during the Pearce exercise.

We are aware that the British government is using some gullible Africans in Zimbabwe by persuading them to come to terms with Ian Smith. Large sums of money from the British purse are being made available for this hopeless venture. The Smith regime is being used, of course, as an agent of the British government. The people of Zimbabwe are quite aware of this unholy league between the settler regime and Britain, who have now been talking secretly on how best to hoodwink the Africans.

ZANU wishes to expose this evil plot meant to liquidate the majority wishes for ever. This unpardonable complicity between the imperialist Britain and the settler bandits cannot go by unexposed. ZANU will resolutely succeed in foiling the strategy of the British imperialists in their attempts to ignore and destroy the revolutionary spirit and wishes of the people of Zimbabwe. The people of Zimbabwe will not accept anything short of immediate majority rule in Zimbabwe, and ZANU will endeavour to fulfil this national wish. Our immediate wish and aim is to crush the settler regime and obtain the liberation and independence of Zimbabwe.

ZANU will never be persuaded to believe that the settler dictatorship and the British government can work out a satisfactory solution to the Zimbabwe problem. These people cannot preside at the liquidation of their political power and economic interests.

We wish to unreservedly condemn the British government for its failure, because of its kith and kin policy, to hand over Zimbabwe to the rightful owners. The armed struggle now being waged by ZANU and supported by the masses of Zimbabwe will continue and be intensified until we have won.

Our firm faith in the victory of the revolution and our fervent revolutionary passion, our firm revolutionary principle and our strong fighting spirit cannot be broken by any negotiated settlement which gives the African anything short of majority rule.

ZANU wishes to warn those of our brothers who have styled themselves 'leaders of the people' and are now involved in illicit contacts with the enemy at the direction and approval of the British government, that they will face the wrath of the people should they prove to be nothing else but puppets of the imperialist Britain and her accomplices.

The revolution is on and Britain must be told in no uncertain terms that nothing will stop the wheel of revolution until the desired objective is attained.

42 Zimbabwe African National Union: memorandum submitted to the OAU Co-ordinating Committee for the liberation of Africa meeting in Mogadishu, Somalia, 15–20 October 1973

Your Excellencies,

Be it recalled that after changing its strategy in 1969, ZANU went into three years (1969–72) of intensive, arduous, secret, underground preparatory work for a relentless and continuous war of liberation against the settler racists in Zimbabwe.

During the three years, ZANU—through its military wing, the Zimbabwe African National Liberation Army (ZANLA)—worked at the grassroots in Zimbabwe, mobilizing the masses to participate fully and physically in the war of liberation, recruiting new cadres (men and women) for training outside and on the spot, organizing underground transportation groups for carrying weapons, foodstuffs, medicines and clothing and hiding them in safe strategical operational areas and, above all, infiltrating hundreds of fighters into well surveyed operational zones.

The preparatory work was very successful. By the end of 1972 we launched an unprecedented war against the settler racists—such as they never expected. It is remembered that the enemy, because of the severe blows he received from ZANLA forces, admitted by 21 December 1972 that there was a grave war situation in the north-eastern area of Zimbabwe. He revealed his casualties of his own accord. Ever since that time ZANLA forces have continued to fight gallantly without a stop. We scored victory after victory against the enemy. The fight spread to other areas in the north, north-eastern, north-western and eastern areas of Zimbabwe and as we consolidate our position in these areas we also expand and open new fronts.

Our forces struck at the enemy's so-called security forces, at the settler farmsteads used as operational and supply bases, at every armed man used by the enemy; they mined roads, destroyed bridges, police stations and enemy administrative centres used for suppressing Africans. We shot planes used to attack us. During our fights we killed 249 enemy forces.

Details thereof have been given in our communiqués. More have been killed ever since we issued our last communiqué—No. 4. Another communiqué will be issued soon. We captured a white intelligence officer, Gerald Hawksworth, on 8 February 1973 (purportedly reported by the enemy as a land inspector). We captured four black puppet British South Africa police. They are all in our custody. We captured weapons, radios, spectacles, clothing and money.

The area we are operating in is very large—north, north-eastern, north-western and eastern areas of Zimbabwe which we are expanding at the same time as we open new fronts—and in this operational area there are approximately three million Africans living there who are working hand in hand with our forces, supplying foodstuffs, cover, information about the enemy and physically fighting alongside our forces and carrying weapons to strategical operational areas.

As would be expected, the enemy panicked and reacted to our offensive in a very crude and barbaric manner: Smith deployed his entire regular defence force—army, air force and police and reservists—to the war zone in a bid to rout our elusive fighters. He failed dismally. He then brought in thousands of South African forces to assist him. This has also failed.

He then desperately acted most stupidly by closing the border with Zambia on 9 January 1973 in a bid to strangle Zambia's economy and pressurize her to stop giving us passage facilities. Thanks to the government and gallant people of Zambia who refused to be blackmailed but chose to suffer and sacrifice in order to uphold Africa's noble cause.

The enemy then resorted to most fascistic and draconic last ditch suppression methods against the African people—the masses—for supporting, giving food, cover, clothing and information to our forces about enemy activities and mobility. They arrested both men and women, put them in barbed wire concentration camps, reminiscent of Hitler's concentration camps, shot and killed men, women and children in cold blood, burnt down and destroyed homes and granaries, raped women, passed regulations for collective punishment and impounded cattle and property of the masses, closed schools, hospitals, clinics and shops, and uprooted whole villages from purportedly guerilla zones to new so-called inaccessible areas. We have lost about 24 of our gallant heroes in the battlefield—nine of them were hanged. Many civilians have been killed in cold blood under the guise that they were guerillas.

The result of this reign of terror is that the whole African population in these areas looks to our forces for protection and care. Some of the masses whose homes were destroyed and burnt down fled into the bushes naked and without food or any means of livelihood. Our forces had to provide them with food, clothing, and medicines. This situation continues. All these people are the responsibility of our party. But contrary to the enemy's expectation, all his fascist methods have, instead of cowing down our masses, strengthened and steeled their will to fight against the enemy to the end until victory is achieved. Hundreds of men and women—including teachers, nurses and students—have enlisted to go for military training. Our training camps are full to capacity, hundreds are waiting in transit camps to go for training. Our army has grown up enormously. We have formed a women's detachment to fight hand-in-hand with their male counterparts. Besides, we also have in transit camps old men, women, and children who are either too old or too young to train and those who have either been injured in battle or shot at random as the enemy encircled and destroyed villages.

One of the most heartening and spectacular achievements in this war is that through physical action and contact in the field we have united the masses in these areas. All of them without exception who came into contact with ZANLA forces—whether they were ZAPU or ANC or any other organization—gave themselves to fight under the banner of ZANU which is spearheading the fight through its military wing. This unity, carved in action and cemented in blood, forms the basis and permanent solution towards complete unity of the people of Zimbabwe.

We wish this august committee to give full support and encouragement to the people of Zimbabwe in this promising unity which is being forged in action.

Beside uniting people in Zimbabwe, people outside Zimbabwe have been coming to join ZANU in great numbers. To mention just a few cases:

(a) Ten military cadres who previously were ZAPU have joined ZANU. We have re-orientated them and trained them. Three of them have risen to very important positions of commanders.

(b) Over 30 former FROLIZI members resigned and joined ZANU. Many more have joined without issuing press statements.

(c) One, Comrade Wilfred Pasipanodya Nyashanu—formerly a top ZAPU official and later in FROLIZI—resigned and joined ZANU. He has been given an important assignment in the party.

(d) Comrade Edison Zvobgo, who was ANC Director for External Missions, has resigned to join ZANU.

(e) Cadres, formerly ZAPU, who are in detention have written to our party requesting that they be accepted to join ZANU.

It is, therefore, evident that through action in the field ZANU has managed and can unite the people of Zimbabwe.

While we welcome advice from our friends on the question of unity, it is our submission that the final decision should be left to the people of Zimbabwe who are specifically engaged in the fighting.

DIFFICULTIES ENCOUNTERED

During this period we have encountered lots of difficulties:

(a) *Weapons*

Although we received some assistance from the OAU, the weapons we got fell short of our requirements in the field, and in many cases we did not get the suitable type of weapons we needed and did not get them in good time as the situation warranted. We did not also get enough and suitable weapons and equipment for training in our training camps.

(b) *Food*

Food has been another problem and a major drawback. We were very short of food to feed our forces, the underground transportation teams and the masses whose homes and granaries had been burnt down and destroyed by the enemy troops.

(c) *Medicines*

Although the OAU and other friends abroad have contributed some medicines, drugs, etc., this has not been enough to cater for our injured and sick fighters, underground transportation teams and masses whose hospitals and clinics had been closed by the enemy troops and had to look on us for medical facilities and all other necessities of life.

(d) *Clothing and uniforms*

Clothes and uniforms have become a major problem. We did not have enough uniforms to cater for our forces in the field and in camps. It was very difficult for us to raise enough clothing to cater for the underground transportation teams and the masses who fled their homes naked or with hardly enough clothing to cover themselves when the racist troops burnt and destroyed their homes. Boots for the fighters were a very big problem. They cover a very long stretch of land on foot from the Zambia border with Mozambique to Zimbabwe through Mozambique and for operation in the bush in Zimbabwe.

(e) We also had serious difficulties with transport to carry our materials to the entry points. We had no transport to carry the injured from the receiving points to clinics and hospitals in Zambia. Thanks to Zambia who have often come to our assistance in carrying our sick and treating them in their own institutions.

(f) *Funds*

We were very short of funds to cater for the needs in the field, i.e.

(i) To provide financial needs for the fighters for operation, food, clothing and mobility. Although the masses tried to help, as the fighting intensified, the enemy harassed the masses, and in many cases the masses were no longer able to help the fighters but instead when they were rendered homeless and went to the fighters for assistance.

(ii) The army had grown very big since we have been training some of the cadres on the spot to replenish and build the army. We had to provide all the facilities necessary.

(iii) We had to buy foodstuffs and clothing to cater for masses who were under our care in transit camps and to cater for the cadres who were on their way to the training camps.

N.B. The assistance given by the OAU to cater for the fighters as they leave training camps going to Zimbabwe is very minimal and only caters for a few days. Thereafter, we did not receive any aid to maintain the fighters in the field. This gives us a very big problem which hampers the progress of the war.

THE ENEMY

1. The Smith regime, shaken by the successful operations of the ŻANLA forces, is consolidating its military alliance with South Africa and Portugal with the backing and connivance of Western big powers—Britain, America, West Germany and other NATO countries.

2. Aware that they are losing in the war and that the morale of its security forces is very low, the Smith regime has resorted to bribing the soldiers and police by increasing their earnings.

3. The Smith regime in connivance with Britain is trying to dupe the Africans through the ANC that there will be a constitutional settlement. This is a very subtle and dangerous manoeuvre aimed at confusing the Africans in Zimbabwe and certain OAU countries, and to stop them supporting the armed struggle.

4. Certain OAU countries are working hand in hand with the Smith regime, e.g. Gabon is allowing Smith's planes to operate there.

5. The enemy is using certain OAU countries to propound and support the theory of dialogue. This is dangerous as it confuses our people and divides the support of the African countries for armed struggle.

INFORMATION

It is with great pleasure that we inform the OAU that ZANU held its bi-annual review conference from 14–16 September 1973. For the first time since we started operating from outside in 1964, the conference was attended by delegates from home, including chiefs and fighters who fully participated in the deliberations. It was also attended by representatives of the Zambian government, the director of OAU Sub-Regional Office in Lusaka, and most recognized liberation movements in Zambia.

Our requests
1. Given the difficult nature of our struggle and the description of our programmes and activities outlined above, we submit that the funds and system of giving funds to ZANU have so far been extremely inadequate. Our mode of operation has changed. We therefore propose that a more comprehensive system be adopted whereby funds given to ZANU will not only cover administrative expenses but also such things as maintenance of fighters in the field, of people who have been dispossessed in the operational zones, our transit camps, transport and general political mobilization and propaganda inside the country (Zimbabwe).
2. We request for more arms, accessories, medicines, foodstuffs, uniforms, clothing, and transport.
3. We request that the OAU once again states clearly and unequivocally that only armed struggle is the only solution to the Zimbabwe problem and that the OAU supports unreservedly freedom fighters waging the armed struggle in Zimbabwe.
4. While welcoming other fronts used hand-in-hand with the armed struggle to dislodge the enemy, it is our submission that if sanctions have to be effective, they should apply to Rhodesia, South Africa and Portuguese territories.

APPRECIATION

Our party, through your committee, would like to express our heartfelt gratitude for the concrete support given to us by OAU countries both materially and diplomatically, and, in addition, we would like to thank those neighbouring countries who have suffered and sacrificed so much for the sake of the oppressed and suffering people of Zimbabwe and Africa, without whom we would not have succeeded in our operations.

But we would like to state that the stage we have reached is very critical indeed and calls for unwavering commitment and concrete support by the OAU for our action. It is through action only that we can liberate and unite the people of Zimbabwe. Any relaxation of concrete and unwavering support by the OAU will give opportunity to the enemy to re-organize and consolidate his shaken position. The OAU cannot afford the luxury of a wait-and-see attitude. We, on our part, shall play our role effectively in the battlefield.

Let OAU be united in this sacred resolve.

Long live the People's Armed Struggle!

Forward with Chimurenga (War of Liberation)!

Long live Organization for African Unity!

43 African National Council: presidential address to inaugural congress by Bishop Abel Muzorewa. Stodart Hall, Harare, 2 March 1974

Mr Chairman, sons and daughters of Zimbabwe, this is an historic hour and a time of reckoning! While Zimbabwe is gathered here to take a thoughtful look at the continuing struggle for our freedom, we gather fully aware of the presence of Almighty God and with full blessing of those political martyrs and heroes in Zimbabwe's struggle for self-determination. The names of Drs Samuel Parirenyatwa, Elisha Mutasa, Mr L. Takawira and all those pioneer leaders of the struggle rotting in indefinite detention and restriction whose names cannot be mentioned by the dictators of the so-called laws of this country, are remembered by all of us with loving concern and inspiration.

I greet you with great admiration, gladness and gratitude. Your presence from the four corners of Rhodesia, from branches and the eight provinces representing the very grassroots of people of this country through the ANC, the organization of the masses, is a clear demonstration of your deepest desire to have Zimbabwe free. And your presence is evidence of the unquestionable overwhelming majority which we have always claimed. Last but not least I welcome all the invited guests and observers present, and all those of goodwill among us today.

While I am still thinking of those to whom I am indebted, I trust you will agree with me that I should include those who have continually given us moral support and exerted their political pressure in our favour at home and abroad. The free African states cannot go unmentioned for their concern toward our need for liberation. For example, Zambia has gone out of its way, and sacrificed economically for our liberation. The same goes for other OAU member states.

Now, Mr Chairman, ladies and gentlemen, it should be my primary task to praise and thank you and all those who sent you here to this congress, for despite the evil forces that laboured to divide us, you remained calm, determined and united. At a time when some of our brothers endured detention without trial, harassment and intimidation by the authorities and in the face of the murder of our innocent and unnamed brothers and sisters by the RF Government troops in the cities of Umtali, Salisbury and Gwelo at the time of the Pearce Commission, you faced it all with an indomitable courage. And still you continued to carry out your duties with determination. Here I want to stand up and pause and in a moment of silence remember those who died while exercising their democratic right by registering their 'No' vote to the Pearce Commission.

While talking about troops, I call for a joint ANC-Government Commission to go into the question of the relationship between security forces and civilians in the north-east border and alleged atrocities which have repeatedly come to our ears.

Furthermore, you have persevered in the face of the most discouraging and harsh circumstances. You amazed me for your insight and assessment of the political dynamics of our country. Your ability to distinguish genuine African leaders from the money seekers is praiseworthy.

Now as you are all aware the purpose of our organization and of this congress is to seek for and try to achieve majority rule and end the RF totalitarianism and fascism which have haunted us for the last painful and wasted 11 years. This period has created miserable conditions for Africans, and since the Pearce Commission left, more segregatory and repressive laws have been passed. In my opinion the most damaging, and inhuman one is the cruel collective punishment. Our people are being damaged mentally, physically and economically. The RF government may never realize that by these deplorable actions, they are writing the blackest chapter in the history of this country. This black chapter will not only be printed as history but stamped indelibly in the hearts and minds of the African people of this and future generations. In short, let me emphasize that laws such as these engender feelings of hostility between races, the government and the Africans.

When we stop to think that there are people who are languishing in prisons, detention and restriction camps and of the innocent persons dying in the north-eastern border area, we are motivated incessantly to demanding our immediate emancipation. We often cry out 'When Lord, will we be a free people? When? When Lord?' I wonder whether the blood of our innocent brothers and sisters will permit us to rest, to enjoy ourselves in our comfortable positions as African businessmen, teachers, lawyers, doctors, ministers of religion, Members of Parliament, nurses, policemen, students, even money mongers and Africans of all walks of life in Rhodesia while the country continues to be devoured by the oppressive laws which haunt us from the cradle to the grave!

To mention a few I repeat the most terrible so-called law of (1) collective punishment, (2) the Land Tenure Act (3) the stupid Stupa Bill, (4) the practice of job reservation and now (5) the Settlers for '74 Campaign, (6) day-to-day humiliation and insults through racial discriminations.

Although the above oppressive measures are directed to persecuting the Africans, let me remind you that the black people are not the only ones who need to be freed. White people need freedom, too, now and especially in the future. But of course, the way they are treating Africans now will determine how free they will be in the future. For instance, the whites in the north-eastern border area know more and better than I do how much they desperately need freedom. They are fast becoming slaves of fear. As we read, they are a people who go to bed and hide behind a wall of sandbags; a people who are scared of their employees day and night; a people who hesitate to use the roads they helped to construct; a people who leave their comfortable beds and pets to suffer overnight and return home the next morning. Such a people cannot claim to be psychologically, socially and politically free.

When we presented our evidence to the Pearce Commission, the ANC had enough foresight and we duly warned the country of the violence and bloodshed that have now become the order of the day particularly in the north-eastern border area, but it was received with scorn and shrinking resistance. For instance, when I was in London in February 1972, while I was speaking to the Members of Parliament in the House of Commons, a woman MP reacted with emotion to my prediction.

She alleged that I was merely threatening the whites in Rhodesia. I told her that I was not praying for the coming of the dark days in Rhodesia, but I was only making a sincere analytic observation of a serious concern. One of her colleagues asked me when I thought that racial hatred and confrontation would deteriorate to the stage of bloodshed. I said then in five years time. But I was proved wrong—it came in a matter of months. It has continued intermittently and there is no sign of it ever stopping in spite of the dangerous wishful thinking that the security forces are 'getting on top of the situation'. At times I wonder what is getting on top of what. Can the white Rhodesians continue to ignore our call for a concerted effort to iron out our dispute and stalemate as a people in one country?

Now Mr Chairman and countrymen, as we try to solve our problems and pursue the cause of freedom and justice we must be aware of the enemies of Zimbabwe's freedom. You will sadly remember that some of the enemies of our cause once succeeded in working out a split and put us in a political coma while setting back the clock of Zimbabwe's freedom ten years. I am sure, as certain as the fact that we are here meeting in Stodart Hall, that we should have been a free nation by now if we had remained bound together in the name of unity. However, let us not cry over spilt milk. Let us beware of being nose-dragged into the same kind of pit we fell into before.

You know there are some people who have prayed to the devil for our split. Count how many times for example we have read and heard the words about the 'ANC Split', in the white-owned and controlled news media. The reasons are clear. That this is something some of them would have printed in bold headlines if it had happened and the RBC would have put it in the loudest possible volume, and the RF would have danced on top of Milton Buildings if the split had taken place. These news media have also written a few times the word 'ousted' in reference to your President. The ANC, like any other democratic organization, believes in changing its leaders whenever necessary. But it must be made clear that our enemies must not think that by repeating falsehoods about the change of leadership they can change it. Our enemies have failed in the past to detract the African people from their true leadership. They will fail now and will continue to do so in the future.

I want to stress that the forces that can cripple this organization for Zimbabwe's freedom are lively at work. Now therefore watch out for people who are intoxicated and obsessed with tribalism—people who see everything through tribal spectacles. Take note of the people who seem to think that chickens, pigs, and cows raised among their own tribe produce eggs, pork and milk which taste better and sweeter than those of other tribes. Watch out for people who have ill and cheap ambitions in so much that they backstab their colleagues, highlighting their faults without appreciating their strong points. There are the people who are mainly interested in enhancing their personal prestige at the expense of the freedom of the masses. Such people do not know what loyalty means except when they want others to be loyal to them. Watch for leaders who do not know how to follow other leaders. Don't forget to watch for those whose gods are their stomachs—those who worship their bellies like the Biblical Judas Iscariot who would sell even persons to get money. Again, people like Esau of the Old Testament who sold his own precious birthright for a plate of porridge. These are materialistic people who are moved by the money-pulse. Watch out for people who tragically lack self-respect and suffer severely from that old disease of inferiority complex. Don't forget the cowardly who do nothing because they are afraid. Beware of the cheap informers. Watch out for people who are counting on what position they will hold personally, or their friends or their tribe in the event of majority rule—people who are more personality- and party-politically-centred than purpose-centred.

Countrymen, our only serious purpose should and must be the freedom of Zimbabwe. We must have the purpose clearly defined and in full focus. And we must accept the fact that if it should be a healthy struggle, it cannot be one man's struggle, it cannot be a struggle for an individual, organization or movement, or any party or group. It must be, and is, a struggle of all the people of Zimbabwe, by all the people of Zimbabwe, for all the people of Zimbabwe, to paraphrase Mr Abraham Lincoln.

And yet Mr Chairman and countrymen, I, for one, am not in any doubt as to the precious loyalty to the struggle of you ANC members— true sons and daughters of this land which you have demonstrated beyond doubt over the last two years now.

We must not be like five brothers who sent out hunting and when they saw a kudu almost pausing for them, they started quarrelling. One started demanding that he would have the chest, the other one said the chest would be his and so on until they started fighting. The kudu ran when it heard the noise of the fighting brothers. Now countrymen, let me remind you again that this happened before with our politics and it can happen many times over if we are not clever and wise enough to learn by our past mistakes. You know the English adage, 'A wise man learns by the mistakes of others, but a fool will never learn.'

Before I turn directly to speak on some points surrounding the settlement issue I want to clear the air about a number of things. First, Mr Smith said recently that some Africans who had been talking to him had said they were being intimidated not to settle by people from outside. I can assure you that this does not include the ANC. If the ANC were susceptible to intimidation by anybody we would have been intimidated into accepting the 1971 settlement proposals. Also, I have heard that there are people who dislike our idea of talking with other political bodies, including the government, while our brothers are in detention. I have stated before, and I want to repeat it now, that whatever discussions we are having with the Rhodesian Front government and other political bodies, we are aiming at the total emancipation of all our people. We are not indifferent to the continued detention of our brothers. My thinking and feeling is that those of us who are out of gaol and detention should help bring about majority rule, and have everybody free, i.e. those who are in prisons and restriction and those who are refugees in other countries as well. Brothers and sisters, that is our goal—total liberation of Zimbabwe.

Consistent with our stand of not negotiating in public, I do not believe it is politically wise at this stage to go into details of what has transpired so far in the talks we have held with the RF and the RP. Suffice to say that we want to continue to talk until we reach a happy solution. All I can do at present is to assure you that we will press and strive for justice to be done. There will be no settlement which will be acceptable unless it is an honourable and just settlement.

There can never be a sellout. There can never be a betrayal of the aspirations of the African people. Anyone suggesting that is engaging in cheap political propaganda.

Before I go any further, I want to say that all true members of ANC know this by now, that our organization is committed to achieving our goal of freedom by non-violent means. It means that we need to know what tools and non-violent weapons we should and must use to achieve our goal peacefully. It means we must talk, or negotiate on constitutional problems that should be put right or the elimination or amendment of such documents. It means we must always be ready to exercise our voting rights whenever or wherever it is wise and beneficial to do so. It means we must give our service to ANC whenever the country's interest and necessity calls for it. It means we use our money where it is needed in the promotion of the cause of our freedom. It also means making a stand by speech, and writing where one's civil rights may be violated against. It means we have to be individuals endowed with psychological liberty, self-respect and dignity. You would be surprised by how fast we would gain our freedom if more people than we have now were aware of who they were and had pride in themselves.

Although it is the declared policy of the ANC to pursue the goal of freedom non-violently, yet a violent situation has already been created in our country. And we are, unfortunately, in a civil war now. We want to state that there is no country anywhere in the world which can survive and make progress through the tempest of a civil war.

Past and contemporary political history proves we are in the right by advocating non-violent action in solving our constitutional difficulties. Citing a few examples around the world—the Israelis and the Arabs started by an exchange of fire across the Suez Canal, but they are now at a negotiating table—talking. Capitalist America and Communist Russia have regarded each other traditionally as ideological and economic enemies. They have actually fought a bitter war in Vietnam but they ended in France at a negotiating table. And now America and Red China have exchanged high level diplomats and official visits and yet in the past they were hostile to each other. You can multiply more such examples of the modern world where fighting ended by talking. Some people think it is weakness to talk to your enemy or someone you do not agree with.

This is why we think the present confrontation should come to a conference table. Are we going to wait and inevitably come to the negotiating table in wheel chairs, with broken arms and spines, limping and struggling to talk about the atrocities which we could well avoid now before it is too late? I believe with goodwill, political integrity and statesmanship we can do it now.

While I am still on this issue of civil war, I must discuss as false the recurring sentiment that puts the blame for the whole civil war on external forces, which they call communism. I want to be brutally frank and say that these people are Rhodesians by birth and are motivated to fight the oppressive legislation and deprivation of their self-determination. And those who fight from inside are also Rhodesians. Where are the Communists then? It seems, therefore, that to remedy the situation we need to eradicate the internal, rather than the external, anomalies that have provoked the situation.

Mr Chairman, we have so far been talking about every important issue which affects the achieving of our independence. I want to refer again to the settlement issue. We cannot help starting by reminding ourselves of the fact, which is known universally, that we rejected the 1971 settlement proposals. We have reiterated for the last two years why we rejected the terms. Now we need not take time to repeat the reasons. Suffice it to summarize in one sentence that the proposals were unacceptable and from an overall observation and analysis—a sellout.

The time we rejected the proposals was, and is, similar to the time of preparation in the renovation of a house. A builder may tear down a building in order to rebuild. Hence in the same spirit we rejected the terms in order to build an acceptable deal. We, therefore, called for a constitutional conference, a period of negotiation, and dialogue of reflection and talks. We also made it clear that we would welcome talking to anybody, black or white, individual or group, that was interested in achieving a just and honourable settlement. We also maintained that we would not negotiate in public. In fact your President was and is very surprised when some people criticize him for not letting them know what has been going on in regard to the talks. How could this be done without negotiating in public? At any rate we don't rush to the public with little things. Time will be ripe when there are important things to share with everybody in public. . .

. . . But it must be stressed that the ANC does not believe in a constitution that would deprive the white man of all political influence.

The ANC does not aim at driving the white man out of the country or of confiscating his property. We believe in a constitution that will safeguard the rights of all and will ensure all races that they have a place here if they wish to stay.

But the white man must accept the fact that the ANC insists on a Common Roll. We believe in a franchise qualification that will give the vote to the majority of the people of Rhodesia as a whole. We will accept representation in parliament which is a satisfactory sharing of power. We believe that once representation and the franchise have been satisfactorily dealt with, the other matters which are normally part of a constitution would be easy to deal with.

I, therefore, repeat the ANC call to a constitutional conference, and have it immediately, as the only way we can achieve a permanent and healthy solution.

In view of the fact that the issue of the detainees is a hyper-sensitive one, and that it has been too long since these people have been deprived of leading a normal life, we call the government in the name of humanitarianism and justice to review their cases with immediate effect.

. . . I want to call upon all the people of Rhodesia to work hard in their respective areas and capacities of work.

We call upon the African businessmen to support the organization of the people, their own organization, the ANC.

We call upon the African teachers, doctors, nurses, policemen, youths, students and the Africans from all walks of life, to support their organization very seriously, morally, intellectually, and financially. On a financial point I want to challenge the whole African population and other races of goodwill, to each give a special donation. Do you know that if every adult African would give at least 10 cents this month, ANC would raise over $20,000 in addition to the normal subscriptions! Now I call upon you to contribute to this special fund in cash or in postage stamps and send it to the Treasurer-General, ANC Headquarters, P.O. Highfield, in Salisbury.

We call upon our churchmen to do more than praying for the country. They should help make their people politically aware of themselves as persons in need of freedom. I wish to remind you that it was the Christian church which remained the whole voice of justice during the days of Nazi Hitler. A similar situation is here in Rhodesia now.

I want to draw your attention to a matter of politics as an ethical concern. Countrymen, the struggle for freedom is a very serious business which demands characters of high morality with a high degree of self-control and personal integrity, dedication, and commitment to our cause. One of the practices that we must try to refrain from is excessive drinking.

We cannot afford to lose the brains we need to think clearly, and to perform intelligently the great task for leading people from their political bondage to their political promised land. Think of the thousands of dollars that the men and women of our land are wasting throughout the country by drinking. Think of the children and wives who are living like widows and orphans because their bread-winners have become slaves of liquor, and it seems as if they are dead. How can we succeed in our struggle if we are crippled in this way? We need to be our very best physically, intellectually and economically. Liquor does not help us.

I call upon each of you here and in the country as a whole to observe Sunday, 10 March 1974 as a day of mourning for all our country.

Finally, I want to summon all of us to march with perseverence, courage, endurance, determination and in unity as one people of Zimbabwe. And though thousands fall by arbitrary detention, restriction, imprisonment and wanton murder, though a thousand are scattered homeless in the Inyanga Mountain area and in refugee camps elsewhere in the world, though our membership cards and parties get banned, though our people are harassed from time to time, let not the struggle of the freedom of Zimbabwe be given up, but let the struggle be vigorously pursued until the freedom chimes ring from the tower of Zimbabwe. Free—Free—Free—Zimbabwe shall be free!

44 Zimbabwe African National Union: address by Herbert Chitepo, national chairman, to the sixth Pan-African Congress. Dar-es-Salaam, Tanzania, 19–27 June 1974

SIGNIFICANCE OF THE SIXTH PAN-AFRICAN CONGRESS

The Sixth Pan-African Congress is an historic event. It meets at a momentous stage in the decolonization process in Africa, Asia and Latin America.

Many important events have taken place since the last Congress held in 1945. Anti-imperialist and anti-colonialist forces in the Indian sub-continent and Indo-China have scored numerous victories. British, French and American imperialism and colonialism have been given shattering blows in these years.

The period after 1945 has also seen the liberation of the people of African origins in the Caribbean and the resurgence of black power in

North America. But perhaps the most important development since 1945 has been the liberation of large parts of the African continent and the formation of the Organization of African Unity. The only remaining part under colonialist and imperialist domination is southern Africa. Even in these areas which were at one point considered impregnable, the situation is ripe for revolution.

National liberation forces are dealing heavy blows to the white fascists and cracking the wall of the unholy alliance of Lisbon, Pretoria and Salisbury. The military coup in Portugal on 25 April 1974 was a result of the battering of Portuguese soldiers by revolutionary forces in the Portuguese colonies and has thrown the regimes in Salisbury and Pretoria into utter confusion and disarray.

By this measure alone, Africa, the people of African origin and progressive people everywhere have travelled a long way; it is not sanguine to hope that at the next Pan-African Congress there will not be any liberation movement of the kind we know today. It will be a conference of leaders of black governments as well as leaders of black people of African origin in everywhere in the world; liberation movements fighting slavery, colonialists or racism will have come to an end.

But the struggle for African dignity, personal and national worth, the struggle for progress and improving the quality of life will not have come to an end. It will continue. The evil spirit in man that led to slavery, colonialism, capitalism and racism will not have been exorcized. The past can help to predict the future. When slavery became odious and unacceptable, its perpetrators turned to colonialism in order to continue to exploit; and today there exists the Vorsters and Smiths, who pursue the policies of racism for the same reason in order to continue to exploit the black man.

We must expect that even after racism has been dug up and buried exploiters will rise under different guises. That is how the struggle in which we are engaged becomes part of the historical world wide struggle between the forces of progress and those of reaction, between the exploiting classes and the exploited classes, between the bourgeoisie and the working class. That is how we came to identify our struggle with the struggle of the Vietnamese, Palestinians and other progressive forces in Asia, Africa, Latin America and North America. So our struggle merges with the historic social contradictions which have characterized the story of man. Indeed the struggle seeks to resolve these basic social and economic contradictions.

MEANING OF PAN-AFRICANISM

To us Pan-Africanism is the sense of solidarity, unity and identity of African and peoples of African descent wherever they may be. Black people everywhere are united by their colour, history and cultural heritage. Pan-Africanism is also an expression of the African and peoples of African origin's desire to free themselves from the shackles of racism, capitalism, and imperialism so that they can be in a position to decide and determine their future without any strictures.

Pan-Africanism to us is also linked with the just struggle being waged by peoples all over the world against racism, capitalism and imperialism. Pan-Africanism is therefore linked with the struggle for human equality and dignity.

We agree with the late brother George Padmore when he said that Pan-Africanism '. . . rejects both white racism and black chauvinism. It stands for absolute equality and respects human personality. Pan-Africanism looks above the narrow confines of class, tribe and religion.'

It is only by linking the African peoples struggle with the struggle of all exploited peoples in Asia, Latin America and even in capitalist countries that our struggle will be meaningful and will receive universal support. We would like to make it clear that Africans and people of African origins are not fighting for exclusive rights but for universal rights for human equality and dignity. It is the ardent hope of us in Zimbabwe fighting under the leadership of ZANU that this conference will formulate a general strategy for the revolutionary change in Africa and in the world.

GLOBAL STRATEGY AGAINST IMPERIALISM

Given the fact that the Pan-African struggle is fundamentally a struggle against racism, capitalism and imperialism, what should be our global strategy to defeat imperialism?

The basic approach we submit is both to give more material assistance to national liberation movements of Africa and simultaneously to launch our attacks on capitalism and all its manifestations in all fronts—in the developing areas and in the heart of capitalism in North America and Western Europe.

We in ZANU believe that this double pronged approach constitutes the best strategy to attack and defeat racism, capitalism and imperialism. Each movement, each country, or each nation should shoulder the main burden of liberating itself. However, since imperialism has its weakest links in the periphery in Asia, Africa and Latin America, we think that more concerted efforts should be made to defeat imperialism in these areas. Once these areas are liberated they will become bases for the final assault on imperialism at its centre—in other words, underdeveloped areas would provide revolutionary bases from which revolutionaries launch their attack on imperialism. By cutting off the tentacles of imperialism in the periphery, we will deprive the white working class in capitalist countries of their high standards of living they have enjoyed because of the super profits that multi-national companies reaped in underdeveloped countries. It is only when the exploited working class of both black and white realize that they have a common enemy, a common oppressor, and a common exploiter that they will unite to overthrow the capitalist system. This is our global strategy against capitalism, racism and imperialism.

THE ZIMBABWE REVOLUTION

Let us now turn to our concrete situation and experiences in Zimbabwe. For our part in Zimbabwe, we consider our struggle a small contribution towards the liberation of the African continent, the liberation of the people of African descent and the liberation of mankind.

The struggle in Zimbabwe and indeed in southern Africa as a whole is fundamentally between an exploiting class and an exploited class. The exploiters who control political, military and economic power are wholly whites and the exploited and powerless are wholly Africans. Because of this division along racial lines, the struggle in Zimbabwe is also racial. But we must be quick to point out that white racism is only a result of the irrationality of capitalism. Capitalism, to us, has been the major source of economic and social conflict. The concentration in a few hands of the ownership of the means of production and the unequal distribution of the produces of human labour have resulted in a tragic situation where a few countries in Western Europe, USA and Japan have established political, economic, military and cultural hegemony over many parts of the world not yet developed.

There is therefore nothing peculiar with our situation in Zimbabwe. Our society, like any human society, has been in the process of historical development. As this process has unfolded classes and class struggles have emerged with different class position, different class interests, and different ideologies. What this means for us is that as we struggle to change our society in Zimbabwe, we also struggle to change ourselves. This revolution—this total transformation of men on a mass scale, is necessary not only because the ruling racist class cannot be overthrown in any other way, but also because the national liberation movement seeking to overthrow it must rid itself of the muck of ages if it is to be fitted to form the new society of man. We call our revolution 'Chimurenga'—meaning total war of liberation—total transformation of the Zimbabwe society, and the Zimbabwe people.

While our party is guided by the Marxist-Leninist theory of revolution, we are painfully aware that the road from today's settlerism and colonialism in Zimbabwe to socialism is a big jump, and that half way we will have to pass through the transitional stage of national democratic revolution. By this we mean our revolution embraces in its ranks not only the workers, peasants and the urban petty bourgeoisie, but also the national bourgeoisie and other patriotic and anti-imperialist democratic forces. In our present struggle against imperialism, it is absolutely necessary to rally all anti-imperialist patriotic forces that can be united.

The African people of Zimbabwe first in the ANC (African National Congress 1957-9); NDP (National Democratic Party 1959-61) and ZAPU (Zimbabwe African People's Union 1961-2) sought political power through reformist methods of discussion and negotiation with imperialists but to no avail. So they created ZANU on the slogan of Confrontation which is now deployed into today's CHIMURENGA—ARMED STRUGGLE.

ZANU launched armed struggle in Zimbabwe on 28 April 1966. Using modern weapons for the first time the Zimbabwe African National Liberation Army (ZANLA) the military wing of ZANU, inflicted heavy loss on the enemy. Between 1966 and 1969, our forces fought bravely and gallantly at Sinoia, at Hartley, at Lomagundi and in numerous other places. But these initial battles were fought in a social climate in which our people had not been given full political ideology and line. As a result our successes were limited and scattered. The struggle lacked continuity.

The first major lesson we drew from our experience during this first phase of our armed struggle was that support by the masses cannot be taken for granted. We should not assume that because the people are oppressed they will automatically follow us without our winning them to our side.

The second lesson is that we cannot expect to wage guerilla warfare successfully without mass support. As Lenin said: 'The masses who shed their blood on the battlefields are the factor which brings victory in a war;' and as Mao also said: '. . . the masses are the bastion of iron'.

With the experiences gained during the first campaign, ZANU was able between 1969-72, to develop a sophisticated strategy that has produced the north-east front in Zimbabwe. In those three difficult years advance units of ZANU secretly penetrated into Zimbabwe and carried out intensive practical political programmes. By the end of 1972 we had established political cells in many parts of the north-east of Zimbabwe, had recruited many peasants and workers for military training, for assisting in carrying weapons and supplies and in reconnaissance and movement of the enemy.

Towards the end of 1972, ZANU opened its campaign and battles. We have been able since to maintain a level and pace of activity which has driven Ian Smith into panic. Not a week passes without any reports of land mines blowing up a vehicle, an ambush, or a battle. In the period of almost two years, we have extended our activity to cover some 50,000 square miles and embracing some two million Africans. The area is ever expanding. We call these operational zones. In those zones we exercise in relation to our people almost complete control and provide them with some of the services normally provided by government.

The effectiveness of our campaign in Zimbabwe has produced a lot of panic among white settlers. Smith has realized that the real secret of our success is the espousal by the freedom fighters and the peasants and workers alike of a common political ideology and line. And the masses have correctly identified the enemy. Smith has used every trick known to the book of oppression to achieve a divorce between the freedom fighters and the peasants and workers. He has intimidated the people by closing their schools, hospitals and markets; confiscating their property, destroying their homes by indiscriminate bombardment and ruthless uprooting of whole communities. More recently Smith has resorted to cold blood shooting of innocent Africans.

Salisbury prison has become the human butchery where Africans are hanged for opposing his regime. He has also introduced forced labour and so-called protected villages—in fact concentration camps. To give effect to this large programme, his defence budget is ever rising, the armed forces are fully mobilized and more territorials (reserves) are called out for longer and longer periods. An attempt has been made to form a second African regiment and to purchase more mercenaries from Europe for the white army. All to no avail. The African people of Zimbabwe under the leadership of ZANU will not be intimidated or cowed. In spite of their support from South Africa in men and supplies, the settler forces have got bogged down.

The victories that ZANU has so far scored against the fascist forces in Zimbabwe have been the result of constant review of our successes and failures, strategies and tactics, and adapting our strategy to suit our concrete situation. 1969 was therefore a watershed in our revolutionary struggle in Zimbabwe. In the year we reviewed all our previous strategies and tactics and mapped out the strategy which has produced the north-eastern offensive in Zimbabwe. First, political mobilization carried out by advanced units of ZANLA among the workers and peasants succeeded in commiting our people to wage a protracted armed struggle. Second, by involving our people we have made our struggle a people's war and a people's war is invincible. Third, we have succeeded in combining the political and military struggle which is one of the hallmarks in guerilla warfare. Both struggles are waged simultaneously with an accent on the political struggle. To us, the party commands the gun. Our combatants are not only fighters but are also social reformers who register and respond to the grievances of the people. The combination of political and military struggles has worked against the tendency toward militarism in our struggle. Four, we have also succeeded because our strategy has been focused on the rural areas. Just as the underdeveloped areas are the weakest links of imperialism and the rear bases so are rural areas the weakest links and the rear bases of our fight against the minority regime in Salisbury. The countryside provided broad areas for our revolutionary forces to manoeuvre freely. Finally, we are scoring victory after victory because of the material support we have received from progressive African countries, socialist countries and progressive groups and organizations in northern America.

However, one of the major lessons we have learnt in our struggle in Zimbabwe is the policy of self reliance. Africans and peoples of African descent invariably support each other in their struggles against racism, capitalism, and imperialism. Socialist countries and all progressive forces in the world are duty bound to support and assist national liberation struggles and the peoples who have not yet achieved freedom. But international support, no matter how large it may be, can only play a supplementary role. The key to the liberation of Zimbabwe lies with our own strength, our own sweat, our own blood and creativity, particularly our own ability to adapt the revolutionary experiences of others to our own concrete situation. It is only through our reliance on the strength of the masses in our own country and our preparedness to carry on the fight independently that we can achieve genuine independence. As our President, Comrade Ndabaningi Sithole declared ten years ago: 'Independence is not ours unless we liberate ourselves. There is no such thing as being liberated by others. Others can only help us to liberate ourselves. We are our own liberators.' We are our own liberators has since become the cornerstone of ZANU's policy.

Finally, we would like to take this opportunity to warn Ian Smith that his days in Zimbabwe are numbered. ZANU will relentlessly increase the onslaught on white settlers in Zimbabwe. Smith must not deceive himself that he can bypass the armed revolutionary struggle launched by ZANU by trying to hoodwink Bishop Muzorewa or the ANC into accepting the legalization of his regime. And if Muzorewa of the ANC accepts offers which compromise the Zimbabwe peoples' rights to total independence they are not true successors of the spirit which created Pan-Africanism . . .

SECTION IV

THE PERIOD OF ARMED STRUGGLE AND DETENTE 1974-1976

The fourth and last period in this analysis witnessed the co-existence of armed struggle and detente in order to achieve majority rule in Zimbabwe.

The so-called Vorster-Kaunda detente exercise resulted in the Lusaka Declaration of Unity of 7 December 1974; the release of African leaders from detention; the frustration of armed struggle and the abortive Victoria Falls bridge talks. After the resumption of armed struggle the United States intervention in southern Africa—the so-called Kissinger peace initiative—resulted in the latest constitutional talks which began in Geneva in October 1976.

Unity and leadership questions were also dominant.

CHAPTER TEN

FROM LUSAKA TO VICTORIA FALLS

45a Zimbabwe Declaration of Unity. Lusaka, 7 December 1974

ZANU, ZAPU, FROLIZI, and ANC, hereby agree to unite in the ANC.

2. The Parties recognize the ANC as the unifying force of the people of Zimbabwe.

(a) They agree to consolidate the leadership of the ANC by the inclusion into it of the presidents of ZANU, ZAPU and FROLIZI under the chairmanship of the President of the ANC.

(b) ZAPU, ZANU and FROLIZI shall each appoint three other persons to join the enlarged ANC executive.

4. The enlarged ANC executive shall have the following functions:

(a) To prepare for any conference for the transfer of power to the majority that might be called.

(b) To prepare for the holding of a congress within four months at which—

(i) A revised ANC constitution shall be adopted;

(ii) the leadership of the united people of Zimbabwe shall be elected;

(iii) a statement of policy for the new ANC will be considered.

(c) To organize the people for such conference and congress.

5. The leadership of the ZAPU, ZANU and FROLIZI call upon their supporters and all Zimbabweans to rally behind the ANC under its enlarged executive.

6. ZAPU, ZANU and FROLIZI will take steps to merge their respective organs and structures into the ANC before the congress to be held within four months.

7. The Leaders recognize the inevitability of continued armed struggle and all other forms of struggle until the total liberation of Zimbabwe.

Signed: ABEL TENDEKAYI MUZOREWA   *President of ANC*
Signed: JOSHUA MQABUKO NKOMO   *President of ZAPU*
Signed: NDABANINGI SITHOLE   *President of ZANU*
Signed: JAMES ROBERT CHIKEREMA   *President of FROLIZI*

State House,   Lusaka

45b Salisbury Declaration, 11 December 1974

Recognizing the paramount need for unity in the Zimbabwe liberation struggle, the executive committees of ZAPU, ZANU, FROLIZI and ANC have met in Lusaka to discuss the aims, objectives, and methods to be pursued. Full agreement was reached on the following points:

1. We have agreed to unite under one organization with immediate effect. We have agreed further, that this organization shall be the African National Council.
2. We shall be working for the independence of our country. We assume that on this demand for independence there is no difference among Rhodesians of all races. But there has until now been a difference on the kind of independence which Zimbabwe must have. The Rhodesian Front has, in the past, sought independence on the basis of minority rule. We reject that. The independence we still seek, is independence on the basis of majority rule.
3. For the purpose of achieving that objective we have always been ready to enter into negotiations with others concerned. Now that some of us have been released from detention, we believe the time is ripe for us to repeat this offer. Without pre-conditions on both sides we are ready to enter into immediate and meaningful negotiations with leaders of the Rhodesian Front, and with the British government in Britain, on the steps to be taken to achieve independence on the basis of majority rule.
4. As a demonstration of our sincerity, all freedom fighters will be instructed, as soon as a date for negotiations has been fixed, to suspend fighting.
5. We are not racialists. We accept the right of white Rhodesians to live in Rhodesia and share the same rights and obligations of citizenship as their fellow Rhodesian of the majority community, without any discrimination on grounds of race, colour or creed.
6. We call upon all Rhodesians, and all who reside in Rhodesia, to remain calm, maintain peace and to go about their normal business, while these matters are being considered, and while any negotiations are proceeding.
7. We call upon all Zimbabweans, wherever they are, to remain united behind the demand for independence on the basis of majority rule, and to give full support to the African National Council.

8. We appeal to all our friends in Africa and abroad to continue their support for our struggle until independence is achieved on the basis of majority rule.

Signed: ABEL TENDEKAYI MUZOREWA   *President of ANC*
Signed: JOSHUA MQABUKO NKOMO   *Former President of ZAPU*
Signed: NDABANINGI SITHOLE   *Former President of ZANU*
Signed: JAMES ROBERT DAMBADZA CHIKEREMA
            Former President of FROLIZI

46   Resolution on Zimbabwe by the 24th session of the Council of Ministers of the OAU

A. Reaffirming the new strategy adopted by the Liberation Committee in Dar-es-Salaam on 8-14 January 1975 which gives priorities to the liberation of Zimbabwe and Namibia;

B. *Appreciating* the initiatives taken by the Presidents Kenneth Kaunda Julius Nyerere, Seretse Khama and Samora Machel to achieve the attainment of majority rule;

C. *Noting* with satisfaction the Unity Declaration adopted by the nationalist movements of Zimbabwe on 7 December 1974 in Lusaka and current efforts to consolidate it;

(a)   *Recommends* substantial increase in the financial support to the United Movements under the ANC in order to enable the people of Zimbabwe to intensify their armed struggle until total liberation is achieved;

(b)   *Calls upon* all states to adhere strictly to the UN and OAU resolutions on economic sanctions and diplomatic isolation of the illegal regime;

(c)   *Condemns* South Africa for her military presence and assistance to the illegal regime and call upon her to withdraw her troops forthwith.

(d)   *Requests* the four presidents to increase their efforts to find a solution to the Zimbabwe problem based on one man one vote.

(e)   *Congratulates* Zimbabwe nationalist movements for their achievements of unity and urges them to institute all immediate measures to strengthen and consolidate their unity.

47 African National Council: a broadcast appeal to Zimbabweans at home and abroad, by Bishop Abel Muzorewa, President. Lusaka, Zambia, 19 March 1975

I speak to you tonight with a very heavy and grieved heart, because of the untimely death of our dynamic and dedicated comrade, Herbert Chitepo.

Bearing in mind this tragic event, and the need for rededication to the struggle for majority rule in Zimbabwe, I appeal to you to pay special attention to what I will say tonight.

In 1963 at the time of the split a demon invaded Zimbabwe, and in particular the African townships of Harare and Highfield in Salisbury, Mpopoma and Luveve in Bulawayo, Mkoba in Gwelo, and Mucheke in Fort Victoria only to mention a few of the haunted areas. The demon ravaged the entire country petrol-bombing to death and maiming innocent children, men and women. The monster also killed and crippled our livestock, plundered our business and burnt down church and school buildings. Our beautiful daughters lost their virginity through organized thuggery and rape.

Eleven year old illegitimates from madiro are still a shameful legacy of those turbulent years. Magnificent houses and beautiful cars were stoned and destroyed. The educated and the affluent were victimized. To have a differing political opinion was tantamount to witchcraft and as a result some of us lost confidence in ourselves and sacrificed self-rule.

What was the cause of that dramatic tragedy? Surely it was the calculated split between ZAPU and ZANU which occurred in 1963. The then Southern Rhodesia became HELL on earth. People did not have to die to go to HELL—HELL had descended upon us.

In fact, we were in the same situation as the people in Northern Ireland find themselves today where people of the same blood and colour live like cats and dogs locked in the same kennel or in reality where peace and unity do not exist.

Furthermore, we deprived ourselves of black majority rule for the next 11 years while the Rhodesian Front successfully manipulated these tragic events to the entrenchment of oppressive rule and segregatory legislation thereby sabotaging the early achievement of our freedom.

Let us be brutally frank and swallow the bitter truth that the masses breathed a big sigh of relief when PCC and ZANU were banned in 1964. That was not because we condoned Rhodesian Front rule. No. But because we condemned our fearful and self-destructive actions. . . .

I, therefore, summon every Zimbabwean wherever and whoever he is, at home and abroad, to come forward in the name of God Almighty and all the saints of Zimbabwe and for the sake of the struggle for our freedom, to observe with honesty the Declaration for the Unity of Zimbabwe made at State House here in Lusaka, Zambia, on 7 December 1974. I entreat each one of you to make the letter and spirit of that declaration a living reality and certainly the best and most effective way to do that is to be absolutely purpose-centred and not self- or tribe-centred.

ONE NOBLE PURPOSE

My observation in the African National Council for the last three years has been that when people are motivated and united under one sole purpose they can perform miracles, in harmony and peace with one another.

For example, the ANC was born out of a real threat of political assassination, posed by the Smith-Home settlement proposals. It was then that ZAPU, ZANU, NPU, the trade unions, churches, the foresighted African civil servants and the masses who were not committed to any organization, stood with ONE voice and with ONE NOBLE PURPOSE, to reject the now defunct settlement proposals.

Thus, that Zimbabwe characterized by apathy, disunity and fear of both ourselves and police was spontaneously transformed into ONE purpose-centred people.

Under the banner of unity and purpose in the ANC we regained our self-confidence. We succeeded in liberating the minds of those who were slaves of fear and disunity. We healed those who were politically wounded. And under our policy of non-violence we did not coerce people to support the organization and the cause. Under that policy we learned to respect each other. We tolerated even the destitutes and the so-called settlement groups who, backed by the white industrialists, ravaged the country advocating the acceptance of the Smith-Home proposals against the will and the stand of the people of Zimbabwe.

There was a new and positive relationship and mutual respect between the nationalist movement and the church. Generally under the acceleration of self, social and political awareness, we witnessed an amazing amicable relationship among ourselves as a people of one blood and colour ought to do. We demonstrated to our enemies, to each other and the world how democratic we could be if we became a government. In fact, we behaved like a government in waiting.

By our democratic stance we shattered the smearing campaign against us and the reputation posed by imperialists that all African people are 'hooligans, agitators, intimidators, irresponsible and rabble rousers'. We remained resolute and uncompromising in spite of these incessant recriminations.

NOTHING SHORT OF MAJORITY RULE

As the present united ANC, let us remind ourselves of what that continuing PURPOSE must be and is—namely, that we seek to achieve majority rule. People with self or tribal interest have liked to divide us by saying that ANC was not interested in majority rule. Take it from me today, that it is a red and dirty lie. If we didn't like majority rule, what is it that we are struggling for?

Now, countrymen, is there anything else short of majority rule under the sun or in the name of sanity, sanctity or goodwill that should predominate or preoccupy our struggle?

I want to state here and now, in the name of total liberation of Zimbabwe that if there is any person or leader, whether he be on the branch, district, provincial or national level in the ANC, exiled or anywhere in the world labouring for anything other than the achievement of majority rule, that person or leader must be the arch enemy of Zimbabwe's freedom. What would that person struggle for? Personal gain or power? Disunity? Perhaps an agent and spy for the enemy?

Let me reiterate and remind you of what I said at the inaugural congress of the ANC in March 1974, how we should be aware of the enemies of Zimbabwe. Knowing them as you do, I still maintain that we should all be on our guard and overcome those enemies of our freedom, by everything at our disposal.

WE MUST BE ON GUARD

Let us therefore:

Watch out for the people whose chief aim and ambition is to enhance their personal prestige at the expense of the peace and freedom of the masses of Zimbabwe. People who do not know how to follow the wish of the masses and other people's leadership.

Watch out for people who are neither loyal to the country nor to their leaders, except to themselves.

Watch out for people who suffer from the power-hungry leprosy; people who count upon what positions they will hold personally or their relatives and friends or their tribal groups or even former party or organization. You must overcome them for they delay our inevitable majority rule.

Watch out for the people whose primary purpose is to gain credit for what they may have achieved or contributed to the struggle and those that seek prestige for its own sake.

Watch out for the people who are actively working against the peace and unity we painfully acquired.

Countrymen, how else can we regard the persons who spend their time, energy and money senselessly dividing Zimbabwe and literally setting its good people at each other's throats?

Watch out for people who in one breath condemn white racism against blacks and in the next practise tribalism against their own people who have the same culture, colour and country.

Watch out for our own people who, because they have been tragically brainwashed by colonialism, look at the inevitability of majority rule as a physical impossibility. Those are crippled personalities who thrive on cowardice and worship other races. Such people suffer from an inferiority complex.

UNITY AND URGENCY

Let me re-emphasize that from the very beginning right up to the time when the detente exercise was called for in southern Africa, we have always called for a peaceful solution to the independence issue. We have in the same call repeatedly warned that failure to achieve that goal in a non-violent way would result in unnecessary bloodshed to both black and white.

The South African Prime Minister merely echoed our policy when he said that 'the alternative to any peaceful constitutional change in Rhodesia is too ghastly to contemplate'.

And when we presented the Declaration of Unity for Zimbabwe at State House in Lusaka we categorically stated that 'we recognize the inevitability of armed struggle, should our endeavours for peaceful change fail'.

Sons and daughters of Zimbabwe, there are those of us who indulge in pretentious talk and say that we are prepared to suffer even more as we have suffered so much before, in the struggle to achieve our freedom. Some of those people forget that they speak and play their politics from the ivory towers of the big cities and universities of the world and in the cities of oppressed Rhodesia. These same people sleep on the most comfortable beds, eat the most delicious meals and drive in large luxurious cars. Sometimes we pathetically overlook the fact that our sons and daughters at our borders are at the mercy of mosquitos, snakes, lions and leopards. And our people in the so-called protected villages and war-zones are dying from torture and disease. Yes, we must be willing to suffer for the real cause. But we must not allow suffering for the sake of suffering.

If we can hasten the end to this suffering and senseless loss of life, the better for our people in Zimbabwe. Brothers and sisters, let us tackle the Zimbabwe crisis in the spirit of purpose, unity and urgency. And think of what methods will deliver the goods of majority rule quicker.

THINK UNITY, ACT UNITY

In reality that spirit of UNITY calls us to recognize appreciatively that several factors have induced the imperialists to show signs of wanting to talk with us. Those factors presuppose the United Nations backed economic sanctions against Rhodesia, and the involuntary isolation of Rhodesia from the international community, also the commendable resilient attitude of our people living in the zones of armed conflict, who have suffered and continue to suffer more than some of us and the world realize, and of course the armed struggle. Let us not forget the masses of Zimbabwe who overwhelmingly rejected the Smith-Home proposals for a settlement without whom Rhodesia should long have been recognized. The political detainees and prisoners cannot go unmentioned for they have always stood tall among us as symbols of our solidarity and freedom. These efforts and sacrifices have, of late, brought the spirit of detente with its chief architects the honourable presidents of the Republics of Zambia, Tanzania, Botswana, and of Frelimo, the Prime Minister of South Africa, the Organization of African Unity and all those who helped and continue to help us financially, morally and otherwise.

Furthermore, the spirit of unity calls us to accept the fact that the freedom fighters are children of Zimbabwe who were motivated by nothing else but the profound desire to see Zimbabwe free. They, therefore, decided to communicate with our enemy through the language of physical confrontation. Unselfish people would therefore readily acknowledge that the young men and women are the children of Zimbabwe by birth from different parents scattered all over Zimbabwe, and fighting for Zimbabwe. There is no one particular person or group who can boastfully claim that this young blood has been and is being shed for a particular individual or individuals. The blood is being shed for Zimbabwe's liberation. Their precious lives should not be diverted from the noble purpose to a civil war among blacks themselves.

The same spirit of unity and humility does not permit the attitude that those who were and are in prison or detention deserve the highest places in the coming kingdom of Zimbabwe by virtue of their being where they are. With all due respect if we seriously, objectively and honestly entertain that view then the people who must be considered for such lofty places at all in future Zimbabwe are none other than those fighting and languishing in the bush.

We are challenged to make every effort to reconcile ourselves in thought, word and deed, to live under a new motto: MOTIVATED BY UNITY. THINK UNITY, ACT UNITY.

THE SPIRIT OF BROTHERHOOD

Let us behave like faithful parties in wedlock. We should not be like a bride who uses her maiden name soon after the marriage ceremony. In other words, let us stop this unfaithfulness to our recent political bond of marriage—UNITY.

The letter and spirit of our Declaration of Unity forbids that we indulge in futile divisive conversation in pubs, clubs, hotels and all other public places. Let us engage ourselves in constructive talk which culminates in working out peaceful ways and means of achieving majority rule.

I remind you that the stride toward our freedom is a tempting exercise. We should refuse to be divided into the so-called camps of 'militants', 'extremists', 'moderates', 'freedom fighter', or 'nationalists', by the enemies of unity and freedom. Neither should we be deviated from the course of our unity by intimidatory tactics such as arrests or imprisonments similar to the recent detention of our colleague and fellow struggler, the Rev Ndabaningi Sithole, and the death of Comrade Chitepo.

Let us be mature and wise enough to embrace each other in the spirit of brotherhood and unity in our struggle. The grassroots people in our organization and country have demonstrated during the last three years that they are peace-loving and purpose-centred followers.

Such a good loyal people deserve a good, dedicated purpose-centred and united leadership. . . .

TOTAL EMANCIPATION OF ZIMBABWE

Onward we march in our struggle with one aim of overcoming our enemies. We can only do that by the powerful weapon of unity. Our bickering and disunity can only be time-consuming, destructive and make us lose our goal. We should learn from our past experiences as the old English proverb says: 'Wise men learn from other people's mistakes but fools do not'. . . .

Let us, therefore, forgive and forget our past differences. Let us bury our grudges in the abominable tomb of disunity. Let us sink our hatred in the deep ocean of the past. Let us throw away our bitterness, resentment and dissensions.

I have no apology to make when I appeal to you in the name of Great Zimbabwe to stop any acts of enmity and disunity.

Let us concentrate on getting back the country from the imperialists first and then leave the good people of Zimbabwe to choose their leadership in the normal, peaceful and democratic way.

Let no one misunderstand me. I, in no uncertain terms, desire with all my heart and spirit the total emancipation of Zimbabwe and conscientiously look forward to the establishment of majority rule. But, and it is a very big BUT, I pray, and hope you do the same, that we all move to that historic day in harmony and peace one with another. The happiness, power and prosperity of Zimbabwe ultimately depends upon our love and dedication for unity, and that unity must be made real NOW.

MAJORITY RULE IS INEVITABLE

Having addressed myself chiefly to black Zimbabweans, let me direct a few remarks to whites in Rhodesia in particular, and those in southern Africa in general. The coming of majority rule is inevitable. This is fact and no fiction.

With this in mind whites must ask themselves whether they wish to make this part of the world their permanent home. Obviously, those who want to stay can help by promoting the achievement of majority rule and the detente movement instead of sabotaging the efforts to bring about peaceful change in Zimbabwe and southern Africa.

Whites will have to change their racialistic attitudes. They will have to change their discriminatory legislation and practices such as job reservation, and the inequitable distribution of wealth. But let me assure you that we are not fighting whites. We are fighting evil and oppression.

Let it be made clear now that the dignity of all Zimbabweans must be respected.

In conclusion, let me point out that we want to correct the present abnormal situation whereby a minority tries, with little success, to protect the rights of the majority. Instead, the majority should take the responsibility of ruling and protecting the rights and properties of the minority. And make no mistake, this we are capable of doing, and have the spirit and will to execute it. I, therefore, call upon the blacks, whites, coloureds and Asians to work together now for one community and one nation based on peace and understanding.

Lastly, let me say how extremely grateful I am to my very dear comrade, His Excellency President Kenneth Kaunda, his party and government for their hospitality and dedication to our struggle in Zimbabwe.

Were it not for the Zambian government you would not have had the opportunity of listening to this broadcast, because the Salisbury regime has denied us these facilities.

48 President Kaunda's broadcast message to Zambia. Lusaka, 31 March 1975.

As you know, Zambia recently witnessed one of the worst criminal acts perpetrated against the people of Zimbabwe and their struggle, and against Zambia's boundless efforts in support of that liberation struggle. This was the brutal assassination of the late Herbert Chitepo, one of the most leading nationalists of Zimbabwe.

We are shocked. We are still grieved and angered. We remain bitter against the murderous act, bitter against the murderers—the enemies of the Zimbabwe revolution, the enemies of Zambia and Africa. Many Zambians are, to say the least, very dismayed and justifiably irritated by statements made by some Zimbabwe nationals. Some, even nationalist leaders, have shown no concern whatsoever for the assassination of Mr Chitepo. To them Mr Chitepo has been assassinated and that must be the end. Instead of calling upon the party and government to track down the killers of this gallant fighter, they are either completely silent, while others virtually demand that we stop the investigation altogether and thereby shelter the assassins and their imperialist paymasters. This is really asking imperialism and racism to continue corrupting the minds of freedom fighters and to deal a heavy blow on our struggle. Can we stop the investigation? I say categorically, NO. We are going ahead with full strength till we find the culprits and identify the real agent bent on disrupting armed struggle.

Why must the investigation continue?

First: Because Mr Chitepo was not an animal. He was first and foremost a normal human being.

Second: He was a prominent leader of his people, a fighter for peace, freedom and justice. He sacrificed so much in his own life for the good of the people of Zimbabwe.

Third: He was not killed in the battlefield but at his house, not inside Zimbabwe but on Zambian soil. So we are taking full responsibility for finding the culprits. Under our law, murder is a grave offence punishable by death. So we have a duty to find the culprits and that duty we will fulfil. But let me say this. We know ultimately the responsibility for the tragic and untimely death of Mr Chitepo squarely rests on Ian Smith's shoulders. He cannot escape that responsibility.

Smith created the unhealthy condition which led Mr Chitepo to leave his motherland.

Smith declared UDI which has led to the bitter armed conflict between African nationalists and the rebel regime.

Smith has continued to create conditions for the escalation of the armed struggle and closed all avenues for peaceful change.

Smith has left only one way to achieve peace based on majority rule and that is violence which in process has taken Mr Chitepo's life. Thus Mr Chitepo's assassins are clearly the creation of Ian Smith.

It is our national and international duty to seek these agents out, expose them and bring them to book. We have a duty to investigate the cause of Mr Chitepo's death and we intend to carry out that investigation with the thoroughness of a toothcomb. We will leave no stone unturned.

We have already taken some measures. We have rounded up a number of people including some Rhodesian nationals and their leaders.

In the present conditions we must take into account the following:

(a)   Smith has agents among freedom fighters just as we know of his agents among Zambians.

(b)   Imperialists have agents among freedom fighters as they have among Zambians.

(c)   Among those who shout loudest about revolution and armed struggle are found, well-camouflaged, the most dangerous counter-revolutionaries and saboteurs.

(d)   Reactionaries often hide behind revolutionary rhetoric to cover up their counter-revolutionary and diabolical intentions and actions. Reactionary elements can be more extreme in advocating revolutionary actions which are in fact designed to take the masses along the wrong political line and lead fighters into an ambush by the enemy.

(e)   Finally, it requires no special talent to criticize and insult. Even the stupid, the ignorant and the insane can and do criticize. Zambians must not be unduly perturbed by insults.

We know we are a sovereign state. We are independent. We want others to attain independence. We are committed to give all possible assistance to the oppressed in order to overthrow their oppressors and achieve independence like us. We have demonstrated in practical terms our commitment to the cause of the oppressed in Southern Africa and elsewhere in the world. No price has been too high to pay for the freedom of others.

In this great African endeavour to liberate the rest of Africa, there is no struggle which has been as expensive for Zambia as that currently waged in Zimbabwe. We have spent millions of Kwacha. We have lost more lives and property to assist the Zimbabweans in their liberation struggle than we have lost in the armed struggle to free Mozambique and Angola.

The sacrifice we have made in terms of development is greater in respect of Zimbabwe than the amount of sacrifice made in the struggle for independence in Mozambique and Angola. Zimbabweans themselves know that whatever successes have been achieved in the armed struggle have depended on what sacrifice Zambians have been able to make. We do not dispute the fact that the future of Zimbabwe will be decided by Zimbabweans. This is what we are fighting for. But it is a fact that no country, no people in the world apart from Zimbabweans themselves, have suffered more for the freedom of Zimbabwe than Zambians. We have paid and we will continue to pay a just price for the freedom of our brothers and sisters. But to suggest that we are frustrating the struggle by investigating the assassination of Mr Chitepo is not only to show no regard for this prominent leader, but also to add very grave insult to the irreparable injuries sustained by Zambians in their unequivocal support for majority rule in Zimbabwe.

We have nothing to hide from Zimbabwe, the OAU and the world. I have thus, on behalf of the Party, government and people of Zambia, decided to establish a Special Commission of Inquiry to carry out the investigation. The Special Commission will consist of a team selected from UNIP, Central Committee and Cabinet. I am also inviting some members of the OAU Liberation Committee and its Executive Secretary as well as representatives of Botswana, Zaire, Congo (Brazzaville), Malawi, Tanzania and Frelimo, to be members of the Special Commission. Zambia Security Services will be at the disposal of the Commission in its investigation.

I want the Special Commission to thoroughly study the events leading up to Mr Chitepo's death. To this end, I invite anyone, anywhere in Zambia, Zimbabwe and the rest of the world who has any evidence to help the Commission to come forward. I especially invite leaders in Zimbabwe and their compatriots in the world who feel very strongly about our actions to come to Zambia and give the Commission the facts. We will provide a full report to the OAU following the findings of the Commission.

As always, we in Zambia want to be completely honest about the recent events. We will be honest in the interests of the struggle we have vowed to support until victory is won in Zimbabwe.

At the same time, this Inquiry will not interfere with the criminal proceedings through a court of law if the assassins are found. We view Mr Chitepo's death with utmost gravity.

Finally, let me say that we understand the situation in Southern Africa very well. We know what we are doing. We know every step we are taking. The armed struggle in Zimbabwe has not ended, it will continue; it will be intensified unless majority rule is achieved. Smith must not be under any illusions whatever. 1975 is a year of decision.

Only his positive decision can help avert the escalation of war which he is bound to lose. Victory is on the side of the majority and Zambia will spare no efforts and time to guarantee that victory. I call upon Zambians and the rest of Africa to rally together and unite their efforts to bring about the victory now overdue. With God's guiding hand and His inspiration we will win as long as we are united in our national and international purpose.

God bless the republic.

Good night.

49 Rev Ndabaningi Sithole: on the assassination of Herbert Chitepo and ZANU. 10 May 1976

Dear Zimbabwean,

Since the assassination of Mr Herbert Chitepo on 18 March 1975, I have been silent on the whole matter for obvious reasons of not wishing to appear to be meddling in the affairs of Zambia and of not wishing to prejudice in any way the international investigation that was going on.

But now I feel free to speak out my mind on the matter since the *Report of the Special International Commission on the Assassination of Herbert Wiltshire Chitepo* has been released to the public. I have studied the *Report* very carefully, and I must say that the findings of the Commission confirm my own findings of April–May 1975, which I have largely kept to myself.

There can be no doubt that the events that took place in ZANU in December 1974 and January to March 1975, constitute a black chapter in the annals of the liberation of Zimbabwe, but we should learn a few important lessons from our mistakes of the past so that we may avoid these in future. To close our eyes to our own serious mistakes and blunders would be to do our own nation of Zimbabwe great disservice. Let us admit our blunders and let us resolve not to repeat them in future. Only in this spirit can we learn from our past mistakes.

In this long letter, I wish to make a careful analysis of the true nature of the problem that faces us as a nation. We cannot afford to think and act small without tragic consequences for ourselves and for our country.

The main thesis of my letter is that ZANU as we had first formed it became constantly subjected to a process of tribalization or regionalization that it lost completely the national perspective with the result that unprecedented kidnappings and killings within ZANU took place and culminated in the assassination of Zimbabwe's greatly esteemed and admired Herbert Chitepo who was regarded as a man of great national stature by all Zimbabweans who knew him.

In order that we may see the true nature of the problem that faces us as a nation, I wish to analyse first the Dare to which the ZANU Central Committee in detention had delegated power to prosecute the armed struggle, and, secondly, the High Command which was a practical implementation of part of that armed struggle.

1. After the biennial review conference of April 1969, the Dare at its full strength comprised three Manyika or easterners; three Zezuru or north-easterners; and two Karanga or south-easterners.

    This means that the Dare was 37.5 per cent Manyika or eastern; 37.5 per cent Zezuru or north-eastern; and 25 per cent Karanga or south-eastern.

2. When the 1971 ZANU conference was held at Kafue, Zambia, for election to the Dare, the Dare at its full strength comprised four Manyika or easterners; three Karanga or south-easterners; and one Zezuru or north-easterner.

    This means that the Dare was 50 per cent Manyika or eastern; 37.5 per cent Karanga or south-eastern; and 12.5 per cent Zezuru or north-eastern.

3. After the review conference of September 1973, the Dare at its full strength comprised five Karanga or south-easterners; and three Manyika or easterners.

This means that the Dare was 62.5 per cent Karanga or south-eastern and 37.5 per cent Manyika or eastern.

4. After the so-called Nhari rebellion of December 1974 the Dare comprised five Karanga or south-easterners; and one Manyika or easterner.

This means that the Dare was now 83 per cent Karanga or south-eastern, and 17 per cent Manyika or eastern.

5. By January, 1975, the Dare, for all practical purposes had become nearly completely tribalized or regionalized as the following diagram illustrates:

Year	Karanga or south-eastern		Manyika eastern		Zezuru or north-eastern	
	No	%	No	%	No	%
1969	2	25	3	37.5	3	37.5
1971	3	37.5	4	50	1	12.5
1973	5	62.5	3	37.5	—	—
1974	5	83	1	17	—	—
1975	5	83	1	17	—	—

6. When we formed ZANU in 1963, it was called the Zimbabwe African National Union, but by 1974 and at the beginning of 1975, it had become in practice 'Zimbabwe African Tribal Union' masquerading under the respectable garbs of the ZANU of 1963. The tribalized or regionalized Dare had therefore ceased to represent ZANU as we knew it. It had come to represent in effect ZATU (Zimbabwe African Tribal Union) or ZARU (Zimbabwe African Regional Union).

7. Even a superficial examination of the ZANU military High Command also shows a corresponding process of tribalization or regionalization.

8. After the review conference of 1973, the High Command comprised five Karanga or south-easterners; three Zezuru or north-easterners; and one Manyika or easterner.

This means that ZANU's High Command was 55 per cent Karanga or south-eastern; 34 per cent Zezuru or north-eastern; and 11 per cent Manyika or eastern.

9. After the so-called Nhari rebellion of December 1974, ten new additions were made to the High Command so that at its full strength it comprised 15 Karanga south-easterners and one Manyika or easterner.

This means that the new High Command of December 1974, was 79 per cent Karanga or south-eastern; 16 per cent Zezuru or north-eastern; and five per cent Manyika or eastern.

10. At this point the High Command had become completely tribalized or regionalized. It had therefore lost its true ZANU character. It had become a ZATU or ZARU High Command. A tribalized or regionalized Dare could not possibly avoid an equally tribalized or regionalized High Command.

11. By December 1974, both the Dare and the High Command had become completely tribalized or regionalized, and the liberation politics of ZANU then followed tribal or regional lines resulting in the present confusion among former ZANU supporters. The tribe or region, instead of the new nation of Zimbabwe, became the centre of ZANU politics which have had tragic consequences vis-à-vis the organization itself and the armed struggle which is our only credible alternative.

12. The following table shows clearly tribalized or regionalized Dare and High Command:

Year	Karanga or south-easterners		Manyika or easterners		Zezuru or north-easterners	
	% Dare	% High Command	% Dare	% High Command	% Dare	% High Command
1973	62.5	55	37.5	11	—	34
1974	83	79	17	5	—	16
1975	83	79	17	5	—	16

It should be noted that after Chitepo's death, the Dare became 100 per cent tribalized or regionalized.

13. The present High Command which was formed without consulting and involving the ANC leadership consists of nine ex-ZANU and nine ex-ZAPU officers. All the ex-ZANU officers have connections with the tribalized or regionalized Dare and belonged to the tribalized or regionalized High Command of the former ZANU.

14. The so-called Third Force which has been unfortunately projected as a rival of the ANC (Z) has had the effect of resuscitating the tribalized or regionalized Dare and High Command which have already resulted in armed conflict since the majority of the cadres are utterly opposed to the whole idea of the Third Force.

15. It is significant that ex-ZANU supporters in the UK, USA and Zambia who refuse to work within the ANC as required by the Zimbabwe Declaration of Unity of 7 December 1974, are those who strongly and effectively promoted the tribalization or regionalization of the Dare and the High Command which resulted in the kidnappings and killings within ZANU culminating in Chitepo's assassination in March 1975.

16. The problem which we now face as a new nation is essentially a tribal or regional one. The advocates of tribalized or regionalized political and military leadership can help us in this matter by joining us in the effort to detribalize or deregionalize the attitudes and outlooks of those who have been tragically misled to believe that one tribe or one region can ever be the centre of the politics of Zimbabwe. No one tribe or region can be the centre of Zimbabwe. In other words our basic problem is to untribalize or unregionalize Zimbabweans whose present efforts are grossly misdirected and are a discredit to the whole national effort.

17. If the death of our Herbert Chitepo is to be associated with any 'ism', it cannot be directly or immediately be with colonialism, imperialism or capitalism, but rather with tribalism or regionalism. This is to say tribalists or regionalists are responsible, for Chitepo's death. If it is to be associated with any race, it can only be the African race. If it is to associate with any political party it can only be with ZANU which had been perverted into ZATU or ZARU. If it is to be associated with any persons, it can only be with those who worked closely with him within ZANU itself.

18. Those who have essayed to justify the kidnappings and killings within ZANU culminating in the assassination of Herbert Chitepo have put forward a punitive thesis which is not acceptable on the following grounds:

(i) If those who had been killed as a matter of disciplinary measure had been dealt with when the ZANU Central Committee had been in prison or detention the punitive thesis would probably be acceptable. But as it is the Dare to whom the Central Committee had delegated power to prosecute the armed struggle during their period of detention took an extreme punitive measure *when the ZANU Central Committee was out of prison or detention and free to attend to such matters.*

(ii) The fundamental question then arises: Why did the Dare have to take such an extreme action when the Central Committee from which they derived their power was free to attend to such matters?

   The answer to this question is self-evident. With the tribalization or regionalization of ZANU, the Central Committee had ceased to exist in the minds of the tribalized or regionalized Dare and the High Command and the Dare had, by a process of usurpation become the Central Committee to the exclusion of the real ZANU Central Committee. In other words, the genuine ZANU Central Committee had become irrelevant to the Dare and hence the latter took such serious matters into its own hands to the exclusion of the former.

(iii) A new orientation had already been introduced in ZANU that the gun commands the party, and not the party the gun. The present High Command which was formed without consulting and involving the ANC leadership is in fact a continuation of this new and foreign thesis that the gun commands the Party. Our fundamental teaching in ZANU was that the Party commands the gun, and not the gun the Party. In Zimbabwe we maintain without reservation that the gun cannot decide the question of national leadership, but the collective will of the people of Zimbabwe. The so-called Third Force is also an unwitting extension of this wrong-headed doctrine that the gun leads the Party instead of the Party leading the gun. National leadership through the barrel of the gun is anathema to the people of Zimbabwe.

19. My earnest appeal to all Zimbabweans is that we forget the past and resolve to start on a clean slate and go forward together in our task of liberating Zimbabwe, that we cease to tribalize or regionalize our own liberation struggle and that those who continue to do so be regarded as enemies of the Zimbabwe we fight for, we suffer for, and we die for. We cannot afford tribalism or regionalism in

matters that involve life and death. The present effort to promote one tribe or region in our political and military life effectively undermines our armed struggle and delays the day of Zimbabwe's freedom and independence. The blood that is flowing in the grim struggle to liberate our country flows from all the tribes and regions of Zimbabwe and not from one tribe or one region.

I want everyone to know that this tribalism or regionalism which went on in ZANU did not originate from the people at home, but from the people outside Zimbabwe. The Karanga, Manyika, Zezuru, Korekore, Ndau, Ndebele, Kalanga and other tribes in Zimbabwe are solidly united and determined to become one nation. Our only hope lies with those people from all the tribes of Zimbabwe who have made up their minds to think and act together as one nation rather than as various tribes.

Yours in the struggle,
NDABANINGI SITHOLE

50 African National Council: address by Bishop Abel Muzorewa, President, to the Commonwealth Heads of Government conference. Kingston, Jamaica, April 1975

Mr Chairman, distinguished Presidents, distinguished Prime Ministers, distinguished Commonwealth Secretary-General, Heads of Delegations, ladies and gentlemen:

On behalf of the fellow oppressed and politically wounded people of Zimbabwe and myself, my first obligation is to express my heartfelt gratitude, deep and sincere appreciation for the kind invitation extended to me by the Hon Prime Minister of Jamaica, Michael Manley, to come as a special guest of his Government and to be among the hospitable people of Jamaica.

Although Jamaica seems to be geographically far from Africa those of us who live there know that they are our neighbours in spirit, word and in generous actions towards the struggle of the oppressed, even Zimbabwe.

Jamaica has had a long and serious relationship with the Freedom

Fighters of Africa. The name Jamaica stands proud and high among the countries of Africa.

I am extremely grateful for the opportunity offered to me by Commonwealth leaders to speak to the people of the world from a platform of the Heads of Government Conference now being held here. I trust that there are some here who will take the Zimbabwe sick and deteriorating situation more seriously to be able to deal with it conclusively. For the problematic Rhodesia this must be the year, the month and week of conclusion, the period of final decisions; the time to give the Rhodesian white minority the final non-violent blow so that the independence of Zimbabwe can become a reality.

The African National Council of Zimbabwe (Rhodesia) representing the unified voice of the people of Zimbabwe, demand immediate self-determination on the basis of majority rule, expressing the inalienable and universal right and dignity of every man to participate in his own government. Committed, without reservation, to the achievement of this principle, the ANC—with the fraternal support and encouragement of African Commonwealth States, and the OAU—has dedicated itself to make every effort to attain its end by peaceful negotiation. In doing so, the ANC is equally committed, aware and conscious that failure to achieve self-determination by negotiation inevitably involves a reintensified armed struggle as the only alternative.

Against the changed background of a new independent Mozambique, there are increased opportunities for international co-operation to ensure much more effective economic sanctions. The additional prospects of success in negotiating for peace and freedom, we believe, will be increased by the unequivocal moral and material commitment of all Commonwealth states to this historic enterprise—enthusiastically accepting and endorsing the imaginative and positive initiative of the Commonwealth leaders of Botswana, Tanzania, and Zambia. They must also face the inextricable link between this opportunity and the armed struggle, and be equally prepared to give endorsement and support to that alternative if it must be resorted to in order to end the illegal declaration of independence, and the oppression which is sought to perpetuate.

Looking forward to the aftermath of independence under majority rule, the ANC is deeply conscious of the host of problems, which must be faced in every field. In this we seek Commonwealth support in taking active steps to prepare for that time, especially through increased educational assistance for our people.

PEACEFUL CHANGE OR ARMED STRUGGLE

The African readiness to co-operate with South Africa in seeking a peaceful solution to transfer power from a white minority settler Rhodesian government to a majority rule Zimbabwean government—involves enormous dangers which must be faced up to, if only because the alternative may result in greater risks of human suffering.

The current initiatives by Africa must be understood as the sole alternative to prolonged armed struggle. It has been brought about by the emergence of the increasingly effective military struggle for liberation. Its potential success is entirely dependent upon the liberation movement's effective ability to return to armed confrontation. Thus states endorsing detente must be prepared to provide the facilities and support to ensure the military readiness of Zimbabwe, to declare this and to act immediately to implement it realistically.

i.   insistence (by Britain especially) that the illegal regime should recognize the political basis of the violence aimed at it and those associated with it. It should treat its political opponents, and especially those who have engaged in combat against it as prisoners of war. No further criminal prosecutions for political violence should be initiated, and all already convicted should be treated as prisoners of war. Special efforts should be made to prevent any further execution of freedom fighters, and both sides be pressed to apply the 1949 Geneva Conventions.

ii.   Commonwealth states should take every step to ensure that the illegal regime receives no support from individuals who may be their nationals, whether by legislating to exclude from passports rights citizens who enlist in the Rhodesian police or armed forces, as well as providing criminal sanctions against them.

iii. Rhodesian Front intransigence is to some extent maintained by the fact that even those sections of the minority who no longer support it, or who are now convinced that it cannot maintain white supremacy indefinitely, cannot leave the country. Severe restrictions on expatriation of funds means that would-be emigrants face virtual destitution. Commonwealth countries, especially those to which such voluntary emigré groups would be attracted by reason of cultural and historical links (Australia, Canada, New Zealand and the United Kingdom) should be encouraged to support, if necessary stimulate, such emigration and provide for their rehabilitation. This would not only provide a humane alternative to people whose indoctrination has placed them in an impossible situation, it would also provide additional graphic evidence in an area which is meaningful to the Rhodesian Front, that the time for evasion is past, and the most efficient, positive and rapid means of achieving majority rule must be pursued.

The ANC has made it clear that it does not seek to repatriate any of its minority, who have a role in the rehabilitation and development of Zimbabwe; equally it would not wish to enforce continued residence upon those who do not welcome the inevitable change.

EDUCATIONAL PREPARATION AND HUMANITARIAN ASSISTANCE

Successive settler governments in Southern Rhodesia, have denied educational opportunities to the African people of Zimbabwe for political reasons. They were aware that African educational advancement would stimulate political, economic and social progress and threaten white supremacy. European education has since 1930 been compulsory and virtually free, while African education is still voluntary and subject to strictly enforced fee payments weighing heavily upon an African population whose average earnings in 1965 was R$246 (compared with R$2576 for Europeans), which in 1971 has risen to only R$315 (compared with R$3387 for Europeans). It must also be noted in this connexion that about 40 per cent of the African population are employed in agriculture, where average income was only R$124 in 1971 (and 35 per cent of that was paid in kind and not cash). Government expenditure on education has always discriminated by a factor of approximately 10:1 in favour of European education. In 1972 R$21,388,451 was budgeted for 69,162 European enrolled pupils and only R$19,912,435 for 724,444 African enrolled pupils. The *per capita* expenditure of R$309,25 per European pupil compared with R$27.48 per African pupil, shows that this rate has in fact worsened. Equally, if not more significant is the deliberate bias in Rhodesian Front policy to restrict secondary and thus higher technical education for Africans. Of the total African enrolment 695,432 were in primary school (where average expenditure per capita was R$19.58) and only 22,012 were in secondary schools (where average expenditure per capita was R$159.59, compared with R$398.25 in European secondary education). A deliberate and arbitrary Rhodesian Front decision to peg spending on African education two per cent of the gross national product and concentrate on 'basic education' only, will produce the desired effect of imposing a crippling burden on a majority rule government, unless the enormity of the problem is realized and commensurate efforts made to avoid its consequences. The Rhodesian Front policy is *designed* to ensure only 50 per cent of African primary school leavers enter secondary school at all, and the majority of these will receive only two years non-academic education in so-called Junior Secondary Schools. Thus, only 12.5 per cent of black children can look forward to receiving four years of secondary schooling.

Education through industrial training and apprenticeship is equally discriminatory against Africans. Not only in industry concentrated in the white urban areas, and virtually non-existent in the Tribal Trust Lands (where the majority of the African population still lives), but black apprenticeships are hardly provided for. In 1971 there were 1,974 white apprentices, 148 Asian and Coloured apprentices and only 59 African apprentices registered!

COMMONWEALTH CO-OPERATION AND PREPARATION

A free and independent Zimbabwe will need more and better manpower than this system provides, both in scale and diversification.

a. Commonwealth countries are urged to expand their existing programmes to meet the challenge in terms of both size and variety of education and training opportunities. Specific efforts to provide for both technical training and 'in service' experience for Zimbabweans, are urgently needed.

b. Freedom of movement for Zimbabweans is essential to enable them to take advantage of such preparations. Proper planning is hampered by their present doubtful status as British citizens, and the Commonwealth is urged to encourage Britain to match the urgency of this very special problem with decisive and deliberate action. Zimbabweans should be provided with passports without restrictions, undignified delays or unnecessary discriminatory conditions. The 'Catch-22' vicious circle of unprivileged citizenship should be changed for a deliberate organized programme to take maximum advantage of the interim period to train and prepare for the future.

ECONOMIC SANCTIONS

The people of Zimbabwe have never accepted sanctions as the appropriate method of solving the political crisis created by the illegal declaration of independence. Military intervention by Britain (the international responsible power) was demanded if only to open the way for a properly representative constitutional conference, which alone could provide a solution acceptable to all our people. However, sanctions are a form of pressure to help bring the Rhodesia Front regime to negotiate, and for this reason must be maintained and indeed intensified, until negotiations for majority rule and independence have been successfully concluded.

Commonwealth governments already know that many of the hopes and estimates of the effectiveness of sanctions have been frustrated by loopholes and wilful non-compliance by both selfish individuals and internationally irresponsible states. Both the Commonwealth Sanctions Committee and the United Nations Sanctions Committee have done much to reveal and repair these. They have disclosed an elaborate and complex collaboration developed to accomplish sanction busting exercises, some of the most important of which need to be mentioned.

The unfortunate delays involved in detecting even massive sanctions breaking, is revealed by one of the most recent cases exposed: the scheme to finance, to the tune of R$42,500,000, the expansion of the RISCOM steel plant with European capital and technology. Banks and companies including state controlled concerns) in Austria, Bermuda, West Germany, Switzerland and South Africa were involved with agencies in Rhodesia, directly or through 'convenience' and undercover corporations. The scheme was evolved at a rendezvous in France in August 1972, with all the trappings of international business.

In 1973 three Boeing 707 airliners were sold to Rhodesia (providing a significant boost to the profitability of the Rhodesian airline) by agents in Switzerland and South Africa.

For several years *Afretair* and *Air TransAfrica* operated, with the co-operation of Gabon and the military regime in Greece, carrying Rhodesian beef to Greece and the Netherlands, and returning with imports from Europe.

An elaborate and secret network to circumvent sanctions has been set up by the Smith regime. This includes the Zephyr network unearthed with great efficiency by the Netherlands Anti-Apartheid Movement in Amsterdam. This reveals that almost every state unconsciously or otherwise has been used and involved in the complex web, either as a supplier of goods for, or a market for goods from Rhodesia.

A COMMONWEALTH RESPONSE TO A NEW OPPORTUNITY TO ENFORCE SANCTIONS

These examples reveal that the regime's success in counter-sanctions operations can be attributed to:

i.   some States' willingness to actively assist Rhodesia
ii. lack of an efficient international policy system to discover and plug the loopholes.

To remedy this action is required on three levels; political, economic, and social.

The most significant assistance in undermining sanctions, both positive and negative, has been from South Africa and the former Portuguese government in Mozambique. They provided the lifeline which sustained the Smith regime, its rebellion and the arrogant self-confidence which has prevented any meaningful negotiations with representatives of African opinion, and strengthened Rhodesian Front contempt for world opinion, the Commonwealth and the United Nations. Today, however, significant changes have occurred and the new opportunities must not be lost if sanctions, as an alternative tool to achieve international order, are not finally and forever to be discredited. These changes make it necessary and urgent that the Commonwealth Heads of State and Government should seriously consider taking the following actions:

i. *Mozambique*

The rail links between Rhodesia and the ports of Beira and Lourenco Marques were secure under a Portuguese government; only elaborate schemes to blockade the ports would have prevented them serving as the major outlets of Rhodesian exports and thus the vital means of earning foreign exchange for the regime.

The welcome establishment within a matter of weeks of the conference, of an independent Mozambique under the Frelimo government means that these routes are controlled by an administration committed to majority rule in Zimbabwe and to supporting and enforcing sanctions as a means of achieving that end. However, the cost to the new state will be great, and will fall upon it at a most crucial period. Loss of revenue resulting from merely disallowing sanctions-breaking Rhodesian traffic will be in the region of £20 million per annum. The Commonwealth in co-operation with the United Nations member states should cushion this loss, and, in particular, ensure that food supplies obtained with these earnings are provided for, preferably in advance of the loss. Thus,

(a) A crash relief economic programme for a specific period should be set up.

(b) Commonwealth states may also consider providing expert personnel to carry out the documentary checks to ensure that sanctions are complied with by traffic using the railways and ports. The ANC itself would be willing to provide whatever assistance in manpower it may have, to assist in the administration burden sanctions enforcement would involve.

(c) It should be noted that this action by a Frelimo administration would make Britain's Beira patrol quite unnecessary. It is appropriate that if Britain thus withdraws the patrol, she could re-direct the revenue thus released directly to Mozambique, who will be taking over the burden.

ii. *South Africa*

South Africa's support for the Rhodesian Front regime in transport, finance, travel, trade and military facilities has been the single most significant pillar of the maintenance of the illegal minority government in Rhodesia. Her moral support in social and sporting relations has also been important. Effectively, South Africa has not been sanctioned for this overt defiance of world opinion even by her closest associates including important members of the Commonwealth. While it is clear that South Africa cannot buy African friendship or acquiescence as long as she practices the abhorrent policy of *apartheid,* it must be made even more clear that the prospect of a peaceful transition and change in Southern Africa, which is offered by Africa's acceptance in good faith of the current initiatives is dependent upon a clear and open South African commitment to refrain from effective interference in Rhodesian affairs by continuing its active (or passive) support for sanctions breaking. To do otherwise is total contradiction of detente, dedicated as it is to the serious attempt to achieve majority rule in Zimbabwe by negotiation rather than long and inhuman war. Every extra hour during which the Rhodesian Front believes sanctions can be avoided with help from South Africa, means another hour's delay in their final decision to enter meaningful discussions for peace and majority rule. We urge the Commonwealth and especially Britain, whose relations with South Africa are strong and whose continued responsibility is still unequivocal, to help the South African government to understand and act upon this inescapable fact. Its full re-admission to the community of nations is dependent upon the pre-condition that it respects and applies sanctions, (which are intended to achieve the majority rule which Mr Vorster proclaims is his own ideal solution for the problem in Rhodesia) as it is dependent upon South Africa's finding a humane solution to changing itself.

The ANC and the people of Zimbabwe are anxious to take their part not only in the solution of their own national problems, but look forward equally to participating with their fellow Commonwealth peoples in a constructive and resolute effort to face and solve the multiple international issues facing us all. We hope and pray that the efforts made by Heads of State and Governments at this conference and within the next few months will bring us closer to the goal; in this spirit we urge your most serious and dedicated support. We also urge the Commonwealth Heads of State and Government to support Africa's strategy on Southern Africa as clearly set out in the Dar-es-Salaam Declaration of 10 April 1975.

51 Rev Ndabaningi Sithole: address in Switzerland, 15 June 1975

I am sure most of you have been following our struggle in Zimbabwe and, probably, there is no need for me to repeat myself on the geography and history of Zimbabwe. I am sure the various groups which work here, have given you enough information on Zimbabwe . . .

We all know that all nations regardless of their colour and culture, love singing. And we in Zimbabwe, who are engaged in our liberation struggle like to sing certain songs and this is one of the songs that we sing in Zimbabwe. The language in which this song is sung, is called Shona. Shona is the principal vernacular we have in Zimbabwe. The next one is Ndebele which is very akin to Zulu. I have lost my tuning phone and therefore if the tune will go a little out of the way, you should be able to understand it.

Ngat'batane pamwe chete,
Ngat'batane pamwe chete.
Ngat'batane—pamwe—chete,
Ngat'batane pamwe cmete,
Ngat'batane pamwe chete.

Iyo nguva yakanaka,
Iyo nguva yakanaka.
Iyo—nguva—yaka-oma,
Iyo nguva yaka-o-ma-,
Iyo nguva yakaoma.

Ndiyo nguva yeChim'renga,
Ndiyo nguva yeChim'renga.
Ndiyo—nguva—yeChim'renga,
Ndiyo nguva yeChem're-nga,
Ndiyo nguva yeChim'renga.

These words are generally sung by our people in Zimbabwe, urging all the people to unite so that they may prosecute their struggle to a successful conclusion.

Now, many of you might ask the question: Why is it that the people in

Zimbabwe are fighting? Why can't they do something else in order to get what they want without having to fight?

One has to understand fully the situation in Zimbabwe to appreciate what is happening. Sometimes I find that people do not understand the nature of the problem that confronts Zimbabweans. For instance, I have been urged by many people that the people in Zimbabwe should not fight, because fighting, naturally, sheds blood. And it is quite normal that people do not, as a rule, like to fight. They want to live in peace. People do not fight for the sake of fighting, because all fighting hurts. . . . But when all means of settlement of such problems have failed, then they have no other alternative other than to fight. . . .

In 1957, for instance, the African National Congress of Southern Rhodesia was formed, but when it became very popular with the African people, it was banned in 1959. In 1961 the National Democratic Party was formed on the wrecks of the African National Congress, but when it became popular with the people, it was banned at the end of that year. In 1962 the Zimbabwe African People's Union was formed, but when it became very popular with the African people, it was banned again. In 1963 the PCC and ZANU were formed, but when they became popular with the people, they were banned in 1964. So that all legitimate political means of realizing their only aspiration in the land of their birth, were turned down. The African people, naturally, turned their backs on the peaceful settlement of problems that were facing the country. So that today the gates are crashed, physically crashed between African people and the white people.

Some people may ask this question: Will the African nationalists succeed to realize their freedom and independence through the armed struggle? Well, history provides us with many examples. In Algeria, for instance, the colonial powers tried to suppress the people's struggle for independence, but they failed; in Kenya they tried to suppress the struggle of the people, but they failed; in Guinea-Bissau they tried to suppress the struggle of the people, but they failed; in Mozambique they tried to suppress the struggle of the people, but they failed and in Angola they tried to suppress the struggle of the people, but they failed. We can go outside Africa to see what history has for us. In Vietnam itself they tried to suppress the struggles of the people, but they failed. And we, in Zimbabwe, believe that those who try to suppress the legitimate struggle of the people will be defeated.

Some people have been wrongly informed that the struggle in Zimbabwe is against the white people as such. They have been told that the African nationalist movement is anti-white as such. Of course, that is wrong. We are not fighting the white man as such. We are fighting against an oppressive social and political system.

Our basic policy is one of non-racialism. We believe that man is man the world over regardless of the colour of his skin and culture. White people are welcome to our free and independent Zimbabwe, but we are quite uncompromising on the question of white supremacy. We do not subscribe to the theory that some human beings are more human beings than others. *We believe that human life is the same the world over.* So that those of you have been wrongly informed that we are fighting against the white man as such must forget it. Our battle is against oppression; our battle is against injustice; our battle is against man's inhumanity to man. What we would like to see established in a free and independent Zimbabwe is a government elected by the people and responsible to the people.

Some people look at what is going on in Zimbabwe and just come to the conclusion that the African people should not be taking up their arms against the present illegal regime. Whenever we see such acts as are going on in Zimbabwe, we should ask ourselves the question: Why are the people of Zimbabwe fighting? The reason for the fight will either justify the fight or disqualify the fight. Are the people in Zimbabwe fighting to oppress others? Are they fighting in order to maintain a system that is oppressive to the majority of the people? Are they fighting in order to set up a system based on racial consideration? Are they fighting for the sake of shedding blood? Of course, the answer is no. They are fighting to free themselves. What people among you here will not fight in order to be free? Would you consider any people, people in the sense of the word, if they did not fight in order to be free? One young African put it very bluntly to me one day. He said to me, 'President Sithole, if we are denied the ballot box, we shall rush into the battlefield.' They fight to capture the ballot box which is presently denied to them. They want to have a say in the land of their birth. They want to terminate the status of third rate citizenship in their own land . . . It is a struggle to bring about the rights, the legitimate rights of a people who are presently being denied those rights. So that the armed struggle should be seen in the light of the redemption of a people's rights.

So much about why the African people are fighting in Zimbabwe.

Now, I would like to speak for a moment on the question of the unity pact that was concluded on 7 December 1974 in Lusaka. Many of you, I am sure, have been following the events in Zimbabwe. Those of us who were in detention for the last ten years were suddenly told that we would be released and flown to Lusaka. And there we were supposed to discuss the future of Zimbabwe. When we were told, naturally, we were very happy for these wonderful things after ten years of detention. We were taken to Salisbury military airport and there we were told to wait until the Zambian aeroplane would come to take us to Lusaka . . .

When we got to Lusaka, our main problem was the subject of unity. The four presidents, i.e. Kaunda, Nyerere, Samora Machel and Sir Seretse Khama emphasized to us the need for all Zimbabwean political organizations to come together so that we might fight better. After a protracted argument, we finally decided that this unity would be a practical one. We were not interested in unity for its own sake. We are interested in unity that would enable us to liberate Zimbabwe. There were two schools of thought. There were some who believed that we could get our independence by talking with the British people or the white settlers, but there was another group which believed that we could never get what we demanded by mere talking. They pointed out to the history of 80 years during which talking had not produced freedom and independence in Zimbabwe. And so we insisted that a certain clause should be included in the unity pact. The ZANU group, for instance, refused to sign the unity pact until that particular clause was included in the pact. The opposite group did not want that to be included. They strongly sensed that if they were included, people would be arrested. And we pointed out that if the people are afraid to be arrested, then they have no right to fight for their independence, they have no right to demand their independence. If people are afraid to suffer for their own right, then there is something wrong with them. If a people have no course to fight for, to suffer for, then there is something wrong with them. Now, because we refused to sign the unity pact until that clause was included, there was a great difficulty with our course in Lusaka. But finally it was agreed that, that clause should be included. That clause was the inevitability of armed struggle.

In the last paragraph of the unity pact, there are these words: '*The new ANC recognizes and respects the inevitability of armed struggle.*' In other words, our unity pact is based on the important proposition of armed struggle if we are to realize our freedom and independence in the land of our people.

After this unity pact was signed, we returned home in three days. Our whole meeting was described and talked with the illegal regime and we tried to find out ways and means of arriving at a peaceful settlement of the problem that exists on Rhodesia. It had been agreed in Lusaka that the African nationalist leaders would be allowed to hold public meetings; that all political detainees would be released; that the African nationalist leaders would try to act within the framework of the law. But on the other hand, the African nationalists were supposed to observe certain conditions too. For instance, there was the question of the ceasefire.

The question of ceasefire was discussed at great length in Lusaka. It was agreed that the ceasefire would fall into two stages, there would be a *de facto* ceasefire which would result in a big de-escalation of guerilla activities in the country; then there would be a *de jure* ceasefire, which would be announced when the date for the constitutional conference was set, and which would be announced when talks reached a meaningful stage. But as soon as we left Lusaka, the illegal regime dropped leaflets over the operational zones in the north-east, ordering our fighting men to surrender themselves and their arms to the district commissioner, to the police and also to the soldiers. The leaflets further ordered our fighting men to withdraw into Zambia and Mozambique. In other words, the Rhodesian government interpreted ceasefire in terms of surrender, but the nationalists interpreted ceasefire only as meaning to stop fighting. Again and again, the government appealed to us to give ceasefire orders because there was no reason to do this. I remember pressure was brought to bear upon me as Commander-in-Chief of the ZANU forces to give out ceasefire orders or else I would return into detention. *They thought that a personal threat to me would change my mind, but I made it quite clear that with detention or without it, the fight goes on.*

There would be no reason whatsoever for anybody in his right mind to give ceasefire orders just because he was afraid himself to be in trouble. The only thing that will cause our men and women to stop fighting is when they get what they want. Because the government felt that I was not co-operating, they re-detained me in March. But that did not stop the fight that was going on. Our forces kept fighting and *are still fighting up to this day,* until majority rule comes to Zimbabwe.

When I was in detention for the second time, naturally, I was saying to myself: 'Well, I shall remain there for the next ten years again.' But I was left in no doubt whatsoever that the struggle would go on with or without me, because during the last ten years I was in detention, the struggle has been going on. And I was quite satisfied that it would continue to go on for the next ten years I would be in my second detention. But to my surprise one morning I saw a detective officer come to my cell. He said to me,

'You are invited to attend a conference in Dar-es-Salaam!'

I looked up and said, 'Dar-es-Salaam!'

He said, 'Yes, an invitation is being extended *to you.* Would you like to attend the conference?'

I pretended of course to be reluctant. And finally I said,

'All right, I can go.'

Then the detective officer said,

'But you must clearly understand that after the conference, you will come back here in prison.'

I looked up and said,

'Oh, quite naturally!'

He said, 'Good!'

And in my heart I said, 'It was good for me.'

This was on a Friday, and I couldn't believe my ears; I couldn't believe that the invitation had been extended to me. So I waited until Saturday morning. And, indeed, the detective officer did come to take me to the airport. The way I was received on my second release was widely reported in the international media. At Dar-es-Salaam airport, I was met by an excited crowd of hundreds of Zimbabwean patriots and well-wishers, who carried me shoulder high through the tarmac to the airport hall. This must have greatly embarrassed the Rhodesian government, which thought that it had inflicted damage on my personality by heaping a lot of false charges against me; one of the charges having been that of an assassination plot against what it termed my 'political rivals'.

Since the Rhodesian Prime Minister's pledge to release all political prisoners was made, more African nationalist leaders have been arrested and our active supporters have since continued to languish in Rhodesian prisons; our captured freedom fighters are still being hanged; the number of people in concentration camps (the so-called protected villages) is still increasing. They now number over 120,000 people. And yet we have been talking with the Rhodesian Prime Minister. Is it that we believe we can get something out of the talks? Of course nobody does. The only reason why we are attending the present talks is that we want to demonstrate to the people in Zimbabwe and to the world at large that nothing can be got out of the talks with the illegal regime. If we got something, that will be all right, of course. But we know we can't get anything from these talks. And yet we can get something if we fight hard like other men.

For instance. I will give you an example of what happened about these talks. Before I was detained for the second time, we met the Prime Minister with four items to discuss. The first item was the venue of the conference, the second was the chairmanship of the conference, the third was the timing and the fourth was the size of the delegations. We were only able to agree on the size of the delegations and not on the other three items. The Prime Minister insisted that the conference should be held inside Rhodesia. But the nationalists also insisted that it should be held outside the country. The reason for this is that the nationalists feared to be victimized, since there is a state of emergency in Rhodesia. We wanted the ANC delegation and the government delegation to meet on a footing of equality, but the Prime Minister refused. On the question of chairmanship of the conference, the Prime Minister insisted that he should be chairman of the conference. We said that he was an interested party and therefore could not possibly be an impartial chairman. He said that we should trust him. Then, of course, we reminded him that he had torn up the 1961 constitution. So there was a deadlock even on the mechanics of the conference. Only last week, another meeting was held between the ANC delegation and the Prime Minister. It was agreed that there should be a conference, but there was no agreement on the venue of the conference and also on the chairmanship. In other words, *the Prime Minister is just playing for time.* He wants the whole problem to drag on until he reaches his retirement age.

This explains why most of our people don't believe that we can have anything concrete from these talks. This is why more and more of our young people are going out of the country to train and return to fight to establish majority rule.

Now, this problem that is facing Zimbabwe is one of majority rule as against minority rule. The white people feel that the present problem could be solved by having a House of 66 people and then 22 of them should be Africans. This is what they call a blocking third. But the African people have turned this solution down. Another solution which has been put forward by the Rhodesian government is the parity solution. They say that in a House of 100 representatives, there should be 50 Africans and 50 Europeans. Their argument is that this will prevent one race dominating over the other. The African feels that this is all wrong arithmetic. 50 Africans representing six million Africans could not possibly be equal to 50 whites representing 230,000 whites. Proportionally this means 25 Africans are equal to one white man. Furthermore, the African people argue that this formula of parity makes the African people inferior and the whites indefinitely superior. So that *the parity formula has been rejected by the African people.*

Now, the next solution which the Rhodesian government has put forward is one of majority rule in principle. They say, 'All right we accept majority rule in principle.' What is the attitude of the African people towards majority rule in principle? We reject totally and utterly majority rule in principle. No African in his right mind accepts majority rule in principle. Majority rule in principle is for the birds, as they say in America. What we demand is not majority rule in principle; we demand majority rule in practice!

I think that distinction should be quite clear to all of you, ladies and gentlemen. We all accept in *principle* that a one year baby one day will get married, but in *practice* it can't get married at the age of one. For instance in 1890 the white settlers accepted majority rule in principle; in 1923 when Southern Rhodesia was granted self-determination, the government accepted majority rule in principle; in 1953 when the Federation of Rhodesia and Nyasaland was formed, the government accepted majority rule in principle; in 1965 when UDI was declared, the illegal regime accepted majority rule in principle; the 1971 proposal by the British and Rhodesian governments also accepted majority rule in principle. But from 1890 up to 1975, no majority rule has been established in Zimbabwe, in spite of the fact that it has, all along, been accepted in principle. That is why we demand *MAJORITY RULE NOW*.

To us, that proposition 'Majority Rule Now' has two important parts. The first part is 'Majority Rule'. Majority Rule is not negotiable. It must be accepted that majority rule is *the thing* for the African people or for the majority of the people. But what is negotiable is that little word 'Now'. The delegates to the conference must spell out what the little word 'Now' means. In other words, the African people accept the principle of a transitional period. The question is how long is that transitional period to be. All of us want that period to be not more than 12 months. We feel it should be along the same line as the formula of Mozambique. Side by side with this principle of transitional period, is the composition of the provisional government. We feel strongly that the provisional government should be dominated by African representatives so that they can facilitate majority rule for Zimbabwe. . . .

52 African National Council: statement of basic policy. 1 August 1975

WHEREAS,

1a. On 7 December 1974, the people of Zimbabwe brought to an end a history of internal divisions and internecine rivalries and agreed on having only one national organization, the African National Council (ANC), to operate as the sole political and military instrument for the liberation of Zimbabwe, colonized by British imperialism in 1890;

b. There is need to continue the struggle started by our forefathers in 1890 against colonialism, imperialism and settlerism, intensified in the War of Resistance of 1896 and thereafter continued in various forms and by the guerilla war campaigns launched after the Unilateral Declaration of Independence (UDI) made by the fascist Rhodesian regime on 11 November 1965;

c. The Rhodesian settler regime continues to consolidate its position both politically and militarily;

2a. The first duty of a true revolutionary is to identify the enemy clearly and properly and get to know his nature;

b. The fascist regime of Rhodesia is a product and a special form of capitalism and world imperialism whereby Britain, the arch-enemy of the people of Zimbabwe, granted a licence for white dictatorship;

c. Settler-colonialism in Zimbabwe is in fact sustained by a vast imperialist partnership which includes Britain, the United States of America, France, the Federal Republic of Germany, other NATO countries, Japan, South Africa and Switzerland;

d. The Rhodesian regime is the direct enemy of the oppressed and exploited people in Zimbabwe;

e. The chief character of Rhodesia's settler colonial society is capitalism whereby the means of production are owned by a numerically insignificant white settler community (200,000), while the rest of the population (6,000,000 Blacks) is, except for a handful of petty-bourgeois elements, a proletariat made up of workers, peasants and squatters who own nothing but create by their labour incommensurable incomes for the capitalists and the settler class;

NOW, THEREFORE—

CHAPTER ONE: NATIONAL UNITY

1. The party, which is the vanguard of the revolution and the main instrument in the hands of the people in their fight for national liberation and independence, stands for solid and unshakeable total national unity for a national struggle against the enemy of the nation.

2. All the people of Zimbabwe must unite in the national struggle, irrespective of ideological, political, religious or sectarian differences. The unity of the people is absolutely necessary for the efficient and successful prosecution of the armed struggle and the realization of the revolutionary cause.

3. The Party seeks to involve all the oppressed people of Zimbabwe, not only in the national purpose of fighting against foreign domination and settler rule; but also in detailed preparation for the new order.

CHAPTER TWO: ARMED STRUGGLE AND THE NATIONAL ARMY

1. Aware that:

a. the conflict between the people of Zimbabwe and the Rhodesian white settlers cannot be resolved without the use of force;

b. in a revolutionary situation, capitalist and imperialist powers never relinquish power voluntarily;

c. there will be no real change in Zimbabwe without armed revolution;

The party upholds the continuation of revolutionary armed struggle as the only means of overthrowing oppression and establishing a people's democratic and socialist rule in Zimbabwe.

2. The Zimbabwe Liberation Army shall play a full part in production, and in mobilizing and educating the population in tasks of nation-building and economic development.

3. The Zimbabwe Liberation Army shall be part and parcel of the people and their system of social organization, and will be part of the political system and process. The party insists upon democratic centralism within the military.

4. The party commands the army.

CHAPTER THREE: FOREIGN RELATIONS

1. The party foreign policy shall be determined by two cardinal principles: to fight against imperialism and neo-colonialism, and to unite with the revolutionary and progressive forces of the world.

2. The party shall make the people aware of their oneness with other peoples struggling against imperialism and oppression in Africa, Asia, the Middle East, Latin America, North America and Europe.

3. The party upholds the charter of the Organization of African Unity. It shall explore all avenues and take every opportunity for all possible forms of co-operation with other African peoples.

4. The party upholds the United Nations in its support of oppressed and exploited peoples the world over.

CHAPTER FOUR: NATIONAL AND SOCIAL REVOLUTION

1. The party stands for total national liberation through armed revolution to achieve revolutionary independence.

2. The party seeks to change totally and completely the existing social and political system and establish a new society altogether which is not based on private ownership of the means of production, a socialist society in which, naturally, the democratic process is to be exercised in such a way that the most exploited masses have control of political power, since they alone can go furthest in establishing proper rights and liberties for all.

3. The party stands for a society in which all classes and all prejudices or

privileges shall be combatted and weeded out.

4. Any person regardless of his or her race, ethnic origin, culture, sex, racial background or nationality who shall identify himself or herself with a socialist Zimbabwe will have expanded opportunities to contribute fully towards the development of the country and live as a human being; but no one shall be permitted to exploit or oppress other free and equal citizens for his or her own benefit, or to receive material or financial benefits that do not derive from his or her own efforts.

CHAPTER FIVE: POLITICAL ECONOMY

1. The economic system in Zimbabwe today is geared to benefit the settlers and capitalists, and international capitalism. The economy of a socialist Zimbabwe shall be designed to meet the basic needs of each worker and peasant in accordance with living standards, and to develop abilities to the full.

2. All means of production, distribution, exchange, and communications shall be placed fully in the hands of the people of Zimbabwe as a whole. The economy shall provide for the greatest dominance of worker-peasant interests throughout the system.

3. Labour, which is the greatest asset of Zimbabwe, shall be used for the fulfilment of the personality of every Zimbabwean, enabling him or her to lead a decent life.

4. The economic system shall enable every worker and peasant to make the greatest possible contribution to his or her own and the country's development.

5. Exploitation and privileges shall not be allowed by and among free citizens of Zimbabwe. Property as a commercial or exploitative factor shall be abolished.

6. Economic development shall be determined by the state using socialist methods and techniques of planning.

7. Incomes shall accrue in accordance with the amount of labour each one contributes to society.

8. There shall be minimum and maximum wage levels determined by the state.

CHAPTER SIX: LAND

1. All the natural resources of Zimbabwe—the land, minerals, water, flora and fauna—belong to the people of Zimbabwe, and shall be administered by the state.

2. There shall be no private ownership of land or natural resources.

3. There shall be land reform and an agrarian revolution geared to meet the needs of the peasants, co-operatives, and collective and communal programmes at every stage of development in the nation.

CHAPTER SEVEN: EDUCATION

1. Every Zimbabwean shall have the opportunity to acquire free, compulsory and good education commensurate with his or her capacity and desire to learn, and in consistency with the manpower needs and capacity of the society.
2. The party's aim shall be to educate the citizen for responsibility and participation in the economic, political, cultural or social life of the country.
3. In a free Zimbabwe, the party shall advocate and stress technical and science education.

CHAPTER EIGHT: CULTURE

1. A new Zimbabwe culture drawn from the best in our heritages and histories and developed to meet the needs of the new society shall be encouraged.
2. Zimbabwe culture shall stem from Zimbabwe creativeness.

CHAPTER ELEVEN

FROM VICTORIA FALLS TO GENEVA

53 Michael Mawema: memorandum on realistic approach to the Zimbabwe political revolutionary settlement

The revolutionary and fighting people of Zimbabwe, through their national liberation movement and vanguard of Chimurenga (war of liberation), the Zimbabwe African National Union (ZANU), together with other militants engaged in the war of national liberation against the racist and fascist white minority regime of Ian Smith, wish to express their continuing confidence in your support for the Zimbabwe People's Revolution. The people of Zimbabwe would like to underscore their sincere satisfaction in the national commitment and sacrifice by the gallant and heroic people of Tanzania and Mozambique in their support for our struggles against colonialism, imperialism and racism and in pursuit of national independence.

The Zimbabwe People's Revolution suffered great setbacks over the past year due to errors of judgement by some of our African leaders and also due to over-confidence in the good virtues of the enemies of our revolution. We approach you with wounded minds, with fractured souls, with dislocated nationalism and crippled African pride dangling from the so-called 'Southern African detente'. We are full of doubt and frightful expectations that our revolution may be traded and auctioned off once again to our enemies as happened in 1974–5. We fearfully watch and listen to renewed dialogue between you and our enemies, the arch-imperialist and colonialist Britain and her allies. Presently our revolution is writhing with painful experiences from the ashes of detente engineered by the arch-*apartheid*ist John Vorster of South Africa and the arch-racist and fascist Ian Smith in 1974–5. We have no doubt that you are committed to Chimurenga as the only means by which genuine national independence will be achieved in Zimbabwe, but the consistent call given by reconciliationists and accommodationists under the guise of 'voices of reason' appealing to you once again disturbs us very seriously.

To the militants of Zimbabwe any call for discussion with the supporters of Ian Smith is counter-revolutionary and is as counter-productive as was the 1974–5 detente. Any suggestions for renewed talks with Ian Smith on anything other than surrender terms is a conspiracy against our revolution. Our experiences from the 'Southern African detente' are painful and may be summarized as follows:

1. That detente was manufactured by our oppressors and their collaborationists and reconciliationists who supported non-violence

as the means by which oppression would be removed from the Zimbabwe soil. For that reason it was supported by all opportunists, religionists, liberals, the local African petty-bourgeois class and all racists and fascists who claimed that it was the most 'conventional' way by which Africans may get to majority rule.

2. It created a false sense of victory by the liberation forces and surrender by Smith when there was a call for a constitutional conference between Smith and our African leaders.

3. It destroyed the ZANU-ZANLA revolutionary forces by failing to acknowledge ZANU's successes and recognizing its leaders as the only political power-group that would set terms for any negotiations. By releasing other African leaders who had no fighting forces and giving them prominent positions, detente stole the thunder and force of the ZANU Chimurenga.

4. It promoted collaborationists and reconciliationists who were puppets of the oppressors and prostituted the lives and blood of all of the Zimbabwe freedom fighters of ZANU who had died.

5. It divided the people of Zimbabwe and created feelings of doubt among the revolutionaries and their forces. ZANU militants were divided and ZANU was infiltrated by international opportunists and spies of Ian Smith and John Vorster.

6. It destroyed confidence between our supporters and the party and created a situation of contradiction between our commitment to the armed confrontation and our vulnerability to political derailment.

7. It divided the members of the OAU who had been totally committed to supporting ZANU and the Zimbabwe revolution based upon our policy of Chimurenga into two groups. One group accepted the cunning of the white oppressors and was then used to propagate the politics of the 'voice of reason and responsibility' and one group supported our Chimurenga but with a 'wait and see' attitude.

8. By creating false hopes in one section of ZANU, detentists brewed a conspiracy in the Party which resulted in the 1974 attempted coup aimed at eliminating the 'hard liners' in the party. The conspirators then decided to assassinate Comrade Herbert Chitepo, the Party National Chairman, who was the vanguard of Chimurenga. His assassination was tactically followed by a mass swoop and arrest of all Dare members (members of the ZANU Military High Command), ZANLA commanders and party Central Committee members and cadres. This was intended to be the final devastating and crushing blow on ZANU and Chimurenga. Up to this day all ZANU military leaders are incarcerated in Zambian prisons as victims of detente.

9. It threw open the whole struggle to the international opportunists

and their academicians who have now become pseudo-nationalists and can claim to be 'experts' of the Zimbabwe revolution. Before the detente exercise Zimbabwe revolutionary spokesmen were limited and restricted to those aligned with activists but now academicians and political careerists have assumed a higher role in our struggle.

10. It gave time to Ian Smith to regroup his army which was fighting a running battle with ZANLA. Since 1974 the fascist and racist forces of Ian Smith have received an unlimited supply of arms of aggression from the colonialist and imperialist countries of Europe and North America. NATO has concentrated its forces in the southern hemisphere with the purpose of giving military support to Southern Rhodesia and South Africa. Besides receiving free arms, the Smith forces are supported by large mercenary forces from South Africa, Western Europe and the United States of America.

11. It brought about the Lusaka Declaration of Unity of 7 December 1974 which led to the birth of the enlarged umbrella organization the African National Council led by Bishop Abel Muzorewa. This unity was broken up by counter-revolutionary machinations of pseudo-nationalists supported by international opportunism. The formation of the Zimbabwe Liberation Council (ZLC) as the ANC's external wing became the final blow against the unity declaration. ZANU militants refused to be represented by counter-revolutionaries who had been politically excommunicated from the party and were believed to have conspired against ZANU and its military leadership with the enemies of Chimurenga. ZAPU militants objected to being made the underdogs in the ZLC structure.

The other problem that ZANU faced was the issue of direct usurpation of its party, its military structure, its honour and its tradition by a group of non-revolutionaries. The ZLC structure was set up in such a way as to whittle away all authority and power of ZANU and invest into the hands of counter-revolutionaries who had been known as public critics of Chimurenga. The ZLC imposed upon the ZANU freedom fighters a military hierarchy composed of reactionaries and international opportunists most of whom had collaborated with the Zambian police in the arrest and detention of the ZANLA commanders. There was sufficient evidence that the ZLC was a conspiratory organization against ZANU. It failed to take a position against the arrest and continued detention of our members by the Zambian government. It refused to pay defence costs for our ZANU detainees. It refused to issue a protest statement against the shooting to death of 15 ZANU cadres at Mboroma by the Zambian army; it refused to pay rent or to give food to the families of the detainees; it refused to give food and clothing to the detainees in Zambian prisons; it took and expropriated ZANU property with the complicity of the Zambian authorities; ZLC officials demanded the dissolution of ZANU and sought the support of the Zambian government to enter ZANU military camps and issue orders of authority. Whilst the ZLC was prostituting with the revolution in Lusaka, the domestic ANC of Joshua Nkomo put the whole Zimbabwe revolution on the international stock exchange. What the ZLC did not achieve in practice it claimed in public statements. Its leaders claimed unending military victories by the army which they did not know and had refused to support. The ZLC has no army. It has never had any army. The ZLC has no communication with our army and it has never given service to the army. The ZLC paper, the *Revolution*, discusses no revolutionary politics, but concerns itself with the denunciation of its opponents.

We have no doubt that you will not succumb again to the false calls for a 'peaceful settlement' after you were led up the garden path by South Africa in 1975. We believe that you will not listen too to the calls for a ceasefire by our enemy. In your dialogue with reactionary governments we believe that you will not compromise the principle of majority rule now and that you will continue to uphold Chimurenga as the only method by which genuine national independence shall be won. We need no more compromises, we do not accept the loud voices from international opportunists who will request you to pick and impose non-revolutionary leaders to speak on behalf of our army. We believe too that you will cut the old apron strings of attachment you have with certain persons who claim to be the only national heroes of the Zimbabwe revolution and rather that you will recognize the fighting men to speak for themselves.

The militants and people of Zimbabwe declared that 'We are our own liberators!' In committing ourselves to the battles of self-determination we demand the right to choose our own revolutionary leadership to represent us at all conferences; we demand the right to determine our own destiny and through our own elected leadership to enter into discussion with the enemy to set terms and conditions for final surrender and for final structuring of our national independence. As we resist superpower intervention on the Zimbabwe body-politic, we also resist most vehemently any benevolent dictatorship by or from any of our African brothers. We need material and financial support to prosecute the war of liberation but we want to fight our own battles and win our own war against our enemies so as to ensure genuine independence in Zimbabwe. The people of Zimbabwe have filled the training camps and they would love to smell the gunpowder for themselves. But, because the enemy is now supported by international imperialism and international opportunism, the Zimbabwe people's revolutionary army will welcome the support from all independent African states under the auspices and command of the OAU African Military High Command.

In his call for international imperialist support for his racist and fascist regime to counteract the ZANU freedom fighters in their continued defence of the masses, Ian Smith said: 'The aim of ZANU is to secure domination (liberation) over all the people of Rhodesia, including their black rivals, and to do so by means of terrorism (Chimurenga). Hence they must be defeated, and decisively defeated, irrespective of whether or not the constitutional discussions reach a successful conclusion'. (*Times of Zambia*, 6 February 1976).

Ian Smith knows that his enemy is ZANU, that it wants to liberate Zimbabwe, and that it enjoys the total support of Zimbabweans. What seems to be ridiculous in our revolution is that organizations without the army want to claim leadership for the army. We have no doubt that you will not mistake trees for the forest.

We have no doubt that you came out of the past detente machinations by the racist and fascist minority regime of Ian Smith with enriched but painful experiences like ourselves. You saw that the effort to sponsor revisionists, reconciliationists and accommodationists and their microphone revolutionaries into leadership has caused the greatest setbacks in the Zimbabwe People's Revolution. We do not believe in the qualities of leadership heralded by our enemies; we do not believe in the virtues of our oppressors; we do not subscribe to the same philosophies of life as our oppressors and for that reason we refuse to be conditioned to their so-called 'conventional way to independence'. We believe that peace, majority rule now and national independence will be born from the barrel of the gun, through Chimurenga.

Comrades, the African people of Zimbabwe believe that there is not one man in the Zimbabwe revolution who has a monopoly of wisdom. We believe in collective and democratic leadership born upon the dictatorship of the masses. We believe too that there is no one man with a key to the door to our national independence. Our independence shall be won by co-operative effort of all Zimbabwe revolutionaries. We believe too that leaders come and go but the nation lives forever and that no leader in the Zimbabwe revolution is indispensable. We urge you to accept and continue to recognize the ZIPA leadership and all those who promote and support it. To refuse to support the fighting men upon whom our total liberation is dependant is to be reactionary and counterproductive. We believe that you will not submit to political blackmail by reactionary elements who base their claim to leadership on past history rather than on active commitment and support of the present fighting forces. The war against the racist and fascist white minority settlers in Zimbabwe will not be won by arm-chair politicians but by the ZANLA forces and their counterparts in ZIPA. We do not want another constitutional conference but in the event of the need to discuss surrender terms with the enemy, much needs to be said immediately.

SUGGESTED ACTION IN THE EVENT OF SURRENDER DISCUSSIONS

We have no doubt that you are being canvassed once again to join the continuing conspiracy against the Zimbabwe People's Revolution. We would like to sound our revolutionary opinions on this issue before you can be forced into opening discussions with our enemies. Our views are consistent with the operation of the war effort and recognize only those involved actively in the present war effort. We suggest that:

1. The revolutionary and fighting people of Zimbabwe will not accept any call for a ceasefire in the present armed conflict.
2. That any negotiations must be preceded by the release of all ZANU revolutionary leaders presently in Zambian prisons.
3. That we will not recognize any group of persons claiming to represent ZANLA and ZIPRA forces other than those truly elected and appointed by the fighting forces.
4. That ZANU militants and loyalists together with their ZAPU and ZIPA militants will elect a delegation to negotiate with the enemy any surrender terms. This means that ZANU will be represented by its members of the Central Committee; Dare and ZANLA commanders; and will be led by Robert Mugabe. Central Committee members: Robert Mugabe, Morris Nyagumbo, Edson Sithole, Eddison Zvobgo, Edgar Tekere, Michael Mawema, Morton Malianga, Simon Muzenda, Henry Hamadziripi, Crispen Mandizwidza and Enos Nkala. (Comrade Ndabaningi Sithole represents the ZLC, Dare and ZANLA: Mukudzei Mudzi, Rugare Gumbo, Josiah Tongogara, Kumbirai Kangai, etc. ZAPU militants representation will be composed of Jason Moyo, George Silundika, Edward Ndhlovu, Dagangwa, etc. ZIPA forces representation will be composed of the 18 ZIPA commanders led by Comrade Solomon Nhongo.)

We realize the importance of the ANC led by Bishop A. Muzorewa without the ZLC. We recognize that the ANC as a 'protest and politicizing organization' in Zimbabwe deserves a place in the final conference, but its position in the conference must be established by the fighting men. It is politically erroneous to believe that the Muzorewa ANC in Zimbabwe is the same organization in the name of ZLC.

It is only from the above group that an acceptable delegation of the revolutionary forces of Zimbabwe can be elected. It is only this group that represents the grassroots revolutionary spirit of the Zimbabwe masses. This is the only group that is not tied to the social aprons of stagnation and revisionism; a group that has no tribal influences; a group that knows the evil machinations of the enemy; a group committed to Chimurenga and that is engaged in the war today; a group that represents a true and effective unity of the people of Zimbabwe.

The supporters of the Zimbabwe people's struggle must know the true facts of our revolution. The world must know that the ANC-ZLC has no army nor contacts or information about the present forces of liberation. No ANC-ZLC can step foot in our military establishments since July 1975 (team of Nkomo, Sithole, Muzorewa and Chikerema). All ANC-ZLC leaders who live in Mozambique live in hotels in Maputo and have never met one freedom fighter. Their ZLC Military High Command is resident in Lusaka and Tanzania terrorizing ZANU supporters. After the establishment of the joint military force (ZIPA) in November 1975 the OAU recognized it and supports its operational budget. The world must know that all funds raised by the ANC-ZLC have never been given to the Zimbabwe forces but have been used to pay hotel bills and purchase cars for ANC-ZLC officials in Zambia, Tanzania, Malawi and Mozambique. It is therefore criminal for any true revolutionary and supporter of the Zimbabwe People's Struggle to continue to disseminate and propagandize false claims by the enemies of our revolution.

CONCLUSION

We would like you to know that it will be a disinvestment of time and a waste of human resources as well as a further incitement to a protracted blood-bath in Zimbabwe if, in the event of negotiations with the enemy for the terms of surrender leading to the establishment of majority rule now, for you to invite persons outside the ZANU and ZAPU militants who support the United Zimbabwe People's Army (ZIPA). Any action to the contrary is divisive, reactionary and counter-revolutionary. To continue to fraternize with the ANC-ZLC in its pretence as a revolutionary and militaristic organization committed to Chimurenga is criminal and destructive of the Zimbabwe People's Revolution.

In our demand for majority rule and our commitment to Chimurenga we show our supporters and friends that we are our own spokesmen. We have no doubt that you will desist from the old colonial system of 'we, the whites, know what the African wants'.

The gallant and heroic people of Mozambique led by their revolutionary President Samora Machel have stood resolutely in support of the Zimbabwe People's Revolution with a commitment that deserves our praises and honour. We have no doubt that as Mozambique commits itself to our support that the OAU and all of its member-nations will commit themselves to the OAU charter in spirit and action. We recognize the war declared by Southern Rhodesia on Mozambique and the people of Zimbabwe will not fail in their mission to fight in defence of Mozambique as their forces increase attacks on Southern Rhodesia.

In the event of negotiations, nothing short of meeting the following conditions will help in solving the political problems in Zimbabwe.

(a)   The immediate release of all ZANU leaders from Zambian prisons so that they can participate in the conference.

(b)   No call for a ceasefire during negotiations.

(c)   Recognition of the fighting forces and their acceptance as the constituent element in negotiations with the enemy.

(d)   Convening of a ZANU-ZAPU-ZIPA militants conference to elect their delegation to negotiate with the enemy. The mediating African countries will help in facilitating the conference.

There may not be a mathematical formula to solve the Zimbabwe situation but the above is as near a magic formula satisfying all of the fighting peoples expectations as is politically possible. The correct solution to our issue is to seek immediate consultations with the militants. Any delay on your part in calling the above groups to advise you on the correct line may cause our revolution irreparable harm.

54   Tanzanian delegation to the OAU Liberation Committee conference: statement on Michael Mawema. Maputo, Mozambique, 9 May 1976

Mr Chairman,
On behalf of the Tanzania delegation, I wish to make a brief statement on an issue which, if not elaborated on could give a wrong impression.

Today's *Daily News,* a Tanzanian government newspaper, has published an article with the title *Zimbabwe Fighters call for OAU recognition: ANC Leaders denounced.*

As distinguished delegates are aware, this article is printed from a document circulated here in Dar-es-Salaam by one person who calls himself a supporter of the Third Force of Zimbabwe. I am sure distinguished delegates have received or have seen copies of this document.

I should like to state here, that the Tanzania government has not sanctioned either the printing or the circulation of the said document. It has been circularized clandestinely.

Upon investigations, the government of the United Republic of Tanzania has discovered that the author of the document has already left the country, on 5 May 1976, for Europe and United States. Investigations have further revealed that the author of the document, Mr Mawema, has in fact been expelled from the ANC for his anti-party activities.

Because the document has been widely circulated here in Dar-es-Salaam, presumably by Mr Mawema himself or/and his collaborators, it would have been an error to pretend otherwise. Hence the publication of the document in the *Daily News* of today.

The Tanzania government treats the document and contents therein with the greatest contempt. We are certain it will be treated as such by all people who are familiar with the current situation in Zimbabwe. The document is malicious and vicious, intended only to create confusion and division within the ranks of the ANC freedom fighters. Factually it is totally incorrect.

As distinguished delegates are well aware, the Heads of State of Botswana, Mozambique, Tanzania and Zambia have already stated that they support the armed struggle of Zimbabwe waged by the freedom fighters of the ANC. The OAU which recognizes the ANC as the only authentic and legitimate liberation movement of Zimbabwe, has endorsed the current armed struggle in Zimbabwe waged by the freedom fighters of the ANC. The four Heads of State have always recognized the freedom fighters as members of the ANC. It should be emphasized very strongly that the four Heads of State have all along been one and the same in their total support for the freedom fighters of the ANC.

Mr Mawema, who purports to be a supporter of the liberation struggle of Zimbabwe has clearly demonstrated, by this document, that he, in fact, is an enemy of that struggle. He is an agent of imperialism, confusionism and division. He has set out to serve the interests of the enemies of the freedom struggle in Zimbabwe rather than the true interests of the people of Zimbabwe or third force. Mr Mawema has exposed his true colours for all to see.

At the same time, we hope that the genuine freedom fighters of

Zimbabwe united under the ANC will have learnt a lesson from the document in question; that there are many people who masquerade in various guises. Now that the struggle has entered a critical phase, vigilance by the freedom fighters must be intensified.

On its part the government of the United Republic of Tanzania rejects and denounces in its entirety the contention put forward by Mr Mawema in respect of the ANC.

55 The Nkomo faction's view:
Facts about the ANC

What compounds confused assessment of the Zimbabwe liberation movement today is the sole reliance on the pieces of information and statements put out by propaganda media out of context with historical backgrounds or even a slight analysis of the motivation to determine fact from fiction. Some supporters of the Zimbabwe liberation struggle have been grooved or, in their subjective interests, have grooved themselves into fabricated and dangerously false notions such as:

(a) the ANC outside Zimbabwe and the ANC inside Zimbabwe—sustaining, thereby, a thoughtless and superficial basis of assessment that a leader by himself constitutes an organization and where he is, physically, is necessarily where the organization is;

(b) the Reverend Ndabaningi Sithole, the leader of the so-called 'militants' merely because he has tunefully repeated the 'slogan' of 'armed struggle' and Joshua Nkomo labelled a 'moderate' merely because he has insisted on consistence and honesty in honouring conclusively, agreed and signed lines of policy including that of tactical pursuit of negotiations with the Rhodesian regime;

(c) the leadership is divided but the cadres are united: a truth manipulated purposefully to cover up the fact that the Reverend Ndabaningi Sithole and Bishop Muzorewa have been exposed and rejected by cadres and lost the command of the cadreship on which they based their hollow propaganda of the 'armed struggle'. The truth is also skilfully misapplied to lend an impression that the cadres under the leadership and command of Comrade Joshua Nkomo are united with the others against his leadership as well. This is a pure and unmitigated lie—whose motivation is clearly that 'the Reverends must not sink alone, Joshua Nkomo must be plunged in as well by hook or crook' . . . .

The decision to launch an armed liberation struggle in Zimbabwe was made at the beginning of the early sixties. The decision did not descend from the blue. It was a direct consequence of or a development from the realization, through experience, that political pressures such as constitutional demands and active boycotts, strikes and demonstrations by themselves, could not dislodge minority rule and its oppression. It is significant and necessary to note that this conclusion and the decision to launch the Zimbabwe struggle along the armed struggle were made by Comrade Joshua Nkomo at the time as President of the National Democratic Party—predecessor of Zimbabwe African Peoples Union and the present African National Council. He proceeded thereafter to seek the support and co-operation of external forces towards realization of this policy in Zimbabwe. It is equally important to note that but for Kenya and Algeria, at the time, because of the tide of national independence which was sweeping Africa through constitutional struggle, Mr Nkomo's advocacy for the armed struggle in Zimbabwe was least understood, doubted and often opposed by some leaders of present day Africa who, in their belated realization of Mr Nkomo's vision then, now claim it against him.

Equally within the Zimbabwe leadership (NDP and ZAPU) there were elements then, like the Reverend Ndabaningi Sithole, which opposed the idea of the armed struggle (1963); they linked with the wavering and doubting external forces and made common cause already then to ditch Mr Nkomo's leadership as an attempt to offset the burden of the armed struggle he advocated for. This is how the Reverend Sithole caused the split (ZANU) in the Zimbabwe liberation movement, a split which but for support witting and unwitting by some external forces would not have developed to the tragic proportions that it is today and the resultant tragically confused assessment of the Zimbabwe liberation struggle.

It was hardly a year from the event of the split (1963–1964) that the march of events proved Mr Nkomo right in his advocacy of the armed struggle. The Rhodesia Front regime grew more ruthless in its suppression, imprisonments and detentions of African political leaders whilst the African masses grew equally violent in their resistance to violent oppression (1964). Mr Nkomo and hundreds of other political leaders were detained and put out of the active scene in April 1964 leaving the opposing forces—the minority regime and the struggling African masses—fully geared towards intensified violent conflict which he had visualized and prepared for as inevitable as far back as 1960.

The elaborate and only political machinery in Zimbabwe covering every element of the country and every corner of it which kept the Zimbabweans in this frame of effective struggle was ZAPU (PCC) under the leadership of Comrade Nkomo. Following years of intensive organization of the African National Congress, the National Democratic Party and the Zimbabwe African Peoples Union itself which constituted a continuity despite bannings by the regime, ZAPU was rooted in deep levels of organization for survival in carrying the struggle through hazards and harrassments from the regime. It is through this resilience that it emerged as the main base of the African National Council (1971) and as the decisive power in the total rejection, through the Pearce Commission, of the Smith-Douglas Home fraudulent constitution in 1972. It is through this power that, but for the temporary disturbance through the abortive emergence of FROLIZI only four years (1971) ago, ZAPU all along was the main fighting force in the field of the armed struggle in Zimbabwe. It is as recent as 1973 after the formation of the JMC that our brothers of ZANU also came effectively on the fighting scene through their north-eastern district operations.

The point for illustration here is that both in the political scene and that of the armed struggle, forces of former ZAPU constitute the only background for the organized coherence of the Zimbabwe nation. It is on this basis as already indicated, that the African National Council (ANC) emerged in 1971 with Bishop Muzorewa put as leader. It is on this basis that the ANC as constituted pressed for an organized congress which finally took place on 27-28 September 1975 and re-established itself under the leadership of Mr Nkomo. . . .

In January, 1975, the Organization of African Unity Liberation Committee in Dar-es-Salaam was presented with a formal application of the African National Council (ANC) for recognition as the sole representative organization of struggling people of Zimbabwe in place of the dissolved former organizations ZAPU, ZANU and the tiny FROLIZI. The application was based on the Lusaka Declaration of Unity of 7 December 1974, which established a single organization out of the various previous Zimbabwe liberation movements. The Lusaka Declaration of Unity was a culmination of the hardest ever possible synthesis of divergent attitudes. It must be pointed out for those who easily or conveniently forget, that it was neither the former ZAPU organization nor its leader then, Mr Joshua Nkomo, who were the obstruction to the unity effort; on the contrary, they were the principal basic unifying factor.

What was presented before the OAU for recognition was the organization the ANC. It was not Muzorewa that was presented for recognition and he was therefore never meant to be the condition for the unity of the people of Zimbabwe. To have regarded him as the 'unifying factor' was a tragic misconception of the unity in the ANC as tabled before the OAU. The ANC is the system of organization, in other words, the rules and constitution that govern and bind all its members towards the fulfilment of its objectives. This is what the OAU accepted and recognized in January and subsequently by heads of states. The binding rules and principles of the ANC are contained in the Lusaka Declaration of Unity and the ANC constitution. . . .

We would like hereunder to illustrate how Bishop Muzorewa, as leader of the ANC then, measured to the provisions of the ANC constitution and the principles and programmes of the Lusaka Declaration of Unity of 7 December 1974.

Firstly we quote in full the analysis of the National Chairman of the ANC, Mr Samuel Munodawafa, in his presentation to the ANC Congress of 27-28 September 1975.

CHAIRMAN'S REPORT

Countrymen, Sons and Daughters of Zimbabwe,

It is with much pleasure that I welcome you to this second congress of our great movement, the African National Council. The first was held in March last year. At the same time I wish to apologize for the long delay in holding the congress. As you very well know this congress was supposed, in terms of our constitution, to have been held in March, but, as you can see this is now September. Why has it taken us so long to hold this congress? . . .

. . . At the end of last year all Zimbabwe nationalist leaders, including those who had been in detention for over ten years, suffering for liberation of their country, met in Lusaka, Zambia, and signed what has come to be known as the Lusaka Declaration of Unity. The Declaration, which was signed by Mr Joshua Nkomo, Bishop Muzorewa, Reverend Ndabaningi Sithole and Mr James Chikerema on behalf of their respective former organizations, states in clear terms that a congress of the ANC shall be held in Zimbabwe within four months—that is in March. It allowed the inclusion in the ANC executive of four leaders each from the former ZAPU, ZANU and FROLIZI.

The Declaration also states that at this congress a new constitution of the movement shall be approved, a new policy formulated, and leaders elected. This had to be done because the Unity had brought together four organizations which had previously operated in separation. It had also brought in one fold four leaders all potentially contending for the leadership of the ANC. By this arrangement a new situation and problem had been created which nobody else could solve but congress.

On 12 January 1975, the first enlarged executive of the ANC met in

Highfield and made the item of the pending congress its priority number one on the agenda. Two committees were appointed in anticipation of the congress in March. They were the ANC constitution for the ANC; and the Congress Committee—designed to make all the relevant and necessary preparations for the congress. The same meeting decided on the dates of 9 and 10 March for the holding of the Congress.

At the National Executive meeting held on 17 February our brothers from the former ZANU organization proposed the postponement of the congress dates. They argued that many of their former followers had either been left out of the ANC or had not joined because they did not agree with the policies of the ANC, particularly its non-violence policy. The postponement of the congress dates would give the former ZANU members an opportunity to join the ANC and to be present at the congress.

They said that current branches, districts and provinces were dominated by former ZAPU members. The proposal was rejected by the majority of the National Executive members who argued that:

1. At the initial stages of the ANC the National Executive Committee was dominated by former ZANU members who logically had the effect of attracting former ZANU members into the ANC.

2. The first National Organizing Secretary of the ANC was a former ZANU leader who by the nature and logic of things was bound to attract more former ZANU members into the ANC than former ZAPU members.

3. It was strongly argued that the real reason why the former ZANU members and many other Africans did not come forward to assume official positions in the ANC was fear of arrest and detention, since in those early days of the ANC, those who accepted official positions in the organization did so at their own peril. Thus the proposal was formerly rejected by way of a vote.

At the executive meeting of 2 March the same issue was raised again and almost the same arguments were advanced for the postponement of congress. Even if the meeting rejected the arguments, it was eventually felt that in the interest of the fledgling unity and of Zimbabwe the complaints of the former ZANU people, though they were patently groundless, must be investigated and, where necessary, righted. So a committee was appointed and charged with the task to investigate existing complaints in branches, districts and provinces from former ZANU officials who felt that they had been left out of the ANC for one reason or the other.

The committee sat at Kambuzuma and Glen Norah from where complaints had been received by the committee. But to the shock surprise of the committee it was discovered that those people who had made complaints did not care to attend the committee meetings even though they had been given sufficient notice to attend.

At the same time former ZANU leaders were holding secret meetings, outside the established organs of the ANC at which efforts were made to revive the former ZANU. They visited various areas trying to form ZANU branches parallel to ANC branches. The former ZANU leadership took the position that they could not go to or allow the holding of a congress until and unless they had formed sufficient ZANU branches in all places to counter the ANC branches which, they alleged, were full of former ZAPU members.

What this amounted to was that they would not allow the holding of congress unless they were thoroughly sure of winning the leadership contest. And they said so in clear terms.

It was in these circumstances that an inter-provincial meeting was held and called upon the Branch Investigation Committee to stop proceedings forthwith. They also resolved to have nothing to do with the committee's proceedings. The National Executive Committee met on 27 April and called for an end to the Branch Investigation Committee's proceedings and for the fixing of a new date for the holding of a congress. No formal decision was taken on the matter, and it was formerly agreed that a special executive meeting must be urgently convened at which the sole item on the agenda will be the question of congress. The meeting was to be convened within two weeks' time.

The President, Bishop Abel Muzorewa, gave notice that he had been invited to the Jamaica Commonwealth Conference and he would therefore be absent from the special meeting, but the meeting should go ahead, chaired by the Vice-President Dr E. M. Gabellah. But Dr Gabellah did not convene the special meeting urgently as had been decided by the executive—that is, within two weeks. Instead, he convened the meeting for 1 June, and what was most astounding was that he had deliberately omitted the most important items of congress from the agenda. The meeting demanded that the item be included as a top priority. This was done. . . .

The national executive committee on this 1 June unanimously decided on holding this year's ANC Congress, and set 21 and 22 June as the dates for the congress. It was resolved to do away with the Branches Investigation committee, and instructions were given that the committee stop any further investigations and proceedings.

Expectedly the former ZANU leaders declared their hostility to congress and stated that they were going to boycott the congress. This was no surprise to us.

What greatly surprised us was that when the Bishop came back from Jamaica through America, he defied the decision of the majority executive and sided with the anti-congress minority of largely former ZANU leaders. He pulled up a new defensive theory stating that the question of congress must be decided by four signatories to the Lusaka Declaration of Unity. He could not say where the four signatories derived the right and power to impose their will on the national executive and on the people of Zimbabwe since neither the ANC constitution nor the Declaration of Unity gave them those powers.

Later on the Bishop said he was going to convene an emergency meeting of the national executive to discuss the question of congress with a view to changing the dates (21-22 June). Since the emergency meeting the Bishop called, some of us went with them to Dar-es-Salaam under the false guise that they were wanted there by Presidents Nyerere, Seretse Khama, Kaunda and Samora Machel, and yet he was the one who had invited the presidents.

Ever since that trip to Dar-es-Salaam in early July the Bishop has not returned home to his people. He has not told his national executive about his desire to stay in Zambia and he has not given any reason for doing so. Some say he is afraid of being arrested and detained if he comes. Some say he has some work to do in Zambia. What work is it which he does not want to tell his executive? We are left guessing. Is it the proper thing for a president to stay away from his people? I leave that question to you to answer. . . .

No report has been given about the Jamaica Commonwealth meeting; no report has been given about the David Ennals meeting; no report has been given about the Dar-es-Salaam meeting where several recommendations were made; no report has been made about the trip to Mozambique for the independence celebrations; no report has been given about the historic constitutional talks on the Victoria Falls Bridge; and no report has ever been given about the moneys of the organization. How the moneys are being spent is a closely guarded secret known only to a privileged few—a small clique within the organization. This is a most abnormal way of running an organization, let alone a people's movement.

When I used my constitutional powers to convene a meeting of the executive committee on 7 September 1975 it was in response to a popular call by various organs of your movement, and it was with the intention of reviving the powers of the national executive which is the supreme decision making organ after congress. We made no new decision about the congress. The decision was made by the executive meeting of 1 June and what we merely did on 7 September, was to set new dates for the congress.

Now I come to the question of the congress. There are some people who say they do not want a congress and they accuse others of wanting a congress. It is quite clear that most of these people have little or no experience about the organizations. No organization can survive for long without a congress. Congress is the people; it is the totality and unified will of all the people belonging to an organization. To say that there should be no congress for an organization is as good as saying there should be no people in that organization.

Congress is the link between the led and the leaders; congress rejuvenates the organization; it removes the dead wood from the organization; it shows the real power of the people; it acts as a check on the dictatorial inclination of the leaders. It is through congress that the people maintain a concrete control over their leaders who are in actual fact their servants and not their masters.

That is why congresses are enshrined in all constitutions of all organizations. In our organization, the ANC people who are anti-congress are divided into two; there are those who fear congress because they have never been popular with the common man-in-the-hut and they therefore know that by going to congress they are putting their political heads on the chopping block; and there are those who fear congress because they have no political history or record and they have also committed many political sins, both of omission and commission. . . .

Our president Bishop Muzorewa has done a good job. He led us ably and successfully against the iniquitous Home-Smith constitutional proposals. He united all the people of Zimbabwe. He correctly and honestly told all and sundry that he was filling the gap of the detained leaders. He made many political mistakes but we turned a blind eye, preferring only to see his good side rather than the other.

But let me say that of late the Bishop has taken up the wrong path. He has linked up with one group of the ANC against the other, instead of maintaining his neutralist and central position acting as a centripetal rather than centrifugal force. By doing this he is responsible for undermining the unity that we had built. By keeping away from his people and trying to run the organization from Zambia he has become a liability rather than an asset. He has attempted to usurp power from the people and to repose it in a clique of three people.

The Bishop's greatest blunder was his attempt to remove Mr Joshua Nkomo from the liberation struggle. Whoever advised him to do that must be his greatest enemy. I am stating an objective fact when I say that the liberation of this country has been associated with Mr Nkomo for the past 20 years.

He started the struggle when most of us were at school or

unconcerned, and taught us how not only to fight, but also to suffer and sacrifice for the liberation of our motherland. It is most uncalculating and callous for the Bishop to think that he can uproot Mr Nkomo from the struggle just by the waving of a magic wand. I can only hope the Bishop will think better than that.

I wish to reiterate our position on the question of a constitutional settlement. We want majority rule now. We shall not accept any constitutional settlement that leaves effective power still in the hands of the white minority. Our desire has already been stated and is well known. But let me assure you that whatever settlement we arrive at shall be subject to approval by you, through a special congress that shall be convened for the purpose.

The world is watching today's deliberations with keen interest and I hope that you will tackle the task before you with enthusiasm, wisdom and foresight.

(End of the Chairman's Report.)

The Lusaka Declaration of Unity added twelve to existing 57 members of the National Executive of the ANC, making the total 69. Considering those in prisons and the FROLIZI quota (four) which had no substitute within the country, the National Executive membership in regular attendance was 57.

On the 'National Conference'—which is Congress under the ANC constitution—Clause 7 provides that:

> It shall meet in ordinary session *once every year* provided that it may at any time meet in extra-ordinary session if so summoned by the president or at the requirements of at least two-thirds of the Central Committee members, National Assembly and the Provinces or the Branches.

As can be observed, there is no provision for any officer or organ of the ANC, for any reason, to postpone the stipulation for the annual National Conference (Congress) to any period beyond its limit; on the contrary there may be more congresses within the period. Accordingly the congress was scheduled for March—precisely 2 March 1975.

It was in recognition and taking advantage of this provision that the 'Lusaka Declaration of Unity' laid down that, as from 7 December 1974, Clause 4 provides:

> The enlarged ANC executive shall have the following functions:
> (a) To prepare for a conference for the transfer of power to the majority that might be called.
> (b) To prepare for the holding of Congress within four months at which—

    (i)   a revised ANC constitution shall be adopted.

    (ii) the leadership of the united people of Zimbabwe shall be elected.

    (iii) a statement of policy for the new ANC will be considered.

(c)   To organize the people for such conference and Congress.

None of the signatories of the Lusaka Declaration of Unity was coerced to attach their signatures to this declaration and from all evidence everyone of them and their supporters was within their five senses in binding themselves to this programme.

The next stage was implementation. The National Executive session which took place on 1 June 1975, and set the date of the Congress (21-22 June 1975), though belated was attended by the full complement of 55 National Executive members (Muzorewa absent). In setting the congress date, in spite of the vocal opposition by the former ZANU minority, at voting only Dr Edson Sithole voted against and the abstentions were two, Enos Nkala and Morton Malianga. This left 52 members finally voting for the date of the Congress. . . .

It was in the face of these constitutional and popular demands for the congress that Bishop Muzorewa faltered and took risks against the popular will within the organization in the misguided hope that he could use external support as a leverage to turn the tide against congress and thus warm the seat of presidency a little longer to gain sufficient votes to make him the final compromise candidate for ANC leadership. He increasingly suffered dangerous illusions on Zimbabwe leadership which were anchored (for their own purposes), by experienced intriguers—the Rev Ndabaningi Sithole and James Chikerema—and warmed by the hospitality and regard of capitals of independent African states.

In an attempt to reach at his illusions and painfully conscious of the fact that he was acting outside the rules and regulations of the ANC and worse still against the popular will within the organization, Bishop Muzorewa

(a)   made common cause with the Rev N. Sithole and James Chikerema assumed the 'POWER' of decision of the ANC.

(b)   exiled himself from Zimbabwe and the people he was supposed to lead by seeking sanctuary in neighbouring independent states.

(c)   fabricated the excuses that he stayed away from Zimbabwe for fear of arrest because of 'statements' to the press on the armed struggle and that in any case he had accepted president Nyerere's advice to stay out of Rhodesia.

(d)   he failed to fulfil his executive duty of convening national executive meetings from 15 June to 1 September 1975. . . .

(e)   acting on false assumptions and on the typical style of imperialist inspired *coups-d'état*, the Bishop, in common cause with the Rev N. Sithole and James Chikerema, conspired to seize the externally based machinery—the Zimbabwe Liberation Council (ZLC)—which had been planned to seek international support for the Zimbabwe struggle and to promote the armed struggle. He believed the Zimbabwe armed forces were just inanimate instruments which could be picked and rattled to silence opponents and stand upon them as pinnacles of prestige for exclusive leadership. Still their target for this move was Mr Nkomo; hence their exclusion of all officers who saw truth and honesty in Nkomo's leadership.

(f) the Bishop has remained a presiding director of a Zimbabwe factory for the manufacture of the most filthy political lies—through pen and propaganda. The object of hate is Mr Nkomo and the source of fear being the Zimbabwe masses and the Congress—the concrete base of Mr Nkomo's leadership.

(g) unable to hold back the tide to hold congress and misled by the fiction of a leadership which does not submit itself to the mandate of the people the Bishop took the precipitate step of 'expelling' Mr Nkomo. Picking on Mr Nkomo for a political tide generated by the people themselves pin-pointed the Bishop as an enemy of the peoples' will and Congress became even more inevitable.

It was in this atmosphere that the executive of all the eight provinces of the ANC met in August under the chairmanship of the then Secretary-General Gordon Chavunduka and made it very clear that their patience had run out and that unless the national executive met and set out a final date for congress, they would suspend it and assume that task. Bishop Muzorewa received this clear message of these organs of the ANC through more than 70 telegrams whilst in Zambia and abroad.

The anti-congress elements have made allegations that the national Chairman's convention of the National Executive on 7 September 1975 was unconstitutional. The constitution of the ANC on the National Executive provides under Clause 6: 'It shall meet in ordinary session once every two months but shall meet in extra-ordinary session when summoned by the president or *at the request of at least half its* members.'

From the last session of 1 June to 7 September, three months had expired without Muzorewa calling even the ordinary session of the National Executive—when by the course of events, he should have convened extra-ordinary meetings for his Commonwealth conference report in Dar—July fraudulent meeting he convened. In addition *more than half the members* of the ANC National Executive had petitioned for the National Executive meeting.

Clauses 7 and 8 under provisions on the National Executive, the ANC constitution lays down:

> 7. 'President shall preside over all meetings. In his absence the Deputy President or, in the absence of both, a person elected for the purpose shall preside.'
> 8. 'Its quorum shall be half its members.'

For the national executive session of 7 September 1975, the national chairman, Mr Samuel Munodawafa was not only the highest officer available by order of precedence but was also elected by the national executive members present—who were in excess of the quorum *laid down—to preside.*

On the National Conference—Congress—the national chairman, Comrade Samuel Munodawafa, was within his constitutional right and obligations to preside over congress because the ANC constitution provides under clause 9:

> 9. 'The national chairman or in his absence the deputy national chairman or in the absence of both, a person elected for the purpose, shall preside'.

Thus the congress was constitutionally convened, constitutionally presided over and therefore took constitutional decisions. . . .

We wonder at the mentality of people who expected the majority of the national executive and other organs of the ANC to continue after eight months of patience to stand watching whilst the Bishop and his junta usurped the powers of the organization, rendered every other organ useless and irrelevant, refused completely to implement the programme on which the unified ANC was founded. This was reducing the ANC as a liberation movement into a churchdom in which the powers of the hierarchy descended from heaven and not from the people to the leader. To have expected any more patience from the membership of the ANC was contempt and insult to the intelligence of the people of Zimbabwe.

ON THE MUZOREWA CONSULTATIVE MEETING

The reasons put forward by the Muzorewa faction for their opposition to a congress of the organization were that:

(a)   a decision to disengage from the constitutional talks and embark solely on the armed struggle had already been taken.

(b)   in the circumstances a congress of the people was a luxury and had to await the victory of the armed struggle.

In order to angle for FRELIMO's support they put across the fictitious theory that all movements committed to liberation through armed struggle have had to postpone congresses until after victory of the armed struggle. They instanced FRELIMO to substantiate their case. This was an argument which was as mischievous as it was dishonest and opportunistic.

Firstly, notwithstanding the different historical processes and conditions of the development of the political struggle in Mozambique and Zimbabwe, it is an historical fact that FRELIMO is democratically based and has resolved its problems in the course of the armed struggle, through Party congresses to which former ZAPU was represented as observers. In any case all genuine revolutionary movements, past and contemporary, relied and do rely on congresses as their cardinal stages of development. It is equally an historical fact that only fascist dictatorships (Franco-Spain, Hitler-Germany, etc) opposed peoples' congresses because they were conscious of the unpopular line they were pursuing.

Secondly, no decision to disengage the constitutional talks with Rhodesian regime was ever taken by *any organ* of the ANC. The legitimate organ to take such a decision is the National Executive of the ANC. It never sat anywhere to reverse its decision to engage in talks with the regime.

Thirdly, the ANC never, at any time, reduced its policy over a complex struggle like the Zimbabwe one to a simple choice between the armed struggle and talks with the enemy as alternatives as if they were opposites in strategy. The ANC has never regarded talks with the enemy and the armed struggle as mutually exclusive processes of struggle. On the contrary the ANC regards talks and the armed struggle as complementary depending on the objectives created by the circumstances of that given phase of the struggle.

As it should be clear that the reasons put forward by the Muzorewa junta in opposition to congress were a pack of dangerously misleading lies, the real reason must now be exposed. Each one of the junta— Muzorewa, N. Sithole and James Chikerema, separately, under all sorts of guises, had a burning pathological desire for the leadership of the ANC and therefore that of Zimbabwe. The stark reality among the people was that, popularly, whether combined as a junta or separately as individuals, they had no chance whatever. They were conscious and bothered by this painful fact. The only thing they shared, hated and feared in common was the rooted and popular standing of Mr Nkomo with the masses and consequently the inevitable choice for leadership of the ANC and that of Zimbabwe. They could not relent. They gambled for their political fortunes on the path of discrediting Mr Nkomo, deceiving and dodging the Zimbabwe public, engaging in political deviousness and prolific lying and counting on certain sentimental external forces for propaganda and financial support.

Though lies are fast in capturing a moment, they, however, cannot withstand the truth in the long run. This is one of the complexities of the Zimbabwe struggle. Realizing that the so-called expulsion of Nkomo had no effect and was, in fact, irrelevant to the march of the people towards congress, the Muzorewa junta, using Dr Gabellah and Dr Chavunduka inside Zimbabwe, decided to make a cautious test of its strength among the people by convening what was called a 'Consultative Meeting' of branches and provincial executives of whatever was left in their support. Discovering that they had lost almost everything and could not draw any response from the formal structure of the organization, they turned to the public in the streets of Salisbury and to the church followers of Muzorewa inviting everyone and anybody to a rally at the Gwanzura stadium, the venue of the supposed 'Consultative Meeting'. Having no formal delegates they were selling at five cents delegates' labels to anyone curious enough to hear what sermon was to be preached in the stadium. True enough they drew large crowds to the stadium. The limit of 6,000 allowed them by the Rhodesian regime as had been allowed to the ANC congress was exceeded. But what did that mean in political terms? The crowds were not an organization, they were not representative of anyone but curiosity as crowds milling around a circus lion. Dr Gabellah was aware of this and realized that he could neither effect discipline nor conduct even a 'Consultative Meeting' with a crowd whose credentials he did not know. He decided to make the quantity of the people the issue. He created a farce over numbers with the police as a way out and, on that excuse, dismissed the crowd, despite the fact that his junta group had accepted a written permit for a limit of 6,000.

The group has noticed that drawing a crowd against formal organization by whatever deceitful methods has a confusing effect on some supporters. It is thus currently engaged in trying to carry out another experiment on crowd-catching without giving the people any chance of telling it off.

ON THE CONSTITUTIONAL TALKS

A delegation of the ANC led by comrade Joshua Nkomo is currently engaged in constitutional talks with the Rhodesian regime. The talks are a continuation of the talks which broke down on the South African coach at the Victoria Falls on 25 August 1975. All these talks are sequel of talks originally initiated by Bishop Muzorewa in April 1974. At that time Bishop Muzorewa as leader of the ANC pulled into the talks a non-member Chad Chipunza to assist him. Chad Chipunza is a distinguished traitor in Zimbabwe. The results were tragic. Bishop Muzorewa found himself signing a deal with the racist leader Ian Smith which accepted the 1971 Douglas Home-Smith constitutional fraud as a basis for finding a settlement.

The National Executive of the ANC met on 2 June 1974 to consider the deal. It was thrown out. Bishop Muzorewa offered to resign. The National Executive pardoned him and asked him to continue as leader.

In the fever of the fall of Portuguese colonialism on 25 April 1974 and the brilliant victories of the PAIGC and FRELIMO, the frontier states in Southern Africa, Botswana, Zambia and Tanzania judged the moment ripe to test the racist regimes—Vorster and Ian Smith—on the demands of the Lusaka Manifesto, an OAU and United Nations policy document for Southern Africa. Their immediate objective was how best they could salvage the talks initiated and later plunged by Bishop Muzorewa himself. The initiatives of these states led to the release of the leaders in prisons—Joshua Nkomo and others to Lusaka first and finally on 12 December 1974, to Rhodesia. Before their release the 'Lusaka Declaration of Unity' was initiated on 7 December, constituting the unified ANC and laying down a definite programme of future development. . . .

Quite naturally there was some concern within the OAU as to whether the talks being fostered by the frontier states with Ian Smith through contact with Vorster were being carried out on an acceptable interpretation of the Lusaka Manifesto. This led to the Special Council of Ministers' meeting in Dar-es-Salaam on 7 April 1975. The Council of Ministers emerged with a Dar-es-Salaam declaration which laid down—
(a)   that the racist regimes should talk to liberation movements first.
(b)   contact between OAU states and the racist regimes could be made providing this did not suggest 'detente' with these regimes.

The OAU summit conference held in Kampala in July 1975 endorsed the Dar-es-Salaam Declaration. This cleared the atmosphere for the frontier states and for the ANC (Zimbabwe) on the talks. It was in this African context that the talks on the South African coach were held at the Victoria Falls bridge at the end of August 1975.

We would like to stress that the talks at the Victoria Falls bridge broke down on the mechanics, in other words procedural question, of the conference and NOT on the substance of the talks. It has always been understood as a matter of elementary logic that the vital point of breakdown can only be considered on the matter of substance—majority rule itself—and not the question of immunity which was just a tactical question which could be varied considering that the future of Zimbabwe could not hang on a few individuals outside whatever their rank. The refusal of the British government to allow the Hon Mbiu Koinange to enter the constitutional conference for the independence of Kenya in spite of the spirited tactical pressure of KANU did not end the constitutional conference nor did it prevent the independence of Kenya.

Once congress was held on 27–28 September 1975 it was up to the new national leadership of the ANC to decide how best to respond to the overtures of the racist regime for the resumption of the talks. In the event the talks were resumed with the ANC aiming at three immediate objectives—

(a) clearing the immunity hurdle,
(b) eliminating the factor of South African involvement in the talks,
(c) reaching the substantive issues to determine as to whether it is any worthwhile to continue the talks.

This is where the talks are at present. This is what comrade Joshua Nkomo has always meant by saying these talks should be carried to their logical conclusion.

We have to repeat that these talks are being deliberately conducted on the clear approach that they are neither a substitute nor an obstruction to the armed liberation struggle. The talks will not stop just to appease destructive speculators and the armed struggle will not stop just because there are talks being conducted with the regime.

Allegations have been made by the Muzorewa junta that the peoples' leader, comrade Joshua Nkomo, has a deal with the racist leader Ian Smith on the settlement of the Rhodesian problem. These allegations are pieces of mischievous nonsense manufactured for credulous and cheap minded politicians. No such deal exists, none will ever be made and none has ever been concretely produced but for empty malicious allegations. To believe this nonsense is to be part of the lie and to treat it any further is to waste space and time. Whatever is being talked or negotiated now is being discussed and directed by the ANC National Executive as a whole and the public is kept informed of every stage.

CONCLUSION

It is important to notice that all splitists of the Zimbabwe liberation movement have risen and fallen by common pattern. Every one of them has had their desperate power ambition break open at the pick of entrustment of the highest party duties by the National Leader Joshua Nkomo. . . . At this point every one of them has started their bid for the top post in the nation by smearing the national leader Joshua Nkomo with allegations of weakness, corruption and sell-outism. Every one of them has first attempted an internal coup d'état within the National Executive leadership by trying to usurp powers for an attempt to expel Mr Nkomo. Every one of them has had their plans collapse and fail at this point. On failure every one of them has then resorted to seeking refuge in tribalism, pathological lying and retaining a clique for a split. The favourite theme for stirring tribalism is that original inhabitants of Zimbabwe are Shona speaking peoples; they are the majority after all, having the greatest number of the most highly educated persons who can man government. It is anathema, according to this tribal theory, to tolerate Zimbabwe national leadership moving to government under a person who is not of pure Shona stock.

This is how the Rev Ndabaningi Sithole rose and fell, appointed by Mr Nkomo to take charge of the Party from an external base in Dar-es-Salaam in 1963 and ended up generating a split and forming ZANU finally.

This is how James Chikerema, as vice-president, entrusted by Mr Nkomo with the charge of the party from an external base rose and fell with his FROLIZI, in 1971.

This is how Bishop Muzorewa, appointed by Mr Nkomo, who was then in prison, to lead the unifying ANC, rose and fell in 1975. . . .

It is needless for us to point out that the majority of Zimbabweans have not been taken in by the subversive tendencies of this junta. The danger of the tribal atmosphere they are generating cannot, however, be taken lightly. It is on this issue that we would like to draw the attention of and warn the external forces which have encouraged these elements as to what dangerous tribal brinks they are pushing Zimbabwe to.

Nothing exemplifies the tribal trend of the Muzorewa junta than their bid to control what was supposed to be the external administration of the ANC, the Zimbabwe Liberation Council (ZLC). On 16 August 1975, acting as a tribal force to impose decisions, they compelled Edward Ndhlovu to leave the meeting, at which they remained placing themselves in control of all key external posts.

'ANC—ZLC—MINUTES 16 AUGUST 1975'

Present:
Nyandoro, (Ndhlovu), Mukono, Mtambanengwe,
Munyawarara, Masangomayi, Parirewa, Gamanya,
Parirenyatwa, Chikerema, Sithole (Chairman).
Elections to ZLC:
Chairman: N. Sithole—Ten for.
Vice-Chairman: J. Z. Moyo—Eight for, one abstention, one against.

Secretary: J. R. D. Chikerema—Nine for.

Diplomatic Committee
  (a) Munyawarara, L.
  (b) Mtambanengwe, S. (Chairman—nine for), ZANU
  (c) Nkomo, J.

Finance Committee
  (a) Nyandoro, G. B. (Chairman—nine for), FROLIZI
  (b) Masangomayi, J.
  (c) Muzenda, S.

Publicity Committee
  (a) Masangomayi, J.
  (b) Gamanya, Z. (Chairman), FROLIZI
  (c) Makoni, Rev.

Welfare Committee
  (a) Parirewa, G. S. (Chairman), ZANU
  (b) Nyandoro
  (c) Makoni, Rev.

Party Organization
  (a) Madimutsa, N.
  (b) Tekere, E.
  (c) Mawema, M. (Chairman), ZANU

Military Committee
  (a) Parirenyatwa, S. D.
  (b) Mukono, N. (Chairman), ZANU
  (c) Dabengwa, D.

It is important to conceive and understand properly the operative nature of these tribal dynamics which are concealed in slogans of militancy. When the Muzorewa junta claims majority support it is presuming upon the success of the tribalist mentality it is trying to engender within the Zimbabwe population, in the army and among students—especially abroad.

It is the awareness of this evil movement that has kept the Zimbabwe population tightly together behind Mr Nkomo in order to preserve the gains of national unity achieved under him. Fresh persons on the Zimbabwe political scene and some external forces under the sway of sentimentality and slogans regarding the Zimbabwe struggle must enter into deeper analysis of the historical base and the nature of factors affecting the Zimbabwe struggle before passing judgement on superficial impulse and in this way multiplying confusion.

Finally we would like to clarify the question of unity. It is our standpoint that unity of the people or any quarelling leaders can be solved finally and peacefully by the people of that country exercising their sovereignty in congress. . . . It is then for the external forces to support what the people of Zimbabwe have chosen in congress.

There are people toying with the dangerous idea that the Zimbabwe population must be ignored and that decisions of those carrying arms be imposed on the entire population. These are elements, internal and external, who are, in fact, opportunists and adventurists who want the world to believe that revolution is the gun and that the man with the gun is the sole revolutionary to the exclusion of the masses. This is treachery to and corruption of the revolution. The people of Zimbabwe with or without guns are a single revolutionary whole in struggle. What prevails in the course of the struggle is their democratic decisions through their organized instrument—the ANC. To suggest anything otherwise is to advocate chaos.

56 Julius K. Nyerere, president of Tanzania: speech given at Oxford University, 19 November 1975

I have talked on the American continent, in Asia and Australia, and in very many countries of Europe, about different aspects of the struggle against racialism and colonialism. I have been doing so since five days after the independence of Tanganyika, when I first addressed the United Nations as the Prime Minister of a free country. I continue to talk about colonialism and racilism not only because, like Mount Everest, they are there, but also because, unlike Mount Everest, we must together remove them from the face of the earth. And I shall be speaking on this subject again today. For Oxford University and its graduates are not unimportant in the development of attitudes; and Britain has more influence in the world than a small, weak, and young country like Tanzania.

We, in Tanzania, have no ambition to be the liberators of Southern Africa. Nor do we ask other countries to undertake this task. We do not believe that one country can ever free another. We do not believe that any people can be given liberty. They can only be assisted or hindered in getting freedom for themselves. Equally, however, we do not believe that a people can ultimately be denied liberty. For man is so constituted that he will not rest unless he feels that he has freedom and the human dignity which goes with it. Otherwise he will, sooner or later, by one means or another, fight for his own freedom within his society, and for the freedom of his society from outside domination. The history of the world, and of every nation, is at bottom a story of man's struggle to reconcile the need for order in a technologically changing society with his demand to associate as a free individual on terms of equality with other men.

Tanzania's interest in the freedom movement of Southern Africa therefore does not arise out of any belief that our peoples have a God-given mission to free others. If that were the case, the world would rightly look upon Tanzania as the African danger to its peace; messianic concepts of duty have done more damage to real liberty in the world than any deliberate evil intention. And, as I hope to make plain before I finish speaking, we have not yet solved the problems of making freedom a reality within our own borders.

Yet we are free in one sense. We govern ourselves. We elect our own government and Parliament; we determine the direction of our own development. We make our own mistakes, and achieve our own successes. For Tanzania is one of the many states of Africa which owes its present existence to the world-wide anti-colonial movement after the 1939-45 World War. We campaigned for our independence. We would not have achieved it in 1961 had we not campaigned with determination. But our celebration was not just a consequence of our own efforts. We benefited from the fact that colonialism had become unacceptable to the world; its inconsistency with the principles of human equality and freedom had become widely acknowledged. And even now, our continued independence owes more to broad acceptance of the principles of national freedom than to any defence capacity of our own. So anything which strengthens the acceptance of the principle of national independence is of importance to us; anything which weakens it is of concern to us.

Thus, as we see it; the right to independence either exists for every nation, or it does not exist for Tanzania. Tanzanians have no superhuman virtues which are denied to the people of Rhodesia. The people of Namibia have no less right to solve their problems of disunity for themselves than have the people of Portugal, of Lebanon, or any other long-independent state whose peoples are divided along linguistic or ideological lines. And black men in Dar-es-Salaam or Lusaka or Lagos, have neither more nor less right to human dignity than those of Johannesburg or Pretoria or Cape Town. What we claim for ourselves we have to accept as the right of others. While others are denied such rights our own hold over them must be insecure.

But, although our weakness and our blackness makes obvious our responsibility to support other Africans when they struggle for freedom, the same connexion exists for older nations and peoples of other colours. Europe has had the evils and dangers of racialism terribly demonstrated within its own borders. And colonialism in Africa is only an older—and more long-lasting—version of the attempt made by Nazi Germany to occupy, dominate, and control the rest of Europe in its own interests. Africa is not unique in its problems. Nor is it any more possible to confine them to Africa than it was to limit the effects of the European conflict to the borders of that continent. Racialism and colonialism in Africa are of world wide relevance. The question which has yet to be answered clearly is how the rest of the world is going to react to the freedom struggles in Southern Africa.

For the peoples of Rhodesia, Namibia, and South Africa do not accept their subordinate human status. In South Africa, the struggle in its modern form goes back to the formation of the African National Congress in 1912. In Rhodesia the first African Congress was established after the 1914-18 war. And, although nationalist organization is more recent in Namibia, the efforts of the traditional African leaders to get redress for their grievances goes back to the beginning of the League of Nations Mandate.

The demands for dignity and freedom made by these organizations were expressed peacefully—and were time and again met with violence. Yet the effort to organize politically continued—and indeed still continues. Serious people are very reluctant to revolt against their government, however unrepresentative and unjust it may be. While there is any hope of change for the better they will normally work for that change within the law as laid down, whoever has made that law. But when all hope of change is denied because the very principle of freedom and equality is denied, and when the laws prevent the peaceful expression of opinion, then the people are confronted with a clear choice. They either acquiesce in their oppression and humiliation, or they commit themselves to an armed struggle.

The Lusaka Manifesto of 1969 was, therefore, merely restating the obvious when it said that over the objective of freedom and racial equality 'We would prefer to negotiate rather than to destroy, to talk rather than kill. We do not advocate violence; we advocate an end to the violence against human dignity which is now being perpetrated by the oppressors of Africa.'

Yet the armed freedom struggle had already started. The peoples of the Portuguese colonies had been driven to acknowledge that without a willingness to kill, and be killed, their demand for freedom would make no progress. The Rhodesians had come, with even more hesitation, to the same conclusion, and were preparing themselves for war. The Lusaka Manifesto was thus a twelfth hour offer to talk. It stated clearly—almost in words of one syllable—'If peaceful progress to emancipation were possible, or if changed circumstances were to make it possible in the future, we would urge our brothers in the resistance movements to use peaceful methods of struggle even at the cost of some compromise on the timing of change.'

The Lusaka Manifesto was drawn up by the states of East and Central Africa. It was endorsed by the Organization of African Unity, and the United Nations. The Liberation Movements accepted it. But the governments of South Africa, of Rhodesia, and of Portugal ignored it.

So the armed struggle in the Portuguese colonies was intensified. The preparations for a guerilla war in Rhodesia were speeded up. And the result we now know. As a direct consequence of the fighting in Mozambique, Angola, and Guinea Bissau, the Caetano Government in metropolitan Portugal was overthrown, and the new army regime accepted the principle for which the freedom movements had been fighting. So the fighting stopped. The independence of Guinea-Bissau—already declared and operative in large parts of the country—was recognized. FRELIMO agreed upon a transitional handing-over period of ten months, and negotiated about the details of Mozambican independence. In Angola, however, the damage of the Portuguese struggle to retain power could not be undone; the disunited nationalist forces came together only for long enough to get agreement on a date for independence, and then began fighting each other. The people of that unhappy country are now paying the price of succumbing to the tactics of those who seek to dominate others by dividing them.

Independence in Mozambique appeared at first to achieve what the Lusaka Manifesto had failed to do. The government of South Africa indicated a willingness to talk, on one subject, on the basis we had set out—that is, on the basis of how, not whether, majority rule would come in Rhodesia. In accordance with the Lusaka Manifesto the governments of Tanzania, Zambia, and Botswana therefore accepted the responsibility of acting as intermediaries with the Rhodesian nationalists, with Vorster accepting a similar function with the Smith regime. It is these discussions which gave rise to talk of a detente by South Africa, and our denial of detente.

In accepting this function, my colleagues and I were facing up to the facts of life in Southern Africa, and the tripartite nature of the problem there. Rhodesia is a British colony. For all practical purposes, however, Britain surrendered its power there to a racial minority in 1923; it has consistently refused since then to reassert its authority. Knowing this, the

African states still refused to recognize the declaration of Rhodesian independence in 1965. We are against colonialism. We have no objection in principle to a unilateral declaration of independence—that was not the problem. But it was no representative of the Rhodesian people which declared independence in Rhodesia. It was a *de facto* authority whose power rests on a racial structure of politics and economics, and which is committed to maintaining that racialist minority domination. Under these conditions we would have refused to recognize the independence of Rhodesia even had the British Parliament legalized it.

As far as we are concerned, therefore, Rhodesia remains legally a British colony. But in fact, as distinct from theory, it is quite obvious that the issue in Rhodesia will be decided on the basis of comparative power. And the contenders are the minority regime of Ian Smith backed by South Africa, and the nationalist movement backed by the other independent states of Africa and non-racialists elsewhere in the world.

When the South African government let it be known that it was willing to accept the principle of majority rule in Rhodesia, and implied that it would use its influence to that end, it was therefore logical for the free African border states to investigate further. For Rhodesia cannot survive without South African backing; if that were to be withdrawn it appeared likely that there might be no further necessity to fight for freedom in Rhodesia.

I do not need to go through the twelve months of alternate optimism and realism since then. It has become quite clear that even now Smith is not ready to negotiate meaningfully. He has not accepted the principle of majority rule in Rhodesia. And it would be absurd to expect that South Africa will fulfil Britain's responsibility, and will use force to bring about majority rule. South Africa is still refusing even to apply economic sanctions against the illegal regime.

So we are forced back to the alternative strategy outlined in the Lusaka Declaration of 1969. This said 'But while peaceful progress is blocked by actions of those at present in power in the states of Southern Africa, we have no choice but to give to the peoples of those territories all the support of which we are capable in their struggle against their oppressors.' Unfortunately but inevitably, the armed struggle in Rhodesia will have to be resumed and intensified until conditions are ripe for realistic negotiation. And the freedom fighters of Rhodesia, like those of Mozambique, will demand Africa's support.

We very much regret the need for war. It can only bring dreadful suffering to the people of Rhodesia—both black and white. It will, therefore, leave a heritage of bitterness which will make the eventual development of a non-racial democratic society in that country very much more difficult. But we can no more refuse support to the Rhodesian freedom fighters now than Britain could have refused support to the resistance movements of Europe during the 1940s.

In the light of Portugal's changed policy, African states also probed South Africa on the independence of Namibia. For South African leaders had been quoted as saying that they accepted the principle of independence for this Trust Territory. And Namibia is under direct *de facto* South African control. Ian Smith's peculiar stubbornness, and the apparent death-wish of the Rhodesian whites, could not complicate a move towards genuine independence for Namibia. All that is required is for the South African government to accept the decisions of the United Nations, and arrange to pass control of the territory to the UN Commissioner for South Africa.

It has now become clear, however, that the South African government is not thinking in terms of true independence for Namibia. It is not willing to relinquish control to the United Nations; it is not willing to negotiate with the nationalist movement of the territory. Instead, South Africa is intensifying its attempt to divide the people along tribal lines; and it is trying to retain control of Namibia at the same time as posing as a convert to the cause of anti-colonialism.

The evidence for this assessment has mounted in the last few weeks. For South Africa has been using Namibia as a base for its troop incursions into Angola, and as the staging post for mercenary activity in that country.

For the present, therefore, it appears that in Namibia, as in Rhodesia, the freedom movement will have to intensify the armed struggle before any serious negotiations are possible.

In the freedom struggles of Rhodesia and Namibia, the world oustide Africa may dislike the methods adopted by the liberation movements, but it cannot challenge the aim of ending colonial domination. But we also demand freedom in South Africa. Yet South Africa is an independent state. It is absurd to pretend otherwise. And the whole world has accepted—at least in theory—the principle of non-intervention in the internal affairs of independent sovereign states.

Nonetheless, Africa in general, and Tanzania in particular, claims that the world cannot ignore what is happening within South Africa, and that it should act to secure change within that independent state.

South Africa is a tyranny. It is not the only tyrannical police state in the world, nor even in Africa. There are too many of them. Yet we do not urge external intervention in these other states; on the contrary, we have bitterly opposed it. At the height of Tanzania's expressed hostility to the atrocities and the injustices in Uganda, we made it clear that we would nevertheless condemn external intervention. . . .

South Africa is a sovereign state. But the equality and sovereignty of independent nation states must not be accepted as cover behind which racialism can flourish. For racialism is a poison which spreads from man to man and country to country. The victim of racialism too often becomes a racialist himself, and those who sympathize with the victimized are only too prone to take vengeance on others as innocent as themselves. The basic equality of all mankind is too fundamental an issue to the future of the world for other nation states to ignore the racialist structure of South African society.

Politicians and statesmen of the developed countries of the world have been agreeing that *apartheid* is a terrible thing, and condemning it in words, ever since 1948. But they have continued trade, cultural contact, and diplomatic relations with South Africa, as if it were a normal member of the international community. The words have, therefore, been regarded as political face-saving; the South African government has been able to shrug them off as irrelevant. For, if you think a man has smallpox you do not mix with him, treat with him, and ask him kindly to cure himself without passing the disease to you. However, sorrowfully, you isolate him; and if he refuses to take medicine for his disease you force it down his throat for your own protection.

No other single nation state has the right to intervene militarily in South Africa, and certainly Tanzania is not planning a liberation war against that country. But the racialist government of South Africa is, by its daily actions, preparing the conditions for an internal revolution. For, you cannot humiliate and oppress men and women for ever without them asserting their humanity in the only way left open to them, that is, by revolt. So there are now, and there will in the future be, South Africans—of all colours—who risk torture and death in the fight against the whole structure of the racialist society.

We, in Tanzania, believe that those who are genuinely opposed to racialism should help those who fight racialism. Because South Africa is an independent state, some governments and organizations may feel inhibited from direct support of those who seek to overthrow the South African system. But nothing in international law demands that the rest of the world should support the South African government in this conflict of principles, and help it in the struggle between racialism and non-racialism. At the very least, they should refrain from strengthening the supporters of *apartheid*.

Yet all those who invest in South Africa, or trade with South Africa, or otherwise treat it as a respectable member of the international community, are giving support to *apartheid,* and everything which follows from it. Institutions and individuals do not invest in a foreign country out of philanthropy. They invest to make a profit or to get interest on their money. And by investing for these purposes they have bought, (together with the stocks or shares) an interest in what is called 'political stability'—which in this case means the maintenance of *apartheid*. Their interest in this will be the greater the larger the amount they invest, and the greater the return on their investment. And the stronger the South African economy, the larger the resources which the South African government can devote to upholding racial privilege.

The more South Africa can attract outside investment, therefore, the more allies it obtains—quite regardless of any fine words about opposition to apartheid. And investment is attracted by high returns. So the greater the surplus South Africa can extract from the labour of its working people, the greater will be the attraction to new investment. Far from undermining apartheid, foreign investment's contribution to expanding the South African economy makes the intensification of exploitation on racial grounds the more inevitable. We would hear a great deal less of the argument that economics must be separated from morality if the dividends from South Africa were to fall.

The investors in South Africa and the traders with South Africa, help to pay the cost of *apartheid*. They contribute to the growth of the economy of apartheid, at the same time as they benefit from it. And in the process they are themselves corrupted by *apartheid*; they are participants in it however far distant they may live, and however non-racial they may be in their personal relationships.

Opponents of *apartheid,* and of racialism as a state doctrine, have no honest choice but to isolate South Africa. By doing so they will be at least refraining from adding to the present strength of the South African state. That seems to be the least which a non-racialist can do to help those who are, and will be, fighting racialism on our behalf and at great cost to themselves.

In talking about Southern Africa today I have said nothing which is new or startling. For I have no magic solution to the problems of entrenched racialism, and I cannot foresee the details of the future course of the liberation struggle in that area. All that I have been trying to do is to explain the situation as we see it in Tanzania, and to indicate the manner in which we shall support the struggle for human dignity in that area of our continent, and those three countries.

57 African National Council, Zimbabwe: address to the OAU African Liberation Committee by Bishop Abel Muzorewa, President. Lourenco Marques, 19 January 1976

Mr Chairman, your excellencies, distinguished delegates and fellow freedom fighters: I feel greatly honoured to have this opportunity of addressing for the first time this august session of the African Liberation Committee of the OAU.

Mr Chairman, we in Zimbabwe attach great importance and significance to this meeting being held in this beautiful city of Lourenco Marques in the newly independent people's republic of Mozambique whose brave and gallant men and women fought heroically and won their freedom and independence through armed struggle. Their example serves as an inspiration and encouragement to us in Zimbabwe who are still struggling under the ruthless yoke of colonialism, white settlerism, and racism. It is more so because we share a long common border and a long common history with the People's Republic of Mozambique. We are one people and we regard their victory as ours. We greatly appreciate the correct line they followed in the prosecution of the armed struggle which is a shining example for us in Zimbabwe.

Mr Chairman, I would like to say how grateful the ANC of Zimbabwe is for the very generous hospitality offered us by our comrades in FRELIMO, government and people of the people's republic of Mozambique.

On behalf of the African National Council, the vast masses of the people of Zimbabwe and indeed on my own behalf, I wish to take this opportunity to thank the OAU through the African Liberation Committee for the practical, moral, financial and diplomatic assistance they have rendered to the liberation movement of Zimbabwe in the past and in the present. .

A. MILITARY—THE ENEMY

I. Aims and objectives of the enemy

1.(a) *Aims*

   The aim of the enemy today is to prevent the ANC (Zimbabwe) from consolidating and expanding into a fighting politico-military force.

   (b) *The objectives of the enemy*

The enemy would like to see independent Africa:

i.   stop providing centres and facilities for the training of ANC (Zimbabwe) military cadres;

ii.   stop being rear revolutionary bases for the ANC (Zimbabwe);

iii.   stop giving arms and war equipment to the ANC (Zimbabwe);

iv.   make ANC (Zimbabwe) turn in all arms and war equipment and relinquish vital rear bases and reinforcement and supply corridors;

v.   order ANC (Zimbabwe) not to continue armed struggle intensification;

vi.   stop recognizing armed struggle;

vii.   remove all ANC (Zimbabwe) cadres from their national territories;

viii.   stop ANC (Zimbabwe) propaganda broadcasts to the oppressed Zimbabwe population.

2. To eliminate all ANC (Zimbabwe) recruitment rings.

3. To turn the population against ANC (Zimbabwe).

4. To stop cadres from being loyal to ANC (Zimbabwe).

5. To cut all ANC (Zimbabwe) infiltration and supply routes at the border areas.

II. Activities of the enemy

1. Since the call for ceasefire:

(a)   The regime has been and is striving to acquire more and up-to-date military hardware.

(b)   The regime is taking in more and more recruits.

(c)   The regime is hiring more and more mercenaries and military experts from USA, Europe and South Africa.

(d)   The regime is thoroughly reorganizing its armed forces to a new and higher level of combat effectiveness as clearly stated by General G. P. Walls, commander of the enemy troops in November 1975: 'It would be tragic if we were to allow the advantage to slip away from us by dropping our guard or depleting our efforts.'

2. The gains by the enemy in the operational areas are seen by the fact that whereas one, two, three years ago the enemy tactical units confined themselves to static defence reactions and retaliatory search and destroy operations (scorched-earth policy), now they are undertaking offensive search-and-destroy missions. Some of the new tactical units that have been brought into the field are:

(a)   The Selous Crack Units.

These are specialized in counter-intelligence and counter-insurgence. They are self-contained units armed, clothed and trained 'like' liberation forces. Their speciality is to scour for liberation forces and their bases and to destroy them.

(b) The Mounted Infantry Units (MIU).

These are being raised for mounted charges against liberation forces in mountainous areas in the eastern region of the country and to facilitate transportation in such difficult terrain.

(c) The Sleek-Strikers.

These are being used for search and destroy in deep jungle areas and very rugged terrain. These units are composed of soldiers who know Mozambique terrain very well as they have been recruited from colonial soldiers who fought against FRELIMO forces in Mozambique.

3. The enemy is building electrified fences along the border with Mozambique and also planting fields of landmines along the border.

4. While Rhodesia remains isolated and not recognized by the international community as a state it is encircled by independent African states but for about 150 miles of border, with South Africa. It is South Africa which remains deeply involved in Rhodesian affairs in that:

(a) South Africa has hundreds of military and intelligence personnel operating under cover on Rhodesian soil.

(b) South Africa has large amounts of war equipment in Rhodesia including helicopters, transports, bombers, reconnaissance planes, troop carriers, armoured cars and tanks.

(c) South Africa has stepped up her diplomatic, political and secret service involvement for the benefit of the Rhodesian regime.

(d) South Africa is a channel for support for the Rhodesian regime of British, American, French, West Germany, Swiss and other NATO countries. To illustrate this South African involvement, when Major General Shaw, Chief of Staff of the regime's armed forces, was shot down in the eastern operational zone recently the pilot was a Lieutenant van Reinsberg from Pretoria and the engineer was also a Van Reinsberg from Emello, South Africa, a fact admitted by Radio South Africa.

B. POLITICAL—THE ENEMY

The regime is applying the policy of deception:

(a) The enemy has initiated the bogus settlement so-called 'talks' as a stratagem to gain time, which time it has used to consolidate, expand and improve its military position in terms of recruitment, training, weapons, equipment, tactics and strategic plans, thereby subverting the armed struggle.

(b) As part of this strategy the enemy has used the ceasefire trick to prevent the advance of the guerilla offensive, to encircle liberation forces in the field in a bid to wipe them out and to disrupt regular flow of reinforcements, supplies, equipment and weapons.

(c) The strategy is used to dupe and hoodwink the outside world into believing that it is possible that we will get our independence through peaceful means and confuse the supporters of our armed struggle, which to us is the only way to bring majority rule based on genuine freedom and independence. The strategy is also to establish a puppet neo-colonialist so-called multi-racial government and integrate into the Rhodesian security forces so-called 'willing' former guerillas brought into the system by African political hirelings or quislings in the so-called multi-racial system of government.

C. ECONOMIC—THE ENEMY

The United Nations economic sanctions which were supposed to solve the Rhodesian problem have been on for the last ten years but they have been ineffectual in the achievement of their main objective. Some western powers including South Africa have fully co-operated with Rhodesia's illegal regime to bust the UN sanctions. As an instrument of settling the Rhodesian problem peacefully we might as well forget that sanctions will bring down the minority regime.

D. OUR SITUATION

I. Internal Situation

When the ANC was formed on 7 December 1974 all the people of Zimbabwe welcomed the new unity and this position has basically not changed. Those who try to deviate from it run the risk of losing the support of the people of Zimbabwe.

There has been mischievous talk about so-called two ANCs, one led by Bishop Abel Muzorewa and one led by Mr Joshua Nkomo. It should be made clear that the majority of the people of Zimbabwe whether living inside or outside follow the ANC as formed on 7 December 1974 and led by Bishop A. T. Muzorewa. This was clearly demonstrated by the fact that Nkomo's so-called 'Congress' could only attract not more than 5,000 people while the consultative meeting of the ANC drew over 100,000 people who came, in spite of the regime's intensive and extensive intimidation, to demonstrate their full support for the leadership of the ANC and the *armed struggle for which it stands.*

The ANC has overwhelming support both inside and outside Zimbabwe and acknowledges the leadership of the ANC as constituted on 7 December 1974.

Since the formation of the ANC its approach to the problem facing Zimbabwe has been one of a double strategy, namely that there should be negotiations for peaceful settlement and if talks fail to yield majority rule now then armed struggle would be intensified.

At a review meeting in Dar-es-Salaam in July 1975 attended by the four heads of the front-line states and the leaders of ANC drawn from inside and outside Zimbabwe, it was unanimously agreed that talks be de-escalated and the armed struggle escalated.

Prior to the Dar-es-Salaam conference of July 1975 there was a series of talks held between the Rhodesian government and the leaders of the ANC in Salisbury which culminated in the abortive Victoria Falls conference. Following this abortive conference there was a summit meeting held in Lusaka in September 1975 where it was agreed unanimously between the four Presidents of the front-line states and the leaders of ANC that there shall be *no more talks* with Mr Smith but that there shall be an intensification of the armed struggle.

At the same summit meeting it was agreed that in view of the fact that the projected congress of ANC would inevitably divide the people of Zimbabwe it should not be held and that the main concentration should be focussed on the liberation of Zimbabwe rather than on the congress which was regarded as a secondary matter.

Past experience has convinced the leaders of the ANC and the people of Zimbabwe generally that majority rule now cannot be established in that country through peaceful negotiations. We cannot accept any constitutional arrangement which is less than Majority Rule Now, because in our situation, unlike that of other ex-British colonies which had the colonial power to supervise progress towards majority rule, there is no such external power to supervise the progress towards Majority Rule Now. Our situation calls for an immediate transfer of power from the white minority to the black majority. The situation in Zimbabwe is unique in that of all the British colonies, Rhodesia was the only colony allowed self-government and control of an army and security force of its own.

It is political *naiveté* to expect the present illegal regime which seized independence unilaterally in 1965 to preside over its own liquidation. They did not seize that independence to hand it over to the African majority but to keep it for themselves for all time.

E. ANC STAND

The leaders of the ANC are convinced that armed struggle is the only correct and effective means of solving the present independence problem facing Zimbabwe and have, therefore, solemnly decided on an intensified armed struggle. This conviction and decision are not only confined to the leadership of ANC but shared basically by the majority of the people of Zimbabwe who are presently leaving the country in their thousands to go to train for the serious armed struggle that lies ahead.

It is in this respect, Mr Chairman, that for practical and urgent assistance we make requests details of which are contained in a document dated 31 December 1975 submitted to the Liberation Committee Secretariat to enable us to implement effectively and successfully, this solemn decision—to achieve Majority Rule Now.

VIVA OAU.

VIVA PEOPLE'S REPUBLIC OF MOZAMBIQUE.

VIVA SOLIDARITY WITH ALL REVOLUTIONARIES THE WORLD OVER.

58 African National Council: an open letter from ANC-ZLC (Z) to sons and daughters of Zimbabwe living abroad. Mozambique, 23 January 1976

Dear comrades,

This is an historic letter in that it is our first joint communication to you since our former organizations merged in December 1974. We send you fraternal greetings with the confidence that it will not be long before we start to exchange such comradely salutations inside a free and independent Zimbabwe.

The ANC is the political and military instrument for wresting economic and political power from the white settlers in Zimbabwe. It provides a role for every dedicated Zimbabwean who wants not only to continue, but also to intensify and complete the revolutionary struggle against the racist regimes which was started by our forefathers. This grandiose task of liquidating colonialism and racism requires firm affirmation by everyone of us to fight to win full economic and political independence and a tireless cultural fight to assert our African personality. Our dignity and self-respect demand that we condemn marginal and opportunistic organizations which, because of their dubious sponsorship, search for compromises with the enemy in secret while making brave declarations publicly to try and hoodwink and dupe Zimbabweans into believing that they are genuine liberation movements. These divisionist, imperialist lackeys serve only one purpose—to confuse the masses of Zimbabwe and by that very token delay the liberation of our people and country. We can assure you here and now, comrades, that as sure as day follows night, these confusionists will pay a heavy price to Zimbabwe. The ANC opposes the manoeuvrings of these reactionary forces resolutely and will forge ahead with its chosen course of revolutionary armed struggle. Because this is a correct line, the ANC has received support and encouragement from progressive countries of the world and more importantly from the African Liberation Committee of the Organization of African Unity which is the blood-bank of genuine African liberation and solidarity.

We now wish to dispel once and for all the mischievous talk of two ANCs which is being fanned widely by the international capitalist communications media. The naked lie put out is that there is an ANC inside Zimbabwe and purportedly led by one Joshua Nkomo, and another ANC outside Zimbabwe led by President Muzorewa. But comrades, you know it just as much as we do that there is only one ANC which was constituted in December 1974 which continues to enjoy mass support of Zimbabweans both inside and outside Zimbabwe. These very communications media of our oppressors did report the unprecedented turn-out of Zimbabweans to 26 October 1975 consultative meeting to show their support for the ANC leadership and the correct line of armed struggle.

These agents of imperialism and colonialism have used every trick in the book to try and subvert our efforts to prosecute the armed struggle. They have put out falsehoods regarding the Zimbabwe Liberation Council stating that the ZLC is a separate and independent entity from the ANC. We know you are aware of the true facts but for the record we shall mention briefly the relationship between the ZLC and the National Executive of the ANC. The ZLC is the external wing of the ANC created as a result of a decision to do so by the National Executive. The ZLC is therefore one of the legitimate organs of the ANC. The present Chairman and Secretary of the ZLC, comrades Rev Sithole and Chikerema respectively, are members of the National Executive.

We return now to what we said earlier on that the ANC has a role for every dedicated Zimbabwean to be involved actively in his or her respective way in the revolutionary march towards freeing ourselves and our country. It is not only the country that needs freeing from foreign rule, we too need to be freed from colonial values and hang-ups through a correct political orientation. We implore you therefore, in the name of Zimbabwe to join us in this our chosen course and goal. We challenge you therefore in the name of the soil of Zimbabwe that your country awaits your joining with us to tackle this Herculean task we have set for ourselves.

Lastly, we would like to mention that we are constantly asked, if not tutored, about the need for unity within the ANC. You may be experiencing similar situations from these so-called know-it-alls. The position is that these prophets of doom or Jeremiahs should be reminded that the ANC was born out of the essence of unity and has been nurtured in the milieu of unity and thrives on unity as our joint communication to you today proves that point beyond all doubt. We are not only a united organization, but a disciplined organization so the expulsion of reactionary collaborators should not be misconstrued as disunity. No sensible person can blame a doctor for removing cancerous tissue from the body of a patient because by that action he makes the patient healthier. The leadership of the ANC cannot, in like manner, be accused when they remove characters that collaborate with the enemy from among their midst.

We wish you well.

(Signed):

Bishop Abel T. Muzorewa
        President
(Dr) Elliott Gabellah
        Vice-President
Rev Ndabaningi Sithole
        Chairman, ZLC and Member of the National Executive
James Chikerema
        Secretary, ZLC and Member of the National Executive
(Dr) Gordon Chavunduka
        Secretary-General

59 African National Council: speech by Dr Gordon Chavunduka, Secretary-General, to Zimbabweans in London.
7 February 1976

Comrade chairman, sons and daughters of Zimbabwe, and friends, I have come today in my capacity as Secretary-General of the African National Council. I was asked by the Central Committee of the African National Council to do a number of things while I am here. Firstly, to give you all a full report of the ANC activities at home and abroad. Secondly, to hear your views on the numerous issues that face us in Zimbabwe today. And finally to carry with me to the Central Committee as well as to the Zimbabwe Liberation Council any suggestions that you may have.

My work in the ANC has not been easy since December 1974. December 1974 is the time when unity was achieved in our movement. From that time we have moved from crisis to crisis in the African National Council. At times we have had to abandon the struggle in order to deal with enormous internal human problems that confronted us from time to time.

The Zimbabwe Declaration of Unity made at Lusaka, Republic of Zambia, in December 1974, says, among other things, that, 'ZANU, ZAPU, FROLIZI, and ANC, hereby agree to unite in the ANC. The parties recognize the ANC, as the unifying force of the people of Zimbabwe. The leaders of the ZAPU, ZANU, and FROLIZI call upon their supporters and all Zimbabweans to rally behind the ANC under its enlarged executive. ZAPU, ZANU, and FROLIZI will take steps to merge their respective organs and structures into the ANC before the Congress to be held within four months.'

Lastly, the document states that the leaders recognize the inevitability of continued armed struggle and all other forms of struggle until the total liberation of Zimbabwe.

Comrade chairman: It has, therefore, been my responsibility as Secretary-General to implement these measures.

Between December 1974 and March 1975 it became clear to me, however, that the leaders of ZANU were unwilling to implement fully the Lusaka agreement which I have already described.

It became clear from the statements made from time to time by former ZANU leaders at that time that they did not recognize the ANC as the unifying force of the people of Zimbabwe. Secondly, the former leaders of ZANU failed at that time to call upon their supporters to rally behind the ANC. Thirdly, the former leaders of ZANU failed to take steps to merge their organs and structures into the ANC. Former ZANU members continued to publish their own newsletters. They continued to maintain their own transport system. They failed to surrender their bank account to the ANC Treasurer-General and they employed their own organizing secretaries.

Thus at that time former ZANU leaders made it impossible for total unity to be achieved, and accordingly we warned them that they would have to face expulsion unless they took immediate steps to implement the Lusaka agreement in full. In fact, we came very close to expelling former ZANU leaders around March 1975. Fortunately, some serious attempt was then quickly made by the former ZANU leaders to conform to the Lusaka agreement. During that time former ZAPU and FROLIZI leaders appeared to be making satisfactory progress towards the achievement of total unity.

One issue remained which eventually led to the expulsion of Mr Joshua Nkomo and a few of his supporters—this is the matter concerning the holding of a congress early in 1975.

The President and I and the whole ANC administration argued against the holding of a congress at that time because of a number of reasons. The most important reasons were:
1. That certain leaders of former organizations had not had sufficient time in which to call upon their supporters to rally behind the ANC.
2. That certain leaders of the organizations had not yet taken adequate steps to merge their respective organs and structures into the ANC.
3. That the ANC branches, districts and some provinces were un-representative at that time. These unrepresentative structures had been brought about by unrepresentative manoeuvres at the inception of the ANC organs and by the reluctance of the former ZANU supporters to identify themselves actively with the ANC which they considered non-violent and therefore contrary to the pursuit of ZANU abroad.
4. Moreover, following the abortive Victoria Falls conference, a summit meeting was held in Lusaka in September 1975 where it was agreed unanimously by the four Presidents of the front-line States and the leaders of the ANC that in view of the fact that the projected congress would inevitably divide the people of Zimbabwe, it should not be held and that the main concentration should be focussed on the liberation of Zimbabwe rather than on the congress which was regarded as a secondary matter.

Mr Nkomo and his friends, however, became impatient and wanted a congress to be held without delay. Nkomo had expected to win the leadership of the ANC if such a congress was held because of the unrepresentativeness of the main branches, districts and some provinces. Thus Nkomo and his friends went ahead on their own and arranged a congress at which Nkomo was elected President. The majority of the branch, district and provincial officials did not attend. Under these circumstances the President of the ANC, Bishop Muzorewa, had to act or abdicate. He decided to act. Mr Joshua Nkomo was expelled from the ANC.

We now know that Mr Nkomo did not act on his own. He acted in accordance with a plan drawn for him by members of the Rhodesian regime. The regime wanted a moderate African party to emerge and thus attempt to eliminate the militants in their future contacts.

This, in fact, was publicly admitted by Mr Smith and Mr Sutton-Pryce—a deputy Minister in Mr Smith's office.

Mr Sutton-Pryce, addressing a meeting of the Justice and Peace Commission in Salisbury in June 1975, stated that if it became impossible to reach a settlement with a united ANC, they would work hard to split the ANC so that they could talk with a splinter African opinion such as the chiefs. He also stated at that meeting that they had had contacts with Nkomo and his aides, and that if it had not been for the former ZANU and ZAPU elements now agreeing with the ANC, a settlement could be easily reached with Nkomo. His only fear was that such a settlement might not be accepted by the British government and the United Nations. He however, thought that with the backing of Nkomo, a nationalist of long standing, this obstacle could be overcome.

Comrades, I am glad to report that the departure of Mr Nkomo and his friends was in a way a blessing in disguise. It was a blessing in disguise for two main reasons:

1. Their positions in the ANC have now been taken by men and women of ability, dedication and character. The dead wood departed with Nkomo.

2. It is also clear that the political views held by Nkomo and his friends were not in line with those of the majority.

Mr Nkomo seems to be looking for a place in the sun only for himself and his friends. The present Smith/Nkomo talks provide enough evidence in support of this assertion.

In the ANC we would like to see a complete overhaul of the whole social, economic and political system. In the ANC, we are engaged in a project—a project whose aim is to secure for ourselves and all our fellow citizens the full blessings of Zimbabwean life.

Our first duty in this regard has been to identify our enemy clearly and properly and to get to know his nature. We have already done this, and our analysis runs something like this:

> The regime in Rhodesia is a product and a special form of capitalism and world imperialism whereby Britain, the arch-enemy of the people of Zimbabwe, granted a licence for white dictatorship.
>
> Settler colonialism in Zimbabwe is in fact sustained by a vast imperialist partnership which includes Britain, the USA, France, the Federal Republic of Germany, other NATO countries, Japan, South Africa and Switzerland. But the Rhodesian regime is the direct enemy of the oppressed and exploited people of Zimbabwe.
>
> The character of the Rhodesian settler colonial society is capitalism whereby the means of production are owned by a numerically insignificant white settler community of about 250,000 people, while the rest of the population (that is, about 7,000,000 blacks) is, except for a handful of petty-bourgeois elements, a proletariat made up of workers, peasants and squatters who own nothing but create by their labour incomes for the capitalists and the settler-class.

Thus the ANC seeks to involve all the oppressed people of Zimbabwe, not only in the fight against this domination and settler rule, but also in detailed preparation for the new social, economic and political order.

This new order will be one in which the democratic process is to be exercised in such a way that the most exploited masses have control of political power, since they alone can go furthest in establishing proper rights and liberties for all.

The party stands for a society in which all prejudices or privileges shall be weeded out.

In the new order, any person regardless of his or her race, ethnic origin, or nationality who shall identify himself or herself with a socialist Zimbabwe, will have expanded opportunities to contribute fully towards the development of the country and live as a human being. No one shall be permitted to exploit or oppress other free and equal citizens for his or her own benefit, or to receive material or financial benefits that do not derive from his or her own efforts.

Sons and daughters of Zimbabwe, this how in brief we visualize the future. A committee sitting in Salisbury and Lourenco Marques is already in the process of putting these ideas on paper.

Comrade Chairman, I am also glad to report that we have built up the party again after the disruption caused by Nkomo's activities in 1975. Seven of the eight ANC provinces are now back to full strength. The Matabeleland south province was disrupted more than the others, and many of our organizing secretaries are at present working in that province in an attempt to bring it back to its former strength. Mashonaland south province alone, for example, now has 1,224 branches and 153 districts.

All this has been achieved in the face of considerable hostility on the part of government and town authorities as well as most of the newspapers.

Despite the support that Mr Nkomo received from the authorities and newspapers he has failed to get off the ground. What support he has comes mainly from one province—the Matebeleland south province.

As a result of political education which our people have received over the years, there are two things that people in Zimbabwe want more than anything else today—unity and the freedom of Zimbabwe. Talking about tribalism or regionalism is committing political suicide in Zimbabwe today. Talking about ZANU or PCC or FROLIZI is equally committing political suicide in Zimbabwe today. And any activities that appear to frustrate our attempts to free Zimbabwe will be resisted very strongly by the people of Zimbabwe today. If anybody here does not believe this: you ask Mr Joshua Nkomo.

I told my audience in Birmingham last Saturday that nowadays at many of our meetings two songs are usually sung—one at the beginning and the other at the end of the meeting. In Shona the first song goes like this:

'Ngatibatane pamwe chete . . .' (Let us be united . . .)
The second song goes like this:

'Nyika yedu tinoitora nebhazuka . . .' (We will liberate our country by force . . .)
These are the two songs. The first is about unity and the second is about the liberation of Zimbabwe—the two important things that people want today. The seven million people who sing these songs are not asking for the revival of ZANU, ZAPU or FROLIZI but for unity. The seven million people who sing these songs are prepared to suffer and die, if need be, not for ZANU, ZAPU or FROLIZI but for Zimbabwe. Comrades, let us then unite and fight against foreign domination and settler rule.

TALKS

I will now say something about the constitutional talks now taking place between Mr Smith and Mr Nkomo. Joshua Nkomo and members of his party have been persuaded by Mr Smith to engage in some sort of constitutional talks.

Our stand in the ANC concerning these talks is clear. We have stated on a number of occasions in Zimbabwe that we cannot allow two minority groups to decide the fate of the Zimbabwe nation. The constitutional talks now going on are therefore irrelevant because the majority of the people are not involved, and we have stated that any agreement reached in these Smith-Nkomo talks will not be binding on the majority of our people. This is the stand we have taken and this stand has been accepted by our people.

In fact we now know that Mr Smith is not interested in any serious constitutional talks at the present time. He has initiated the Nkomo talks mainly as a stratagem to gain time. He needs time to consolidate, expand and improve his military position in terms of recruitment, training, weapons, equipment, tactics and strategic plans, thereby subverting the armed struggle.

While the Nkomo talks have been going on, we know that

1. Mr Smith has been and is striving to acquire more and up-to-date military hardware.

We know that

2. He is taking in more and more recruits.

We know that

3. He is hiring more and more mercenaries and military experts from the USA, Europe and South Africa.

We know that

4. He is thoroughly re-organizing his armed forces to a new and higher level of combat effectiveness.

We know that

5. He is building electrified fences along the border with Mozambique and also planting fields of landmines along the border.

Early last week Mr Smith announced that the present Nkomo talks cannot be rushed. He said they could take several months to complete. This was further evidence of Mr Smith's intention to try and halt or weaken the tide of nationalism. This strategy is also used by Smith to dupe and hoodwink the outside world into believing that it is possible that he will get our independence through discussions with moderates and thus confuse the supporters of the ANC.

Smith must be told that:

Nationalism cannot be halted or weakened. Smith must be told in no uncertain terms that nationalism cannot wait or be postponed until he is ready to accept majority rule. People now want majority rule now.

THE ZLC

This brings us to the Zimbabwe Liberation Council. The ZLC is an external instrument of the ANC instituted for prosecuting the Zimbabwe revolutionary struggle. The ZLC derives its authority from the African

National Council. At present the ZLC consists of 16 members appointed to office for a term of two years by the Party. The Council elects its own chairman, vice-chairman and secretary from among its members who hold office for a term of two years.

In the event of the death, resignation, expulsion or desertion of a member, the ZLC may maintain its composition full by co-option determined by a two-thirds majority of the Council; in such cases informing the party. The ZLC is required to abide by all directives issued to it by the party. Membership of the first ZLC was, however, by appointment in accordance with the Lusaka Declaration. The former leaders of ZAPU, ZANU, FROLIZI and the leader of the original ANC were asked to appoint four persons from their groups to join the first ZLC.

I have mentioned these rules and regulations because there are a few people here who do not appear to understand the way the ZLC functions.

Offices of the ZLC are at present in Lourenco Marques and Dar-es-Salaam.

Thus if any of our members who operate under the ZLC have any complaints, criticisms or suggestions to make concerning the functioning of the ZLC, these must be forwarded to the ZLC for consideration through the ZLC chairman and secretary. If the ZLC fails to resolve the matter satisfactorily, the matter may be sent to the Central Committee through the Secretary-General.

If any members want to be considered for appointment to the ZLC, they must campaign in the normal way bearing in mind that such appointments must be approved by the party, in this case the National Executive Council of the ANC.

I must warn all our members and officials that anyone who engages in activities calculated to weaken, disrupt or frustrate ANC attempts to free Zimbabwe will be dealt with severely. Such an individual will be dealt with firmly, absolutely and without mercy.

Comrades, it is well to remember that many people have died both inside and outside Zimbabwe. There is untold suffering in Zimbabwe particularly in all the operational areas. Men, women and children have died. Crops have been destroyed. Children are without schools, and many people in the operational areas are starving. These people have suffered and died and others will die in future not because they want to promote any leader or a group of leaders, but they have suffered and died so that Zimbabwe might be free.

In Lusaka and London I have met a few people who are talking in terms of reviving ZANU. At home such people would not have a platform anywhere even in a pub or beer hall. People at home, as I mentioned earlier, will resist any attempts to divide them again.

These people who talk in terms of reviving ZANU also seem to think that a ZANU army still exists.

The majority of the young men and women who have gone out of the country for training over the last four or five years were very young during the time of ZAPU or ZANU, nor do they have any emotional attachment to the former leaders of these organizations. The only party they know is the ANC. About three-quarters of the young men and women in the military camps today know no other party except the ANC.

Thus any man or woman in Lusaka or London or Birmingham, who talks in terms of reviving any of our previous organizations is completely out of touch with the realities of Zimbabwean politics.

At this stage it is necessary to comment briefly on the matters raised by our comrade Mr Robert Mugabe in London and Birmingham recently.

Mr Mugabe made a number of criticisms:

1. That the ANC in Lusaka and Dar-es-Salaam was disorganized and inefficient, and had for example failed to get supplies to nationalist camps in Mozambique and Tanzania.
2. That the guerillas were in a state of disarray.
3. That there was poor administration in the camps because of poor leadership.
4. That ANC leaders have not consulted him for a long time, and that
5. Former ZANU members are not properly represented in the ZLC.

Some of the criticisms made by comrade Mugabe may be sound; but was London the right place to present these criticisms?

As a member of the ANC Central Committee Comrade Mugabe should have taken his complaints, criticisms and suggestions either to the ZLC or to the Central Committee.

There were two alternatives open to him as a member of the Central Committee. In fact when Mr Mugabe travelled to London, his colleagues both in the ZLC and the Central Committee were on their way to Lourenco Marques for a joint ZLC-Central Committee meeting. This is where he should be and not in London, unless, of course, he has other motives. I will return to these other possible motives later.

Mr Mugabe left Rhodesia in April last year two days before he was to join an ANC delegation to the OAU. He did not know then that he had been selected by the President as a member of that delegation. He left in order to make his way to the OAU accompanied by Mr Edgar Tekere. They both failed to get to the OAU after all.

For several months, we did not know the whereabouts of Mr Mugabe and therefore could not send him the minutes of Central Committee meetings. We knew he was somewhere in Mozambique.

He himself did not make any attempt to write either to the Secretary-General of the ANC or its President and has not done so up to now.

We have now been told that he wrote to Mr Enos Nkala in Zimbabwe and to Rev Ndabaningi Sithole in Dar-es-Salaam, but these were not official letters to the ANC.

Comrade chairman, I will end by reminding Mr Mugabe and all the sons and daughters of Zimbabwe about the aims and objectives of our enemies now and in the near future. The most important aim of our enemies is:

1. to weaken the African National Council in every way.
2. to try and turn the Zimbabwe population against the ANC.

A number of methods are being used and will be used to achieve this aim. The first is the promotion of opposition groups within the ANC as a way of weakening it.

The Nkomo party is a good example of this. Huge sums of money from local and international organizations were put at the disposal of leaders of that party in order to promote divisions and thus weaken the ANC.

Now that the Nkomo scheme has failed the same western sponsors will turn to the so-called tribal groupings and encourage these to form their own separate organizations. Money for the promotion of tribalism can easily be obtained from London, New York and Toronto.

I also know that there are two or three international organizations that are still willing to finance ZANU, a party which no longer exists. One wonders what their motive is.

Another method used to try and weaken us inside Zimbabwe is to deny the ANC any facilities either in towns or country districts; to deny us any publicity; and to detain our leaders and party workers. Many ANC members are detained and restricted every week in Zimbabwe today. These methods are not new.

What is new is our recent discovery of a Mafia type gang employed by some authority in Zimbabwe whose function it is to kidnap and kill certain leaders of the ANC.

At home we discovered a list of ANC leaders who were to be kidnapped and killed during the months of September, October and November last year. Top on the list was Dr Edson Sithole, then Chavunduka, Enos Nkala, Moton Malianga, Dr Gabellah, Willie Machekano, Crispen Mandizvidza and a few others.

We discovered the list two days before Dr Edson Sithole was kidnapped.

We know the whereabouts of Dr Edson Sithole and Miss Miriam Mhlanga. Two weeks ago both were still alive and in the hands of the kidnappers.

The kidnappers did not kill Dr Sithole when they kidnapped him because a number of things went wrong. Firstly, there was Miriam Mhlanga who was in Dr Sithole's company. Secondly, a certain brother of the Catholic Church whom we now call Brother X was sitting in a car nearby.

For these reasons the kidnappers failed to carry out their mission. But they have held the two persons ever since. We have all the information which we obtained at great cost. But it will be unwise to say more than this at this stage.

I have mentioned these things in order to draw your attention to the dangers that lie ahead. In Rhodesia it is now government policy to promote tribalism and regionalism. It is also the policy of a number of governments and international organizations, and money for this purpose is available.

These divisive factors must be watched and suppressed at all levels and at all times. These two factors—tribalism and regionalism—have never posed serious problems in our political life before and must not be allowed to do so now.

And as we enter this very critical stage in our struggle for freedom, the party will insist, more than ever before, on obedience, loyalty, and discipline.

In conclusion it must be stated that the ANC is now an impressive organization at home. I have attended many meetings of both the Central Committee and the National Executive Council. I have attended many provincial and district meetings. I have also attended many branch meetings. I have been greatly impressed by the dedication, efficiency and enthusiasm of many of the officers and members. The women's wings and the youth wings are in my view the most impressive organs.

There will be problems in the future as I have tried to indicate. But the success of the ANC during the next critical months will depend on the behaviour of all the present office holders—Central Committee, National Executive Council, the ZLC, Provincial leaders, District leaders, Branch officials and also our members.

60 African National Council: press statement by Bishop Abel Muzorewa, President, in response to President Samora Machel's broadcast to the nation. 4 March 1976

On behalf of the ANC, the people of Zimbabwe and indeed, on my own behalf, I wish to convey my condolences to His Excellency, President Samora Machel, FRELIMO, the government and the people of the people's republic of Mozambique on the loss of our brothers and sisters on the border who have been murdered by the racist regime of Ian Smith. I am deeply grieved and remember the people of Mozambique at this moment of bereavement. . . .

The closure of the borders and the immediate application of full sanctions against the racist regime in Southern Rhodesia by the government of the people's republic of Mozambique is resolutely and firmly supported by the ANC and the people of Zimbabwe.

It must be recalled that last April, 1975, the ANC of Zimbabwe requested the member-states of the Commonwealth at the Commonwealth Conference in Jamaica to raise about £50,000,000 as a compensation for our brothers and sisters in Mozambique should the border be closed and the UN mandatory sanctions be applied against the white minority regime in Southern Rhodesia. TODAY, 3 MARCH 1976, THAT TIME HAS COME. I appeal to all Commonwealth countries and progressive peace-loving nations to help our dedicated and gallant brothers and sisters in Mozambique in their sacrificial internationalist duty of assisting in prosecuting the liberation of Zimbabwe to its successful conclusion.

We are ever grateful to the moral, political and material support accorded to us by His Excellency, President Samora Machel, his party and government of the people's republic of Mozambique.

At this grave moment in the history of the liberation struggle of Zimbabwe, I wish to

(a)   call on the African people of Zimbabwe to bury past recriminations and differences and march in unity and strength to fight and defeat Ian Smith and his minority regime;

(b)   call upon those African brothers and sisters who are fighting against their own liberation forces, and side by side with enemy rebel armed forces, police force, special branch to abandon Ian Smith and his forces immediately and fight for the immediate liberation of Zimbabwe. For what does it profit you, brothers and sisters, to sink and die with the enemy at this eleventh, decisive and historic hour? When are you stopping to fight against your own freedom and the freedom of your own brothers and sisters and that of the future generation?

(c) appeal to the white Zimbabweans. I ask you; Are you going to lay down your lives and spill your blood and that of your children in fighting to prevent the freedom of 7,000,000 Africans? For how long will you continue to spill your blood in defence of the sinking ship of Ian Smith?

(d) remind the white people of Zimbabwe that for the last four years the ANC has appealed in vain for peaceful change but now that time is gone. We have to defend ourselves against the random massacre of our innocent people, kidnapping, and harrassment by soldiers of the Smith regime.

(e) reiterate that Ian Smith and his regime must capitulate and surrender to African majority rule now in order to save the impending blood-bath and suffering in Zimbabwe.

The report by Ian Smith's spokesman calling upon the International Red Cross to negotiate for the release of the detained Southern Rhodesia railway men is totally rejected by the ANC. Southern Rhodesia is an international outcast and not a sovereign state. If the International Red Cross accept to mediate for an illegal regime in this affair, then it must equally visit the so-called protected villages—concentration camps in the north-eastern area of Zimbabwe. They are Nazi-like conditions under which over 100,000 people are living. The International Red Cross must also report on the fate of the kidnapped officials of the ANC such as Mr Ethan Dube, Dr Edson Sithole and his secretary Miss Miriam Mhlanga.

DOWN WITH THE FASCIST REGIME OF IAN SMITH!!!

61 African National Council: Smith-Nkomo talks. The ANC's proposals on the major points of principle which must be agreed before detailed committee work can begin. Salisbury, 17 March 1976

INDEPENDENCE CONSTITUTION

1. *Head of State.* The ANC has accepted the Westminster model of a non-executive Head of State.

2. *The legislature.* It is the strong conviction of the ANC and always has been that the only proper franchise is one man one vote on one common roll. But to meet fears expressed by the RF, which the ANC believes to be unfounded, and in a spirit of compromise, the ANC puts forward the following proposals concerning the legislature and the franchise.

The National Assembly will consist of a single Chamber with 144 elected seats:

36 'A' seats elected by voters on a common roll by universal adult suffrage.

72 'B' seats elected by voters on a common 'B' Roll qualification.

36 'C' seats elected by voters on a common 'C' Roll qualification.

Every person qualified to register on the 'C' Roll may at his option register either on that roll or on the 'A' Roll, and in addition on the 'B' Roll. Every person qualified to register on the 'B' roll, and who is not registered on the 'C' Roll may in addition register on the 'A' Roll.

3. *Qualifications.* The following will be the qualifications for the three Rolls:

'A' Roll: Universal adult suffrage.

'B' Roll: The following alternative qualifications, satisfaction of any one of which will confer the right to vote:

(i) *Education.* Completion of one year in Form 2 or the equivalent.

(ii) *Income* at the rate of $60 per month or more at the date of application or in any three of the last preceding six months, including as before an imputation of value for benefits in kind, consorts to qualify on their spouses' qualification.

(iii) *Property.* Ownership or occupation of immovable property of a value of $1440 or more, the value to be the gross value, and consorts to qualify on their spouses' qualification.

(iv) *Status.* Kraal heads with following of 20 families or more, Ministers of Religion.

(v) *Nature of work.* Employment in central or local government service, including the armed forces and the police.

(vi) *Stability of employment.* Persons who at the date of application are in the same employment as they have been for the preceding five years.

'C' Roll:

(i)   Income of not less than $2304 during each of two years preceding date of claim for enrolment, or ownership of immovable property of a value of not less than $4800; or

(ii) (a) Income of not less than $1536 during each of two years preceding date of claim for enrolment, or ownership of immovable property of a value of not less than $3200, and

      (b) completion of a course of primary education of a prescribed standard; or

(iii) (a) Income of not less than $960 during each of two years preceding date of claim for enrolment, or ownership of immovable property of a value of not less than $1600; and

      (b) four years' secondary education of a prescribed standard; or

(iv) Appointment to the office of chief or headman.

NOTES:

(i)   Only citizens will be eligible to vote.

(ii) All the above qualifications are based on voters of 21 years of age or more.

(iii) There will be no automatic upward adjustment for the fall in the value of money or any other reason. All changes will be by constitutional amendment.

(iv) Provision will be included for periodic re-registration.

4. *Delimitation of Constituencies.* There will be an independent Delimitation Commission:

(i)   It will be composed of the chairman, who will be the Chief Justice or another judge appointed by the Prime Minister with the approval of the Chief Justice, and three other members appointed by the Prime Minister with the approval of the Chief Justice.

(ii) It will be convened every five years, or more often if necessary having regard to any substantial change in the distribution of voters.

(iii) Within each Roll the boundaries of each constituency will be determined by the Commission so as to ensure, as nearly as may be, an equal number of voters in each constituency, subject to adjustment of up to 2½ per cent more or less on account of the factors mentioned in the next sub-paragraph.

(iv) In dividing the country into constituencies the Commission will have regard to physical features, community of interests other than racial, tribal or ethnic interests, means of communication, existing electoral boundaries and sparsity or density of population.

5. *Electoral Commission.* There will be an independent Electoral Commission:

(i) Its composition will be the same as that of the Delimitation Commission.

The two could be combined if thought fit.

(ii) Its functions will be:

(a) to prescribe the regulations for and to supervise the registration of voters.

(b) to supervise the nomination of candidates.

(c) to supervise the conduct of elections.

(d) to declare the result of elections.

(iii) There will be provision for election petitions to the High Court.

6. *Executive powers.* Now that the ANC has accepted that there will not be an executive Head of State, there appear to be no difficulties.

7. *The judiciary.*

(i) There will be a separate High Court and Court of Appeal, the number of judges in each to be agreed and stated in the constitution.

(ii) A person will not be qualified to be a judge of the Court of Appeal or the High Court unless:

(a) He is or has been a judge of a superior court in Rhodesia or in a country in which the common law is English or Roman Dutch and an official language is English.

(b) He is and has been for not less than seven years in practice as an advocate or attorney, by whatever name called (including legal service in a government department) in Rhodesia or in a country in which the common law is English or Roman Dutch and an official language is English.

(c) He is a professional magistrate with ten years' experience (including legal service in a government department).

(iii) The Chief Justice and the judges of the Court of Appeal will be appointed on the advice of the Prime Minister.

(iv) The judges of the High Court and inferior judicial officers and officials will be appointed by the Judicial Service Commission comprising:

(a) The Chief Justice

(b) A judge of the Court of Appeal or High Court nominated on the advice of the Chief Justice

(c) The Attorney General (assuming that he is a member of the government) or otherwise the Minister of Justice.

(d) The Chairman of the Public Service Commission

(e) One other person appointed on the advice of the Prime Minister.

(v)   A judge of the Court of Appeal or the High Court may be removed from office only for inability to discharge his functions (whether the inability arises from infirmity of body or mind or any other cause) or for misbehaviour, and then only upon the recommendation of an independent tribunal. The tribunal will be appointed on the advice of the Prime Minister, and will consist of a chairman and at least two other members who have held high judicial office in Rhodesia or in any other country where the common law is English or Roman Dutch and an official language is English.

(vi) Subject as provided above, promotion, transfers, disciplinary control and removal of judicial officers and officials shall be by the Judicial Service Commission.

8. *The Declaration of Rights.*

(i)   There will be a justiciable Declaration of Rights.

The Declaration will open with the following provision conferring positive rights:

'It is recognized and declared that every person in Rhodesia shall be entitled to the fundamental rights and freedoms of the individual, that is to say, the right, whatever his race, tribe, place of origin, political opinion, colour or creed, but subject to respect for the rights and freedoms of others and for the public interest, to each and all of the following, namely:

(a) life, liberty, security of the person, the enjoyment of property and the protection of the law;

(b) freedom of conscience and expression and of assembly and association;

(c) respect for his private and family life.'

(ii) These rights will be protected, subject to necessary exceptions, by common form provisions. The following points, however, arise:

(a) There will be no provision saving pre-existing legislation which would otherwise be repugnant to the constitution, subject to any necessary transitional provisions.

(b) Provisions which make a certificate of a minister virtually conclusive that a case is within an authorized exception will not be included.

(c) The enforcement provisions will provide for legal aid at all stages for a person who claims that his rights have been infringed, subject to safeguards against frivolous or vexatious litigation.

(d) Provision will be made for reference of proposed legislation to a tribunal. On the application of not less than 20 members of the Assembly, the Chief Justice will appoint a tribunal consisting of not less than two persons who hold or have held high judicial office in Rhodesia to consider whether the proposed legislation in question would contravene the Constitution and, if so, to give their reasons.

(e) The Declaration of Rights will contain a common form overriding exception for a state of emergency. But a person detained or restricted without trial will have the following protections. He must be told as soon as practicable and in any case within seven days the grounds for his detention or restriction. Within 14 days the fact and place of his detention or restriction must be published in the *Gazette*. He must have access to legal advisers who may make representations on his behalf. Within the first month of his detention, and thereafter at six monthly intervals he will be entitled to have his case referred to an independent tribunal and to be legally represented at the hearing. The tribunal may make recommendations to the Minister.

9. *Land.* All land belongs to the people. There will be two kinds of land (apart from national parks and other national land):

(i)   open land over which any person of any race will be able to acquire title.

(ii) trust land over which any person of any race will be able to obtain communal rights of residence, agriculture and grazing.

10. *Alteration of the Constitution.* A resolution passed by a majority of two-thirds of the whole Assembly will be required. In addition, certain provisions will be specially entrenched by requiring also a majority of the 'C' Roll members. This protection will apply to:

(i)   the provision for the 'C' Roll seats and the 'C' Roll franchise.

(ii) pensions.

11. *Language.* English will be the official language.

12. *Citizenship.* The requirements for citizenship will be included in the constitution, as they are matters of fundamental importance to individuals. Generally the details can be considered in committee, but the following specific points must be agreed:

(i)   The period of residence required as a qualification for registration will be five years.

(ii) The Minister will have no discretion to dispense with the qualification or abridge it.

(iii) The above provisions will come into force at the same time as the interim government is established.

(iv) Consideration must be given to the possibility of certain categories of person being given the right within a prescribed period to elect to take citizenship of the UK or any other country. As this will involve other governments, there will have to be negotiations with them.

13. *Pensions.* The ANC accepts that pension rights should be included in the Constitution as specially entrenched provisions. These will provide that the law to be applied to the pension rights granted to any person before the new constitution came into force will be the law at the time when the rights were granted or, at his option, any later law.

The ANC will seek a guarantee for payment of pensions from the UK or the Commonwealth.

14. *Service Commissions.* The ANC proposes that express provision should be made in the constitution relating to service commissions, including public and local government, teaching and the police, in addition to the Judicial Service Commission already mentioned. The composition will be a matter for negotiation, but the members will include persons of standing with experience in the particular service. Once this has been agreed in principle, the details can be negotiated in Committee.

15. *House of Chiefs.* The ANC proposes that there should be a House of Chiefs, and that the principal provisions relating thereto should be included in the constitution. Its function will be to consider and discuss any bill or other matter referred to it by the Prime Minister, and it may submit resolutions on any such bill or other matter to the Prime Minister, who shall cause any such resolution to be laid before the National Assembly.

INTERIM ARRANGEMENTS—THE FIRST ELECTIONS

16. The first elections under the new franchise will be held within 12 months after the interim government is established. The first session of the National Assembly then elected will be held within 30 days thereafter.

17. There will be an international Electoral Commission:

(i)   It will be composed of two representatives of the ANC and two of the RF and up to three independent members from abroad to be nominated by the British government, with the approval of the ANC and the RF. One of the independent members will be the chairman.

(ii) The cost of the Commission will be charged on the revenue of Rhodesia.

(iii) The Commission will have the following functions, for which

purpose it will have power to make regulations.
(a) fixing constituency boundaries
(b) advertising the right to register
(c) prescribing the procedure for and supervising the registration of voters
(d) appointing officials
(e) providing for and supervising the nomination of candidates
(f) conducting the election
(g) declaring the result
There will be provision for election petitions to the High Court.
(iv)   The Commission will be responsible to the Executive Council below mentioned.

INTERIM ARRANGEMENTS—INTERIM GOVERNMENT

18. Until the date of the first session of the Parliament elected at the first election under the new franchise, Rhodesia will be governed by an Executive Council of 8 in number, excluding the chairman. The function of the Executive Council will be to prepare for the first elections and to govern the country in the meantime on a caretaker basis. The Executive Council will, apart from the Chairman, comprise the Chief Ministers, Ministers and Deputy Ministers as below provided.
(i)   There will be two Chief Ministers Black and White.
(ii)   In each Department there will be a Minister and Deputy Minister as set out in the following table:

| Department | Minister | Deputy Minister |

[The Departments will be divided equally between the ANC and the RF, each having a Minister from one party and a Deputy Minister from the other.]
(iii) The Executive Council will have powers of legislation limited to those required for day to day administration and in connexion with the first election under the new franchise.
(iv)   There will be a chairman of the Executive Council, who will be appointed by the government of the UK in consultation with the Chief Ministers. In the absence of agreement, the Chairman will be appointed by the government of the UK. Similar provisions will apply to the appointment of a person to fill a vacancy in the office of Chairman.
(v)   The function of the Chairman will be:
(a) to exercise a casting vote upon each of the following matters whenever he shall think fit in order to ensure compliance with the agreed interim policy, if any, on any such matter, or to

ensure the good government of Rhodesia:

(i)   The exercise of emergency powers

(ii)   Defence

(iii) Finance

(iv)   Upon any matter where he shall certify that there is a deadlock in the Executive Council which, if continued, would be prejudicial to the good government of Rhodesia.

(b) to give directions for the implementation of any resolution which shall have been carried by his casting vote, and for this purpose and to this extent to suspend any Minister.

(c) to fill any vacancy in the Executive Council caused by resignation, death or physical or mental incapacity.

(vi) The cost of the Executive Council will be charged on the revenue of Rhodesia.

(vii) The above proposals will be embodied in an interim constitution which may be altered by a resolution of the Executive Council passed by a majority of two-thirds of the whole Council, excluding the Chairman.

62 African National Council: statement on the issues after the breakdown of the Smith-Nkomo talks. Salisbury, 19 March 1976

The ANC believes that the issues between it and the RF should be clearly stated at this stage in order that there should be no misunderstanding. The following points appear to state the position:

1.   The RF has rejected majority rule now. It has accepted the principle of majority rule, but in some indefinite future, too far ahead to be accepted by the ANC.

2.   Assuming that an acceptable settlement is agreed, the RF has proposed immediate parity in cabinet but not in Parliament.

3.   The RF has put forward a proposal for a three tier Assembly in which one-third of the seats would be European; one-third African, and one-third National seats on a common roll with a high qualification.

4.   This arrangement would ensure a European majority of two-thirds or nearly that at first, and a European majority of some kind for an

indefinite period. There are differences of opinion about how long it would be, but it would certainly be far longer than the ANC can contemplate. The RF thinks that it would be from 10 to 15 years.

5. The ANC's strong conviction is that there should be no racial rolls, and that the proper franchise is one man one vote on one common roll. But to meet European fears, which the ANC believes to be unfounded, the ANC will reluctantly be prepared to consider, as part of an over-all settlement and in a spirit of compromise, that, in addition to the national seats, there should be European and African seats, but would require the African seats to be elected by universal adult suffrage. It is understood that the RF will accept this.

6. But the ANC insists on the qualifications on the middle or national roll being in substance no higher than those for the 'B' Roll in the ANC's proposals.

7. The RF has rejected this on the ground that it would lead to majority rule at the first election.

8. Both sides accept that as part of an overall settlement there should be an interim government on a national basis. On its length, the difference between the parties is that the ANC believes that the period should be short: 12 months. The RF believes that it should be part of an evolutionary change to majority rule over an indefinite period as explained above. The ANC believes that this is wrong in principle and dangerous in practice. It is in the interests of the whole nation that the period should be short, so that all can turn to build the new nation and forget the dangerous frustrations of the past, which would continue during any long interim period.

9. On the structure of the interim government, the ANC has pointed out that it would be impracticable and valueless to have parity in the cabinet, as suggested by the RF, whilst having a parliament dominated by a European minority.

10. The RF's argument to meet this objection is: that there would be a national government; the ANC and the RF would go to the country on a national policy; there would be an agreement whereby half the cabinet would be Africans; and the cabinet has the sole right to introduce legislation, so that it could control a possible hostile European majority in Parliament.

11. These arguments are fallacious. Parliament is not confined to considering government legislation only. Members can introduce Bills. They can refuse supply. Parliament would control the situation even against a majority in the cabinet.

12. It is impossible for the ANC to accept the African position under

such a situation. As Mr Nkomo said, the Africans would be hostages.

13. The ANC requires effective parity in an interim government as a step to majority rule as soon as the necessary arrangements can be made under the new constitution, namely within twelve months. The ANC believes that this is in the true interest of all. It believes that over the short period of such an interim government, it should take the form of an Executive Council with legislative powers on which there would be parity. There is nothing legally impossible or impracticable in this. It is a matter of getting the necessary legislation through the UK and Rhodesian Parliaments.

14. The RF is unwilling to consider government without a parliament. A parliament may be necessary over a long period of transition, but not over the short period of twelve months envisaged by the ANC.

15. Again in a spirit of compromise the ANC would be prepared to consider some form of legislature even in the short term of 12 months, so long as there was equal representation.

16. The ANC could not accept a position in which it had parity in the interim cabinet and reverted to a minority position in Parliament under the new constitution. Parity would have to lead to majority rule.

17. In summary the differences are:
    (a) the period before majority rule.
    (b) the character of the interim government.
    But the latter will fall into place once there is agreement under (a). Most of the differences on this point arise from different views about the length of the interim period.

18. The ANC puts the following questions to the RF:
    (a) Assuming an agreed independence constitution, do you accept the principle of an immediate interim parity government, both in the executive and the legislature?
    (b) Do you accept that at the end of the interim period there must be majority rule?
    (c) If so, what is the minimum period you would agree?
    It is clear from the above that the answers to questions (a) and (b) is, no, and question (c) does not arise.

63 African National Council:
press statement by Bishop Abel Muzorewa, President, after the meeting of the ZLC. Lusaka, Zambia, 20 April 1976

. . . We of the ANC (Z) wish to openly declare that we at all times stand for the total unity of the fighting people of Zimbabwe, which is an indispensable requisite for the successful prosecution of armed struggle.

2. We continue to consolidate and strengthen the unity of the masses of Zimbabwe so that we carry the war of liberation to the bitter end. In this respect and in conformity with the stand taken by the broad masses of Zimbabwe under the leadership of the ANC National Executive inside Zimbabwe, we regret that Joshua Nkomo has become so deeply committed to the cause of the enemy in that he has followed the course chartered by the enemy, thereby serving as a broker for Smith's, Vorster's, British and American interests. His case has become irredeemable and, therefore, irrelevant to the unity of the ANC of Zimbabwe.

3. Joshua Nkomo has become irrelevant because:

(a) the unity of the broad masses of Zimbabwe is total and solid both inside and outside Zimbabwe,

(b) there is no such thing as an 'internal' ANC, and an 'external' ANC. There is only one ANC, as constituted on 7 December 1974 under the Zimbabwe Declaration of Unity, and recognized by the Organization of African Unity (OAU).

(c) Joshua Nkomo's recent public pronouncements against coming back to the ANC (Z) only go to prove that the man is totally opposed to unity as constituted in Lusaka on 7 December 1974, at State House.

(d) the so-called Nkomo's ANC was a divide-and-rule weapon of Smith and his allies to undermine the armed struggle by creating an 'ANC' within the ANC.

4. KISSINGER'S VISIT

One of the issues that the African National Council of Zimbabwe has to battle against is American imperialism, which Dr Kissinger is coming down to Africa to fortify. We wish to reiterate that the ANC (Z) has absolutely no business to discuss with Dr Kissinger, because the ANC (Z) is at war with American policy in Africa, particularly in Southern Africa.

We all know that:

(i) the US Government backs white minority regimes in political and diplomatic practice;

(ii) the American government continues to import chrome and encourage its businessmen to invest in Zimbabwe and Southern Africa as a whole in spite of our persistent demands that they should stop;

(iii) the White House is sending Kissinger to prepare ground for the setting up of puppet regimes in those parts of Southern Africa where it thinks majority rule is imminent;

(iv) Kissinger has not recognized the People's Republic of Angola, which is evidence that he is opposed to majority rule.

Furthermore:

(i) Kissinger is the author of the infamous Tar-Baby Plan, which brought about the destructive detente policy of South Africa;

(ii) he is against our war of liberation; he can, therefore, only come to subvert and sabotage it.

(iii) The USA government is allowing mercenaries from America to come to our country to commit atrocities against our people in Zimbabwe;

(iv) The USA government continues to maintain a Rhodesian intelligence office in Washington DC, thereby aiding and abetting the Smith regime;

(v) the primary object of Kissinger's visit to this part of Africa is to subvert the aid and support being given by socialist and progressive countries to the liberation movements in Zimbabwe, Namibia and South Africa.

5. BRITAIN'S RHODESIA POLICY

The African National Council (Z) totally rejects any British political settlement overtures concerning Zimbabwe, and does not want any military intervention by Britain to solve the independence question. The Smith regime is the direct enemy of the people of Zimbabwe, supported by the British government. There is essentially no difference between the Smith regime and the British government: the Rhodesian regime is an outgrowth of British imperialism and colonial policy.

The only talks that the ANC (Z) will attend will be 'surrender talks' for the transfer of political power from the white minority to the African majority.

6. DETENTE IN SOUTHERN AFRICA

We of the African National Council totally reject and condemn detente in Southern Africa and all contacts with the Rhodesian and South African regimes by any country on behalf of the people of Zimbabwe.

Detente has caused confusion in the Zimbabwe Liberation Movement in that:

(i)   it has subjected the struggle to the temperament and mood of the South African regime;

(ii) it has given birth to puppets and traitors in the liberation movement of Zimbabwe;

(iii) it is an attempt to undermine the very liberation movement of Zimbabwe.

64 African National Council: report of the special plenary meeting of the ZLC. Lusaka, Zambia, 17-20 April 1976

I. IDEOLOGICAL—POLITICAL LINE

1. To adequately project our socialist ideology, actively fight capitalist ideas and vigorously advocate for people's power, in accordance with the Organization's revolutionary political programme as drafted in the *Statement of Basic Policy* of August 1975.

II. ORGANIZATIONAL LINE

1. To expand the organization and consolidate unity by seriously getting down to ruthless struggle against enemy infiltration, former-Party hangovers, and tribal intrigues and conspiracies.

2. To consolidate, expand and improve the external strategic and administrative arm of the Organization, the Zimbabwe Liberation Council.

3. To streamline the military front and organize campaigns for the advancement of the armed struggle.

III. POLICY LINE

1. To project the Organization's policy of armed struggle as the only way through which total and complete independence can be established in Zimbabwe.

2. To totally discredit constitutionalist politics and propagate the party's rejection of the policy of talks until such time the enemy accepts to hold formal surrender talks for the transfer of all power from the white minority to the African majority.

IV. FOREIGN RELATIONS LINE

1. To ensure that the Organization is an integral part of the world-wide anti-imperialist movement.
2. To organize and campaign against any British design for a political compromise solution or military intervention to establish such a solution.
3. To wage a consistent struggle against USA objectives and policy in Africa, and in Southern Africa in particular.
4. To campaign against detente or any form of contact with the white minority regimes of South Africa and Rhodesia by any country, no matter how revolutionary, on behalf of the people of Zimbabwe.
5. To ensure that in their struggle for national independence the people of Zimbabwe are their own liberators.
6. To make formal contacts with and visit as many socialist government and progressive movements in the world as possible with a view to establishing concrete and effective relations with them, given that they are the traditional allies of the fighting oppressed people of Zimbabwe.

65 African National Council: memorandum to the chairman of the OAU sub-committee of four front-line states, President Julius Nyerere. 24 April 1976

We can no longer remain silent, Your Excellency. To do so would be an act of gross irresponsibility on our part. We have to state in clear and no uncertain terms that the way some of the heads of front-line states and the OAU Liberation Committee Executive Secretary have been handling the affairs of the fighting people of Zimbabwe and their leaders, clearly because their country is not yet independent, is incorrect and wrong:

> Incorrect because a considerable number of vital national decisions concerning Zimbabwe have been and continue to be taken over and above the heads of the Zimbabwe people and their leaders by leaders

of other nations who have no direct experience with or knowledge of the concrete conditions and situation of our country, an anomaly which is everyday proving costly to our people and country at this phase of our historical development.

Wrong because the people of Zimbabwe are now being deprived of their fundamental right to have the leaders they want and the basic right to be their own liberators. Self-determination, liberation, independence and freedom are swiftly losing meaning for us even before we get our country from the enemy. We hold that so long as there are nation-states in this world, so long as there are national interests, the peoples of various nations should be the ones to determine their own affairs and their own leaders.

In this vein, we would like to point out that what is going on is a gross violation of the OAU principles of respect for the sovereignty and non-interference in the internal affairs of member-states and liberation movements recognized by it (the OAU), which principles are enshrined and reflected in its charter and resolutions.

Your Excellency, our situation leaves a lot to be desired:
1. For some time now there has been and continues to be intolerable interference in the internal affairs of our liberation movement and this has been coupled with unspeakable blackmail:
(a)　For all practical purposes some of the front-line states and the OAU Liberation Committee Executive Secretary, Colonel H. Mbita, have taken it upon themselves to be the decision-makers, the planners, the organizers and the spokesmen of the Zimbabwe liberation struggle. They have taken it upon themselves to decide when, where, how and what for talks or armed struggle should be organized, launched and prosecuted. In this game we have at every important turn been presented with a *fait accompli.*
　　For instance:
(i)　The processing and placing of recruits in training camps without consulting with us;
(ii)　the formation of the so-called third force new high command by the Minister of Defence of Mozambique, Comrade Chipande, and the OAU Liberation Committee Executive Secretary, Comrade Mbita, and its announcement to the world;
(iii)　preparations for and the launching of the armed struggle on 17 January 1976, which was only communicated to us at the Qualimane Summit in February 1976.
Other elements of such interference are:
(i)　Declarations that Mr Nkomo would become irrelevant if his talks failed, on the one hand, and that Bishop Abel Muzorewa

would become irrelevant if the Nkomo-Smith talks succeeded, on the other;

(ii) declarations by President Machel that Mr J. Nkomo and Bishop Abel Muzorewa only represent themselves and that the liberation war must be delayed to change the political mentality of Zimbabwe.

(iii) blockading the ANC leadership from physical contact with the cadres and recruits in the camps and cutting out the ANC leadership from directly delivering supplies to the recruits and the cadres;

(iv) the fact that cadres and recruits who are openly loyal to the ANC leadership are being tortured and liquidated without this being brought to the knowledge of the ANC leadership and that other such cadres and recruits are being sent to labour or refugee camps;

(v) publicization of the strategy of the Zimbabwe fighting forces to the world;

(vi) secretly flying Mr J. Nkomo all the way from Rhodesia to Mozambique in mid-April with a view to imposing him as the leader; contrary to the latest condition by all four heads of front-line states that the camps cannot be visited by the ANC leadership unless all the leaders of former organizations are part of the visiting mission;

(vii) the OAU Liberation Committee Executive Secretary's decision to channel funds and supplies to the ANC cadres and recruits by-passing the authentic leadership contrary to OAU principles procedure and practice;

(viii) the Executive Secretary's assumption of the prerogative of determining the priorities in our struggle and the kind of aid we need.

(b) Zimbabwe leaders now live under the dark cloud of everyday being castigated for ineptitude and ingratitude and under the danger of being deported or character-assassinated if they choose not to conform with the viewpoints or policies of some heads of front-line states, and that in regard to a national liberation struggle that is Zimbabwe.

2. There has been a deliberate subversion and sabotage of our determined efforts to consolidate unity and build a national army.

These obstructive activities have been carried out through:

(a) *The Pretoria Agreement which was concluded and signed behind our backs.* The Pretoria Agreement brought on to the scene two distinct lines standing in sharp contrast and opposition, that is, armed struggle as opposed to talks with Smith. This gave Mr J. Nkomo the pretext and occasion for breaking away from the ANC and go out to openly hob-nob and rub shoulders with Mr Ian Smith in pursuance of their secret deal.

(b) *The abetting and aiding of Mr J. Nkomo's congress campaign and his talks with Mr Ian Smith.* Mr Nkomo continued to get outside moral, technical and man-power assistance for his talks even after the four heads of front-line states had agreed among themselves and with us at the September 1975 Summit in Lusaka that all talks with the enemy stop and armed struggle be taken up as the only course of action to liberate our country.

(c) *The creation of the so-called Third Force or New High Command.* Nobody can tell us that those behind the creation of the 'New High Command' did not know that the ring-leaders of the 45 cadres who were made to meet in President Samora Machel's Palace by the Mozambique Defence Minister, Comrade Chipande, and OAU Liberation Committee Executive Secretary, Comrade Mbita, are die-hard opponents of the Zimbabwe Unity Agreement. Nobody can tell us that those behind the formation of the so-called Third Force did not know that the aim of some of the ring-leaders of the 45 cadres was to strike a tactical alliance, to contract a marriage of convenience, for fighting and smashing the ANC and after that restore the former political organizations. Nobody can tell us those behind the setting up of the 'Third Force' did not know that the ring-leaders of the 45 cadres had as aim to supplant the ANC leadership as constituted on 7 December 1974 as a way to kill the Zimbabwe Unity Accord and revert to the banners of ZANU and ZAPU.

In short the abetting and aiding of the Nkomo breakaway and the creation of the so-called third force cannot be taken as anything else but deliberate acts meant to undermine the unity of the Zimbabwe people and the ANC.

3. There has been blatant deceit and bluff and flagrant distortion of truth. It is simply not true that we have refused to go to the camps and lead the struggle from there, for instance. Here is the true picture of what we have gone through in this particularly important problem area of our struggle:

(a) Way back in April 1975, His Excellency President Nyerere wisely pointed out that all signatories to the Zimbabwe Unity Declaration visit the camps together as a team. We fully agreed on the necessity and importance of the ANC leadership going to the camps. But because we knew that some cadres in one former ZANU camp were violently averse to the concept of unity as agreed upon on 7 December 1974, we decided that the best approach was to have Rev Sithole go alone first to this camp to explain the Unity Agreement and prepare for the coming of all the four leaders together as a team. Reverend Sithole did go alone in advance as we wanted it. We remained behind preparing the mission of all four former presidents to visit the camps together. We are explaining how we handled things in April 1975 to prove that the ANC leadership has never refused to go to the camps. The story going around that the leadership has four times refused to go to the camps to explain things to the cadres and give them direction and guidance is not true. Rather the ANC leadership has been refused access to the camps.

(b)　In July 1975 the ANC leadership on its own initiative embarked on a programme of going to all camps in Zimbabwe, Tanzania and Mozambique together as a team. But in Mozambique hardly had the leaders started to visit the first camp than they found themselves being called back to Lusaka by President Kaunda for the Pretoria Agreement and the Victoria Falls bridge conference.

(c)　At the summit meeting of the front-line states held in Lusaka in September 1975 we were assured by President Machel that we could come to Mozambique and embark on concrete preparations for waging armed struggle. Immediately after the summit the ANC President in the company of two members of our Defence Council left for Mozambique. There our two Defence Council members put forward a programme of action. But they were told that the time was not yet ripe for the ANC leadership to go into the camps and our two men were requested to go back to Lusaka.

(d)　In mid-October 1975 the ANC President and top members of the ANC Defence Council and High Command moved to Tanzania for the purpose of going to the camps and making arrangements for moving our cadres to Mozambique. The team could not get to the camps. It was told by Colonel H. Mbita that the mission was impossible because 'the spirit in the camps is sour'. We have since discovered that Colonel Mbita did not want us to go there at that point in time because he was already in the process of setting up the 'Third Force' high command with dissident elements.

(e)　After a long wait in Tanzania hoping to receive clearance to go to the camps, the ANC President changed his mind and decided to go to the camps in Mozambique. Just as he was making preparations to leave Tanzania he received a message from the Mozambique authorities telling him to remain in Tanzania 'until further notice'.

(f) In the meantime, dissident cadres opposed to unity right from the very beginning and some of whom are criminals were allowed free access to the camps in Tanzania and Mozambique and were having free run all over the camps to preach the gospel of disunity and cultivate a hostile attitude against the ANC and its leadership, against unity as constituted on 7 December 1974, in preparation for the 'inauguration' of the 'Third Force'. The ring-leaders of these dissident cadres included Rex Nhongo, also known as Solomon Mususwa Nhongo. He is the one who became the Chief Commander in the 'Third Force'. Rex Nhongo was involved in the murder of H. Chitepo. The *Report on the Assassination of Chitepo* says Rex Nhongo is the one who supplied the bomb that killed the ex-ZANU Chairman. Other ring-leaders of the dissident cadres such as Dzinashe Machingura (who became 'Third Force' Deputy Army Political Commissar), Elias Hondo (who became 'Third Force' Director of Operations), James Nyikadzinashe (who became 'Third Force' Deputy of Security and Intelligence), were like Rex Nhongo members of the former ZANU High Command which on the evidence of the revelations made by Josia Magama Tongogara (ex-ZANU Chief of Defence) to the Mozambique authorities, was, together with the Dare, responsible for the death of Herbert Wiltshire Chitepo.

Other ring-leaders of the dissident cadres were Alfred 'Nikita' Mangena (who became Chief Army Political Commissar of the 'Third Force') and Clement Munyanyi (who became 'Third Force' Chief of Security and Intelligence). These two are hard-core Nkomo boys who do not accept the ANC leadership as constituted on 7 December 1974.

What is hardest to swallow is that while the dissidents were allowed to do anything they wanted in the camps the authentic ANC High Command Chiefs (John Gwindingwi, the Chief Commander, and Grey Mutemasango the Chief Political Commissar) were being deliberately kept away from the cadres and the recruits.

(g) In November the ANC leadership decided to send an advance party consisting of ANC Defence Council and High Command members to Mozambique. The advance party left Lusaka with five trucks of supplies for the camps in Mozambique. On arriving in Tete the advance party had all the supplies it came with taken away to be given to the 'Third Force' dissidents and was directed to proceed to Maputo to clear itself with the Ministry of Defence. In Maputo our advance party was told by the Ministry of Defence that security conditions were not there for the ANC leadership to work in the People's Republic of Mozambique, and instead of being allowed to go to the camps our advance team was sent for isolation in a place in the country's province of Gazaland. With the exception of two, the team is to this day in that place in Gazaland. On its arrival in Maputo our team was surprised to see Rex Nhongo and Alfred Mangena and their lieutenants in conference. Their presence and the nature of their business was not officially told to the ANC advance team but it was obvious to the team that the dissidents were there as guests of the Mozambique government and Ministry of Defence. In our team's discussions with the Deputy Minister of Defence the dissident group was not mentioned. Our team found this quite odd.

(h) The ANC President got to Maputo around the end of November 1975 and the ANC-ZLC Chairman, Rev N. Sithole also got there on 14 December. Their attempts to join the advance team were for a long time encountered with official delays and it was only at the end of December 1975 that they got in touch with the team. Even after this they were denied access to the camps, in spite of their daily requests to go there.

(i) It was only at the Qualimane Summit in February 1976 that the ANC leadership was told that the question of whether the ANC leader had any role to play in the Zimbabwe armed struggle was a matter for the President of the People's Republic of Mozambique to decide and that in any case the armed struggle had been launched on 7 January 1976. It was argued that the ANC was not united and Nkomo should not have been expelled.

Your Excellency, we would just like to conclude by admitting that we have many faults but point out that at least we cannot in all fairness be accused of having ever been against unity or of ever having refused to co-operate with the front-line states. Equally we cannot in all fairness be accused of ever having refused to be in the camps or, of having neglected cadres and recruits who have been cut away from us and are out of our reach.

We therefore ask that:

1. The ANC as an organization with its leadership and High Command be taken in practice as an independent, sovereign liberation movement by all the front-line states and indeed the entire OAU;
2. the authority of the ANC as a party be allowed to function by the host front-line countries without undue interference in its internal affairs and without blackmail on its leadership;
3. good working relations be restored and that both parties desist from

engaging in vilifications of one another in order to best serve the image of the national liberation struggle in our part of Africa.

66 African National Council: address by Bishop Abel Muzorewa, President, to the 27th regular session of the co-ordinating committee of the OAU Liberation Committee meeting. Dar-es-Salaam, Tanzania, 31 May–4 June 1976

. . . 1. THE ENEMY AND ITS MILITARY ACTIVITIES

Mr Chairman, it is a painful fact to note that since the last meeting of the 26th regular session in Maputo, Mozambique, the enemy in Zimbabwe has become desperate and more ruthless.

(i)   The enemy has become panicky and extremely ruthless: an increase of *wanton murder of innocent civilians* under the pretext that those who are shot are 'curfew breakers' or potential ANC soldiers. For an example, a case in point is that of a pregnant African woman who was shot although she had all the necessary identity documents and was collecting firewood during the right time of the day; and that of a young boy who was shot as he walked from one house to another. Indeed there are numerous cases of wanton murder, torture, rape, death sentences, thousands in prison and the thousands who live under inhuman conditions in the so-called 'protected villages' which are in actual fact concentration camps. These increasing atrocities have been in the operational zones in Zimbabwe.

(ii) There has been a politico-military factor of an *increasing internationalization of the war by the enemy.* Only two weeks ago, over 200 mercenaries arrived from USA, 100 from Britain and some from Australia, Belgium, West Germany, and still there are hundreds of the Portuguese fascists who fled Mozambique, Angola and Guinea-Bissau, and are fighting side by side with the so-called security forces of the Salisbury regime. International intervention by Western forces, specifically NATO countries is also increasing.

(iii) The racist regime now gets most of its war material from Israel through South Africa. Vorster's visit to Israel was aimed at a military bilateral deal, which will carry under its arm-pits the Smith regime. We wish to draw the attention of this committee to the dangerous increase of South African soldiers and military hardware pouring in to consolidate the fascist forces of the Smith regime. That South Africa has withdrawn its military activity from Zimbabwe is absolutely false. The racist white minority regime has desperately tried to set up the South African Bantustan type of separation of races. That is illustrated by the recent appointment of four puppet chiefs and their deputies to ministerial posts in the regime's cabinet. These puppet chiefs in the mind of Smith operate as heads of separate Bantustans. The racist regime banned the issue of receipts in place of the ANC membership cards which were also banned.

The regime is convinced that ANC is raising a lot of money from within the country which is supporting the armed struggle now being gallantly waged by ANC fighters inside Zimbabwe.

(iv) The regime has desperately stepped up a psychological war against our armed struggle; for example, a daily propaganda programme in Portuguese denouncing our dear brothers and sisters, the FRELIMO Government, and Comrade President Samora Machel, has been started on the regime's African radio station.

(v) There has been deliberate attempt to build a strategic military base in Zimbabwe in order to exert the influence of American super-power politics. The USA is consolidating its tar-baby policy in Southern Africa—which policy advocates for peaceful change in the remaining territories under white rule. This is a calculated USA policy to undermine armed struggle by the peoples still under white domination and an attempt to install puppet regimes in Zimbabwe, Namibia and indeed South Africa.

Dr Kissinger's visit was in pursuance of the consolidation of this policy.

Our situation: the fighting

It is pertinent to raise the question: *Who is directing the war?* The quickest answer to that question is that the Executive Secretary of the OAU Liberation Committee is directing the war in Zimbabwe. We must be clear about this. The ANC political leadership, responsible for the recruitment and political direction of those soldiers has been effectively isolated through the efforts of the Executive Secretary of the Liberation Committee. The leadership is being denied involvement in the organization of armed struggle. Our stand and our position is that the party directs the gun and not the gun the party.

2. EVENTS LEADING FROM THE LUSAKA SUMMIT OF SEPTEMBER 1975 TO 31 MAY 1976

At an ANC meeting in Dar-es-Salaam in July 1975, the ANC and the four front-line state presidents agreed to stop talks and escalate the armed struggle against the racist regime in Rhodesia.

Following the abortive Victoria Falls bridge talks, a summit of the front-line state presidents was held in Lusaka in September 1975, during which the following decisions were taken:

(i)   That ANC should stop the talks with the racist regime in Rhodesia.

(ii)   That armed struggle should be re-organized and intensified.

(iii) That an ANC Congress should not be held as it would be divisive.

(iv)   The ANC leadership was then invited to Mozambique by His Excellency President Samora Machel to re-organize the army for the intensification of the armed struggle. The leadership gratefully accepted the invitation and prepared to go to the camps in Mozambique and organize for the intensification of the armed struggle.

About a week later, the President of the ANC and two comrades of the High Command of the Zimbabwe Liberation Army went to Mozambique in pursuance of the decision of the September 1975 summit. The comrades were in Mozambique for three weeks during which period they had consultations with the Minister of Defence in Mozambique. They agreed on a working agreement for an immediate military re-organization process. It was agreed that the two comrades should go back to Zambia to collect military personnel data in Zambia, Botswana and Tanzania and return to Mozambique to join the re-grouped cadres in preparation for the launching of the intensification of the armed struggle. In October 1975, the ANC President together with some of the top ANC military comrades came through Dar-es-Salaam to collect military personnel data in the camps in Tanzania and then proceed to Mozambique. It was during this period that we discovered the Executive Secretary of the Liberation Committee of the OAU had already started secret discussions with some dissident cadres from our camps in Tanzania and created an 18-man High Command drawn from former ZAPU and ZANU consisting of nine each. This was a creation of a joint military command which is well known to this Committee. All this was done behind the back of ANC. Having discovered this plot, Rev Ndabaningi Sithole warned Colonel Mbita of the dangers of his secret manoeuvres. During this period, Colonel Mbita travelled to Mozambique twice leaving our team in Dar-es-Salaam. After this, all our plans arranged with Mozambique collapsed.

In November 1975 we sent an advance party from Lusaka to ANC camps in Mozambique. The team was led by Comrade James Chikerema, Secretary of the Zimbabwe Liberation Council. Included in the party were two members of the ZLC, the ANC Army Commander, and the ANC Political Commissar: the team took five truck-loads of blankets, clothing, camp equipment and radios. When the team got to Tete, Mozambique, they were ordered to leave all the supplies with FRELIMO authorities. The nine comrades were later isolated to Gaza Province in Mozambique where, with the exception of two comrades, six of them are still being held. To be brief, the entire ANC leadership outside Zimbabwe and the ANC High Command personnel are being isolated and some are being victimized. We have been officially told that these six comrades can only be released upon instructions from Comrade Colonel H. Mbita, the OAU Liberation Committee Executive Secretary.

In the meantime a carefully orchestrated vicious propaganda has been mounted to camouflage the subversion of the ANC by the OAU Liberation Committee Executive Secretariat and the dissident cadres. In the context of the ANC, a dissident is:

(i)   one who rejects the unity and authority of the ANC as constituted by the Declaration of Unity of 7 December 1974;

(ii) a person who perpetuates a former movement or movements within the ANC.

There has been propaganda to the effect that:

(i)   the OAU Liberation Committee and the dissidents allege that the ANC leadership refused to go to the camps;

(ii) they allege that we did not take care of our recruits and cadres in the camps.

But the truth is that the ANC sent supplies, material and money to the camps in Tanzania, Mozambique, Zambia and Botswana. A deliberate attempt has been made to conceal the fact, through the propaganda, that the supplies and money were coming from the ANC. A good example is the advance party sent to the camps in Mozambique in November 1975. In spite of the Executive Secretary's non-operation, the ANC has continued to support the cadres. The fact that we have always demanded to go to our camps and be with our army, has always been cleverly concealed.

(iii) Some of the disruptive elements allege that the ANC leadership was disowned by the cadres in the camps.

(iv) They alleged that the ANC leaders are divided and cannot therefore be allowed to be with their cadres in the camps. The allegation that cadres are united while the ANC leaders are divided is highlighted in some of the reports before this Committee to justify the hijacking of ANC authority over its army. We wish to state in the clearest terms that there is no unity whatsoever in the Mbita High Command.

There are two distinct groups among the cadres in the camps. The first group consists of the loyalists of the ANC. These constitute more than 90 per cent of the ANC recruits and trained cadres who suffer the indignities of being tortured, killed, denied adequate food and clothing at the hands of the dissident commandership. To make it worse, some of them are deployed into Zimbabwe even without adequate training and equipment as a form of punishment for refusing to be under the Mbita High Command.

The second group, which is a minority, consists of non-loyalists whom we herein describe as dissidents. These are, however, classified into three groups all hostile to ANC and to each other:

(i)   The Nhongo-Sadza group.
(ii)   Gwauya-Hondo group; which consists of former ZANU elements.
(iii) The third one is a ZAPU group which has fragmented into two on the basis of pro-Nkomo and anti-Nkomo.

It is important for this Committee to understand that there are two opposing groups in the camps: one group composed of the majority of recruits and trained personnel on one hand and on the other the minority group consisting of the military hierarchy of the so-called 'Third Force' High Command which is opposed to unity under the ANC. The so-called 'Third Force' High Command numbers only about 40. It is this hostile clique which is terrorizing the majority of the ANC recruits and trained cadres in camps. The clique receives strong financial, material, diplomatic and moral backing from the OAU Liberation Committee Secretariat at the total exclusion of the ANC leadership.

Furthermore, the clique has now degenerated into military factions based on tribal, regional, past and dead political affiliations, as indicated above.

3. INTERFERENCE IN THE INTERNAL AFFAIRS OF THE ANC

Some people want to confuse and distort the Lusaka Declaration of Unity by limiting it to Bishop Muzorewa, N. Sithole, and Joshua Nkomo and deliberately omitting James Chikerema as part of their exercise to create division in the ANC.

As of today and as per the Zimbabwe Declaration of Unity of 7 December 1974, Bishop A. T. Muzorewa is the ANC leader and therefore the only legitimate leader to carry out the business of the ANC of Zimbabwe. Bishop Muzorewa is also the leader of Zimbabwe as per the will of the people of Zimbabwe. In practice, dissidents, break-aways, collaborators are all compounded in the running of the ANC through the authority of the Executive Secretary of this Liberation Committee, Colonel Mbita, in that

(i) The Military High Command appointed by and loyal to the ANC and the leadership were completely ignored and isolated.

(ii) A parallel High Command has been created from among the dissidents resulting in the so-called 'Third Force', behind the back of the ANC (Z).

(iii) The ANC leadership has been refused access to and jurisdiction over its own army.

(iv) International supporters of our struggle have been told to circumvent the ANC when giving material, financial and military help to the Zimbabwe liberation struggle. We have abundant evidence of this, which includes large sums of money.

(v) A definite attempt to impose new leadership on the 7,500,000 people of Zimbabwe is evident.

(vi) It is puzzling that the very people who were instrumental in forging the unity of the political parties of Zimbabwe are actively supporting the dissidents who have never accepted the Unity Accord of 7 December 1974 and all on tribal, regional, and former party political basis.

(vii) Colonel Mbita, the Executive Secretary, has consistently carried out administrative and financial dealings with our cadres behind the back of the ANC leadership even long before the announcement of what is being called the 'Third Force'.

(viii) The recruits and cadres who were recruited by all the former parties (ZANU, ZAPU, FROLIZI and ANC) that merged into the present ANC are now being forced at gun point to denounce ANC, disown their leadership and call themselves by a divisive name like the Zimbabwe Peoples Army (ZPA) as against the official name of the ANC army, the Zimbabwe Liberation Army (ZLA).

(ix) The creation of a High Command from the dissidents and behind ANC and its leadership has indirectly given licence to the repetition of wanton torture and murder of recruits and cadres loyal to the ANC and it is causing more ANC casualties than the enemy is inflicting. It is in a sense the continuation of the barbarous murder of over 200 recruits and cadres and other activists in the former ZANU, which culminated in the assassination of Herbert Chitepo.

(x) The creation of a High Command from among the dissidents hostile to the ANC and its leadership is leading to a highly explosive counter-revolutionary crisis of conflict in that:

(a) while the massive and grass root political organization of the people of Zimbabwe regard the ANC as their politico-military wing, and are supporting the ANC army materially and financially, the people are now being told that their soldiers are now a 'Third Force', opposed and hostile to the national leadership. The people of Zimbabwe earnestly ask the question, and we join them in asking those questions:

WHO IS THE THIRD FORCE?

WHY A 'THIRD FORCE'?

FOR WHAT PURPOSE AND WHOSE INTEREST THAT 'THIRD FORCE'?

(xi) The creation of a High Command, opposed to the ANC and its authentic High Command and its leadership, which ironically draws its support from the ANC masses is unfortunate.

(xii) The creation of a High Command behind the ANC and its leadership is tantamount to setting a time bomb which will tragically explode into a civil war in independent Zimbabwe. We must therefore state clearly that it is not the contact of the Zimbabwe political leadership with its army that will cause a civil war, rather it is this isolation of the national leadership from its army.

Mr Chairman, I want to pose a serious and heart-searching question: Is this responsible Liberation Committee, the OAU, all Africa and the progressive countries of the world prepared to let the present grim, explosive and potentially dangerous situation now being created, continue unchecked?

Mr Chairman, on behalf of the people of Zimbabwe, this question must be answered by this Committee.

4. OUR POSITION

(i) Our position is that the ANC of Zimbabwe is a massive grass-root organization of the people of Zimbabwe which was first launched on 16 December 1971 with the immediate task of fighting and rejecting the then sell-out Smith-Home proposals. The task was executed in the unity and strength of all tribes and former political parties that existed in Zimbabwe then. The unity of the people of Zimbabwe was founded by the people of Zimbabwe themselves on 16 December 1971 in Mutanga Hall, at Highfield, Salisbury, Zimbabwe. The unity and sovereignty of ANC was re-affirmed and consolidated by the Zimbabwe Declaration of Unity at the State House, Lusaka, Zambia on 7 December 1974 and fully recognized by the OAU.

(ii) Our position is that the Zimbabwe recruits and cadres were recruited and trained by the ANC as established by the Declaration of Unity and are therefore, and should be, and must be under the direct control of the party, the ANC (Z). The army is an instrument for a political objective, i.e. transfer of political power to Zimbabweans. As such an instrument, the army should only perform its duty in perfect loyalty to and in harmony with the party. Any attempt therefore to make that instrument a separate entity hostile to the people's party can only be subversive, counter-revolutionary and can cause unnecessary tragic consequences during the prosecution of the struggle and even after the common enemy is defeated.

(iii) Our position is that the creation of a hostile High Command behind the back of the ANC leadership and the people's party is gross violation of the OAU principle of no-interference in the internal affairs of a liberation movement.

(iv) The creation and support of a High Command hostile to the ANC and its leadership is undermining the Zimbabwe Declaration of Unity at a time when we are relentlessly working to consolidate the unity of the organization. The act is reactionary and creates conditions favourable to our enemies both politically and militarily. Setting the army against the party and the masses of Zimbabwe creates a time bomb in that it can result in a bloody civil war in an independent Zimbabwe.

(v) Our position with regard to unity is that the ANC united all different political organizations of Zimbabwe—former ZANU, ZAPU, FROLIZI and ANC—on 7 December 1974 at State House, Lusaka, Zambia. This position has not changed and continues to be the position accepted by the people of Zimbabwe and to this end ANC of Zimbabwe is working to consolidate. As a step towards this consolidation and soon after the 26th Session of the OAU Liberation Committee in Maputo, the President of the ANC wrote a letter to Colonel Mbita with copies to the four front-line presidents expressing a genuine desire that the ANC was willing to accept Joshua Nkomo into the ANC as constituted on 7 December 1974.

Subsequently, at a meeting in Lusaka, Zambia, the ANC President met Joshua Nkomo and repeated what he had told the Heads of State.

(vi) Our position regarding the armed struggle has never wavered—we stated it after the abortive Victoria Falls bridge talks, restated it in various meetings with the front-line states, vehemently maintained it in Maputo and Addis Ababa Ministerial Conference in 1976. Now we wish to reiterate categorically before this Committee that there is and shall be no other way to liberate Zimbabwe except through armed struggle.

While we appreciate the training facilities being offered by the front-line states, we wish to state that we have made bi-lateral arrangements with some of the OAU member states for general and specialized training of our cadres. We wish therefore to state that:
(a) the ANC be given the latitude to undertake such bilateral arrangements;
(b) the transit facilities for ANC cadres be provided.

5. PROPOSALS

1. We request the OAU to respect and recognize the sovereignty of the ANC of Zimbabwe over all matters pertaining to the liberation of Zimbabwe.
2. We request immediate control of all our armed forces wherever they are.
3. All aid destined for the ANC (Z) must be channelled through the ANC of Zimbabwe and not through the OAU Liberation Committee. The OAU's role is to facilitate receiving and conveyance of such aid.
4. We wish to reiterate the often repeated position of the OAU that the role of the OAU and individual member states and friends of the struggle of Zimbabwe is only to assist the liberation movement.

THE FINAL OAU RESOLUTION ADOPTED ON ZIMBABWE

The OAU Co-ordinating Committee for the Liberation of Africa, meeting in its 27th Ordinary Session in Dar-es-Salaam, from 31 May to 5 June 1976
(a) Having reviewed in detail the situation prevailing in Zimbabwe, in particular the armed struggle going on in that territory,
(b) Noting with satisfaction the progress made by fighting cadres of the ANC of Zimbabwe,
(c) Realizing the importance of unity among the ranks of the liberation movement of Zimbabwe,
(d) Noting with profound satisfaction and gratitude the assistance given to the liberation forces of Zimbabwe by the front-line countries in particular,
    1. Commends the fighting cadres of the ANC of Zimbabwe for their gallant successive victories over the fascist minority regime

of Ian Smith and expresses its total unconditional support for the armed struggle going in Zimbabwe. Hails the unity, the determination of the fighting cadres which has made these victories possible;

2. Urges therefore, all member states of the OAU and all other states which have assisted and continue to assist the liberation struggle in Zimbabwe to increase their assistance and channel it through the OAU Liberation Committee;

3. Appeals once again to the ANC political leadership to bridge their differences and to unite in order to contribute towards the liberation of their country. Calls upon that leadership to refrain from taking any steps which might undermine the current armed struggle in Zimbabwe and the unity of the fighting cadres.
   (The ANC reserved its position on this resolution.)

4. Commends the government of the peoples republic of Mozambique for the sacrifices they are making towards the liberation struggle in Zimbabwe and calls upon all OAU member states and the international community to render all possible assistance to the young republic to overcome the economic problems arising from that struggle;

5. Expresses its profound gratitude to the heads of state of the front-line countries, namely, Botswana, Mozambique, Tanzania and Zambia for their self-sacrifices and support for the liberation struggle in Zimbabwe. Appeals to these heads of state to continue in their constructive role to bring about the reconciliation of the various factions in the ANC leadership with a view to consolidating all liberation efforts under one strong, united and viable for the intensification of the armed struggle against the racist minority of Ian Smith;

6. Expresses its appreciation to the OAU Liberation Committee Executive Secretariat for the excellent work done in support of the liberation struggle in Zimbabwe and instructs the Secretariat to continue to assist provisionally the fighting cadres in accordance with the pertinent OAU Resolutions.

67 *Rev Ndabaningi Sithole: speech before the UN Committee of 24. New York, 8 June 1976*

. . . First, I wish to thank you, Mr Chairman, and your colleagues, for affording me this opportunity to participate in this debate on Rhodesia, whose freedom and independence are long overdue.

Secondly, I wish to express, on behalf of the African National Council of Zimbabwe . . . our appreciation for the work of this Committee in particular and the United Nations in general. There can be no doubt that the United Nations as such serves as the moral conscience of the world in which we live, move and have our being. In this age and era of atomic power, the immoral use of which can easily lead to the extinction of millions of people in a few seconds, this world moral conscience of the United Nations is all the more appreciated.

Thirdly, I wish to express our sincere thanks for the moral and material support the United Nations has given and promises to give to the people's republic of Mozambique to cushion off the adverse economic effects consequential upon its closure of its borders with Rhodesia. That was a courageous act on the part of the people's republic of Mozambique, and it is most encouraging that the United Nations recognizes this noble act with moral and material support which the young republic so badly needs.

The closure of the Mozambican border with Rhodesia, while not decisive in itself, has definitely had a direct effect in accelerating the process of the decolonization and liberation of Zimbabwe. This brave and noble step has created very favourable conditions in the process of liberating Zimbabwe.

Fourthly, let me take this opportunity to express our gratitude for the assistance and advice given to us by the four front-line states—Zambia, Tanzania, Mozambique and Botswana—and by the Liberation Committee of the Organization of African Unity. Owing to Zambia's close proximity to Zimbabwe, it has borne the worst brunt of Zimbabwe's liberation struggle, and Mozambique will be no exception in this regard. Without the willing co-operation of these front-line states, our liberation struggle would be faring very badly.

Fifthly, I wish also to take this opportunity to thank the various socialist governments and political parties throughout the Eastern bloc and the various progressive organizations throughout the Western bloc that have morally, materially and financially committed themselves to the liberation of Zimbabwe. I wish also to tender our thanks to all those who have regularly supplied us with arms, the lack of which has been the main reason for our subjection in the land of our birth and the possession of which is now breaking loose the shackles and fetters of colonialism and imperialism.

I now wish to turn to the main burden of my presentation to this Committee. I need not bore the Committee with the history of the liberation struggle in Zimbabwe. I am sure it is well known to this Committee. I am therefore going to deal only with the current problems affecting the liberation struggle of Zimbabwe. In any conflict situation there are always problems caused internally, and there are also problems caused externally. What is happening inside Zimbabwe is largely the result of the interplay between internal and external factors. I propose to deal first with the internal factors, and after that with the external factors.

I turn now to the question of unity within the African National Council. By the Zimbabwe Declaration of Unity of 7 December 1974 the four political organizations of Zimbabwe united as the African National Council of Zimbabwe. The purpose of this unity pact was to provide a united front against the enemy in our search for majority rule. Without exception, the people of Zimbabwe welcomed this new unity, and up to this day they still treasure it. They are opposed to anyone who threatens it.

But, in spite of that, this unity has been violated by the fact that one of the signatories of the unity pact broke away and formed his own group. However, the vast majority of the people of Zimbabwe have remained firmly on the side of unity within our liberation movement, which is recognized by the Organization of African Unity (OAU) as the only legitimate movement for the people of Zimbabwe. The ANC has, however, kept the door open for the breakaway group to return, if it so desires.

I should like to point out here that too much has been made of the fact of our present disunity within ANC. It should be remembered that three of the four signatories are still together, so that one can say that at least 75 per cent of the unity is still intact; therefore, in practical, rather than in idealistic terms, we have unity within ANC. It should be remembered that we cannot have 100 per cent unity in any human situation. It should also be remembered that there is now complete agreement on our quest for majority rule now and on the question of the armed struggle, an agreement which did not exist substantially before the breakdown of the Smith-Nkomo talks last March.

I should also point out that our disagreement on the question of majority rule now did encourage the enemy to divide us, and that a similar disagreement on the armed struggle had the same effect. This Committee should bear in mind that within the ranks of ANC there were always two schools of thought: one maintained the principle of majority rule now and the other that of substantial constitutional changes, without spelling out what they were or should be. There were also two schools of thought on the question of armed struggle. One consistently maintained that only armed struggle could bring about majority rule, while the other maintained that majority rule could be achieved by peaceful, constitutional means. The breakdown of the Smith-Nkomo talks has removed the grounds for these disagreements, and this is why we believe that the so-called disunity within ANC is superficial rather than substantial. This is partly due to an idealistic approach which does not take cognizance of the fact that unity is something that grows in actual action and consolidates itself with achievement. No action, no unity; no achievement, no unity. Apart from that idealistic approach, over-emphasis on the disunity within ANC has been largely due to leadership preferences.

The second factor with which I should like to deal, the internal factor, is the people of Zimbabwe themselves, because ultimately whatever political changes are brought about will be brought about only by the people of Zimbabwe themselves. Therefore, I felt it important to try to tell the Committee something about the people of Zimbabwe.

The people of Zimbabwe have remained solidly united behind ANC, which is led by its Vice-President and his colleagues inside Rhodesia, while its President remains outside the country. Their demand is for majority rule now, by hook or by crook. They desire to be free and independent like the people of other independent African countries around them. They strongly feel that their independence is long overdue, and that feeling has produced in them a fierce determination and a high sense of sacrifice in the full pursuit of their national objective.

While they believe in majority rule now, they do not for a moment believe in peaceful talks, but only in an intensified armed struggle. Those who believe in peaceful talks and who do not believe in the armed struggle are the exception rather than the rule. There are thousands of men, women and young people who have left Zimbabwe for the sole purpose of undergoing military training with a view to returning to Zimbabwe physically to liberate their country in which they are at present treated as non-citizens or as third-rate citizens. Our people are quite convinced that they cannot achieve majority rule now by any other means than an intensified armed struggle. That explains why and how thousands of them have voluntarily left Zimbabwe for military training.

It should be made clear to this Committee that our people have committed their very lives to the liberation of Zimbabwe, and there can be no greater commitment than that. They have long moved away from the politics of threats and from deceitful politics of talks about talks to politics of direct physical confrontation with the enemy. They have demonstrated that they are quite prepared to fight and to die to be free like other people elsewhere in the world.

The whole liberation movement of Zimbabwe, therefore, derives its strength and resilient, self-perpetuating vitality from the very being of the people themselves. Without this communal commitment to the struggle, the enemy could have easily silenced the whole movement. Our freedom fighters are effectively fighting deep inside the country because they have the co-operation of the people who are fully committed to the liberation of Zimbabwe and who have, as a matter of duty, given their own sons and daughters to fight, suffer and die for their country. This is the true nature of the spirit of the people of Zimbabwe, and it is on this spirit that our fighting forces depend in our grim struggle to be free in the land of our birth. It is a whole people fighting.

The third internal factor to which I should like to draw the Committee's attention is the white settlers themselves. We believe that if the situation in Zimbabwe is to be understood in its correct perspective the white-settler factor must be made known to the outside world and to those who are keenly interested in what is going on inside Zimbabwe.

The white settlers who make up five per cent of Rhodesia's population and who have ruled that country since 1890 feel greatly threatened by the present intensified armed struggle. Although many of them see the handwriting on the wall, many of them are determined to hold their own, come what may. It is inconceivable to them that a white man should live under black rule; that they should give up a position of privilege that obtains nowhere else in the world; that they should be treated as equals of the black man; that they should earn the same wages for the same job as black workers even when the qualifications are the same; and that they should be made to share with the black man the common things of this life. To many of those white settlers who had created for themselves an altogether different world based on their philosophy of 'Europeans high, Africans low', it is better to be dead than to face up to the inevitability of majority rule in Zimbabwe.

In their determination to hold their own, the white settlers have been joined by thousands of Portuguese die-hards who have moved to Rhodesia from Mozambique, Angola and Guinea-Bissau and are digging in against African majority rule in that part of the world. To strengthen the white-settler ranks Rhodesia's illegal régime has now embarked upon an extensive programme of recruiting mercenaries from the United States of America, Britain and West Germany, as well as from South Africa. In order to make the African population completely submissive, the illegal régime has embarked upon secret trials not only of the freedom fighters caught in action but also of civilians suspected of co-operating with them. In those courts people are sentenced to death secretly and they are executed secretly. Sometimes whole villages have been bombed to dramatize visibly to the villagers the power of the illegal régime.

The point which this Committee should underscore here is that the blacks and the whites in Rhodesia have set for themselves diametrically opposite and opposed objectives far beyond reconciliation's reach. The whites are using guns to entrench their white rule, and the blacks are also using the same means to achieve majority rule in the land of their birth. They have to shoot each other to attain their objectives. This is the cause of the problem which faces Zimbabwe today. The blacks have to shoot to end white oppression, which has been with them since 1890, and the whites have to shoot to maintain their system of oppression of the black man. The possibilities of a racial war are writ large in the present situation. As more whites are killed, white consciousness will be raised across the globe, white sympathy may find itself on the side of oppression, and another global war is not inconceivable under such circumstances.

The fourth internal factor to which I should like to draw the Committee's attention is the actual fighting inside the country. I should have loved to give a lot of details to this Committee, but I do not want to be found guilty of injudicious remarks by those who are engaged in the actual struggle over matters of life and death; so that members will excuse the calculated superficiality in my approach to this particular factor.

Our freedom fighters are infiltrating into Zimbabwe along a border of 900 miles and they have gone deep inside the country. They are making a real impact on the enemy. The detente exercise, which disrupted the armed struggle during the whole of 1975, had the serious effect of frustrating and demoralizing our freedom fighters, and the enemy gained great advantage over our forces, which then had no fresh supplies for a full year. But with the intensification of the armed struggle since the middle of January this year, the morale of our freedom fighters is now very high, and they are creating the necessary pressures on the enemy. I should have liked to give this Committee details of the good fight that our freedom fighters are putting up, but for obvious military reasons I deliberately refrain from such a course. It is a matter of life and death, and not one of cheap propaganda.

As a result of the fight of our freedom fighters, last month Rhodesia lost 800 whites in net emigration; the whites who had been exempted from military service are now being called up; there is talk of conscripting blacks into Rhodesia's army; only last week South Africa sent 400 white workers into Rhodesia to take the places of those who had gone to the front to fight our forces, and more are on the way with the conscious help of the South African government. More white farms are being deserted; more white houses are being placed on sale at unusually low prices. There can be no doubt that there is considerable panic among Rhodesia's white settlers, and the full credit for shaking Rhodesia's philosophy of white supremacy to its very foundations goes to our determined freedom fighters. If the present pressures are kept up, it will only be a matter of not too long a time before the paradise of oppression folds up, to the great delight of the 95 per cent of Rhodesia's population who are denied normal freedom and rights in the land of their birth.

Now I come to some of the external factors that impinge on the current Rhodesian situation; and I will not bore you with a long account, because I know that the Committee has many things to attend to. Although what goes on in Rhodesia can only be determined finally by internal factors, none the less it can also be greatly influenced by external factors, and it is to these that I now wish to draw the attention of this Committee, so that our struggle may be seen in its right context.

The first external factor I shall deal with here is South Africa. South Africa has taken a keen interest in Rhodesia's conflict between blacks and whites, and it has done so on the side of the latter, which means it has supported white domination and, therefore, black subjection in Rhodesia. In 1967, for instance, it sent its troops into that country, and at one time these numbered between 4,000 and 5,000 men. South African troops were not withdrawn from Rhodesia until August 1975. In the interest of white supremacy, South Africa repudiated its own principle of non-interference in the internal affairs of its neighbours. During the so-called constitutional talks between the illegal régime and African nationalist leaders of Zimbabwe, South Africa insisted on a cease-fire to weaken the bargaining position of the latter, and hence strengthen the position of the former. It has helped Rhodesia's illegal régime to defeat the United Nations sanctions. At present it supplies the illegal régime with weapons, helicopters and military planes. We are left in no doubt that South Africa is committed fully to the cause of white minority rule or white supremacy in Rhodesia.

Our contention is that if South Africa had never intervened militarily in Rhodesia, the illegal régime would long have come to terms with the legitimate political demands of the African people. South African military intervention unnecessarily prolonged the present armed struggle, without solving the basic problem. It gave the illegal régime the false feeling that it could hold its own, when in fact it was South Africa that was holding things for the régime. South Africa's military and economic intervention in Rhodesia has been highly prejudicial, not only to an early settlement of Rhodesia's problem, but to any peaceful solution, and its continued intervention cannot fail to bring about a racial war in southern Africa, and hence ignite a global war, with all its dire consequences. South Africa complicates the problem facing blacks and whites by its unnecessary intervention in the affairs of Rhodesia. It is not interested in solving the problem so that we can build a non-racial state, which is our fundamental policy, in a free and independent Zimbabwe. Its overriding concern is the preservation of white supremacy in Rhodesia, as in South Africa; whereas our burning concern is the termination of oppression, explicit and implicit, in the philosophy of white supremacy.

Now I come to the next external factor, which is Britain. I have already made my remarks, but I would like to add to what I have already stated. During the last ten years, Britain has consistently refused to intervene militarily in the Rhodesian situation, although the international community recognized it as the ultimate colonial power over Rhodesia. There is no British presence in that country and, although at present blacks and whites are slaughtering one another, the so-called colonial power over Rhodesia has neither the will nor the capacity to intervene. This is due largely to the fact that the element of kith and kin politics is fundamental to the thinking of the British government. Neither the Zimbabwean forces nor the Rhodesian forces are under the command of the British, the so-called colonial power over Rhodesia. There is now a growing feeling among the people of Zimbabwe that the recognition of Britain as the colonial power by the international community is most unrealistic in effective terms. Britain's non-intervention has justified the armed struggle upon which the people of Zimbabwe have now embarked and from which they will not desist until their national objective is attained.

The last factor which I should like to present to this Committee is that of the armed struggle. I think that it is very important that this Committee be made sensitive to this aspect of our struggle. I should like this Committee to believe that when we embarked on the armed struggle it was not out of lightmindedness, it was not because we enjoy fighting. We do not. It was a very painful thing to do. It was not a light thing. It took us months, it took us years to come to this decision. All normal people would like to live in peace, but no normal people would like to live in subjection indefinitely.

Since the armed struggle has now been accepted as the only credible alternative at our disposal, it is necessary that I should say a few words about this. Britain, the United States and South Africa have stated again and again that they prefer a peaceful solution to a solution attained through armed struggle. They prefer non-violence, notwithstanding the fact that Britain used violence during the Second World War to protect British shores. The United States used violence in 1776 to end British colonialism and imperialism. South Africa used violence to dispossess the African people of their land and basic human rights and freedoms.

Too often there is a tendency in the West especially to think of those of us who believe without apology in armed struggle as warmongers or bloodthirsty people. We tried the peaceful method, but since 1890 it has not worked because the white settlers were armed while we were not. What people which is armed to the teeth can really listen to an unarmed people? Since 1890 the white settlers have always been armed against the unarmed blacks. It occurred to us, therefore, that the reason for this was that the white settlers armed themselves in order to concentrate all effective power in their hands to our indefinite disadvantage, and so we began to arm ourselves to match those who were armed against us.

I want this Committee to note that we do not want war for its own sake, and that no right-minded people would want war for its own sake. We have adopted the way of armed struggle not out of light-mindedness or lack of respect for the sanctity of human life. We came to that decision not as a matter of personal choice, but as a matter of national duty in the face of the determination of our people to become free and independent in the land of their birth, and we came to that serious decision as a result of the enemy's determination to hold down our people for all time. We love peace as does any other people elsewhere in the world, but we do not love the peace that is to be found among slaves. We do not love peace at the expense of our freedom and independence.

I should also like this Committee to know that no one, either inside or outside of Zimbabwe, can stop the present armed struggle. We are committed to majority rule now, and it is only the fulfilment of this demand that can put an end to the present armed struggle. Our people have defied death itself in order to achieve this just demand in their own country. Only established majority rule can induce our men and women to lay down their arms. Therefore, those who are speaking about talks in order to undermine our armed struggle should bear in mind that our men and women are committing their very lives to bring about majority rule in the land of their birth.

We need arms in order to decolonize Rhodesia. We need them in order to redeem ordinary human freedoms and rights which are at present denied our people. We need them in order to reassert the human personality and dignity of our people, which have been trampled underfoot for the last 86 years. We need arms in order to ensure that power is transferred from a fear-ridden white minority to the majority. We need arms in order to end our own 80-year old subjection which has caused those who have arms to treat us like non-persons in our own native land. We need arms so that we may effectively make good our claim to self-determination, to which all the peoples of the earth are fully entitled. The armed struggle has become our only credible instrument for our freedom and independence.

In conclusion, I should like to state once more that we do not want armed struggle for its own sake. We want armed struggle in order that we may become free and independent like all other peoples throughout the world.

68 African National Council—Zimbabwe Liberation Council. Address by Luke Munyawarara, deputy-Chairman of the Diplomatic Committee: address before the UN Committee of 24. New York, 9 June 1976

The report of the *Ad Hoc* Committee is correct in identifying, among other factors, the absolute necessity and importance of escalating the armed struggle and consolidating unity for the liberation of Zimbabwe. It reflects a job well done. Again, we should like to congratulate the group. The only sad thing, is that, because of political factors beyond its control, it could not go to Rhodesia where it would have seen that the impression being created outside that the ANC is divided does not correspond to reality. But first of all, before I go further, I should like to make a few remarks to amplify the basic issues which our delegation raised.

The first point concerns the character of our armed liberation struggle and the role of Britain as the administering power in our country. I want to be absolutely frank on this point: the Zimbabwe liberation struggle is not being fought to attain a neo-colonialist solution in Zimbabwe. The ANC is no longer interested in British-style constitutional talks, for fear of getting a parcel with a live leopard wrapped in it. What the people of Zimbabwe want today is a straightforward transfer of political power from the white minority to the black majority.

Politically, the Rhodesian state machinery is a blatantly violent one. Our people are being butchered in cold blood, all civil rights have been denied the black population, the best of our land has been expropriated, and our livestock has been virtually confiscated. Our workers are by and large, receiving slave wages, the freedom to strike is non-existent—in fact strikers are liable to be sentenced to death. The Rhodesian régime is striking terror into the hearts of the freedom-loving people of Zimbabwe, whom Ian Smith used to say were the happiest beings on earth simply because, temperamentally, they normally display a cheerful face which hides the deep wounds of colonialism in their hearts.

What then has a neo-colonialist solution in store for the Zimbabwe masses? We will be compelled to inherit the violently anti-people state machinery, comprising the colonial army, police and air force, and a judiciary accustomed to sentencing Africans to death in order to safeguard settler-colonial interests in the area. One does not need a crystal ball to foretell that the colonial machinery which we shall inherit will no doubt massacre our military cadres who are fighting relentlessly to uproot colonialism from the face of our motherland. Equally, other Zimbabwean revolutionaries will have no chance in our country. They will doubtlessly be systematically massacred. This is the concrete reality of a neo-colonial solution in Zimbabwe. We fully realize that many former British colonies did not follow the same course that Rhodesia, with its large resident European settlers is following. Hence the superficial and unrealistic call for a neo-colonial solution.

Economically, British companies and others from the imperialist heartland are ravaging our resources while paying Africans wages below the subsistence level which we choose to call slave wages. The best land is in the hands of British companies and corporations and individual settler farmers.

Economically, what is in store for the African population in the event of a neo-colonialist solution? Concretely, it will be almost meaningless. Inevitably, the revolution will be compelled to continue. It will be a harder struggle. A few more blacks may have been assimilated into the neo-colonialist system in which the resident settlers will still have an upper hand in things of this life that matter, the economy being underpinned by an inherited colonial-state power.

The position of the United Nations appears to be one of taking Britain to be the administering power in Rhodesia. Reverend Ndabaningi Sithole, Chairman of the Zimbabwe Liberation Council of the African National Council, spent a lot of time exposing the myth that Britain is the administering power. What has remained visible is the British economic system ravaging our motherland. A call on Britain to intervene in Rhodesia is, to the people of Zimbabwe, mischievous. Asking Britain to play an active role in guarantee the safety of its economy in the area, on African soil, on Zimbabwe soil, is not acceptable to the people of Zimbabwe.

But what is the relationship between the Rhodesian régime and the British establishment? The Rhodesian régime is an agency of the British establishment which is faithfully safeguarding British economic interests in the area. The quarrel between the Rhodesian régime and the British is a quarrel between father and son.

The Africans are fighting the British in Rhodesia. The British army invaded Rhodesia by force of arms in the 1890s and has since maintained power by the gun. Asking the British to intervene in Rhodesia to safeguard a people they have reduced to servitude is like asking the Devil to rescue God . . .

Coming to the question of unity, we should like to point out that the consolidation of unity is being made difficult by external forces. The emphasis placed on disunity in the African National Council leadership by certain external forces arises from the leadership and former party preferences of those external forces. But the truth is that historically the people of Zimbabwe have always been for unity in fighting the common enemy, colonialism, which has developed into a rule of terror. The quest of our people for unity became very evident in the 1960s, soon after the liberation movement was split into two bitterly opposed camps.

The formation of the African National Council was, therefore, enthusiastically welcomed by the Zimbabwe people as a whole. It must be pointed out that this union under the African National Council was originally conceived for the purpose of extracting constitutional concessions from the oppressive régime in Rhodesia.

However, under the conditions of a rule of terror that had characterized Rhodesia, no Zimbabwean had any illusions that the settler colonial régime would hand over political power to the Zimbabwe masses on a golden platter.

The small group which broke away from the African National Council in September 1974 to advocate a solution by constitutional means did so for opportunistic reasons. The vast majority of the people of Zimbabwe remained in the African National Council. They favour unity for armed struggle to liberate the motherland.

It is the avowed aim of the African National Council to unite all forces interested in waging armed struggle in Zimbabwe for the establishment of full and complete independence based on the power of the people. Unfortunately, there are some elements who continue to be intransigent against unity. These are the type of people who can agree to unite with others only if they are the leaders of the movement.

The most surprising thing is that it is the African National Council which is today being victimized for the intransigence of these divisive elements. It is the African National Council which is today being condemned for the divisive attitude and anti-unity activities of these elements. It is the African National Council which is being asked to grovel for unity before these elements.

As if this were not enough, some external forces have gone even further and introduced a completely philistine element into the question of leadership. It is being urged that the military should become the political leadership of the African National Council on the completely unfounded and false argument that the soldier is better material for correct leadership. All I can say on this point is that a military system cannot help but be a reflection of the political system of which it is an aspect.

In a nutshell, the African National Council maintains that the standard and criterion of leadership is to be found in ideology, as reflected in service to the people, and in general political orientation . . .

From the above it is quite clear that there is a conflict between the African National Council and the outside world over the question of unity and other important issues, and that the matter may very easily become a complicated affair.

We want to state here that there are now two distinct positions in fundamental contradiction over the issue of the effectual means of ensuring unity. One of the positions is that of the African National Council leadership, which holds that the real basis and genuine criterion of unity is the political stand of the Zimbabwe masses inside the country, masses which have since 1971 remained united in their overwhelming numbers under the African National Council and the leadership of Bishop Muzorewa. The other is that of certain outside forces which want the aforementioned military command to be accepted as the uniting factor and the actual political leadership of Zimbabwe.

On the basis of first-hand experience, the African National Council delegation here would like the following points to be heard and noted.

The Third Force Military Command is not on its own a structure capable of holding the African National Council together because of the nature of its composition. Therefore, to insist on it as the political leadership alternative is tantamount to insistence on the destruction of the African National Council, which would result in total disunity.

It is our view that the masses of Zimbabwe are the real and actual force that has stood the test of time as far as commitment to unity is concerned and that they are the only valid standard and true criterion of unity . . .

The real and central problem around which all others cluster is, therefore, that there are external forces which are determined to stop at nothing to smash and destroy the African National Council leadership in order to impose their own style of political structure and leadership on the masses and the rank-and-file combatants of Zimbabwe. As a counter-measure, the African National Council is today saying that the people of Zimbabwe will not take orders from other people, nations or countries, no matter how revolutionary they may be. The African National Council has no choice but to state its stance very clearly, irrespective of the dangers involved.

But the African National Council leadership does not want to create antagonism between it and anyone, big nations or small nations. The Council is dedicated to its basic principles.

The African National Council and its leadership wish to create excellent relations with the front-line states, the Organization of African unity, the United Nations and all progressive countries and organizations. We appreciate and will always thank them for their advice and material assistance to us . . . provided such aid and advice does not undermine our right to independence as a liberation movement.

69 United Nations resolution on Zimbabwe (Rhodesia)

The United Nations Special Committee of 24 on Decolonization met in New York from 8 June to 14 June and considered the question of Southern Rhodesia.

RESOLUTION ON SOUTHERN RHODESIA

The Special Committee,

Having considered the question of Southern Rhodesia (Zimbabwe),

Having heard the statements of the representative of the administering power,

Having heard the statements of the representative of the national liberation movement, the African National Council of Zimbabwe (ANC (Zimbabwe)), who participated in an observer capacity in its consideration of the item,

Taking into account the report of the *Ad Hoc* Group established by the Special Committee at its 1029th meeting on 1 April 1976,

Recalling the Declaration on the Granting of Independence to Colonial Countries and Peoples, contained in General Assembly resolution 1514 (XV) of 14 December 1960, contained in General Assembly resolution 2621 (XXV) of 12 October 1970, as well as all other resolutions relating to the question of Southern Rhodesia adopted by the General Assembly, the Security Council and the Special Committee,

Bearing in mind that the government of the United Kingdom of Great Britain and Northern Ireland, as the administering power, has the primary responsibility for as repeatedly affirmed by the Security Council, constitutes a threat to international peace and security,

Taking note of the declared position of the administering power that there shall be no independence before majority rule in Zimbabwe,

Noting that the numerous, arduous efforts jointly made over the past year by the leaders of the African states concerned and other members of the Organization of African Unity, together with those of ANC (Zimbabwe), to secure a peaceful, negotiated settlement in Zimbabwe on the basis of majority rule, have deliberately been frustrated by the illegal racist minority regime, which has constantly resorted to dilatory tactics in order to perpetuate its illegal and racist domination over the territory,

Taking note of the view held by the leaders of the African States concerned and of ANC (Zimbabwe) that the only viable alternative open under existing circumstances for the people of Zimbabwe is to intensify their liberation struggle, and stressing the grave responsibility of the international community to take all possible measures in support of that struggle in an effort to minimize the hardship and suffering of Zimbabweans, in that regard,

Condemning the intensified oppression of the people of Zimbabwe by the illegal racist minority regime, the arbitrary imprisonment and detention of political leaders and others, the illegal execution of freedom fighters and the continued denial of fundamental human rights, including in particular wanton beating, torture and murder of innocent villagers, including arbitrary criminal measures of collective punishment, as well as the measures designed to create an *apartheid* state in Zimbabwe,

Taking note of the firm and unanimously expressed determination of the leaders of the national liberation movement to achieve freedom and independence at all costs and expressing its conviction that their unity and solidarity is fundamental to the rapid attainment of that objective,

1. *Reaffirms* the inalienable right of the people of Zimbabwe to self-determination, freedom and independence and the legitimacy of their struggle to secure by all the means at their disposal the

enjoyment of that right as set forth in the Charter of the United Nations and in conformity with the objectives of General Assembly resolution 1514 (XV);

2. *Reaffirms* the principle that there should be no independence before majority rule in Zimbabwe and that any settlement relating to the future of the Territory must be worked out with the full participation of the national liberation movement of the Territory, the African National Council of Zimbabwe (ANC (Zimbabwe)), the sole and authentic representative of the true aspirations of the people of Zimbabwe;

3. *Strongly condemns* the continued brutal and repressive measures perpetrated by the illegal racist minority regime against the people of Zimbabwe and in particular the wanton killings of Africans carried out by the regime;

4. *Calls upon* the government of the United Kingdom of Great Britain and Northern Ireland, in the discharge of its primary responsibility as the administering power, to take all effective measures to enable Zimbabwe to accede to independence in accordance with the aspirations of the majority of the population and not under any circumstances to accord to the illegal regime any of the powers or attributes of sovereignty;

5. *Commends* the relevant sections of the report of the *Ad Hoc* Group to the administering power for appropriate action;

6. *Firmly supports* the people of Zimbabwe under the leadership of their national liberation movement, ANC (Zimbabwe), in their struggle to achieve majority rule, and emphasizes the importance of maintaining a united leadership within the liberation movement;

7. *Demands:*

   (a) The termination forthwith of the execution of freedom fighters being carried out by the illegal Smith regime;

   (b) The unconditional and immediate release of all political prisoners, detainees and restrictees, the removal of all restrictions on political activity and the establishment of full democratic freedom and equality of political rights, as well as the restoration to the population of fundamental human rights;

   (c) The discontinuance forthwith of all repressive measures, in particular the brutality committed in 'the operational area', the arbitrary closure of African areas, the eviction, transfer and resettlement of Africans and the creation of so-called protected villages;

   (d) The cessation of the influx of foreign immigrants into the territory and the immediate withdrawal of all mercenaries therefrom;

8. *Appeals* to all states to take all necessary and effective measures to prevent advertisement for, and recruitment of, mercenaries for Southern Rhodesia;

9. *Requests* all states, directly and through their action in the specialized agencies and other organizations within the United Nations system of which they are members, as well as the non-governmental organizations concerned and the various programmes within the United Nations, to extend, in consultation and co-operation with the Organization of African Unity, to the people of Zimbabwe and their national liberation movement, all the moral, material, political and humanitarian assistance necessary in their struggle for the restoration of their inalienable rights;

10. *Invites* all governments, the specialized agencies and other organizations within the United Nations system, the United Nations bodies concerned and non-governmental organizations having a special interest in the field of decolonization, as well as the Secretary-General, to take steps, as appropriate, to give widespread and continuous publicity through all the media at their disposal to information on the situation in Zimbabwe and on the relevant decisions and actions of the United Nations, with particular reference to the application of sanctions against the illegal regime;

11. *Decides* to keep the situation in the territory under review.

70 *African National Council: address by Bishop Abel Muzorewa to the 13th summit of heads of state and government conference of the OAU. Mauritius, 2-5 July 1976*

Your Excellencies,

It is with great honour that I feel privileged to submit the following observations on Zimbabwe.

Practically everyone who has talked to me or to whom I have talked about the liberation struggle of Zimbabwe has left me with no doubt that the question of the unity of Zimbabwe is paramount. Without exception, all have expressed the fear that if there is no unity during the struggle, Zimbabwe will suffer the fate of Angola.

Your Excellencies, the OAU treasures the unity of Africa and indeed the unity of liberation movements, in this case the unity of the ANC of

Zimbabwe. It goes without saying that the ANC of Zimbabwe regards the question of unity as paramount—and that the unity we talk of is unity in the armed struggle. It is because of this cardinal point—armed struggle—that it is imperative for me to write this short resumé to Your Excellencies.

You will recall, Your Excellencies, that the ANC of Zimbabwe recognized by the OAU is that ANC formed on 7 December 1974 at State House, Lusaka, Zambia. To the best of our knowledge, there has been no other organization of Zimbabwe which has been entertained and recognized by the OAU other than the ANC formed on 7 December 1974 at State House, Lusaka, Zambia. That Lusaka Declaration of Unity envisaged the holding of a congress within four months, to complete the merger process.

In terms of the agreement between the four front-line states and Ian Smith, this was conditional to the restoration of normal political activities, that is to say:

(a)   the release of all political prisoners;
(b)   the release of detainees, restrictees and those in the so-called protected villages;
(c)   the lifting of the ban on all former political organizations;
(d)   the observance of cease-fire.

On our part, prior to the holding of a congress, we agreed:

1.   to draft and adopt a new constitution;
2.   to engage in the restructuring of the party's organs so as to complete the uniting process.

As matters turned out neither the conditions stipulated between the front-line states and Smith nor the stages that we envisaged were fulfilled when the dead line came. Subsequently and consequently all the people who were involved in the Declaration of Unity met in Dar-es-Salaam in July 1975 to review developments.

On the question of holding a congress, it was agreed that in view of the fulfilment of the conditions pertaining to the granting of general amnesty by the enemy and the total violation of the cease-fire agreement, it was decided to resume armed struggle forthwith. It was agreed that there should be no holding of a congress in view of the non-fulfilment of the conditions stated above and that this would be divisive and destructive to the unity of the people of Zimbabwe. The meeting decided to resume armed struggle and communicated that decision to the front-line states in keeping with the pertinent resolutions of an extra-ordinary Session of the Council of Ministers Conference held in Dar in April 1975; which decision granted option to the ANC to decide whether to talk or discontinue talks with the enemy and resume armed struggle.

The decision not to hold congress and to intensify armed struggle was reaffirmed by the front-line states and the leadership of the ANC at a meeting held at the State Lodge in Lusaka in September 1975. At that same summit meeting I was asked to recall Mr Joshua Nkomo back into the ANC as constituted on 7 December 1974. To that end I have on several occasions publicly and personally asked my colleague, Mr Joshua Nkomo, to comply with the provisions of the agreement as per the Declaration of Unity on 7 December 1974.

In spite of the decisions taken at the meeting in July 1975 and reaffirmed by the September 1975 Summit of the front-line states and the ANC leadership not to hold a congress; to stop forthwith the talks with the enemy, our colleague proceeded to hold a Congress and to talk with the enemy. Furthermore, in spite of what I have said above, I continue to ask our brother, Mr Joshua Nkomo, to comply with the Unity Accord of 7 December 1974 as this is the only basis of the unity of Zimbabwe.

Your Excellencies, I would like to strike a very positive note here by saying that we must address ourselves to the gravity of our situation. We must recognize and we do recognize that the time for recriminations is over. The gravity of the situation in Zimbabwe demands of us all to close our ranks and unite in order to achieve our goal. In this regard, I have been taking positive steps to redress the situation, and among others I have contacted the Chairman of the front-line states asking to convene a meeting of his Committee and the ANC leadership to discuss the question of unity. I am currently in touch with the Executive Secretary of the OAU Liberation Committee on the same subject. Besides, I have contacted my colleague, Mr Joshua Nkomo on several occasions with a view to starting this process of discussion.

Your Excellencies, what is of particular concern to us is that despite all assertions and claims to the contrary regarding unity among the cadres, the situation is even more serious in that area. There are more deaths inflicted among the cadres themselves than those inflicted by the enemy on the battlefield.

We would like to reiterate our policy that the party directs the gun and not the gun the party. As at present, we are required to be directed by the gun.

A successful effort will require a complete re-appraisal of the whole situation in order to achieve complete unity in the party and its army.

I earnestly appeal to the OAU to assist us in our endeavour to this end.

71 African National Council: statement to the 13th OAU summit on the Zimbabwe struggle by Joshua Nkomo, President. 2 July 1976

1. I have the honour, on behalf of the struggling people of Zimbabwe, to thank sincerely the OAU and its member states individually, for the assistance they have given and are giving to the people of Zimbabwe. I would like to assure you that we will sweat to the last drop to put that assistance to honourable and effective use for our liberation.

2. I would like to extend particular and profound thanks to the people and government of Mozambique for having courageously committed their territory and resources to the sacrifices of the Zimbabwe struggle alongside Zambia, Botswana and Tanzania. May I further thank these neighbour states for bearing the brunt of the Zimbabwe struggle and for sacrifices given by them in human lives, economic deprivation and the criminal violation by the Smith regime of their territorial integrity, all for the sake of Zimbabwe liberation.

3. It is with profound feelings that I congratulate the peoples of Angola, Guinea-Bissau and Cape Verde, Comoro Islands, Sao Tome and Principe and lately the Seychelles on having waged victorious struggles and on having thus deserved the assistance by the OAU and other friendly nations.

4. In Zimbabwe today the armed liberation struggle is a raging reality. The OAU should know that we conceived this course of action over ten years ago. For its promotion and prosecution we established an external administration as early as 1963. We are in it until victory.

5. The two crucial questions in the Zimbabwe liberation struggle, today, are unity and the escalation of fighting. Despite frequent interruptions by political and other complications, I must emphasize, for everyone to keep in mind, that my organization has never missed a moment to fight or to effect unity.

6. However, Your Excellencies, we have been subjected to unfair public criticisms and rebukes from some of our brothers in independent Africa. Whilst I acknowledge that criticism is healthy, I must emphasize that it must be honest, sincere and constructive. It appears that an unhealthy and dangerous tradition is developing in Africa which suggests that members of independent states are always right whilst leaders of liberation movements are always wrong. We are in the struggle together and such dogmatic attitudes can disrupt that which we, together, seek to achieve.

7. Let me mention, Your Excellencies, some of the instances:

(a) There has been severe criticism on the Zimbabwe political leadership that we have failed to forge and maintain unity in the face of a formidable enemy;

(b) There have been allegations that some of us have connived with the enemy by carrying out negotiations with the regime;

(c) That the Zimbabwe leaders failed to provide for the armed struggle.

8. Let us briefly look at the unity question. The basic document is 'The Zimbabwe Declaration of Unity at Lusaka, 7 December 1974', whose operative clauses are

'(1) ZANU, ZAPU, FROLIZI and the ANC hereby agree to unite in the ANC

(4) The enlarged ANC Executive shall have the following functions:

  (a) To prepare for any conference for the transfer of power to the majority that might be called.

  (b) To prepare for the holding of a Congress within four months at which (among other things)

    (ii) the leadership of the united people of Zimbabwe shall be elected.

  (c) The leaders recognize the inevitability of continued armed struggle and all other forms of struggle until the total liberation of Zimbabwe.'

This document clearly acknowledges that leaders may propose a form of unity but the decisive authority is the people in Congress who must ratify the unity agreement. The importance and urgency we all attached to the resolution of the issues of unity and leadership was reflected in the stipulation of the period 'within four months'. The unity was an absolute fusion and not an umbrella or a 'front' as clearly defined by paragraph 1 of the unity agreement.

9. When we returned to Zimbabwe from Lusaka our duty was to implement the provisions of the Lusaka Declaration of Unity as stated above. But when some of our brothers (former ZANU leaders later joined by Bishop Muzorewa) discovered that they did not have sufficient political support to capture the vital positions in the hierarchy of the organization, they repudiated the terms of agreement and refused to go to Congress. However, since the document had been published and was now the property of the people, the organization proceeded to implement the terms of the document stated above . . . It is the people, and not Joshua Nkomo, who pressed forward for congress. The congress duly met on 27–23 September 1973; the leadership was elected and thereby fulfilled the Lusaka Declaration of Unity.

10. When people speak of disunity in Zimbabwe, do they realize that the Lusaka Declaration of Unity was fulfilled or do they support those who

deliberately dishonoured an agreement that they had solemnly entered into, for no other reason than that they were unlikely to get the positions that they wanted?

11. It would be hypocritical of me if I did not state frankly that some of our independent brothers, in their cruel-kindness, have, through their preferences of individuals, contributed persistently to the division by encouraging these individuals either to split or opt out of solemn unity agreements.

12. Regarding the talks with the Rhodesian racist regime, it is important to remind you, Your Excellencies, that these talks were started in 1973, when I was in prison. After the massive rejection of the 1971 Smith-Home constitutional fraud, Ian Smith entered into negotiations with Bishop Muzorewa. In 1974 our brothers the Presidents of Tanzania, Zambia, Botswana and the then President of FRELIMO made contact with the Smith regime with a view to discovering whether, after ten years of war, the Rhodesian regime was now ready to transfer power to the majority. In December 1974, they reached a stage at which they secured our release from prison and recommended that we the leaders of Zimbabwe, enter into talks with the regime to discover whether the regime was ready to transfer power to the majority.

13. Although we expressed reservation on the value or success of such talks we, nonetheless, tried, following the advice of our friends. Having started the talks we continued until we proved concretely that the regime was unwilling to transfer power to the majority. In the light of the foregoing, the suggestion that there was connivance on my part was not only false but also an insult.

14. On the question of the armed liberation struggle I would like to bring to your notice, Your Excellencies, that my organization has never spared and will not spare an effort towards its intensification. I must say, however, that whilst going through the report of the Secretary-General on Decolonization, I was shocked at the distortion as to who are involved practically in the promotion of the armed struggle in Zimbabwe as opposed to the struggle by 'Militant Newspaper Statements'. Perhaps this was due to inexcusable misinformation. The imperialist slander that because we were involved in talks with the racist regime therefore we were not for the armed struggle was sadly reflected in this report. The report falls into this cast of propaganda by also reflecting the false labels of 'External ANC' and 'Internal ANC'. There is no such thing as External and Internal ANC. There is only the ANC of the people of Zimbabwe.

15. What are the facts on preparation for the armed struggle? As far back as October 1975, before we had started any talks with the

Rhodesian regime my organization External Administration had already been instructed to start negotiations with former ZANU with a view to setting up a single army to launch the armed struggle. This was duly accomplished in November 1976, following the good offices of the Executive Secretary of the Liberation Committee (Col Hashim Mbita) and the offer of facilities and territory for operations by the Mozambican government. This is how the present Zimbabwe People's Army (ZIPA) which has scored so many victories against the racist regime was formed. The so-called External ANC referred to in the Secretary-General's report had no role whatsoever in the formation of ZIPA and the subsequent intensified armed struggle in Zimbabwe. We have not shouted about this because we believe in action than in words. I must dispel, at the same time, the false impression which has been given much currency that ZIPA was formed as a spontaneous movement in the camps without political leadership. This is not true as indicated above.

16. Whilst the greatest victories are being geared by Zimbabwe fighters from Mozambique, we can no longer conceal the grave problems which have set in within our military wing without detriment to the struggle itself. Intense tribalism as reflected in the Chitepo Report, employing military fascism and masquerading under the label of 'militancy', on the ascendancy in the ranks and is promising our country nothing but chaos and anarchy. As a result, ZIPA is breaking down. We have paid too high a price of human losses in what we considered to be Unity Camps, all in an attempt to achieve unity with elements that have a mania for killing fellow comrades-in-arms.

17. The cause of all this tragedy is the entire line up which controls the former ZANU army. This ZANU military administration, down to camp control, like its political leadership, never accepted the idea of abandoning ZANU for unity, nor abandoning the mass killing mania which finally claimed the life of their leader Herbert Chitepo, as the Chitepo commission amply shows. There was no attempt to clean up the ZANU army of the negative elements as revealed by the report on the assassination of Herbert Chitepo.

18. Theories of the so-called 'third force' and resolutions, praising the 'unity of the cadres' to the exclusion of the unity of the entire people of whom they are part and parcel, have incited some of the destructive elements in the camps to worsen, rather than improve, the stability in ZIPA. We appeal to our friends, Your Excellencies, to avoid mounting divisive theories and resolutions.

19. Having said what I have said above, that is stressing our fulfilment of the Lusaka Declaration of Unity and my brief exposition of the

problems in ZIPA which could affect the armed struggle adversely if not acted upon immediately, I would like:

(a) to appeal to the OAU, its member states individually and its relevant administrative officers to assist us in the solution of our unity problems by advising anyone who claims leadership of the people of Zimbabwe to return to Zimbabwe in accordance with the demand of the Lusaka Declaration of Unity so that there, in Zimbabwe, we should together, dispel the image of disunity and thereby secure the unity of our people. If they are unable to return, their colleagues in Zimbabwe can carry out the task. Our fundamental aim is to secure the unity of all the people of Zimbabwe and not just that of leaders or some functional body. I know that there are some people who do not understand how we go out and return to Rhodesia. It has to be understood that the immense international pressures on the Rhodesian regime, which resulted in our release from long terms of imprisonment, still continue to take effect. In the circumstances, we do take the necessary risks to carry out the tasks of the struggle. Any leader worth his salt has to face these risks.

(b) to suggest, on the problems facing the fighting forces, that an adhoc committee of the OAU, which should include the front-line states, be instituted without delay to assist us to sort out the problems in ZIPA, taking into particular account the revelations in the REPORT OF THE INTERNATIONAL COMMISSION OF THE ASSASSINATION OF HERBERT CHITEPO.

20. Finally, Your Excellencies, may I register once again our position on the question of the channelling of assistance. We cannot agree with the redommendation that assistance should not be channelled through us, provisionally though it may be. Choice of friends and bilateral relations with other countries or organisations is our sovereign right and we cannot therefore agree even to its supposed temporary suspension.

72 The African National Council Accord. Port Louis, Mauritius, 5 July 1976

We, the leaders of the African National Council of Zimbabwe meeting here in Port Louis, Mauritius, during the 13th Summit Conference of African Heads of State and Government;

a. Having listened to and heeding the repeated and urgent appeals of all heads of state and government to close ranks and to unite against our common enemy;

b. Being fully aware of and appreciating the grave and serious situation now facing the people of Zimbabwe during this phase of our struggle for independence;

c. Conscious of the need for total unity as the surest guarantee for success in our struggle;

WISH TO AND DO HEREBY:

1. REAFFIRM our Declaration of Unity of 7 December 1974.

2. STATE our willingness and readiness to take immediate steps to heal all differences that have arisen between us for whatever reason.

3. AGREE AND PLEDGE to meet hereafter as a matter of urgency to discuss and resolve any outstanding problems.

4. REQUEST THE OAU to use their good offices through the Committee of front-line states, that is to say, Zambia, Tanzania, Botswana and Mozambique and any other State to help us to come to a quick resolution of our differences.

5. CONSIDER AND ACCEPT armed struggle as the only way by which we will achieve our goal and to this extent shall take every necessary step to consolidate the unity of the ANC and its army.

73 Statement by front-line Presidents to Ian Smith's proposals for majority rule. Lusaka, Zambia, 26 September 1976

The struggle of the people of Zimbabwe, the African and international solidarity in the implementation of sanctions and co-ordinated action of all anti-colonialist forces and states have together brought the isolation and collapse of the illegal racist minority regime in the British colony of Southern Rhodesia.

The presidents hailed and congratulated the people and fighters of Zimbabwe whose hard and heroic armed struggle forced the rebel regime and the enemy in general to recognize and accept the inevitability of majority rule, the need to establish immediately a transitional government to implement this principle. Thus the victories achieved by the people of Zimbabwe in their armed struggle created the present favourable conditions for the convening of a constitutional conference.

This is a victory for all Africa and mankind and particularly for all those countries and peoples who made sacrifices so that the brotherly people of Zimbabwe can be free.

Now that the pressures of armed struggle have forced the enemy to accept majority rule as a condition for immediate independence, the five presidents call upon the colonial authority, the British government, to convene at once a conference outside Zimbabwe with the authentic and legitimate representatives of the people:

(a)   to discuss the structure and functions of the transitional government.

(b)   To establish the transitional government.

(c)   To discuss the modalities for convening a full constitutional conference to work out the independence constitution.

(d)   To establish the basis upon which peace and normalcy can be restored in the territory.

To achieve these goals two phases are envisaged. The first phase will deal with the establishment of an African majority transitional government. The second phase will be concerned with working out the details of the Zimbabwe independence constitution.

The Presidents have carefully studied the proposals as outlined by the illegal and racist regime which, if accepted, would be tantamount to legalizing the colonialist and racist structures of power. Any details relating to the structure and functions of the transitional government should be left to the conference.

The five Presidents reaffirmed their commitment to the cause of liberation in Zimbabwe and the armed struggle. *A luta continua* (the struggle continues).

BIOGRAPHICAL NOTES

SELECTED CHARACTERS

BANANA, Canaan Sodindo
B. 1936 at Esithezini near Bulawayo. Educated at Inyati and at Epworth
Theological College, Salisbury. Ordained Methodist Minister 1965.
Founder member and vice-chairman ANC 1971-3. Talks with British
Foreign Secretary in London, May 1972, May 1973. Left Rhodesia
without passport to study MA in USA. Returned 1975 and detained.
Executive member ANC.

CHAVUNDUKA, Gordon Lloyd
B. 1936 in Umtali. Educated Domboshava School where he qualified as
an agricultural demonstrator. BA (Univ. of California at Los Angeles);
MA (Manchester); Ph D (London). Lecturer in sociology, Univ. of
Rhodesia 1966- . Member University Senate 1972- . President,
Association of University Teachers of Rhodesia 1974- . President,
National People's Union 1970-2. Secretary-General ANC 1973- .
Publications: *Traditional Healers and the Shona*; also occasional papers
in sociology and contributions to INCIDI, The Rhodesian Journal of
Economics, The Society of Malawi Journal, etc.

CHIKEREMA, James Robert Dambaza
B. 1925 in Zvimba Reserve. Educated at Kutama Mission, Makwiro,
then at Marianhill College and Cape Town University. Politics forced
him to abandon his degree studies. Founder member, City Youth League
1955. Vice-president SRANC 1957-9. Detained 1959-63. Acting-
president ZAPU in exile 1964-70. Founder member, FROLIZI 1971,
President, FROLIZI 1972-4. ANC Executive member 1974- ; secretary
Zimbabwe Liberation Council 1975- .

CHINAMANO, Josiah
B. 1922 in Chinamora Reserve near Salisbury. Taught at Waddilone
Institute. Studied privately for a BA degree with the University of South
Africa. Founder principal, Highfield Community School in Salisbury.
Detained together with his wife 1964-70 and 1972-4. Founder member,
ANC. Vice-president, ANC Nkomo faction, 1975- .

CHITEPO, Herbert Wiltshire (1923-75)
B. near Umtali. Educated at St Augustine's Mission, at Adams College,
Natal, and Fort Hare where he did BA. Then studied law in London.

First African lawyer to practise in the Central African Federation in 1954. Legal adviser to NDP at London Constitutional Conference 1961. Tanganyika's (now Tanzania) Director of Public Prosecutions 1962-6. ZANU national chairman, 1963. Full time leader of ZANU in exile, 1966-74. ANC National Executive member, December 1974-18 March 1975. Killed in Lusaka.

GABELLAH, Elliot
Elliot Gabellah was born at Ntabazinduna near Bulawayo in 1923. Graduated in Divinity and Philosophy in United States (1955-1961) and ordained Minister in African Orthodox Church. Between 1965 and 1968 studied homeopallic medicine in Southern India. Found ANC in 1971, becoming Vice-Chairman 1973, Deputy President 1974 and in 1975 Vice-President of ANC (Muzorewa), attended Geneva Conference in 1976 as member of ANC (Muzorewa) delegation. In August 1977 he joined ZANU (Sithole).

MALIANGA, Morton
Born near Umtali. Educated at Ohlange Institute (Durban) and qualified as an accountant. Founder member and vice-president, NDP 1960. ZANU Secretary for Youth and Culture 1963-4. Detained 1964-74. ANC National Chairman 1975- .

MAWEMA, Michael Andrew
Born near Fort Victoria. Educated at Gutu Mission. Qualified as a teacher. Worked in the Rhodesia Railways. Founder president, NDP 1960. Secretary-general Zimbabwe National Party 1960-1. ZANU Executive member, 1963. Detained 1964-7. Founder member, ANC 1971, and became National organizing secretary. Left ANC in September 1975.

MOYO, Jason Ziyapapa
Born in Matabeleland. Educated at Mzingwane. Qualified as a builder and a carpenter. Vice-president African Trades Union Congress. Vice-secretary general, SRANC 1957-9. Detained 1959-60. NDP executive member, 1960. Treasurer-general, ZAPU (1963-77) and was one of the movement's key figures in exile until killed in Lusaka, January 1977.

MSIKAVANHU, Joseph
B. 1923 in Mazoe District. Worked in Bulawayo. Chairman, Bulawayo African National Congress. Executive member, SRANC 1957-9. Detained 1959. NDP Secretary for Youth 1960. ZAPU External Affairs Secretary, 1961-3. Detained 1964-74 except for a brief period in 1965. Secretary-general ANC, Nkomo faction, 1975- . Obtained BA in

Sociology with the University of South Africa while in detention.

MUGABE, Robert Gabriel
B. 1925 in Zwimba Reserve. Educated at Kutama and Empandeni Mission. Finished BA at Fort Hare in 1951. Obtained B Ed and B Sc (Econ) by private study. Taught in Southern Rhodesia 1952-4, Northern Rhodesia 1955 and Ghana 1956-60. NDP Publicity Secretary 1960. Publicity Secretary, ZAPU. Secretary-general ZANU 1963-. Detained 1964-74. Formed Patriotic Front with Nkomo, October 1976.

MUZOREWA, Abel Tendekayi
B. 1925 in Umtali. Educated Old Umtali and Nyadiri Mission and in the USA. MA (1963) and Hon DD. School teacher 1943-7. Lay preacher in Mtoko district, 1947-9. Ordained Minister 1953. National Director of Christian Youth Movement 1964. Travelling secretary, Student Christian Movement, 1966. Bishop and head of American Methodists in Rhodesia, 1968- . Banned from visiting Tribal Trust (rural) areas 1970. Chairman and later President, ANC 1971- . Unsuccessful negotiations with Smith 1972. UN Prize for Outstanding Achievement in Human Rights 1973.

NKALA, Enos
Born in Filabusi district. Founder member, NDP 1960. ZANU Treasurer-general 1963-74. Detained 1964-74, 1976. Deputy-secretary general, ANC 1975- .

NKOMO, Joshua Nqabuko Nyongolo
B. 1917 in S. W. Matabeleland. Educated at Tsholotsho Government School, Adams College, Natal, and Jan Hofmeyr School of Social Work. Lay preacher. Organizing secretary Rhodesian African Workers Union, 1945-50. Joined United Federal Party (UFP) and attended London Federation Conference 1952. Unsuccessfully sought election into the first Federal Parliament 1953. President, SRANC 1957-9. External Affairs director, NDP, before becoming president in October 1960. President ZAPU, PCC. Detained 1964-74. President of his own faction of ANC September 1975- . Unsuccessfully negotiated with Smith October 1975-March 1976. Formed Patriotic Front with Mugabe in October 1976.

NYANDORO, George Bodzo
B. 1925 near Marandellas. Received only seven years' formal education at St Mary's Mission, Salisbury. Qualified as an accountant privately. Worked in Salisbury and became a trades union official. Founder member, City Youth League 1955. Secretary general, SRANC 1957-9. Detained 1959-63. Secretary general, ZAPU 1963-70. Founder member,

FROLIZI, 1971. Secretary general, FROLIZI, 1972-4. ANC Executive member 1974- , and ANC-ZLC Treasurer-general 1975- .

SILUNDIKA, George
Born in Plumtree, Matabeleland. Studied at Marianhill, the University College at Roma (Lesotho), and Fort Hare. Politics forced him to abandon his studies. Taught at Empandeni Secondary School. Founder member NDP, 1960. ZAPU Executive member, 1963-.

SITHOLE, Edson
Born in Gazaland. Received only four years of formal education. Worked in Salisbury. Founder member, City Youth League 1955; SRANC 1957. Detained 1959-63. ZANU Executive member, 1963-74. Detained 1964-70. Founder member, ANC 1971 and became publicity secretary. Kidnapped 15 October 1975. Nationalists believe he is detained by the Smith regime. Obtained LL B, LL M and Ph D in law during his various periods in detention.

SITHOLE, Ndabaningi
B. 1920 in Gazaland. Educated at Waddilove Institute and Newton College, USA. Obtained BA (SA) and Bachelor of Divinity in the US. President, African Teachers' Association, 1959-60. Church minister. Treasurer, NDP 1960. National Chairman, ZAPU. Founder president, ZANU 1963-74. Imprisoned 1964-74. ANC Executive member 1974-6 and Chairman, ANC-ZLC 1975-6. Left ANC in September 1976 in order to reorganize ZANU. Author of *African Nationalism* (1959), *Obed Mutezo* (1970) and *The Polygamist* (1972).

ZVOBGO, Edson Jonas
Born in Victoria district. Educated at Tegwani Secondary School and later at University College, Roma (Lesotho), but did not complete his studies. Founder member, NDP 1960. Studied law in USA. ZAPU representative at UN, but joined ZANU at split. Detained 1964-70. Founder member, ANC 1971. ANC's External Affairs director 1972. Resigned from the party.

MAIN POLITICAL MOVEMENTS

1. AFRICAN NATIONAL COUNCIL (ANC)
Formed 16 December 1971 to oppose Anglo-Rhodesian settlement proposals: Bishop Muzorewa Chairman and later President. Successfully opposed settlement. Became a political party in 1972. Tried to negotiate with Smith but failed. 7 December 1974: Unity Agreement uniting ANC,

FROLIZI, ZANU and ZAPU. Military wing—Zimbabwe Liberation Council (ZLC)—formed, with N. Sithole Chairman and Chikerema Secretary. Abortive Victoria Falls Bridge talks August 1975. In September 1975 Nkomo left unity movement to continue talks with Smith. September 1976: Sithole resigned to re-constitute his former ZANU. ANC as constituted in 1974 is led by Bishop Muzorewa, Vice-President Elliot Gabellah, a medical doctor, and Secretary-general Gordon Chavunduka.

2. FRONT FOR THE LIBERATION OF ZIMBABWE (FROLIZI)

Launched 1 October 1971 by pro-unity groups from both ZANU and ZAPU. Led by Shelton Siwela. Later Chikerema president. Other leading members—Nyandoro, Stephen Parirenyatwa and Nathan Shamuyarira. Had the smallest army based in Zambia. Forerunner of ANC. Dissolved with the Unity Agreement, December 1974.

3. NATIONAL DEMOCRATIC PARTY (NDP)

Formed 1 January 1960 with Michael Mawema as interim President. In October 1960 Nkomo took over. Continued SRANC's activities but gradually became more and more militant. Attended 1961 London Constitutional Conference. Banned 9 December 1961.

4. SOUTHERN RHODESIA AFRICAN NATIONAL CONGRESS (SRANC)

First African mass political movement. Launched on 12 September 1957 with the amalgamation of the City Youth League and the old Bulawayo African National Congress. President Joshua Nkomo, Vice-president, J. Chikerema, and Secretary-general, George Nyandoro. Opposed Central African Federation and campaigned for racial justice in Southern Rhodesia. Banned 1959 and most leaders detained.

5. ZIMBABWE AFRICAN NATIONAL UNION (ZANU)

Formed August 1963. Split from ZAPU over the question of tactics rather than of principles. Founder president Ndabaningi Sithole, Vice-president Leopold Takawira and Secretary-general Robert Mugabe. Banned 1964 and most leaders detained. In exile ZANU led by national chairman, Herbert Chitepo. April 1966: Sinoia battle, marking the beginning of armed struggle in Zimbabwe. Largest guerilla force. Operated in the north-east. Officially dissolved with Unity Agreement December 1974 but some members continued to operate as ZANU.

6. ZIMBABWE AFRICAN PEOPLES' UNION (ZAPU)

Formed 16 December 1961. Nkomo president, N. Sithole national chairman. Boycotted 1962 elections because of inadequate representation. Banned 20 September 1962. Continued to operate as Peoples' Caretaker Council (PCC) inside. July 1963: serious split leading to the formation of ZANU. Party rivalry and thuggery followed. Both ZANU and PCC banned in 1964 and most leaders detained. ZAPU in exile led by J. Chikerema till 1970. ZAPU organized a small army and operated from north-west Zimbabwe. In December 1974, Unity Agreement. September 1975: ZAPU left Agreement but operates as ANC inside Zimbabwe.

APPENDIX
THE ROAD TO GENEVA

For over a decade the United States had had no comprehensive African policy since the rivalry between Russia and the US over the Congo (now Zaire), during the Cold War years. But after the victory of the Marxist forces in Angola, the main objective of the American Secretary of State, Dr Henry Kissinger, became none other than to '. . . have a stake . . . in not having the whole continent of Africa becoming radical, and moving in a direction that is incompatible with Western interests. That is the issue.' The same view was shared by some African leaders. During his state visit to the US in 1975, Zambia's President Kaunda told President Ford that '. . . the conflict (in southern Africa) with disastrous consequences can be averted, but I submit again, Mr President, there is not much time. Urgent action is required. America must now be in the vanguard of democratic revolution in southern Africa . . .' Propelled by the desire to keep Rhodesia in the Western camp and assured of African co-operation in this venture, Kissinger embarked on his so-called southern African peace initiative which took him to six countries—Kenya, Tanzania, Zambia, Zaire, Liberia and Senegal. The culmination of Kissinger's African safari was in Lusaka where, on 27 April 1976, he delivered his 'message of commitment and co-operation' considered in diplomatic circles as the basis of future American policy on Africa.

Lusaka was chosen for geographical reasons—less than one hundred miles from white-ruled Rhodesia. Kissinger's ten-point plan was expected to bring psychological pressure on the white minority so that they could read the writing on the wall. The plan went as follows:

1. Acceptance of majority rule within two years.
2. No US assistance to the Smith regime in its conflict with African liberation movements.
3. Repeal of the Byrd Amendment, subject to Congress approval.
4. Need for a rapid advance towards majority rule in Zimbabwe.
5. American citizens advised to leave Rhodesia.
6. US aid to Mozambique of $12.5m (about £6.9m).
7. US readiness to assist other countries hit by imposing sanctions.
8. US readiness to help Rhodesian refugees. .
9. US with other nations to provide economic, technical, and educational assistance to a majority-ruled Zimbabwe.

10. US belief that whites as well as blacks must have a secure future in an independent Zimbabwe.

Kissinger's plan endorsed the four-point British plan as laid down by Foreign Secretary James Callaghan on 22 March 1976 soon after the breakdown of the Smith-Nkomo talks. These were:

1. Acceptance of majority rule in principle.
2. Elections to establish majority government to be held within 18–24 months.
3. No independence before majority rule.
4. Negotiations were not to be long-drawn out.

The Lusaka speech appealed for South Africa's support and co-operation in bringing about African rule in Zimbabwe and Namibia. Kissinger also appealed for a peaceful end to *apartheid* in South Africa itself. The promise for economic aid led to speculation that Botswana would close her border with Rhodesia.

But African leaders were deeply suspicious of American motives because of her refusal to back armed struggle in southern Africa. Thus Kissinger's visit was boycotted by Zimbabwe's leaders except Joshua Nkomo, and by Nigeria and Ghana, which he had hoped to visit too. Kissinger himself had ignored John Vorster, South Africa's Prime Minister, the key figure in white-ruled Africa. However, there was little doubt that South Africa had to be involved in any Western diplomatic moves in southern Africa. The result was the Kissinger-Vorster meeting held from 23 June at Grafenau, in the Bavarian mountains in West Germany. That meeting was believed to be the first in 30 years since any official contact had taken place between South Africa and the US at this high level. Among other things the meeting decided that a Kenya-type fund be set up to assist whites who wished to emigrate before the advent of majority rule and those who chose to remain in the country. A senior State Department official was sent to report to the African presidents the outcome of the Bavarian summit.

A second meeting between Vorster and Kissinger took place in Zurich from 4–9 September. Preparation began for a round of 'shuttle diplomacy' between white and black in southern Africa and this finally took place from 13–23 September. The culmination of this so-called peace initiative was Kissinger's meeting with Vorster and Smith in Pretoria on 19 September which took place against the background of the Soweto riots and Nyazonia. Kissinger stated that his deal took into account the views of Britain, the US and black African states. But, surprisingly enough, the views of the Zimbabwe nationalists and guerillas, and of SWAPO had not been sounded. However, after selling the deal to his party and government, on 24 September Ian Smith finally announced his acceptance of the principle of majority rule within two years. Such was the announcement from a man who had declared on many an occasion that there would never be majority rule in his lifetime and not even in a thousand years.

Several factors brought about this dramatic turn but the most decisive one was the pressure from the intensified armed struggle which for the past ten years claimed heavy losses on both sides. Secondly, there is the factor of the internationalization of the conflict in southern Africa. To the West, the conflict was seen as between East and West. Western defeat in Angola with the help of Cuban and Russian assistance could not be allowed to be repeated. South Africa, too, was ready to drop Smith in favour of a 'puppet' black-dominated government in Zimbabwe which would not pose a threat to her own internal and external security. Thirdly, the hard-hit Rhodesian economy was getting worse and worse each day. The critical shortage of currency and of manpower due to the rising loss of migrants were both causes of great concern in government circles.

However, African leaders reacted with great caution to Smith's statement. The major areas of disagreement were spelled out by the front-line Presidents. A 'mini-shuttle' by British Foreign Office Minister of State, Ted Rowlands, and William Schaufelle, the US Assistant Secretary of State, round southern Africa, which included a visit to Salisbury on 4 October, helped to ensure full attendance at the forthcoming Constitutional Conference.

However, the Geneva Conference almost broke down prematurely because of confusion over the details of the 'Kissinger package'. Smith's insistence that the deal was not negotiable and that the conference was merely to find ways and means of implementing the deal was a non-starter to the nationalists. On the other hand, the African viewpoint, as put forward by President Nyerere, was that the proposals were only a basis for negotiations. The status of the Conference chairman, Ivor Richard, Britain's ambassador to the UN, was also a point in question in some nationalist circles. Britain, too, had reluctantly agreed to convene and chair the Conference because of her previous experience in tackling the Rhodesian problem.

The conference, which finally opened on 28 October, remained deadlocked on the independence date issue.

INDEX